FINANCIAL ACCOUNTING

FINANCIAL ACCOUNTING

VOLUME II

Balavant M. Unnibhavi

ATLANTIC
PUBLISHERS & DISTRIBUTORS

Published by

ATLANTIC
PUBLISHERS & DISTRIBUTORS
B-2, Vishal Enclave, Opp. Rajouri Garden,
New Delhi-110027
Phones : 25413460, 25429987, 25466842

Sales Office
7/22, Ansari Road, Darya Ganj,
New Delhi-110002
Phones : 23273880, 23275880, 23280451
Fax : 91-11-23285873
web : www.atlanticbooks.com
e-mail : info@atlanticbooks.com

ISBN 81-269-0421-6 (Vol. I)
ISBN 81-269-0422-4 (Vol. II)
ISBN 81-269-0423-2 (Set)

Printed in India
at Nice Printing Press, Delhi

PREFACE

I am extremely happy to place before the esteemed readers the book entitled *Financial Accounting*. Financial Accounting is said to be the heart of language of business and is more apparent in the Financial Reports. Keeping this in view the two-volume book is designed to cater to the needs of the students of the Indian Universities and those of professional examinations like C.A., I.C.W.A., A.C.S., etc., conducted by the various institutes.

In the best interests of the students who take the different examinations, I have tried to introduce the subject in a simple and lucid manner to enable them to learn and understand the intricacies of accounting in a logical sequence. The concepts have been explained step by step including all minute details and are richly illustrated with graded and appropriate examples, provided in each Chapter, so as to have a concrete understanding of the subject. In addition, short questions, simple problems and practical exercises, selected from the latest question papers of various universities have been given for the benefit of the students. I am optimistic that the book would prove to be a standard textbook on the subject and also worthwhile in enhancing one's knowledge of Accounting.

Although no originality is claimed by me, yet it may be definitely said that it has its own speciality as far as its arrangement, compass and techniques are concerned. I am indebted to all the authors whose works I have referred to and the ideas and thoughts that I have borrowed from.

It would be unjustified if I do not acknowledge the help extended to me by my beloved wife Prof. (Dr.) Pushpa B. Unnibhavi in preparing this book.

I also take this opportunity to express my heartfelt gratitude to Prof. A.G. Sunkad, Head, Department of English, for improving the grammatical standard of the book and for his valuable suggestions which have made the book all the more comprehensive.

I express my profound gratitude to the students, teachers and all my well-wishers whose encouragement has inspired me to bring this book.

Thanks are due to the colleagues and friends of my college for their moral support.

I also thank Dr. K.R. Gupta, Chairman, M/s Atlantic Publishers and Distributors, New Delhi, for taking keen interest in publishing this book.

BALAVANT M. UNNIBHAVI

CONTENTS

VOLUME I

VOLUME II

10

PIECEMEAL DISTRIBUTION

Meaning

When the partnership firm is dissolved, its business comes to an end. Therefore, all the assets of the partnership firm are to be realised on the date of dissolution and the proceeds of the same are to be utilised to discharge the liabilities. But usually, all the assets of the firm cannot be realised on the date of dissolution. With a view of getting better price, the assets of the firm are sold gradually according to the demand for a particular asset. The cash received on the sale of each asset is not kept locked up till the last asset is sold, but it is paid as and when realised to the rightful claimant. The process of realising the assets piece by piece or part by part and distributing the cash to the rightful claimant as and when the cash is received without waiting for the realisation of all the assets of the firm is called piecemeal distribution.

Payment of Liabilities

Naturally the question arises as to whose claim is to be paid first. For this purpose, the Act has laid down the priority for payment as below :

(1) Realisation Expenses : When the cash is received from the sale of assets of the firm, the realisation expenses are to be paid first.

(2) Third Party Liabilities : After the payment of realisation expenses, the available cash is distributed among the various liabilities. If the cash is insufficient to pay all the liabilities, they should be paid in pro-rata. Ex : If the liabilities are— Sundry Creditors Rs. 30,000, Bank Overdraft Rs. 10,000 and Bills Payable Rs. 20,000 and the Cash available is Rs. 6,000, the cash is to be distributed in the ratio of 30,000 : 20,000 : 10,000 *i.e.*, 3 : 2 : 1. It means the Creditors are to be paid Rs. 3,000, Bills Payable Rs. 2,000 and Bank Overdraft Rs. 1,000.

If there are any secured creditors, the cash realised from the sale of assets is first used in payment of such creditors and remaining cash is used in payment of others. Similarly, if there is any contingent liability (*e.g.*, a bill discounted), the amount for such a liability is set aside before paying cash to any other claimant and if it does not turn into a liability, the amount set aside is used for the payment of other claimant.

(3) Partners' Loans : After the payment of outside or third party liabilities, the partners' loans should be paid. If the available cash is insufficient to repay the loans of all the partners at a time, the available cash is distributed on pro-rata basis as is done in item 2 above.

(4) Partners' Capital : After payment of all outside liabilities and partners' loans, the capital of the partners are to be paid. While distributing the cash among the partners, the question crops up as to how to distribute such cash among partners for return of capital. While distributing the cash it should be noted that the balances of capitals finally left unpaid should be in their profit sharing ratio, because these balances represent the loss on realisation. If the cash is distributed in profit sharing ratio, the final capital balances will not be in the profit sharing ratio unless the capitals are in profit sharing division. If the cash is distributed in capital proportion, the final capital balances will also be in the same capital ratio but not in profit sharing ratio. It will be clear from the following example.

Example : X and Y are partners with capitals of Rs. 75,000 and Rs. 50,000 respectively. After paying off all the creditors, two further instalments were collected— one of Rs. 45,000 and the other of Rs. 15,000. They share profits and losses as X 2/3rd and Y 1/3rd.

Show how the discrepancy arises when the cash is distributed (a) in profit sharing ratio and (b) in capital ratio.

Solution :

(a) If cash distributed in profit sharing ratio :

	X Rs.	Y Rs.
Profit sharing ratio	2 :	1
Capital balance to be paid	75,000	50,000
First instalment of Rs. 45,000 distributed in the profit sharing ratio of 2 : 1	30,000	15,000
Balance due	45,000	35,000
Second instalment of Rs. 15,000 distributed in the ratio of 2 : 1	10,000	5,000
Balance being loss on realisation	35,000	30,000

This loss of Rs. 35,000 to X and Rs. 30,000 to Y also is not in the profit sharing ratio of 2 : 1, hence, this method of distribution of cash in the profit sharing ratio is wrong.

(b) If cash distributed in capital ratio :

		Rs. X	Rs. Y
Capital balance to be paid		75,000	50,000
First instalment of Rs. 45,000 distributed in the ratio of capital *i.e.*, 3 : 2		27,000	18,000
	Balance due	48,000	32,000
Second instalment of Rs. 15,000 distributed in the ratio of 3 : 2		9,000	6,000
Balance being loss on realisation		39,000	26,000

This loss of Rs. 39,000 to X and Rs. 26,000 to Y also is not in the profit sharing ratio, hence, the above method of distributing the cash in the profit sharing ratio is defective.

While making the payments to the partners, it must be seen that no partner either receives over payment or is put to heavy loss. Therefore, the distribution of cash is required to be made in such a manner that the balances on capitals left unpaid are in the profit sharing ratio. But in the above two methods final loss on realisation is not shared in the profit sharing ratio. In order to achieve the correct result, it is necessary to make the capitals of partners proportionate to their profit sharing proportion. Following two methods may be applied to achieve the above result.

(i) Surplus Capital or Proportionate Capital Method

(ii) Maximum Loss Method.

I. Surplus Capital Method

Under this method we have to find out which partner has the highest capital i.e., more than proportionate to other partners' capital in view of profits sharing ratio. Distribute the available cash to the partner who has first highest to bring down his capital in proportionate to that of second highest. Then, distribute the available cash to these two partners in their profit sharing ratio until their capitals brought to the level of the third highest. The cash then available is distributed to all the partners in proportionate to their profit sharing ratio. This process is continued till the available cash is distributed fully. Finally the balances of capital accounts represent profit or loss on realisation and this will be in the profit sharing ratio of each partner. This is the proof of correctness of distribution of cash piece by piece. It will clear from the following examples.

Example 1

X, Y and Z are partners having capital of Rs. 20,000, Rs. 10,000 and Rs. 5,000 sharing profits in the ratio of 2 : 2 : 1. Calculate the surplus capital and put the note how the distribution is made.

Solution :

Statement Showing Surplus Capital

	X	Y	Z
Profit sharing ratio	2 :	2 :	1
Actual capitals	20,000	10,000	5,000
Capitals of partners on the basis of Z's capital, his being the lowest capital	10,000	10,000	5,000
Surplus Capital	10,000	—	—

Note : After paying the surplus capital of Rs. 10,000 to X, the remaining cash should be distributed to all the partners in their profit sharing ratio of 2 : 2 : 1.

Example 2

A, B and C are three partners having capitals of Rs. 12,000, Rs. 15,000 and Rs. 20,000 respectively. The profit and losses are divided in the ratio of 3 : 2 : 1. Calculate the excess capital and put the note as how to distribute the available cash of Rs. 29,000.

Solution :

Statement Showing Surplus Capital

	A	B	C
Profit sharing ratio	3 :	2 :	1
Actual capitals	12,000	15,000	20,000
Capitals of partners on the basis of A's capital, his being the lowest capital	12,000	8,000	4,000
Surplus capital	—	7,000	16,000
Surplus capital of 'C' on the basis of 'B' surplus capital	—	7,000	3,500
Final Surplus Capital	—	—	12,500

Note : First pay the excess capital of Rs. 12,500 to 'C'. After paying the excess capital of 'C', the capital of 'B' and 'C' will be in their profit sharing ratio (*i.e.*, 2 : 1). Further after paying the excess capital of B— Rs. 7,000 and 'C'— Rs. 3,500 in their profits sharing ratio, the remaining cash of Rs. 6,000 should be distributed to all the partners in their profit sharing ratio.

Illustration 1

A, B, C and D are partners sharing profits and losses in proportion of 4 : 3 : 2 : 1 respectively, and their capitals are Rs. 48,000, Rs. 1,20,000, Rs. 1,50,000 and Rs. 20,000.

The partnership is dissolved and the proceeds of sale of assets are received in three instalments of Rs. 2,00,000, Rs. 58,000 and Rs. 30,000 respectively at intervals of 3 months.

Prepare a statement showing how much each instalment should be divided between the partners so as to ensure that no partner at any time receives more than his ultimate share, bearing in mind that final profit or loss on realisation will not be known until the receipt of the final instalment. Assume that all outside liabilities have already been discharged.

Solution :

Statement Showing Distribution of Cash

	A	B	C	D
Profit sharing ratio	4 :	3 :	2 :	1
Capital Balances	48,000	1,20,000	1,50,000	20,000
I. Instalment received Rs. 2,00,000 :				
Rs. 70,000 paid 'C' to bring his capital in proportionate to that B	—	—	70,000	—
Rs. 1,30,000 Balance	48,000	1,20,000	80,000	20,000
Rs. 60,000 paid to 'C' and Rs. 40,000 paid to 'B', bring down their capitals in proportionate to that 'D'	—	60,000	40,000	—
Rs. 30,000 Balance	48,000	60,000	40,000	20,000
Paid Rs. 30,000 to B, C & D in their profit sharing ratio	—	15,000	10,000	5,000
Balance	48,000	45,000	30,000	15,000
II. Instalment received Rs. 58,000 :				
Paid Rs. 18,000 to B, C and D in their profit sharing ratio to bring down their balances in proportionate to that 'A'	—	9,000	6,000	3,000
Rs. 40,000 Balance	48,000	36,000	24,000	12,000
Paid Rs. 40,000 to all partners in their profit sharing ratio	16,000	12,000	8,000	4,000
Balance	32,000	24,000	16,000	8,000
III. Instalment received Rs. 30,000 :				
Paid Rs. 30,000 to all partners in their profit sharing ratio	12,000	9,000	6,000	3,000
Realisation Loss	20,000	15,000	10,000	5,000

Illustration 2

Ranga, Sanga and Ninga are partners in a firm sharing profits and losses in the ratio of 3 : 2 : 1. The following is their Balance Sheet as on 31-12-1995.

	Rs.		Rs.
Capitals :			
Ranga	39,000	Fixed Assets	30,000
Sanga	25,000	Stock	25,000
Ninga	9,000	Debtors	18,000
	73,000		73,000

The firm was dissolved on 31st December, 1995 and the assets were gradually realised and distributed amongst the partners on a piecemeal basis.

The following are the realisations made on January, 1996 Rs. 800, February, 1996 Rs. 4,700 and March, 1996 Rs. 37,500.

Set out the distribution of cash among the partners.

Solution :

Statement Showing Distribution of Cash

	Ranga	Sanga	Ninga
Profit sharing ratio	3 :	2 :	1
Capital balances	39,000	25,000	9,000
I. Amount Realised on Jan., 1996 Rs. 800 :			
Paid Rs. 800 to Ranga	800	—	—
Balance	38,200	25,000	9,000
II. Amount Realised on Feb., 1996 Rs. 4,700 :			
Rs. 700 paid to Ranga to bring down his capital to the level of Sanga	700	—	—
Rs. 4,000 Balance	37,500	25,000	9,000
Paid Rs. 4,000 to Ranga and Sanga in their profit sharing ratio	2,400	1,600	—
Balance	35,100	23,400	9,000
III. Amount Realised on March, 1996 Rs. 37,500 :			
Paid to Rs. 8,100 to Ranga and Rs. 5,400 to Sanga to bring down their capitals to the level of Ninga	8,100	5,400	—
Rs. 24,000 Balance	27,000	18,000	9,000
Paid Rs. 2,400 to all partners in their profit sharing ratio	12,000	8,000	4,000
Balance being loss on realisation	15,000	10,000	5,000
In profit sharing ratio	3	2	1

Illustration 3

Kamala, Vimala and Sumala were partners in a firm. They dissolved the firm on 1-1-1995 when their position was as follows :

Liabilities		Rs.	Assets	Rs.
Creditors		50,000	Cash	35,000
Bills Payable		20,000	Debtors	90,000
Bank Loan		30,000	Stock	1,50,000
Kamala's Loan		15,000		
Vimla's Loan		10,000		
Reserve Fund		30,000		
Capitals :				
Kamala	50,000			
Vimala	40,000			
Sumala	30,000	1,20,000		
		2,75,000		2,75,000

It was decided that the net realised amount should be distributed as and when cash received. The realisation and the expenses thereon were as follows :

Date	Debtors	Stock	Expenses
31-1-1995	20,000	51,000	1,000
28-2-1995	10,000	40,500	500
31-3-1995	32,000	42,000	2,000

The stock have been completely disposed of, it was agreed that Kamala should take over the remaining debts at Rs. 3,000.

Prepare the statement showing the distribution of cash.

Solution :

Statement Showing Distribution of Cash

Profit Sharing Ratio						1 :	1 :	1
Particulars	**Creditors**	**Bills Payable**	**Bank Loan**	**Kamala's Loan**	**Vimala's Loan**	**Kamala's Capital**	**Vimala's Capital**	**Sumala's Capital**
Balance as per Balance Sheet	50,000	20,000	30,000	15,000	10,000	50,000	40,000	30,000
Add : Reserve to partners equally	—	—	—	—	—	10,000	10,000	10,000
						60,000	50,000	40,000
Cash in Hand Rs. 35,000 : Paid to Creditors, B/P and Bank Loan in the ratio of 5 : 2 : 3	17,500	7,000	10,500	—	—	—	—	—
Balance	32,500	13,000	19,500	15,000	10,000	60,000	50,000	40,000
Cash received Rs. 70,000 on 31-1-1995 : Paid Rs. 65,000 to Creditors, B/P and Bank loan in full	32,500	13,000	19,500	—	—	—	—	—
Rs. 5,000 Balance				15,000	10,000	60,000	50,000	40,000
Paid Rs. 5,000 to Kamala's loan and Vimala's loan in the ratio of 3 : 2				3,000	2,000	—	—	—
Balance				12,000	8,000	60,000	50,000	40,000
Cash received Rs. 50,000 on 28-2-1995 : Paid Rs. 20,000 to loan of Kamala and Vimala in full				12,000	8,000	—	—	—
Rs. 30,000 Balance						60,000	50,000	40,000
Paid Rs. 10,000 to Vimala to bring down her capital to the level of Vimala						10,000	—	—
Rs. 20,000 Balance						50,000	50,000	40,000
Paid Rs. 20,000 to Kamala and Vimala equally to bring down their capitals to the level of Sumala						10,000	10,000	—
Balance						40,000	40,000	40,000
Cash Received (on 31-3-1995) Rs. 72,000; *Add :* Value of assets 3,000; 75,000								
Paid Rs. 75,000 to all the partners equally						25,000	25,000	25,000
Realisation Loss						15,000	15,000	15,000

Notes : (i) Cash received is calculated at below :

Date	Debtors		Stock		Expenses		Cash received
31-1-1995	20,000	+	51,000	–	1,000	=	Rs. 70,000
28-2-1995	10,000	+	40,500	–	500	=	Rs. 50,000
31-3-1995	32,000	+	42,000	–	2,000	=	Rs. 72,000

(ii) Rs. 25,000 paid to Kamala includes the value of remaining assets taken over by her Rs. 3,000.

Illustration 4

Arun, Kiran and Charan were partners in a firm sharing profits and losses in the proportion of 2 : 1 : 1 respectively.

Balance Sheet as on 31-12-1995

Liabilities		Rs.	Assets	Rs.
Creditors		12,000	Cash	10,000
Income Tax		3,000	Machinery	40,000
Loan from Bank		25,000	Furniture	15,000
(secured by pledge of stock)			Stock	12,000
Kiran's Loan		5,000	Debtors	8,000
Capitals :			Motor Car	15,000
Arun	22,000		P & L Account	4,000
Kiran	21,000			
Charan	16,000	59,000		
		1,04,000		1,04,000

The firm was dissolved on 1st January, 1996.

(1) Bank could realise only Rs. 17,000 on disposal of stock.

(2) A sum of Rs. 2,000 was spent for repairs of furniture to get better price.

(3) Other assets were realised as follows :

Jan.	1996	Rs. 18,000
Feb.	1996	Rs. 6,000
March	1996	Rs. 15,000
April	1996	Rs. 16,000
May	1996	Rs. 12,000

Solution :

Statement Showing Distribution of Cash

Month	Particulars	Income tax	Bank Loan	Creditors	Kiran's Loan	Arun's Capital	Kiran's Capital	Charan's Capital
	Balance as per Balance Sheet	3,000	8,000	12,000	5,000	22,000	21,000	16,000
	Less: P&L Dr. balance to partners in P & L ratio	—	—	—	—	2,000	1,000	1,000
	Balance	3,000	8,000	12,000	5,000	20,000	20,000	15,000
Dec., 1995	**Cash in hand Rs. 10,000 :**							
	Paid Rs. 2,000 for repairs to furniture and Rs. 3,000 for income tax	3,000	—	—	—	—	—	—
	Rs. 5,000 Balance		8,000	12,000	5,000	20,000	20,000	15,000
	Paid Rs. 5,000 for Bank loan and creditors in the ratio of 2 : 3		2,000	3,000	—	—	—	—
	Balance		6,000	9,000	5,000	20,000	20,000	15,000
Jan., 1996	**Cash received Rs. 18,000 :**							
	Paid Rs. 15,000 to Bank loan and creditor in full		6,000	9,000	—	—	—	—
	Rs. 3,000 Balance				5,000	20,000	20,000	15,000
	Paid Rs. 3,000 to loan of Kiran				3,000	—	—	—
	Balance				2,000	20,000	20,000	15,000
Feb., 1996	**Cash received Rs. 6,000 :**							
	Paid Rs. 2,000 for Kiran 's loan and Rs. 4,000 to Kiran				2,000	—	4,000	—
	Balance					20,000	16,000	15,000
Mar., 1996	**Cash received Rs. 15,000 :**							
	Paid Rs. 1,000 to Kiran to bring down his capital to the level of Charan					—	1,000	—
	Rs. 14,000 Balance					20,000	15,000	15,000
	Paid Rs. 10,000 to Kiran and Charan to bring down their capitals to the level of Arun					—	5,000	5,000
	Rs. 4,000 Balance					20,000	10,000	10,000
	Paid Rs. 4,000 to all partners in their profit sharing ratio					2,000	1,000	1,000
	Balance					18,000	9,000	9,000
April, 1996	**Cash Received Rs. 16,000 :**							
	Paid to all the partners in P & L ratio					8,000	4,000	4,000
	Balance					10,000	5,000	5,000
May, 1996	**Cash Received Rs. 12,000 :**							
	Paid to all the partners in P & L ratio					6,000	3,000	3,000
	Realisation Loss					4,000	2,000	2,000
	In profit sharing ratio					2	: 1	: 1

Notes : (i) Income-tax being preferential is paid first.

(ii) Bank recovered Rs. 17,000 from stock given as security. The unrecovered balance of Rs. 8,000 being bank loan paid along with creditors proportionately.

Illustration 5

A, B and C carrying on business in partnership and sharing profits in the ratio 4 : 2 : 1 decided to dissolve it on and from 30th September, 1990. The following was their Balance Sheet on that date.

Liabilities		Rs.	Assets	Rs.
Capitals :			Fixed Assets	45,000
A	40,000		Current Assets	42,000
B	10,000		Bank	10,000
C	20,000	70,000		
General Reserve		7,000		
Creditors		20,000		
		97,000		97,000

As per the agreement with the Bank the partners were entitled to withdraw an amount of Rs. 5,000 only at present and the balance amount of Rs. 5,000 could be drawn only after 1st December, 1990.

It was decided that after keeping aside an amount of Rs. 2,000 for estimated realisation expenses, the available cash should be distributed.

The following were the realisations :

	Fixed Assets Rs.	Current Assets Rs.
31st October, 1990	10,000	19,000
25th November, 1990	24,000	20,000
20th December, 1990	10,000	10,200

Actual realisation expenses amounted to Rs. 1,300 and paid on 20th December, 1990.

Prepare a statement of distribution of cash and show necessary Ledger Accounts.

(Shivaji, B.Com. & Sagar, B.Com.)

Solution :

Statement Showing Distribution of Cash

Date	Particulars	Creditors	A's Capital	B's Capital	C's Capital
	Balance as per Balance Sheet	20,000	40,000	10,000	20,000
	Add : General Reserve to partners	—	4,000	2,000	1,000
	Balance	20,000	44,000	12,000	21,000
1-10-90	**Cash in Hand Rs. 3,000 :**				
	(Rs. 5,000 – Rs. 2,000 set aside for expenses) Paid to the creditors	3,000	—	—	—
	Balance	17,000	44,000	12,000	21,000
31-10-90	**Cash Received Rs. 29,000 :**				
	Paid Rs. 17,000 to creditors in full	17,000	—	—	—
	Rs. 12,000 Balance		44,000	12,000	21,000
	Paid Rs. 10,000 to 'C' to bring down his capital in the ratio of A		—	—	10,000
	Rs. 2,000 Balance		44,000	12,000	11,000
	Paid Rs. 2,000 to A and C in the ratio of 4 : 1		1,600	—	400
	Balance		42,400	12,000	10,600
25-11-90	**Cash Received Rs. 44,000 :**				
	Paid Rs. 18,400 to A and Rs. 4,600 to C to bring down their balances in proportion to that of B		18,400	—	4,600
	Rs. 21,000 Balance		24,000	12,000	6,000
	Paid Rs. 21,000 to all partners in their profit sharing ratio		12,000	6,000	3,000
	Balance		12,000	6,000	3,000
20-12-90	**Cash Received** **Rs. 25,900** (Rs. 20,200+5,000 from Bank + 700 remained out of Rs. 2,000 reserved for expenses)				
	Less : Total of Capitals Rs. 21,000				
	Profit on Realisation 4,900		2,800	1,400	700
	Balance		14,800	7,400	3,700
	Cash paid Rs. 25,900 to all partners		14,800	7,400	3,700

Notes : (i) If the cash available for distribution is more than the total of capitals, the difference is treated as profit.

(ii) On 1-10-90 Rs. 5,000 withdrawn from Bank as agreed is used for payment of creditors and reserved for expenses.

Ledger Accounts

Realisation Account

Dr. Cr.

Date	Particulars	Rs.	Date	Particulars	Rs.
1-10-90	To Fixed Assets	45,000	1-10-90	By Creditors	20,000
	To Current Assets	42,000	31-10-90	By Bank	29,000
1-10-90	To Bank (Creditors)	3,000	25-11-90	By Bank	44,000
31-10-90	To Bank (Creditors)	17,000	20-12-90	By Bank	20,200
20-12-90	To Bank Expenses	1,300			
	To Capital Accounts : (Profit transferred)				
	A — 2,800				
	B — 1,400				
	C — 700	4,900			
		1,13,200			1,13,200

Partners' Capital Accounts

Dr. Cr.

Date	Particulars	A Rs.	B Rs.	C Rs.	Date	Particulars	A Rs.	B Rs.	C Rs.
31-10-90	To Bank	1,600	—	10,400	1-10-90	By Balance b/d	40,000	10,000	20,000
25-11-90	To Bank	30,400	6,000	7,600	1-10-90	By Gen. Reserve	4,000	2,000	1,000
20-11-90	To Bank	14,800	7,400	3,700	1-10-90	By Realisation (Profit)	2,800	1,400	700
		46,800	13,400	21,700			46,800	13,400	21,700

Bank Account

Dr. Cr.

Date	Particulars	Rs.	Date	Particulars	Rs.
1-10-90	To Balance b/d	10,000	1-10-90	By Realisation	3,000
31-10-90	To Realisation	29,000	31-10-90	By Realisation	17,000
25-11-90	To Realisation	44,000	31-10-90	By A's Capital	1,600
20-12-90	To Realisation	20,200	31-10-90	By C's Capital	10,400
			25-11-90	By A's Capital	30,400
			25-11-90	By B's Capital	6,000
			25-11-90	By C's Capital	7,600
			20-12-90	By Realisation	1,300
				By A's Capital	14,800
				By B's Capital	7,400
				By C's Capital	3,700
		1,03,200			1,03,200

Illustration 6

Ananth Associates is a reputed firm. On account of certain misunderstandings between the partners, it was decided to dissolve the firm as on 31st Dec., 1990. Their Balance Sheet as on 31st Dec., 1990 was as follows :

Balance Sheet

Liabilities		Rs.	Assets	Rs.
Creditors		2,00,000	Land and Building	7,00,000
Bank O.D.		3,00,000	Other Fixed Assets	3,00,000
Mortgage Loans		3,00,000	Stock-in-trade	2,00,000
Other Loans		2,00,000	Debtors	4,00,000
Kumar's Loan		2,00,000	Bills	1,50,000
Capitals :			Goodwill	30,000
Ananth	3,00,000		Cash	20,000
Kishore	2,00,000			
Kumar (Minor)	1,00,000	6,00,000		
		18,00,000		18,00,000

It was decided that Mr. Ananth shall be in-charge of realisations. He shall set apart Rs. 10,000 towards expenses. He shall be paid a remuneration of 5% on the amounts distributed to the partners towards their contributions, other than loans. Assets realised as under :

1-1-90	Debtors	Rs. 3,50,000
15-1-90	Fixed Assets	Rs. 4,00,000
1-2-90	Debtors	Rs. 50,000
15-2-90	Bills	Rs. 1,40,000
1-3-90	Fixed Assets	Rs. 50,000
15-3-90	Land and Buildings	Rs. 8,00,000

Prepare a statement showing how the monies received on various dates will be distributed assuming :

(a) The actual expenses of realisation amounted to Rs. 20,005.

(b) The firm is solvent.

(c) The profit sharing ratio was as under :

	Profit	Loss
Ananth	2	1
Kishore	2	1
Kumar	1	Nil
	5	2

(d) The final dissolution is made on 15th March, 1990.

(Delhi, B.Com.; Panjab, B.Com. and C.A. Inter, 1977)

Solution :

Statement Showing Distribution of Cash

Particulars	Mortgage Loan	Bank O.D.	Other Loan	Creditors	Kumar's Loan	Ananth's Capital	Kishore's Capital	Kumar's Capital
Balance as per Balance Sheet	3,00,000	3,00,000	2,00,000	2,00,000	2,00,000	3,00,000	2,00,000	1,00,000
Cash in Hand Rs. 20,000 *Add* : Amount kept for realisation expenses 10,000 Rs. 10,000								
Paid to outsiders in the ratio of 3 : 3 : 2 : 2	3,000	3,000	2,000	2,000	—	—	—	—
Balance	2,97,000	2,97,000	1,98,000	1,98,000	2,00,000	3,00,000	2,00,000	1,00,000
First Realisation Rs. 3,50,000 (on 1-1-1990) Paid to outsiders	1,05,000	1,05,000	70,000	70,000	—	—	—	—
Balance	1,92,000	1,92,000	1,28,000	1,28,000	2,00,000	3,00,000	2,00,000	1,00,000
Second Realisation Rs. 4,00,000 (on 15-1-1990) Paid first to Mortgage Loan of Rs. 1,92,000 being secured	1,92,000	—	—	—	—	—	—	—
Rs. 2,80,000 Balance		1,92,000	1,28,000	1,28,000	2,00,000	3,00,000	2,00,000	1,00,000
Paid to outsiders (3 : 2 : 2)		89,143	59,429	59,428	—	—	—	—
Balance		1,02,857	68,571	68,572	2,00,000	3,00,000	2,00,000	1,00,000
Third Realisation Rs. 50,000 : (on 1-2-1990) Paid to outsiders (3 : 2 : 2)		21,429	14,285	14,286	—	—	—	—
Balance		81,428	54,286	54,286	2,00,000	3,00,000	2,00,000	1,00,000
Fourth Realisation Rs. 1,40,000 : (on 15-2-1990) Paid to outsiders (3 : 2 : 2)		60,000	40,000	40,000	—	—	—	—
Balance		21,428	14,286	14,286	2,00,000	3,00,000	2,00,000	1,00,000
Fifth Realisation Rs. 50,000 : (on 1-3-1990) Paid to outsiders (3 : 2 : 2)		21,428	14,286	14,286	—	—	—	—
Balance					2,00,000	3,00,000	2,00,000	1,00,000
Sixth Realisation Rs. 7,89,995 (on 15-3-1990) : Paid Rs. 2,00,000 to Kumar's Loan					2,00,000	—	—	—
Balance						3,00,000	2,00,000	1,00,000
Amount available for partner is Rs. 5,89,995 *Less* : Ananth's Commission $\left(\frac{5,89,995 \times 5}{105}\right)$ = 28,095 5,61,900								
Paid Rs. 1,00,000 to Kumar's capital because he suffers no loss						—	—	1,00,000
Rs. 4,61,900 Balance						3,00,000	2,00,000	—
Paid Rs. 1,00,000 to Ananth to make his capital equal to that of Kishore						1,00,000	—	—
Rs. 3,61,900 Balance						2,00,000	2,00,000	—
Paid to Ananth and Kishore equally						1,80,950	1,80,950	—
Realisation Loss						19,050	19,050	Nil

Notes : (i) Value of sixth realisation is calculated as below :

Value of realisation of Land and Building	Rs. 8,00,000
Less : Additional payment of realisation expenses (Actual expenses Rs. 20,005 – Rs. 10,000 set aside)	Rs. 10,005
	Rs. 7,89,995

(ii) Kumar will get 1/5th share of what remains after paying Rs. 19,050 to Ananth and Rs. 19,050 to Kishore out of the realisation of stock-in-trade. If stock does not realise any amount, the unpaid amount to Ananth and Kishore will be treated as realisation loss. Kumar has been paid first because he is not to share any loss on realisation.

II. Maximum Loss Method

It is an alternative method of piecemeal distribution. There is no difference between maximum loss method and surplus capital method so for as repayment of all the outside creditors and partners' loans are concerned. But this method differs from the surplus capital method in respect of repayment of partners' capital.

(1) According to this method, at every stage of realisation, it is presumed that it is the final realisation and no more cash will be realised thereafter.

(2) Maximum loss is ascertained at each stage and distributed among the partners in their profit sharing ratio. 'Maximum loss' means the difference between the total of capitals to be paid to partners and instalment cash received.

(3) After adjusting the maximum loss to the partners' capital accounts, if any partner or partners' capital account or accounts shows/show debit balance, he or they will be treated as insolvent partner or partners and his or their deficiency is to be transferred to the solvent partners in their capital ratio (if *Garner Vs. Murray* principle is followed) or profit sharing ratio (provided *Garner Vs. Murray* principale is not followed).

(4) The amount standing to the credit of the solvent partners after debiting the maximum loss represents the cash to be paid to the respective partners out of the first available cash to them.

(5) After payment of cash, the balances on capitals are brought down and the above procedure is to be repeated until the distribution of the last instalment and the loss shown at the last realisation is the real loss of realisation.

The final loss on realisation suffered by each partner would be the same in case of both the methods of piecemeal distribution.

Illustration 7

A, B and C are partners who share profits in the proportion of 2 : 2 : 1. The following is their balance sheet as on 31-12-1992 on which date they decided to dissolve the firm :

Liabilities		Rs.	Assets	Rs.
Creditors		60,000	Sundry Assets	1,70,000
Capitals :				
A	50,000			
B	30,000			
C	30,000	1,10,000		
		1,70,000		1,70,000

The assets are realised as follows :

First Realisation Rs. 40,000, Second Rs. 30,000, Third Rs. 50,000 and the last Rs. 25,000.

Prepare a statement showing the distribution of cash :

(a) If decision in *Garner* Vs. *Murray* is applied.

(b) If decision in *Garner* Vs. *Murray* is not applied.

Solution :

(a) If rule in *Garner* Vs. *Murray* is applied :

Statement Showing Distribution of Cash

Realisation	Cash Available	Particulars	Creditors	Capitals A	Capitals B	Capitals C
		Balance as per Balance Sheet	60,000	50,000	30,000	30,000
First	40,000	Paid to Creditors	40,000			
	– 40,000					
		(i) Balance Due	20,000			
Second	30,000	Paid to Creditors	20,000			
	– 20,000					
	10,000	(ii) Balance Due		50,000	30,000	30,000
		Total of Capitals Rs. 1,10,000				
		Less : Cash available Rs. 10,000				
		Maximum Loss Rs. 1,00,000				
		Allocated to partners in their profit sharing ratio of 2 : 2 : 1		-40,000	-40,000	-20,000
		(iii) Balance		10,000	-10,000	10,000
		Deficiency of 'B' is transferred to A & C in their capital ratio *i.e.,* equally		-5,000	+10,000	-5,000
		(iv) Balance		5,000	Nil	5,000

(*Contd.*)

		(iv) Balance b/d	5,000	Nil	5,000
	– 10,000	Paid cash to A & C	– 5,000	—	–5,000
		(v) Balance (ii-iv)	45,000	30,000	25,000
Third	50,000	Total of Capital Rs. 1,00,000			
		Less : Cash available Rs. 50,000			
		Maximum Loss Rs. 50,000			
		Allocated to partners in their profit sharing ratio of 2 : 2 : 1	-20,000	-20,000	-10,000
		(vi) Balance	25,000	10,000	15,000
	–50,000	Cash paid to A, B & C	-25,000	-10,000	-15,000
		(vii) Balance (v-vi)	20,000	20,000	10,000
Fourth	25,000	Total of Capital Rs. 50,000			
		Less : Cash available Rs. 25,000			
		Maximum Loss Rs. 25,000			
		Allocated to partners in their profit sharing ratio of 2 : 2 : 1	10,000	10,000	5,000
		(viii) Balance	10,000	10,000	5,000
	– 25,000	Cash paid to A, B & C	-10,000	-10,000	-5,000
		(ix) Balance (vii-viii)	10,000	10,000	5,000
		In profit sharing ratio	2 :	2 :	1

(b) If rule in *Garner* Vs. *Murray* is not applied :

Statement Showing Distribution of Cash

Reali-Sation	Cash Available	Particulars	Creditors	Capitals A	B	C
		Balance as per Balance Sheet	60,000	50,000	30,000	30,000
First	40,000	Paid to Creditors	40,000			
	– 40,000					
		Balance	20,000			
Second	30,000					
	– 20,000	Paid to Creditors	20,000	—	—	—
	10,000	Balance		50,000	30,000	30,000
		Total of Capitals Rs. 1,10,000				
		Less : Cash available Rs. 10,000				
		Maximum Loss Rs. 1,00,000				
		Allocated to partners in their profit sharing ratio of 2 : 2 : 1		-40,000	-40,000	-20,000
		Balance		10,000	-10,000	10,000

(*Contd.*)

		Balance b/d	10,000	-10,000	10,000
		Deficiency of 'B' is transferred to A & C in their profit sharing ratio 2 : 1	-6,667	+10,000	-3,333
		Balance	3,333	Nil	7,777
	-10,000	Paid cash to A & C	-3,333	—	-7,777
		Balance	46,667	30,000	23,333
Third	50,000	Total of Capital Rs. 1,00,000 *Less* : Cash available Rs. 50,000 Maximum Loss Rs. 50,000			
		Allocated to partners in their profit sharing ratio of 2 : 2 : 1	-20,000	-20,000	-10,000
		Balance	26,667	10,000	13,333
	-50,000	Cash paid to A, B & C	26,667	10,000	13,333
		Balance	20,000	20,000	10,000
Fourth	25,000	Maximum Loss Rs. 25,000 (Capital Rs. 50,000 – Cash Rs. 25,000) Allocated to partners (2 : 2 : 1)	-10,000	-10,000	-5,000
		Balance	10,000	10,000	5,000
	-25,000	Cash paid to A, B & C	-10,000	-10,000	-5,000
		Balance	10,000	10,000	5,000
		In profit sharing ratio	2 :	2 :	1

Illustration 8

Anda, Chanda and Nanda who shared profits and losses in the ratio of 3 : 2 : 1 dissolved partnership on 30th June, 1995 on which date their Balance Sheet showed the following position.

Liabilities	Rs.	Assets	Rs.
Sundry Creditors	20,000	Cash in Hand	15,000
Mrs. Chanda's Loan Account	10,000	Stock	20,000
Capital Accounts:		Sundry Debtors	25,000
Anda	20,000	Bills Receivable	3,000
Chanda	10,000	Furniture and Fittings	7,000
Nanda	10,000		
	70,000		70,000

The bills receivable were accepted on 1st May, 1995 payable after three months. The realisations, after deducting expenses were as follows :

	Book Value	Net Proceeds
July 25	Rs. 19,600	Rs. 19,000
Aug. 20	Rs. 24,800	Rs. 24,000
Sept. 28	Rs. 6,500	Rs. 6,000

The Bills Receivable were duly honoured. Prepared a statement showing the distribution of cash and also write up Partners' Capital Accounts.

Solution :

Statement Showing Distribution of Cash

Date	Cash Available	Particulars	Creditors	Mrs. Chanda's Loan	Capital		
					Anda	Chanda	Nanda
		Balance as per B/S	20,000	10,000	20,000	10,000	10,000
June 30	15,000	Cash in Hand					
	-15,000	Paid to Outsiders in the ratio of 2 : 1	10,000	5,000			
		Balance	10,000	5,000			
July 25	19,000	Paid to Outsiders					
	-15,000	in full	10,000	5,000			
	4,000	Balance			20,000	10,000	10,000
		Maximum Loss is Rs. 36,000 (Total Capital Rs. 40,000 – Cash Rs. 4,000) This loss is divided to partners in the profit sharing ratio of 3 : 2 : 1			-18,000	-12,000	-6,000
		Balance			2,000	-2,000	4,000
		Chanda's deficiency allocated to Anda and Nanda in their capital ratio 2 : 1			-1,333	+ 2,000	- 667
		Balance			667	Nil	3,333
	-40,000	Paid cash to Anda and Nanda			-667	–	3,333
		Balance			19,333	10,000	6,667
Aug. 20	24,000	Maximum Loss is Rs. 12,000 (19,333 + 10,000 + 6,667 – 24,000) This is allocated in profit sharing ratio			6,000	4,000	2,000
		Balance			13,333	6,000	4,667
	-24,000	Paid cash to Anda, Chanda and Nanda			-13,333	6,000	-4,667
		Balance			6,000	4,000	2,000
Sept. 28	6,000	Maximum Loss is Rs. 6,000 (6,000 + 4,000 + 2,000 – 6,000) Allocated in profit sharing ratio			3,000	2,000	1,000
		Balance			3,000	2,000	1,000
	-6,000	Paid cash to Anda, Chanda and Nanda			-3,000	-2,000	-1,000
		Balance			3,000	2,000	1,000
		In profit sharing ratio			3 :	2 :	1

Dr. **Partners' Capital Accounts** Cr.

Date 1995	Particulars	Anda Rs.	Chanda Rs.	Nanda Rs.	Date 1995	Particulars	Anda Rs.	Chanda Rs.	Nanda Rs.
July 25	To Cash A/c	667	—	3,333	June 30	By Balance b/d	20,000	10,000	10,000
Aug. 20	To Cash	13,333	6,000	4,667					
Sept. 28	To Realisation A/c (Loss)	3,000	2,000	1,000					
Sept. 28	To Cash A/c	3,000	2,000	1,000					
		20,000	10,000	10,000			20,000	10,000	10,000

Note : In the absence of any specific instruction, students should follow the ruling of *Garner* Vs. *Murray*.

Illustration 9

Ramu, Somu and Raju were the partners in a firm sharing profits and losses in the ratio of 2 : 2 : 1 respectively. They decided to dissolve their firm as from 31st December, 1995 on which date their position was as under :

Liabilities	Rs.	Assets	Rs.
Creditors	20,000	Stock	28,000
Bank Overdraft	18,000	Sundry Debtors	24,000
(Secured by Stock)		Bills Receivable	14,000
Partners' Capitals :		Motor Car	32,000
Ramu	25,000		
Somu	30,000		
Raju	5,000		
	98,000		98,000

There was a bill Rs. 6,000 due on 15th May, 1996, under discount.

They realised their assets gradually and agreed to distribute the proceeds in their due order at the end of each calendar month. The following were their realisations :

Month	Assets	Amount realised
January, 1996	Bills Receivable (part)	Rs. 8,000
February, 1996	Motor Cars	Rs. 16,000
March, 1996	Stock	Rs. 14,000
April, 1996	Bills Receivable (Balance)	Rs. 4,200
May, 1996	Debtors (part)	Rs. 4,200
June, 1996	Debtors (Balance)	Rs. 11,800

The acceptor of the bill under discount met the bill on the due date.

Prepare a statement showing piecemeal distribution of cash assuming Raju is insolvent and that his estate will not be able to pay anything whatsoever.

Solution :

Statement Showing Distribution of Cash

Date	Cash Available	Particulars	Creditors	Bank Overdraft	Capitals Ramu	Capitals Somu	Capitals Raju
		Balance as per B/S	20,000	18,000	25,000	30,000	5,000
31-1-96	2,000	Rs. 8,000 less Rs. 6,000 reserves for bill under discount					
	– 2,000	Paid to creditors	2,000	—			
		Balance	18,000	18,000			
28-2-96	16,000	Paid to creditors	16,000				
	–16,000	Balance	2,000	18,000			
31-3-96	14,000	Paid for Bank over draft		14,000			
	–14,000	Balance	2,000	4,000			
30-4-96	4,200	Paid to outsiders in the					
	– 4,200	ratio of 1 : 2	1,400	2,800			
		Balance	600	1,200			
31-5-96	10,200	Rs. 4,200 plus Rs. 6,000 reserved for bill.					
	2,000	Paid to outsiders in full	600	1,200			
	8,200	Balance			25,000	30,000	5,000
		Maximum Loss is Rs. 51,800 (25,000 + 30,000 + 5,000 – 8,200) This loss transferred to partners in the profit sharing ratio of 2 : 2 : 1			20,720	20,720	10,360
		Balance			4,280	9,280	-5,360
		Deficiency of Raju is transferred to Ramu and Somu in their capital ratio of 5 : 6			-2,436	-2,924	+5,360
		Balance			1,844	6,356	Nil
	– 8,200	Paid cash to Ramu and Somu			-1,844	-6,356	—
		Balance			23,156	23,644	5,000
30-6-96	11,800	Maximum Loss is Rs. 40,000 (23,156 + 23,644 + 5,000 – 11,800) Allocated in profit sharing ratio			16,000	16,000	8,000
		Balance			7,156	7,644	-3,000
		Deficiency of Raju is transferred to Ramu and Somu in their capital ratio			-1,364	-1,636	+3,000
		Balance			5,792	6,008	Nil
	–11,800	Cash paid to Ramu and Somu			-5,792	-6,008	—

Illustration 10

Madan, Mohan and Sadan were the partners in a firm snaring profits and losses in the ratio of 3 : 2 : 1. Their Balance Sheet on 31st March, 1994 before adjusting loss for the year, showed the following position :

Liabilities	Rs.	Assets	Rs.
Sundry Creditors	20,000	Building	26,000
Madan's Loan	8,000	Machinery	15,000
Mohan's Loan	4,000	Stock	10,000
Capitals :		Debtors	20,000
Madan	33,000	Furniture	10,000
Mohan	22,000	Bank	2,000
Sadan	2,000	P & L (1993-94)	6,000
	89,000		89,000

The assets were realised gradually and expenses were paid as under :

Date	Assets	Cash Realised	Expenses Paid
30-4-1994	Building	Rs. 20,800	Rs. 800
31-5-1994	Machinery	Rs. 9,500	Rs. 500
30-6-1994	Stock & Debtors	Rs. 15,900	Rs. 900
31-7-1994	Furniture	Rs. 6,400	Rs. 400

Sundry creditors were paid at a discount of Rs. 1,000. Sadan became bankrupt and only Rs. 1,000 could be recovered from his private estate.

Prepare a statement showing distribution of cash.

Solution :

Statement Showing Distribution of Cash

Date	Net Cash	Particulars	Creditors	Madan's Loan	Mohan's Loan	Capitals Madan	Capitals Mohan	Capitals Sadan
		Balance as per B/S	20,000	8,000	4,000	33,000	22,000	2,000
		Less : P & L (Loss Rs. 6,000)	—	—	—	3,000	2,000	1,000
		Balance	20,000	8,000	4,000	30,000	20,000	1,000
		Less : Discount	1,000	—	—	—	—	—
		Balance	19,000	8,000	4,000			
30-4-94	22,000	(20,800+2,000-800)						
	-19,000	Paid to creditors	19,000					
	3,000	Balance		8,000	4,000			
	-3,000	Paid loan in the ratio of 2 : 1		2,000	1,000			
		Balance		6,000	3,000			

Contd.

Date	Cash	Particulars	Madan's Loan	Mohan's Loan	Madan	Mohan	Sadan
		Balance b/d	6,000	3,000	30,000	20,000	1,000
31-5-94	9,000	Paid loan of Madan and					
	-9,000	Mohan in full	6,000	3,000			
		Balance			30,000	20,000	1,000
30-6-94	15,000	Maximum Loss (Notional loss) is Rs. 36,000 (30,000 + 20,000 + 1,000 – 15,000)					
		This loss is allocated in profit sharing ratio			-18,000	-12,000	-6,000
		Balance			12,000	8,000	-5,000
		Deficiency of Sadan is transferred to Madan and Mohan in their capital ratio of 3 : 2			-3,000	-2,000	+5,000
		Balance			9,000	6,000	Nil
	-15,000	Paid cash to Madan and Mohan			-9,000	-6,000	
		Balance			21,000	14,000	1,000
31-7-94	6,000	Maximum Loss (Realisation loss) is Rs. 30,000 (21,000 + 14,000 + 1,000 – 6,000)					
		This loss is allocated in profit sharing ratio			-15,000	-10,000	-5,000
		Balance			6,000	4,000	-4,000
	1,000	Cash recovered from Sadan					1,000
	7,000	Balance			6,000	4,000	-3,000
		Deficiency of Sadan is transferred to Madan and Mohan in their capital ratio of 3 : 2			-1,800	-1,200	+3,000
					4,200	2,800	Nil
	-7,000	Cash paid to Madan and Mohan			-4,200	-2,800	—
		Balance			16,800	11,200	—
		In profit sharing ratio			3 :	2 :	—

Illustration 11

Anju, Sanju and Manju were the partners in a firm sharing profits and losses in the ratio of 2 : 1 : 1. Their Balance Sheet was as follows :

Liabilities	Rs.	Assets	Rs.
Sundry Creditors	15,000	Plant and Machinery	15,000
Reserve Fund	4,000	Furniture	5,500
Contingency Reserve	5,000	Stock	25,000
Anju's Capital	25,000	Debtors	20,000
Sanju's Capital	15,000	Cash in Hand	4,500
Manju's Capital	6,000		
	70,000		70,000

The firm was dissolved, and the assets were as follows :

First Realisation	Rs. 13,000
Second Realisation	Rs. 26,000
Third and Final Realisation	Rs. 19,000

On the dissolution, there was a contingent liability of Rs. 1,000 against the firm, which was settled at Rs. 600 at time of second realisation. Realisation expenses were estimated at Rs. 1,500 but these actually amounted to Rs. 1,100. The firm was found to pay Rs. 700 out of third realisation for which no provision was made. Sanju took over stock valued at Rs. 1,300 at the time of third realisation.

Prepare a statement showing distribution of cash.

Solution :

Statement Showing Distribution of Cash

Net Cash	Particulars		Creditors	Capitals Anju	Sanju	Manju
	Balance as per B/S		15,000	25,000	15,000	6,000
	Add : Reserve Fund		—	2,000	1,000	1,000
	Add : Contingency Reserve	Rs. 5,000				
	Less : Expected liability	Rs. 1,000				
	Credited to partners	Rs. 4,000	—	2,000	1,000	1,000
	Balance Due		15,000	29,000	17,000	8,000
4,500	Cash in Hand					
1,500	*Less:* Amount kept for realisation expenses					
3,000						
1,000	*Less* : Amount kept for contingent liability					
2,000	paid to creditors		2,000	—	—	—
– 2,000	Balance		13,000	29,000	17,000	8,000
13,000	First Realisation					
-13,000	Cash paid to creditors in full		13,000	—	—	—
	Balance Due			29,000	17,000	8,000
	Add : Profit on contingent liability			200	100	100
26,000	Second Realisation			29,200	17,100	8,100
400	*Add* : Cash saved on payment of contingent liability (1,000 – 600)					
26,400	Maximum Loss is (29,200 + 17,100 + 8,100 – 26,400) which is debited to partners in profit sharing ratio	Rs. 28,000		14,000	7,000	7,000
	Balance Due			15,200	10,100	1,100
-26,400	Cash paid to partners			-15,200	-10,100	-1,100
	Balance Due			14,000	7,000	7,000

(*Contd.*)

	Balance Due b/d	14,000	7,000	7,000
19,000	Third Realisation			
400	*Add :* Cash saved in Realisation Expenses (1,500 – 1,100)			
19,400				
1,300	*Add :* Stock taken by Sanju			
20,700				
700	*Less :* A new liability paid for which no provision was made			
20,000	Maximum Loss is Rs. 8,000 (14,000 + 7,000 + 7,000 – 20,000) which is debited to partners in profit sharing ratio	4,000	2,000	2,000
	Balance Due	10,000	5,000	5,000
-20,000	Cash paid to partners	-10,000	-5,000	-5,000
	Balance Due	4,000	2,000	2,000
	In profit sharing ratio	2 :	1 :	1

EXAMINATION QUESTIONS

(A) Answer the following questions in not exceeding 4 lines each :

(Each Carries two Marks)

(1) What do you mean by piecemeal distribution ?

(Kar., Oct., 1995)

(2) What are the advantages of piecemeal distribution of cash ?

(B'lore, May, 1991)

(3) What is the principle followed under piecemeal distribution of cash ?

(B'lore, April, 1984)

(4) What is the purpose behind adjusting the capitals of partners in their profit sharing ratios in the case of piecemeal distribution of cash ?

(Bombay, April, 1992)

(5) In case of piecemeal distribution, what accounting treatment is given when a partner takes over an asset whose realisable value is in excess of the amount due to him?

(B'lore, Oct., 1993)

(6) Mention the different methods of making distribution of cash among partners.

(M.K.U., Oct., 1994)

(B) Answer the following questions/problems :

(Each Carries eight Marks)

(1) What is piecemeal distribution ? What are its objectives ?

(2) Explain the procedure for distribution of cash among partners.

(Nagpur, April, 1995)

(3) Explain the different methods of making distribution of cash among partners.

(Bombay, Oct., 1989)

(4) State with reasons whether the following statements are true or false.

(i) Under piecemeal distribution, capitals of partners are repaid before repayment of their loans.

(ii) Under piecemeal distribution, cash for a contingent liability is set aside before paying any cash to any unsecured liability.

(iii) Under maximum loss method, deficiency of a partner is charged to other partners in their capital ratio.

(Shivaji, Oct., 1989)

(5) The firm of A, B and C has dissolved when their capitals were Rs. 14,000, Rs. 8,000 and Rs. 3,000 respectively. Their profit sharing ratio was 3 : 2 : 1. After paying off all liabilities, the assets realised as under :

1st instalment	Rs. 7,000
2nd instalment	Rs. 6,000
3rd instalment	Rs. 9,000

Prepare the statement showing distribution of cash.

Ans. : Balance of loss : A–Rs. 1,500; B– Rs. 1,000 and C– Rs. 500.

Hint :	A	B	C
First Instalment	2,000	—	—
	3,000	2,000	—
Second Instalment	3,000	2,000	1,000
Third Instalment	4,500	3,000	1,500

(6) X, Y and Z were partners sharing profits and losses in the ratio of 2 : 1 : 1. The firm was dissolved and the assets were realised gradually, Rs. 2,000 was received once. Rs. 5,500 another time and Rs. 16,000 finally.

Show how each instalment is to be distributed.

Ans. : Balance of loss : X– Rs. 2,000; Y– Rs. 1,000; Z– Rs. 1,000.

Hint :	X	Y	Z
First time	—	2,000	—
Second time	—	500	—
-	2,500	2,500	
Third time	8,000	4,000	4,000

(7) The following is the balance sheet of M/s. A, B and C who share the profits and losses in the ratio of 2 : 2 : 1.

Liabilities	Rs.	Assets	Rs.
Sundry Creditors	15,000	Cash in Hand	2,000
Capitals :		Sundry Debtors	15,000
A	15,000	Stock	29,000
B	12,000		
C	4,000		
	46,000		46,000

The firm is dissolved and the assets realised as under :

1-1-93 Rs. 10,000; 15-2-93 Rs. 15,000 and 31-3-93 Rs. 9,000.

Prepare the statement showing distribution of cash.

(*Bangalore, Oct., 1994*)

Ans. : Balance of loss : A–Rs. 4,000; B–Rs. 4,000; and C–Rs. 2,000.

Hint :	Creditors	A	B	C
Cash in hand	2,000	—	—	—
1-1-93 Rs. 10,000	10,000	—	—	—

15-2-93	Rs. 15,000	3,000	3,000	—	—
		—	4,000	4,000	—
		—	400	400	200
31-3-93	Rs. 9,000	—	3,600	3,600	1,800

(8) Sundar, Chandar and Balan, who shares profits in the ratio of 1/2 : 1/4 : 1/4 decide to dissolve the firm.

Balance Sheet as on the date of dissolution

Liabilities	Rs.	Assets	Rs.
Creditors	35,000	Sundry Assets	1,00,000
Sundar's Capital A/c	25,000		
Chandar's Capital A/c	25,000		
Balan's Capital A/c	15,000		
	1,00,000		1,00,000

The assets realised Rs. 85,000. The proceeds were received in instalments Rs. 35,000, Rs. 25,000 and Rs. 25,000.

Show how the proceeds should be distributed as and when received.

(*M.K.U., April, 1983*)

Ans. : Balance of loss : Sunder– Rs. 7,500; Chander– Rs.3,750; and Balan– Rs. 3,750

Hint :	Creditors	Sundar	Chandar	Balan
I Instalment	35,000	—	—	—
II Instalment	—	—	10,000	—
	—	—	2,500	2,500
	—	5,000	2,500	2,500
III Instalment	—	12,500	6,250	6,250

(9) P, Q and R are partners sharing profits and losses in the ratio of 5 : 3 : 2. They dissolve the firm. It was decide to repay the dues to partners as and when the assets realised. The details of realisation are as follows :

February 1, 1997	Rs. 26,000
April 1, 1997	Rs. 11,000
May 1, 1997	Rs. 10,000

Prepare the statement showing distribution of cash.

Ans. : Balance of Profit : P– Rs. 1,000; Q– Rs. 600 and R– Rs. 400

Hint :		P	Q	R
1-2-97	Rs. 26,000	1,000	6,000	—
1-4-97	Rs. 11,000	2,500	1,500	—
		3,500	2,100	1,400
1-5-97	Rs. 10,000	5,000	3,000	1,000

(10) The firm of M, N and O has dissolved when their capitals were Rs. 10,000, Rs. 7,000 and Rs. 3,000 respectively. After paying off all liabilities the assets realised as under :

1st instalment	Rs. 8,000
2nd instalment	Rs. 7,500
3rd instalment	Rs. 6,000

Prepare a statement of piecemeal distribution of cash.

(Karnatak, April, 1995)

Ans. : Balance of Profit Rs. 1,500 (500 + 500 + 500).

Hint :

	M	N	O
First Instalment	3,000	—	—
	2,500	2,500	—
Second Instalment	1,500	1,500	—
	1,500	1,500	1,500
Third Instalment	2,000	2,000	2,000

(11) A, B and C are partners sharing profits and losses in the ratio of 5 : 3 : 2. The following is the Balance Sheet as on 31-12-94 when they dissolve the firm.

Balance Sheet as on 31-12-94

Liabilities		Rs.	Assets	Rs.
Creditors		40,000	Sundry Assets	1,60,000
A's loan		10,000		
Partners' Capitals :				
A	50,000			
B	15,000			
C	45,000	1,10,000		
		1,60,000		1,60,000

On account of dissolution assets realised as under :

Ist instalment – 30,000; 2nd instalment – 73,000; 3rd instalment – 47,000.

Prepare statement showing the distribution of cash.

(Karnatak, April, 1997)

Ans. : Balance of loss : A– Rs. 5,000; B– Rs. 3,000 and C– Rs. 2,000

Hint :

	Creditors	A's Loan	A	B	C
I. Instalment	30,000	—	—	—	—
II. Instalment	10,000	10,000	—	—	—
	—	—	—	—	25,000
	—	—	20,000	—	8,000
III. Instalment	—	—	5,000	—	2,000
	—	—	20,000	12,000	8,000

(12) A, B and C share profits and losses in proportion of 3 : 2 : 1. On the date of dissolution their Balance Sheet stood as follows :

Balance Sheet

Liabilities	Rs.	Assets	Rs.
Bank O/D	4,000	Sundry Assets	1,00,000
Partners' Capitals :			
A	66,000		
B	24,000		
C	6,000		
	1,00,000		1,00,000

The assets realised as under :

	Rs.
Ist Instalment	28,000
IInd Instalment	15,000
IIIrd Instalment	31,000

Show how the proceeds should be distributed under proportionate capital method.

(*Bangalore, April, 1998*)

Ans. : Balance of loss : A– Rs. 13,000; B– Rs. 8,667 and C– Rs. 4,333.

Hint :	Bank O/D	A	B	C
I Instalment	400	24,000	—	—
II Instalment	—	6,000	—	—
	—	5,400	3,600	—
III Instalment	—	12,600	8,400	—
	—	5,000	3,333	1,667

(C) Solve the following problems :

(*Each Carries 16 Marks*)

(1) The following is the Balance Sheet of the firm of Messers. Tom, James and Warren as on 31st December, 1995 :

Liabilities	Rs.	Assets	Rs.
Capital Accounts :		Fixed Assets	15,000
Tom	31,000	Sundry Debtors	42,000
James	20,000		
Warren	6,000		
	57,000		57,000

The profits and losses are divided in the ratio of 3 : 2 : 1. The firm was dissolved on 31st Dec., 1995 and the assets were gradually realised and distributed amongst the partners on a piecemeal basis.

The following are the realisation made : Jan., 1996– Rs. 500; Feb., 1996– Rs. 2,000; March, 1996– Rs. 22,700.

Set out the distribution of cash among the partners.

(*Shivaji, Nov., 1982*)

Ans. : Balance of Loss : Tom– Rs. 15,900; James– Rs. 10,600 and Warren– Rs. 5,300.

(2) Suresh, Ramesh and Girish are in partnership. The following is their Balance Sheet as on 31-12-1989 on which date they dissolve their firm. They share profits and losses in the ratio of 4 : 3 : 2.

Balance Sheet as on 31-12-1989

Liabilities	Rs.	Assets	Rs.
Creditors	9,500	Cash on Hand	200
Reserve	3,600	Debtors	27,000
Capital A/cs :		Stock	13,000
Suresh	22,400	Furniture	15,800
Ramesh	12,900		
Girish	7,600		
	56,000		56,000

It is decided to repay the amounts due to the partners as and when the assets realised. The assets realise as follows :

	Debtors	Stock	Furniture
I Instalment	2,000	1,000	300
II Instalment	6,000	3,000	2,000
III Instalment	10,000	6,500	5,200
IV Instalment	6,000	1,500	6,000

Prepare a statement showing how the distribution should be made.

(*Kar., Nov., 1980 Sem*)

Ans. : Balance of loss : Suresh Rs. 2,800; Ramesh Rs. 2,100; and Girish Rs. 1,400.

(3) East, South and North are in partnership sharing profits and losses in the ratio of 3 : 2 : 1. They decided to dissolve the business on 31-2-1988 on which date their balance sheet was as follows :

Liabilities	Rs.	Assets	Rs.
Capital Accounts :		Land and Building	30,810
East	38,700	Motor Car	5,160
South	10,680	Investments	1,080
North	11,100	Stock	19,530
Loan Account : North	3,000	Debtors	11,280
Creditors	10,320	Cash	5,940
	73,800		73,800

The assets were realised on piecemeal as follows and it was agreed that cash should be distributed as and when realised :

15-1-89	Rs. 10,380
20-2-89	Rs. 27,900
23-2-89	Rs. 3,600
15-4-89 : North took over investments at a value of	Rs. 1,260
27-4-89	Rs. 19,200

Dissolution expenses were originally provided for an estimated amount of Rs. 2,700, but the actual amount spent on 29-3-1989 was Rs. 1,920. The creditors were settled for Rs. 10,080.

You are required to prepare a statement showing distribution of cash amongst the partners.

(*Gulbarga, April, 1983 and C.A. Inter, 1969*)

Ans. : Balance of Loss : East Rs. 3,600; South Rs. 2,400; and North Rs. 1,200.

Note : (i) The excess provision received Rs. 780 (2,700 – 1,920) paid to East Rs. 390; South Rs. 260 and North Rs. 130.

(ii) Investment of Rs. 1,260 paid to North.

(4) Sohan, Mohan and Ravikant were partners sharing profits and losses in the ratio of 3 : 3 : 2 respectively. On 1st January, 1994 their firm was dissolved. Their Balance Sheet as on that date was as follows :

Balance Sheet as at 1-1-1994

Liabilities		Rs.	Assets	Rs.
Sundry Creditors		20,000	Land	20,000
Mohan's Loan A/c		4,000	Buildings	20,000
Partners' Capital A/cs. :			Machinery	12,000
Sohan	24,000		Stock	15,000
Mohan	15,000		Debtors	5,000
Ravikant	9,000	48,000		
		72,000		72,000

The assets were realised gradually as follows :

	Date	Gross Amount	Expenses	Net Amount
1	15-1-94	11,000	1,000	10,000
2	20-1-94	23,000	3,000	20,000
3	25-1-94	10,200	600	9,600
4	30-1-94	13,000	1,800	11,200
5	10-2-94	12,000	2,000	10,000

Prepare detailed statement showing distribution of realised money as and when received and the final settlement.

(*Shivaji, April, 1984*)

Ans. : Balance of Loss : Sohan Rs. 4,200; Mohan Rs. 4,200 and Ravikant Rs. 2,800.

(5) A, B and C were partners sharing profits and losses in the ratio of 2 : 2 : 1. They dissolved their firm on 1-1-1992 when their position was as under :

Liabilities	Rs.	Assets	Rs.
Trade Creditors	40,000	Land and Buildings	50,000
Bills Payable	30,000	Plant & Machinery	80,000
Reserves	10,000	Stock-in-trade	60,000
Capital Accounts :		Sundry Debtors	10,000
A	40,000	Cash in Hand	10,000
B	60,000	Profit and Loss A/c	5,000
C	35,000		
	2,15,000		2,15,000

Assets were realised and cash was paid to partners as and when received.

The net cash was available each month as under :

End of February 1992	Rs. 50,000
End of March 1992	Rs. 1,20,000
End of June 1992	Rs. 40,000

A part of the stock costing Rs. 20,000 was taken over by B for Rs. 15,000 for his personal use.

Prepare the statement showing piece meal distribution of cash among the partners.

(*Kar., April, 1988*)

Ans. : Balance of Profit : A–Rs. 10,000; B–Rs. 10,000 and C–Rs. 5,000.

(6) The following is the balance sheet of ECON & Co. on 31-12-1989 when their firm was dissolved :

Liabilities	Rs.	Assets	Rs.
Mortgage on Building	5,000	Buildings	22,000
Loan on Investments	8,000	Furniture	5,000
Sundry Creditors	21,000	Investments	5,000
Capital Accounts :		Stock	18,000
E	13,000	Debtors	12,000
C	9,000	Cash	2,000
O	7,500	Profit and Loss A/c	7,500
N	8,000		
	71,500		71,500

The realisation of assets was as under :

	15-2-89	1-3-89	31-3-89	15-4-89
Buildings	7,250	—	12,000	6,000
Furniture	1,000	—	3,100	—
Investments	5,000	—	—	—
Stock	4,000	3,000	5,000	8,000
Debtors	5,000	3,300	2,500	600
Expenses	250	300	100	100

Partners decided to distribute the cash as and when received. Prepare the statement showing how the distribution of cash is made. The partners shared profit or loss in the ratio of 6 : 4 : 3 : 2.

(*Gulbarga, Oct., 1990*)

Ans. : Balance of Profit : E– Rs. 1,200; C– Rs. 800; O– Rs. 600; N– Rs. 400.
Capital ratio of Partners 10 : 7 : 6 : 7.

(7) A, B and C were partners sharing profits and losses in the ratio of 2 : 2 : 1. The firm was dissolved due to bankrupt of C, on which date their liabilities were as under :

	Rs.
Sundry Creditors	20,000
Bills Payable	10,000
Reserve	5,000
Capitals : A	18,000
B	28,000
C	4,000

Assets realised as under :

Ist Instalment	18,000
2nd Instalment	15,000
3rd Instalment	22,000

Applying the decision of *Garner* Vs. *Murray,* prepare the statement of piecemeal distribution of cash and also show the consolidated realisation account, capital accounts and bank account.

(*Kar., Oct., 1989*)

Ans. : Balance of loss : A– Rs. 12,400 (Including C's Capital deficiency of Rs. 400). B– Rs. 12,600 (Including C's Capital deficiency of Rs. 600).
Realisation Loss : Rs. 30,000, Cash A/c. Total : Rs. 79,000.
Cash paid to A– Rs. 19,600 and B– Rs. 29,400 because each partner should bring Solvent Partners Capital Ratio – 2 : 3.

Note : It is solved according to "Maximum loss method".

(8) Anagha, Anita and Alka were in partnership sharing profits and losses as 3 : 2 : 1 respectively. The partnership was dissolved on 30th June, 1991 when the position was as follows :

Liabilities	Rs.	Assets	Rs.
Capitals :		Cash in Hand	28,000
Anagha	1,40,000	Sundry Debtors	2,94,000
Anita	70,000	Stock-in-trade	1,12,000
Alka	14,000		
Creditors	2,10,000		
	4,34,000		4,34,000

There was bill for Rs. 10,000 due on 30th Nov., 1991, under discount. It was agreed that the net realisation should be distributed in their due order (at the end of each month) but as safely as possible. The realisations and expenses were as under :

	Stock and Debtors	Expenses
31st July, 1991	Rs. 84,000	Rs. 7,000
31st August, 1991	Rs. 1,26,000	Rs. 5,400
30th September, 1991	Rs. 70,000	Rs. 4,900
31st October, 1991	Rs. 77,000	Rs. 3,500
30th November, 1991	Rs. 35,500	Rs. 3,500

The stock was completely disposed of and amounts due from debtors were realised, the balance being irrecoverable. The acceptor of the bill under discount met the bill on the due date. Prepare the statement for piecemeal distribution of cash.

(*Bombay, April, 1972*)

Ans. : Balance of Loss : Anagha Rs. 18,900; Anita Rs. 12,600 and Alka Rs. 6,300.

(9) K, L and M are partners who share profits in the proportion of 3 : 2 : 1. Their balance sheet as on Dec., 31, 1991 was as under :

Liabilities	Rs.	Assets	Rs.
Capitals :		Assets :	
K	30,000	Fixed and Current	2,00,000
L	50,000		
M	50,000		
Liabilities	70,000		
	2,00,000		2,00,000

The partnership is dissolved and the assets realised as follows :

First realisation	Rs. 50,000;	Second realisation	Rs. 30,000
Third realisation	Rs. 60,000;	Fourth realisation	Rs. 30,000
and Last realisation	Rs. 15,000.		

Prepare a statement of piecemeal distribution of cash according to the notional or maximum loss method.

(*Bombay, Oct., 1972 and Mangalore, Oct., 1990*)

Ans. : Balance of Loss : K– Rs. 7,500; L– Rs. 5,000 and M– Rs. 2,500.

(10) A, B and C share profits in the proportion of 1/2, 1/3 and 1/6. Their balance sheet is as follows :

Liabilities	Rs.	Assets	Rs.
Capital Accounts :		Assets less liabilities	80,000
A	30,000		
B	30,000		
C	20,000		
	80,000		80,000

The partnership is dissolved and the assets realised as follows :

First realisation	Rs. 10,000
Second realisation	Rs. 15,000
Third and final realisation	Rs. 25,000
	Rs, 50,000

Prepare a statement showing how the distributions should be made applying *Garner* Vs. *Murray* principle.

(*I.C.W.A., Dec., 1976 & B'lore, Nov., 1992 & April, 1995 Mod.*)

Ans. : Third and Final Realisation A– receives Rs. 12,500; B– receives Rs. 8,333 and C– Rs. 4,167.

(11) A, B and C share profits and losses in the proportion of 4/10, 5/10 and 1/10. Their balance sheet is as follows :

Liabilities	Rs.	Assets	Rs.
Sundry Creditors	10,000	Cash in Hand	3,000
A's Loan	6,000	Other Assets	56,000
B's Loan	3,000		
Reserve Fund	6,000		
Contingency Reserve	4,000		
A's Capital A/c	15,000		
B's Capital A/c	12,000		
C's Capital A/c	3,000		
	59,000		59,000

The partnership is dissolved and the assets are realised as follows :

First realisation	Rs. 10,000
Second realisation	Rs. 20,000
Third realisation	Rs. 17,000

On the date of the dissolution, there was a contingent liability of Rs. 1,000 against the firm which was settled at Rs. 700 at the time of second realisation. Realisation expenses were estimated at Rs. 2,000 but those actually amounted to Rs. 1,500. C took stock worth Rs. 500 at the time of third realisation. The firm was forced to pay Rs. 600 out of third realisation for which no provision was made in the books.

Prepare a statement showing how the distributions should be made by following the Maximum Loss Method.

(*Poona, April, 1983, Baroda, Nagpur, Oct., 1974 and B'lore, Oct., 1993*)

Ans. : Balance of Loss : A– Rs. 4,240; B– Rs. 5,300 and C– Rs. 1,060.

(12) Ramesh, Suresh and Umesh were partners in a firm which was dissolved on 31-12-1990. Their position at the time of dissolution was as follows :

Liabilities	Rs.	Assets	Rs.
Capital Accounts :		Building	70,000
Ramesh	30,000	Plant and Machinery	30,000
Suresh	40,000	Furniture and Fixtures	13,000
Umesh	35,000	Stock	12,000
Sundry Creditors	25,000	Sundry Debtors	15,000
Bank Overdraft	10,000	Bank	9,800
Suresh's Loan	10,000	Cash in Hand	200
	1,50,000		1,50,000

The assets were realised and cash was distributed as and when received. The net cash available the end of each month was as follows :

January 1991	Rs. 18,000	February 1991	Rs. 24,000
March 1991	Rs. 41,000	April 1991	36,000

Prepare the statement showing piecemeal distribution of cash showing that the partners shared profits and losses in the ratio of 3 : 2 : 1.

(*Karnatak, Oct., 1991*)

Ans. : Balance of Loss : Ramesh– Rs. 10,500; Suresh– Rs. 7,000 and Umesh– Rs. 3,500.

(13) The following is the balance sheet of X, Y and Z who were sharing profits and losses in the ratio of 5 : 3 : 2.

Balance Sheet as at 1-1-1990

Liabilities	Rs.	Assets	Rs.
Creditors	1,00,000	Building	80,000
Capital Accounts :		Machinery	40,000
X	94,000	Furniture	50,000
Y	66,000	Stock	90,000
Z	60,000	Debtors	60,000
	3,20,000		3,20,000

It was decided to dissolve the firm. The assets were realised as under and the payments were made as and when realised.

1-1-1991	Rs. 60,000
15-1-1991	Rs. 40,000
1-2-1991	Rs. 96,000
28-2-1991	Rs. 1,04,000

Prepare the statement showing distribution of cash.

(*Gulbarga, April, 1995*)

Ans. : Balance of Loss : X– Rs. 10,000; Y– Rs. 6,000 and Z– Rs. 4,000.

(14) The firm of X, Y and Z was dissolved owing the Bankrupt of Z (whose private surplus was nil). The position of the firm on 31-12-1994 was as follows :

	Rs.
Creditors	14,000
Capitals : X	48,000
Y	26,000
Z	12,000
Loss	12,000
Cash in Hand	5,000

The assets realised as follows :

31-1-1995	18,000
28-2-1995	24,000
31-3-1995	12,000

The amount distributed as and when realised. Prepare a statement of distribution of cash. Apply "*Garner* Vs. *Murray*" decision.

(*Karnatak, Oct., 1995*)

Ans. : Balance of Loss : X– Rs. 10,778 (including Z's capital deficiency of Rs. 1,111); Y–Rs. 10,222 (including Z's capital deficiency of Rs. 555).

Note : This problem is solved according to "Maximum Loss Method".

(15) P, Q and R were partners sharing profits in the ratio of 3 : 4 : 5. Their Balance Sheet was as follows :

Liabilities	Rs.	Assets	Rs.
Creditors	10,000	Sundry Assets	36,000
Q's Loan	2,000		
Capitals :			
P	12,000		
Q	8,000		
R	4,000		
	36,000		36,000

The assets realised as follows :

1st Instalment	Rs. 5,000	2nd Instalment	Rs. 10,000
3rd Instalment	Rs. 5,100	4th Instalment	Rs. 6,300
5th Instalment	Rs. 5,700.		

Prepare a statement showing the distribution of cash using maximum loss method.

(*Bangalore, April, 1990*)

Ans. : Cash available after paying the creditors and Q's loan : Rs. 3,000. Maximum Loss : In the second stage Rs. 21,000 (24,000 – 3,000); in the third stage Rs. 15,900; in the fourth stage Rs. 9,600 and in the fifth stage Rs. 3,900.
Balance of Loss : 'P' Rs. 975; 'Q' Rs. 1,300 and 'R' Rs. 1,625.

(16) P, Q and R were partners sharing profits in the proportion of 1/2, 1/4 and 1/4 respectively. Their Balance Sheet on the date of dissolution was as follows :

Liabilities	Rs.	Assets	Rs.
Creditors	10,000	Sundry Assets	60,000
P's Loan	5,000	Cash	1,000
Q's Loan	3,000		
P's Capital A/c	20,000		
Q's Capital A/c	15,000		
R's Capital A/c	8,000		
	61,000		61,000

The assets realised Rs. 65,000, which was received in instalments of Rs. 15,000; Rs. 16,000; Rs. 14,000 and Rs. 20,000. Show how the proceeds should be distributed as and when received by following proportionate capital method.

(*Bangalore, Oct., 1990*)

Ans. : Balance of Profit : 'P' Rs. 2,500; 'Q' Rs. 1,250 and 'R' Rs. 1,250.

Hint : Excess Capitals : P– Rs. 4,000 and Q– Rs. 7,000.

(17) Beru, Kanda and Kombe are partners sharing profits in the ratio of 5 : 3 : 2. Their Balance Sheet on 30th September, 1995 was as follows :

Liabilities	Rs.	Assets	Rs.
Creditors	10,000	Sundry Assets	36,000
Kanda's Loan	4,000	Cash	2,000
Capitals :			
Beru	12,000		
Kanda	8,000		
Kombe	4,000		
	38,000		38,000

They dissolved the firm, and realised the assets gradually and decide to make payment as and when they are realised. The realisation expenses estimated at Rs. 1,500 but actually amounted to Rs. 800. The assets realised as follows :

1st realisation	Rs. 5,000
2nd realisation	Rs. 10,000
3rd realisation	Rs. 5,000
4th realisation	Rs. 6,000
5th realisation	Rs. 5,500

Prepare a statement showing the distribution of cash under proportionate capital method.

(*Bangalore, May, 1991*)

Ans. : Balance of Loss : Beru Rs. 2,650; Kanda Rs. 1,590 and Kombe Rs. 1,060.

Hints : (i) Excess capitals based on Kombe: Beru Rs. 2,000 and Kanda Rs. 1,200.

(ii) Excess capital based on Beru's excess contribution : Kanda Rs. 800.

(iii) Estimated expenses of Rs. 1,500 should be deducted from the available cash and the excess provision received Rs. 700 (1,500 – 800) should be distributed to all the partners.

(18) Monika, Sonika and Romika share profits and losses in the proportion of 2 : 1 : 1. Their Balance Sheet is as follows:

Liabilities	Rs.	Assets	Rs.
Sundry Creditors	10,000	Plant and Machinery	25,000
Sonika's Loan	6,000	Stock	15,500
Romika's Loan	4,000	Furniture	5,500
Reserve Fund	8,000	Sundry Debtors	17,000
Contingency Reserve	6,000	Cash in Hand	6,000
Monika's Capital	20,000		
Sonika's Capital	10,000		
Romika's Capital	5,000		
	69,000		69,000

The firm is dissolved, and the assets are realised as follows :

1st realisation Rs. 12,000

2nd realisation Rs. 25,000

3rd realisation Rs. 19,000

On the dissolution date, there was a contingent liability of Rs. 2,000 against the firm which was settled at Rs. 1,500 at the time of 2nd realisation. Realisation expenses were estimated at Rs. 2,000, but these actually amounted to Rs. 1,200. The firm was bound to pay Rs. 600 out of third realisation for which no provision was made. Sonika took over stock valued at Rs. 1,000 at the time of third realisation. Prepare a statement showing the distribution of cash under 'surplus capital method'.

(*Bangalore, Oct., 1991; April, 1993*)

Ans. : Balance of Loss : Monika– Rs. 4,650; Sonika– Rs. 2,325 and Romika– Rs. 2,325.

Notes : (i) Balance of capital after adjusting reserve fund and contingency reserve : Monika Rs. 27,000; Sonika Rs. 13,500 and Romika Rs. 8,500. Excess capitals : Monika Rs. 10,000 and Sonika Rs. 5,000.

(ii) Contingent liability of Rs. 1,500 should be deducted from the second realisation and stock taken over by Sonika Rs. 1,000 should be added to the third realisation.

(iii) Estimated expenses of Rs. 2,000 should be deducted from Cash in Hand and the excess provision received Rs. 800 (2,000 – 1,200) should be distributed to all the partners. Alternatively, the expenses of Rs. 1,200 can be deducted from the third realisation.

(iv) Further expenses of Rs. 600 should be deducted from the third realisation.

(19) The following is the Balance Sheet of A, B and C who were sharing profits in the ratio of 3 : 4 : 5.

Liabilities	Rs.	Assets	Rs.
Creditors	1,00,000	Sundry Assets	3,80,000
A's Loan	60,000		
B's Loan	40,000		
Capitals :			
A	1,00,000		
B	60,000		
C	20,000		
	3,80,000		3,80,000

They dissolved the firm and assets realised as follows :

1st Instalment	Rs. 50,000;	2nd Instalment	Rs. 1,00,000
3rd Instalment	Rs. 50,000;	4th Instalment	Rs. 10,000
5th Instalment	Rs. 44,000;	6th Instalment	Rs. 6,000
7th Instalment	Rs. 72,000.		

Prepare a statement sharing distribution of cash under proportionate capital method.

(Bangalore, April, 1993 and Oct., 1995)

Ans. : Balance of Loss : A– Rs. 12,000; B– Rs. 16,000 and C– Rs 20,000.

Hints : (i) Excess capitals based on 'C': A– Rs. 88,000 and B– Rs. 44,000.

(ii) Excess capital based on B's excess contribution : A– Rs. 55,000. Therefore A should be paid first out of realisation, Rs. 55,000 to bring his share proportionate to B. Then, A and B should be paid next out of realisations in the ratio of 3 : 4 Rs. 77,000 (33,000 + 44,000) to bring their ratio proportionate to 'C'.

(20) Rashmi, Rakhee and Preethi are in partnership. The following is their Balance Sheet as on 31st December, 1995, on which date they dissolve their firm. They share profit and losses in the ratio of 4 : 3 : 2.

Balance Sheet as on 31-12-1994

Liabilities	Rs.	Assets	Rs.
Sundry Creditors	19,000	Cash in Hand	400
General Reserves	7,200	Sundry Debtors	54,000
Capitals :		Stock-in-trade	26,000
Rashmi	44,800	Plant and Machinery	31,600
Rakhee	25,800		
Preethi	15,200		
	1,12,000		1,12,000

It is decided to repay the amount due to the partners as and when the assets are realised. Assets realised as follows :

Instalments	Debtors Rs.	Stock Rs.	Machinery Rs.
I	4,000	2,000	600
II	12,000	6,000	4,000
III	20,000	13,000	10,400
IV	12,000	3,000	12,000

Prepare a statement showing how the distribution of cash should be made.

(*Karnatak, April, 1998*)

Ans. : Balance of Loss : Rashmi Rs. 5,600; Rakhee Rs. 4,200 and Preethi Rs. 2,800.

(21) 'X', 'Y' and 'Z' are in partnership sharing profits and losses in the ratio of 3 : 2 : 1. They decide to dissolve the business on 31st Dec., 1996 on which date their Balance Sheet was as follow :

Liabilities	Rs.	Assets	Rs.
Capitals :		Land and Buildings	61,620
X	77,400	Motor Car	10,320
Y	21,360	Investments	2,160
Z	22,200	Stock	39,060
Loan A/c 'Z'	6,000	Debtors	22,560
Creditors	20,640	Cash	11,880
	1,47,600		1,47,600

The assets were realised as follows and it was agreed that cash should be distributed as and when realised.

31 January, 1997		Rs. 20,760
28 February, 1997		Rs. 55,800
31 March, 1997		Rs. 7,200
20th April, 1997	'Z' took over the investments at a value of	Rs. 2,520
30th April, 1997		Rs. 38,400

Dissolution expenses were estimated at Rs. 5,400 but actual amount spent was Rs. 3,840. Creditors were settled for Rs. 20,160.

You are required to prepare a statement showing the distribution of cash under Maximum Loss Method.

(*Bangalore, April, 1998*)

Ans. : After paying creditors and Z's loan, the cash available is Rs. 1,080; Maximum loss : In first stage Rs. 1,19,880 (*i.e.*, 1,20,960 – 1,080); In second stage Rs. 64,080; In third stage Rs. 56,880; In fourth stage Rs. 14,400 [*i.e.*, 56,880 – 42,480 *i.e.*, value of investment Rs. 2,520 + Cash realised Rs. 38,400 + Cash surplus of expenses (5,400 – 3,840) Rs. 1,560]. Balance of loss : X Rs. 7,200; Y Rs. 4,800 and Z Rs. 2,400.

11

BRANCH ACCOUNTS

In order to promote the sales and eliminate the middlemen in the chain of distribution, some of the manufacturing and trading concerns open their branches or departments in different areas. When the various divisions of the business concerns are situated in different places of the same city, or different cities, or in the different countries, they are known as 'Branches'. When the various divisions of the business concern are located under one roof, they are known as 'Departments'. A suitable accounting method is to be adopted for recording the business transactions in case of a business having different branches or departments.

Meaning and Objectives of Branch

The term 'branch' means a department which is conducted at a distance. The control and management of such branch or branches is done by Head Office. The concern which is having such branches is known as 'Head Office'. The main idea of opening branches is to increase the existing business and business relation in the country or abroad. The accounting system to be adopted for the branch depends upon the nature and size of the branch and degree of control needed by the Head Office. The main objects of keeping the branch accounts are as follows :

(i) To ascertain the profit or loss of each branch.

(ii) To find out the profitability of each branch.

(iii) To evaluate the performance and progress of each branch.

(iv) To give instructions for improvement in the working of each branch.

(v) To know the goods and cash requirements of various branches.

(vi) To know the financial position of various branches.

Types of Branches

From the accounting point of view the branches may be divided as follows :

I. Dependent branches

II. Independent branches

III. Foreign branches

(I) Dependent Branches

A branch which does not maintain its own set of books is called 'Dependent Branch'. The records of such branches are maintained by the head office. The salient features of such branches are as follows :

(i) These branches sell only such goods which are already supplied by the head office. Usually, they may not be allowed to make purchases from the open market.

(ii) Head office supply the goods to such branches at cost price or invoice price.

(iii) Normally, goods are sold on cash basis. Sometimes, with the instructions of the head office some branches sold the goods on credit basis.

(iv) Cash received by such branches from its debtors is daily remitted to the head office. Usually such branches are instructed to deposit daily cash proceeds into the bank account opened in the name of head office.

(v) All branch expenses are directly paid by the head office through cheques.

(vi) Petty expenses are paid by the branch manager out of petty cash balance. Usually, the petty cash account is maintained on impress system.

(vii) Such branches do not keep any account, accounts are maintained only in the head office books. However, such branches maintain a Debtors Ledger and a Stock Ledger.

System of Accounting

Head office may be kept the accounts of dependent branch in anyone of the following ways :

(A) Debtors system.

(B) Branch Trading and Profit and Loss Account.

(C) Stock and debtors system.

(D) Wholesale branch system.

All these accounting systems are explained in detail in the following or subsequent pages :

(A) Debtors System

This system of accounting is normally adopted in case of branches of small size. Under this system of accounting head office maintains only one account for one branch called "Branch Account" in its books. Branch account is a nominal account in nature. Following accounting entries are to be passed in the books of head office for recording the different branch transactions :

1. **For goods supplied by the Head Office to the Branch :**

Branch Account	Dr.	With the value of
To Goods Sent to Branches A/c		goods sent.

2. **For goods returned by the Branch to the Head Office :**

Goods Sent to Branch A/c	Dr.	With the value of
To Branch Account		goods returned.

3. **For expenses at Branch paid by the Head Office :**

Branch Account	Dr.	With the amount of
To Bank Account		expenses.

4. **For remittances sent by the Branch :**

Bank Account	Dr.	With the amount of
To Branch Account		cash sent.

5. **For goods returned by Branch Debtors to Head Office directly :**

Goods Sent to Branch A/c	Dr.	With the amount of
To Branch Account		goods returned.

6. **For goods sent by branch to another branch at the instructions from Head office :**

Good Sent to Branch Account	Dr.	With the amount of
To Branch Account		goods sent.

Note : It should be treated as goods returned by branch to Head office.

7. **For transfer of balance in Goods Sent to Branch Account :**

Good Sent to Branch Account	Dr.	With balance in
To Purchase/Trading Account		goods sent account.

8. **For assets at the Branch at the end of the accounting period :**

Branch Assets Account	Dr.	With the value of
To Branch Account		assets at the Branch.

9. **For liabilities at the Branch at the end of the accounting period :**

Branch Account	Dr.	With the value of
To Branch Liabilities A/c		liabilities at the Branch

10. **For profit at Branch :**

Branch Account	Dr.	With the amount of
To General P & L A/c		profit of the Branch.

11. **For loss at Branch :**

General P & L A/c	Dr.	With the amount of
To Branch Account		loss of the Branch.

12. At the end of the accounting year the assets and liabilities of the Branch will appear in the Head office Balance Sheet. But in beginning of the next accounting year, they will be transferred to the Branch Account.

In such cases the entry will be as follows :

(*i*) *For transfer of assets to Branch :*

Branch Account	Dr.	With the value of assets transferred.
To Branch Assets A/c		

(*ii*) *For transfer of liabilities to Branch :*

Branch Liabilities Account	Dr.	With the value of the liabilities transferred.
To Branch Account		

When the above entries are posted, the Branch Account will appear as follows :

In the Books of Head Office

Branch Account

Dr. Cr.

		Rs.			Rs.
To Opening Balance :			By Opening Balances :		
Cash in Hand	***		Creditors	***	
Stock (at cost)	***		Any other liabilities like		
Debtors	***		outstanding rent,		
Petty cash	***		insurance etc.	***	****
Furniture	***		By Bank/Cash :		
Any other assets like prepaid			Cash sales	***	
rent, insurance,			Cash received from		
advertisement etc.	****	****	debtors	***	****
To Goods Sent to Branch A/c (at cost)		****	By Goods Sent to Branch A/c (Returns)		****
To Bank (Expenses made by H.O. on behalf of Branch)		****	By Closing Balances :		
			Cash in Hand	****	
To Closing Balances :			Stock (at cost)	****	
Creditors	****		Debtors	****	
Any other liabilities like			Petty cash	****	
outstanding rent,			Furniture		
insurance etc.	****	****	(At depreciated value)	****	
To Profits			Any other assets like		
(Transferred to General Profit			prepaid rent,		
and Loss A/c)		***	insurance etc.	****	****
			By Loss (Transferred to		
			General P & L A/c)		***
		****			****

Points to be Remembered

The following points should be kept in mind while recording the transactions in the Branch Account :

(1) Credit sales made by the Branch, shortage or surplus of stock at the Branch, Discount allowed, Bad Debts etc. are not to be shown in the Branch Account.

(2) Return of goods by the Branch Debtors to the Branch should not be recorded in the Branch Account. When the Branch Debtors return the goods directly to the Hand office, they will be recorded in the Branch Account on the same way as if the Branch has returned the goods to the Head office.

(3) Petty expenses paid by Branch Manager out of petty cash balance are not to be shown in the Branch Account. But reduced petty cash balance is to be recorded on the credit side of the Branch Account. This will clear form the following example :

Opening petty cash balance at the branch	200
Cash sent by the Head office of the Branch for meeting the petty expenses	100
Petty expenses incurred by the Branch	250

In the above case Rs. 300 will be debited to the Branch Account as opening petty cash balance and cash sent by Head office, and Rs. 50 will be credited of the Branch Account as petty cash balance at the end of the accounting year. But the petty cash expenses of Rs. 250 will not be recorded in the Branch Account.

(4) When petty cash is maintained on imprest system, the expenses incurred by the Branch Manager are to be shown in the Branch Account on debit side as the expenses paid by the Head office, because, the amount spent by the branch will be reimbursed by the Head office. At the end of the accounting period the balance equal to the opening balance petty cash is to be shown on the credit side.

(5) Depreciation on fixed assets is not shown in the Branch Account. But assets are to be shown at the depreciated value (*i.e.*, Assets value – Amount of depreciation) on the credit side of the Branch Account at the end of the accounting period.

(6) The Branch may purchase its fixed assets, then the purchased fixed assets are to be added to the concerned asset at the end as it either increases the liability or reduces the cash balance.

(7) When the fixed assets are sold by the Branch, the amount realized on account of sale of fixed assets is remitted to the Head office. Suppose,

if the fixed assets are sold on credit basis, the amount due is to be recorded as debtors at the Branch at the end of accounting period. At the end of the accounting year, the fixed assets are to be recorded as shown below :

Opening balance + Purchases of fixed assets – Sales proceeds of fixed assets.

Profit or loss made on the sale of fixed assets is not considered because the opening and closing balance and the amount realized from the sale of fixed assets are recorded in the Branch Account.

(8) When the stock or any other property insured and they damaged at the branch, the amount received from the insurance company will be remitted to the Head office. Suppose, if the amount receivable from the insurance company is outstanding till the end of the accounting period, that amount will be recorded as an asset on the credit side of the Branch Account.

(9) The Head office may supply the goods to the Branch either at cost price or at a price higher than cost price. When the goods are supplied by the Head office at a higher price than the cost price, that will be termed as invoice price or selling price. The main purpose of supplying the goods at invoice price to the Branch is that the Branch has to sell the goods at invoice price or selling price. When the goods supplied at invoice price to the Branch, certain adjustments will have to be made for excess price included in opening stock, goods sent, goods returned, and closing stock to ascertain the correct profit of the Branch.

The following are the adjustment entries for the removal of excess price :

(i) For adjustment of excess price (loading) included in opening stock :

Stock Reserve Account	Dr.	With the amount of excess
To Branch Account		price

Note : The excess amount already debited to Branch Account is now cancelled.

(ii) For adjustment of excess price included in goods sent to Branch:

Goods Sent to Branch A/c	Dr.	With the amount of excess
To Branch Account		price in goods sent.

Note : The excess amount already debited to Branch Account is now cancelled.

(iii) For adjustment of excess price included in goods returned by the Branch :

Branch Account	Dr.	With the amount of excess
To Good Sent to Branch Account		price in returns.

Note : The excess amount already credited to Branch Account is now cancelled.

(iv) For adjustment of excess price included in closing stock :

Branch Account Dr. } With the amount of excess
  To Stock Reserve Account } price in closing stock.

Note : The excess amount already credited to Branch Account is now cancelled.

The above entries will appear in the Branch Account as below :

Dr. **Branch Account** Cr.

	Rs.		Rs.
To Opening stock (At invoice price)	****	By Closing stock (At invoice price)	****
To Good Sent to Branch (At invoice price)	****	By Good Sent to Branch A/c (Returns from branch to H.O. at invoice price)	****
To Goods Sent to Branch A/c (Loading on returns)	****	By Stock Reserve A/c (Loading on opening stock)	****
To Stock Reserve A/c (Loading on closing stock)	****	By Goods Sent to Branch A/c (Loading on goods sent)	****
	****		****

Methods of preparing the Branch Account under Debtor System

Cost Price Method

Illustration 1

From the following particulars relating to Bombay Branch for the year ending 31st Dec., 1990. Prepare Branch Account in the Books of Head office.

	Rs.		Rs.
Opening Balance as on 1-1-1990 :		Cash paid by the Branch Debtors	
Stock	15,000	directly to the Head office	5,000
Branch Debtors	6,000	Discount allowed to Debtors	500
Petty cash at Branch	200	Bad debts	200
Furniture at Branch	3,000	Goods returned by the Customers	
Prepaid insurance	500	to Branch	300
Outstanding salary	600	Cash sent to Branch for expenses :	
Goods sent to Branch	1,00,000	Salaries	2,000
Goods returned by the Branch	800	Petty cash	1,000
Cash sales during the year	1,50,000	Insurance up to March 31st, 1991	800
Credit sales during the year	20,000	Closing Balance as on 31-12-1990 :	
Cash received from debtors	25,000	Stock	8,000
Petty expenses by Branch	800	Debtors	5,000

Provide depreciation on furniture at 10% p.a. Goods costing Rs. 2,000 were destroyed by the fire and a sum of Rs. 1,500 was received from the insurance company.

Solution :

In the Books of Head Office

Bombay Branch Account

Dr.		Rs.			Cr. Rs.
To Opening Balance :			By Opening Balance :		
Stock	15,000		Outstanding salary		600
Debtors	6,000		By Cash (For remittance) :		
Petty cash	200		Cash sales	1,50,000	
Furniture	3,000		Cash received from Debtors	25,000	
Prepaid insurance	500	24,700	Cash paid by debtors direct to H.O.	5,000	
To Goods Sent to Branch		1,00,000	Received from insurance company	1,500	1,81,500
To Bank (For expenses) :			By Goods Sent to Branch (Returns)		800
Salaries	2,000		By Closing Balance :		
Petty cash	1,000		Stock	8,000	
Insurance	800	3,800	Debtors	5,000	
To General Profit & Loss A/c (Profit transferred)		70,700	Petty cash	400	
			Furniture	2,700	
			Prepaid insurance (1/4 × 800)	200	16,300
		1,99,200			1,99,200

Working Notes :

(1) Calculation of closing petty cash :

Opening balance	Rs. 200
Add : Cash received from the Head office	Rs. 1,000
Total cash with Branch	Rs. 1,200
Less : Petty expenses paid by Branch	Rs. 800
Closing petty cash balance	Rs. 400

(2) Credit sales, Discount allowed to Debtors, Bad Debts and Goods returned by customers to Branch will not be shown in the Branch Account. They will be shown in the Debtors Account.

Illustration 2

M/s Rajan Bros, invoiced goods to their branches at cost, from the following information of Kolkata Branch, prepare Branch Account and calculate profit.

	Rs.		Rs.
Stock on 1-1-1990	5,000	Goods invoiced from the H.O.	15,000
Debtors on 1-1-1990	8,000	Expenses paid by H.O.	2,000
Cash sales for the year	30,000	Expenses paid by Branch	300
Credit sales for the year	10,000	Cash remitted by the H.O. to	
Cash remitted the H.O.	20,000	Branch for the purchase of safe	4,000
Allowances to Customers	500	Stock on 31-12-1990	10,000
Bad Debts written off	200	Returns from Debtors	1,000
Debtors on 31-12-1990	15,000		
Furniture purchased by the Branch	3,000		

Solution :

In the Books of Head Office

Dr. **Calcutta Branch Account** Cr.

		Rs.			Rs.
To Balance b/d :			By Cash Remitted		20,000
Stock	5,000		By Balance c/d :		
Debtors	8,000	13,000	Stock	10,000	
To Goods Sent to Branch		15,000	Debtors	15,000	
To Bank (Expenses)		2,000	Furniture	3,000	
To Bank (Safe)		4,000	Safe	4,000	
To General P & L A/c (Profit transferred)		26,000	Cash	8,000	40,000
		60,000			60,000

Working Note :

Calculation of closing cash in hand with Branch

(i) Dr. **Debtors' Account** Cr.

	Rs.		Rs.
To Balance b/d	8,000	By Cash Received (Balancing figure)	1,300
To Credit Sales	10,000	By Allowances	500
		By Returns	1,000
		By Bad Debts	200
		By Balance c/d	15,000
	18,000		18,000

		Rs.
(ii)	Cash sales for the year	30,000
	Add : Cash received from Debtors	1,300
		31,300
	Less : Cash remitted to Head office	20,000
	Balance of cash with Branch	11,300
	Less : Furniture purchased	3,000
		8,300
	Less : Petty expenses paid	300
	Cash in hand with Branch	8,000

Illustration 3

The Bangalore Head Office supplies to its Hubli Branch goods at cost but with definite instruction to sell the goods at a profit of 25% on selling price.

From the following details of the Hubli Branch, prepare, Branch Account in the Head office books for the month of June 1990.

	Rs.			Rs.
Stock on 31st May, 1990	50,000	Amount received from H.O. (during June, 1990) :		
Debtors on 31st May, 1990	40,000	For Rent	2,000	
Petty cash balance on 31st May, 1990	200	For Salary	4,000	
Goods received during the June, 1990 from H.O.	2,00,000	For Insurance	3,000	
		For Petty Cash	800	9,800
Remittances to H.O. during the June, 1990 (Including Rs. 1,00,000 for cash sales)	2,00,000	Stock on 30th June, 1990		70,000
		Petty cash expenses for the month of June, 1990		500

Solution :

In the Books of Head Office

Hubli Branch Account

Dr. Cr.

		Rs.			Rs.
To Balance b/d :			By Cash		2,00,000
Stock	50,000		(Cash remitted to H.O.)		
Debtors	40,000		By Balance c/d :		
Petty Cash	200	90,200	Stock	70,000	
To Goods Sent to Branch		2,00,000	Debtors	80,000	
To Bank (Expenses) :			Petty Cash	500	
Rent	2,000		(200 + 800 – 500)		1,50,500
Salary	4,000				
Insurance	3,000				
Petty Cash	800	9,800			
To General P & L A/c		50,500			
(Profit transferred)					
		3,50,500			3,50,500

Working Note :

Calculation of Credit Sales and Closing Debtors :

(i) Credit sales

	Rs.
Opening stock (at cost)	50,000
Add : Goods Sent to Branch (at cost)	2,00,000
	2,50,000
Less : Closing stock (at cost)	70,000
Cost of goods sold	1,80,000

Goods are sold at 25% profit on sales.

If the selling price is 100, then the profit on it will be Rs. 25 and cost price will be Rs. 75.

Hence, 75 (cost price) : 1,80,000 (cost price) : 100 (selling price)

$$= \frac{1,80,000 \times 100}{75} = \text{Rs. } 2,40,000$$

Total sales	=	Rs. 2,40,000
Less : Cash sales		Rs. 1,00,000
Credit sales		Rs. 1,40,000

(ii) **Closing Debtors :**

Dr. **Debtors' Account** Cr.

	Rs.		Rs.
To Balance b/d	40,000	By Cash	1,00,000
To Credit sales	1,40,000	(2,00,000 – 1,00,000)	
		By Balance c/d	80,000
	1,80,000		1,80,000

Cost Price and Invoice Price Method

Illustration 4

Mohini Stores of Kashmir had a Branch at Nagpur. Goods are sent by Head office at invoice price which is at a profit of 20% on cost price. All expenses of the Branch are paid by the Head office. From the following information prepare Branch Account in the Head office books :

(1) When the goods are shown at cost price

(2) When the goods are shown at invoice price.

	Rs.		Rs.
Opening balances :		Remittances made to Head Office :	
Stock at invoice price	36,000	Cash sales	25,000
Debtors	4,000	Cash collected from Debtors	50,000
Petty cash	400	Goods returned by Branch	
Goods Sent to Branch at		at invoice price	720
invoice price	72,000	Provisions for doubtful debts	600
Furniture purchased by		Balance at the end :	
Head office for Branch	1,000	Stock at invoice price	42,000
Expenses made by Head office :		Debtors	8,000
Rent	1,200	Petty cash	100
Insurance	800	Write off furniture at 10%	
Wages	500		

Solution :

(a) When the goods are shown at cost price :

In the Books of Head Office

Dr. **Nagpur Branch Account** Cr.

		Rs.			Rs.
To Opening Balance :			By Cash (Remittance) :		
Stock (36,000 – 6,000)		30,000	Cash Sales	25,000	
Debtors		4,000	Cash Collected		
Petty Cash		400	from Debtors	50,000	75,000
To Goods Sent to Branch (72,000 – 12,000)		60,000	By Goods Sent to Branch (720 – 120)		600
To Bank (Furniture)		1,000	By Closing Balances :		
To Bank (Expenses) :			Stock (42,000 – 7,000)		35,000
Rent	1,200		Furniture (1,000 – 100)		900
Insurance	800		Debtors		8,000
Wages	500	2,500	Petty Cash		100
To Provision for Doubtful Debts		600			
To General P & L A/c (Profit transferred)		21,100			
		1,19,600			1,19,600

(b) When the goods are shown at invoice price :

Dr. **Nagpur Branch Account** Cr.

		Rs.			Rs.
To Opening Balances :			By Cash (Remittance) :		
Stock	36,000		Cash Sales	25,000	
Debtors	4,000		Cash Collected		
Petty Cash	400	40,400	from Debtors	50,000	75,000
To Goods Sent to Branch		72,000	By Goods Sent to Branch		720
To Bank (Furniture)		1,000	By Closing Balances :		
To Bank (Expenses) :			Stock	42,000	
Rent	1,200		Debtors	8,000	
Insurance	800		Furniture	900	
Wages	500	2,500	Petty Cash	100	51,000
To Provision for Doubtful Debts		600	By Stock Reserve A/c (Loading in opening stock)		6,000
To Stock Reserve A/c (Loading in closing stock)		7,000	By Goods Sent to Branch (Loading in goods sent)		12,000
To Goods Sent to Branch (Loading in returns)		120			
To General P & L A/c (Profit transferred)		21,100			
		1,44,720			1,44,720

Note : Goods are supplied by the Head office to the Branch at cost plus 20% *i.e.*, at a selling price marked at 120%. Hence, excess price (*i.e.*, Loading) in the opening stock, goods supplied and closing stock is removed at the rate of 20/120 or 1/6 of such selling price.

Invoice Price Method

Illustration 5

Sudhakar of Poona has Branch at Belgaum. The goods are invoiced to the Branch at 20% profit on sales price. All the expenses are met by the Head office except petty expenses which are met by the Branch Manager. From the following particulars prepare Branch Account in the books of Sudhakar of Poona.

	Rs.		Rs.
Opening Balances :		Expenses paid by H.O. :	
Stock (at invoice price)	20,000	Stationery & Printing	650
Debtors	5,000	Wages	400
Cash in Hand	600	Rent	500
Office furniture	2,000	Petty expenses paid by the Branch Manager	300
Goods invoiced by the H.O.	60,000		
Goods returned to H.O.	2,500	Goods damaged at invoice Price (Amount recovered from the insurance company Rs. 800)	1,000
Cash sales	40,000		
Credit sales	35,000		
Cash received from Debtors	35,000	Defective goods written off	500
Goods returned by Debtors	500	Depreciation is provided on Branch furniture at 10% p.a.	
Discount allowed to Debtors	600		

Solution : **In the Books of Head office**

Belgaum Branch Account

Dr. Cr.

		Rs.			Rs.
To Opening Balances :			By Remittances :		
Stock	20,000		Cash Sales	40,000	
Debtors	5,000		Cash Collected from Debtors	35,000	
Cash in Hand	600		Recovered from Ins. Co.	800	75,800
Furniture	2,000	27,600	By Goods Sent to Branch (Returns from Branch)		2,500
To Goods Sent to Branch		60,000	By Closing Balances :		
To Bank (Expenses)			Stock	1,500	
Stationery & Printing	650		Debtors	3,900	
Wages	400		Furniture (2,000 – 200)	1,800	
Rent	500	1,550	Cash in Hand (600 – 300)	300	7,500
To Goods Sent to Branch (Loading in returns)		500	By Stock Reserve (Loading in opening stock)		4,000
To Stock Reserve (Loading in Closing stock)		300	By Goods Sent to Branch (Loading in goods sent)		12,000
To General Profit & Loss A/c (Profit transferred)		11,850			
		1,01,800			1,01,800

Working Notes :

(1) Calculation of Closing Debtors :

Dr. **Debtors' Account** Cr.

	Rs.		Rs.
To Balance b/d	5,000	By Cash (received)	35,000
To Credit Sales	35,000	By Sales Returns	500
		By Discount Allowed	600
		By Balance c/d (Balancing figure)	3,900
	40,000		40,000

(2) Calculation of Closing Stock :

Dr. **Stock Account** Cr.

	Rs.			Rs.
To Opening balance	20,000	By Sales :		
To Goods Sent to Branch	60,000	Cash	40,000	
To Sales Returns	500	Credit	35,000	75,000
		By Goods Returned by the Branch		2,500
		By Goods Damaged		1,000
		By Defective Goods		500
		By Balance c/d (Balancing figure)		1,500
	80,500			80,500

(3) Expenses paid by the Branch are not shown in the Branch Account. However, the cash balance at the end is shown on the credit side of the Branch Account after adjusting the petty expenses.

(4) 20% on sales is 25% on cost (25/125) *i.e.*, 1/5 of the selling price.

Illustration 6

Krishna of Bangalore has a Branch at Hubli. Goods are supplied from the Head office at cost plus $33\frac{1}{3}\%$. Expenses of the Branch except petty expenses are paid directly by the Head office. Petty expenses are paid by the branches which are allowed to maintain petty cash balance of Rs. 400 on imprest system.

From the following particulars, you are required to prepare Branch Account according to the Debtors system :

	Rs.		Rs.
Balance on 1st Jan., 1990 :		Allowances to Debtors	600
Stock in hand at sales price	40,000	Cash received from Debtors	30,000
Debtors	5,000	Cash purchases by the Branch	40,000
Petty Cash in Hand	400	(with the permission of the	
Furniture & Fixtures	6,000	Head office)	
Creditors at Branch	3,000	Cash paid to creditors	6,000
Rent pre-paid (up to		Creditors at the end	7,000
31st March, 1990)	400	Payments made by the Head office :	
Transactions for the year ended		Rent for one year	2,000
31st Dec., 1990 were as follows :		(paid on 1-4-1990)	
Goods sent to Branch	1,00,000	Salaries	3,000
(*Less* : Returns)		Insurance paid for the	
Cash Sales at Branch	75,000	year ending 31-3-1991	400
Credit Sales at Branch	50,000	Payments made by the Branch :	
Bad Debts written off	300	Petty expenses	200
		Balance on 31st Dec., 1990 :	
		Stock at cost	65,000

Write off 10% depreciation on Furniture.

Solution :

In the Book of Head Office

Hubli Branch Account

Dr. Cr.

		Rs.			Rs.
To Opening balances :			By Opening Balance :		
Stock	40,000		Creditors		3,000
Debtors	5,000		By Cash Remitted		59,000
Petty Cash	400		By Closing Balances :		
Furniture & Fixtures	6,000		Stock	65,000	
Prepaid Rent	400	51,800	Debtors	24,100	
To Goods Sent to Branch		1,00,000	Petty Cash	400	
To Bank (Expenses) :			Furniture (6,000–600)	5,400	
Rent	2,000		Rent Prepaid (2,000×3/12)	500	
Salary	3,000		Insurance (400 × 3/12)	100	95,500
Insurance	400	5,400	By Stock Reserve		10,000
To Bank (For petty expenses)		200	(Loading in opening stock)		
To Balance of Creditors		7,000	By Goods Sent to Branch		25,000
To General P & L A/c		28,100	(Loading in goods sent)		
(Profit transferred)					
		1,92,500			1,92,500

Working Notes :

(1) Calculation of Closing Debtors :

Dr. **Debtors' Account** Cr.

	Rs.		Rs.
To Balance b/d	5,000	By Bad Debts	300
To Credit Sales	50,000	By Allowances	600
		By Cash Received	30,000
		By Balance c/d (Balancing figure)	24,100
	55,000		55,000

(2) Calculation of Cash Remitted :

Dr. **Cash Account** Cr.

	Rs.		Rs.
To Cash Sales	75,000	By Purchases	40,000
To Debtors	30,000	By Creditors	6,000
		By Cash Remitted (Balancing figure)	59,000
	1,05,000		1,05,000

Dr. **Creditors' Account** Cr.

	Rs.		Rs.
To Cash	6,000	By Balance b/d	3,000
To Balance c/d	7,000	By Credit Purchases (Balancing figure)	10,000
	13,000		13,000

Dr. **Petty Cash Account** Cr.

	Rs.		Rs.
To Balance b/d	400	By Petty Expenses	200
To Cash	200	By Balance c/d	400
	600		600

(3) Credit purchases and credit sales are not shown in the branch account. But these are considered to find out the debtors and creditors amount.

(4) Petty cash book is maintained on imprest system. Therefore, petty cash expenses must be reimbursed by the Head office.

(5) $33^1/_3$% on cost is 25% on sales. If cost is 100, profit is $33^1/_3$, the selling therefore is $133^1/_3$. Hence the ratio of profit to selling price is $33^1/_3 / 133^1/_3 = ¼$.

(B) Branch Trading and Profit and Loss Account

Sometimes, the student is required to ascertain the Branch profit or loss by preparing Branch Trading and Profit and Loss Account. In such cases the Branch Account should be treated as a personal account and not nominal account. But, Branch Account should be prepared in the same manner as explained in the preceding pages.

Illustration 7

From the particulars given in Illustration 6, prepare Branch Trading and Profit and Loss Account and Branch Account.

Solution :

Branch Trading and Profit and Loss Account
for the year ending 31-12-1990

		Rs.			Rs.
To Opening Stock		30,000	By Sales – Cash	75,000	
(40,000 – 10,000 Loading)			Credit	50,000	1,25,000
To Purchases – Cash	40,000		By Stock at Cost		65,000
Credit	10,000	50,000			
To Goods Sent to Branch		75,000			
(1,00,000 – 25,000 Loading)					
To Gross Profit c/d		35,000			
		1,90,000			1,90,000
To Bad Debts		300	By Gross Profit b/d		35,000
To Allowances		600			
To Rent	2,000				
Add : Paid last year	400				
	2,400				
Less : Paid for next year	500	1,900			
To Salaries		3,000			
To Insurance	400				
Less : In Advance	100	300			
To Expenses by Branch		200			
To Depreciation on furniture		600			
To General P & L A/c		28,100			
(Profit transferred)					
		35,000			35,000

Dr. **Branch Account (Personal A/c)** Cr.

		Rs.			Rs.
To Opening balances :			By Opening balance :		
Stock	30,000		Creditors		3,000
Debtors	5,000		By Cash remitted		59,000
Petty cash	400		By Balance c/d		88,500
Furniture and fixtures	6,000		(Balancing figure *i.e.*,		
Prepaid Rent	400	41,800	Stock	65,000	
To Goods Sent to Branch		75,000	Debtors	24,100	
To Bank (Expenses)			Petty cash	400	
Rent	2,000		Furniture	5,400	
Salary	3,000		Prepaid Rent	500	
Insurance	400		Insurance	100	
Petty cash	200	5,600		95,500	
To Net profit as per Profit			*Less :* Creditors at end	7,000	
& Loss A/c		28,100		88,500)	
		1,50,500			1,50,500

Illustration 8

The Southern Confectionery Co. Ltd., Bangalore has a Branch at Goa. Goods are invoiced to the Goa Branch at selling prices being cost plus 25%.

The Goa Branch keeps it own sales ledger and transmits all cash received to Bangalore daily. All expenses are paid from Bangalore.

From the following details prepare a Profit and Loss A/c of the Goa Branch for the year 1987 :

	Rs.
Stock 1st Jan., 1987 (at invoice prices)	1,250
Stock 31st Dec., 1987 (at invoice prices)	1,500
Sundry Debtors, 1st Jan., 1987	700
Sundry Debtors, 31st Dec., 1987	900
Credit Sales for the year	5,400
Cash Sales for the year	3,500
Cash received for Ledger A/c	3,300
Goods invoiced from Bangalore	9,100
Rent and Rates (paid from Bangalore)	400
Wages (paid from Bangalore)	340
Sundry Expenses (paid from Bangalore)	80

(Berhampur, B.Com., 1970, Patna, B.Com., 1955 & C.A.)

Solution :

Branch Trading and Profit and Loss Account
for the year ending 1987

	Rs.			Rs.
To Opening Stock (1,250 – 250 Loading)	1,000	By Sales – Cash	3,500	
		Credit	5,400	8,900
To Goods Sent to Branch (9,100 – 1,820 Loading)	7,280	By Closing Stock (1,500 – 300)		1,200
To Wages	340			
To Gross Profit c/d	1,480			
	10,100			10,100
To Rent and Rates	400	By Gross Profit b/d		1,480
To Sundry Expenses	80			
To General P & L A/c (Profit transferred)	1,000			
	1,480			1,480

Illustration 9

The City Supply Co. makes purchases at the H.O. and sends the goods bought to the Branch Offices for sale, no stock being retained at the H.O. The Branch office effect sales, keep their own Sales Ledgers, received cash against ledger accounts, and pay in the whole of their cash receipts everyday to the H.O. Branch Office expenses are paid from cash remitted by H.O. to the Branches for the purpose.

From the following particulars, show the Branch Account in the H.O. Books. Also prepare a P & L A/c, showing the net profit made by each branch, and the net profit for the whole concern, assuming that the Head office expenses amounted to Rs. 15,000.

	A	B	C
	Rs.	Rs.	Rs.
Credit Sales	40,500	39,000	34,500
Returns Inwards	300	360	240
Allowances to Customers	75	60	90
Cash received on Ledger Accounts	35,700	36,000	30,000
Cash Sales	21,300	18,750	19,500
Stock at commencement, at cost	8,100	7,200	7,500
Stock at end, at cost	9,300	8,700	7,200
Debtors at Commencement	18,750	18,000	16,500
Debtors at end	22,950	20,430	20,670
Bad Debts	225	150	—

Goods bought by H.O. and Supplied to Branches	31,800	30,900	30,000
Rent & Taxes paid	1,200	1,050	1,125
Wages & Sundry expenses paid	5,700	5,340	5,250

(B.Com., Calcutta, B.Com., Vikram & G.D.A.)

Solution:

In the Books of Head Office

Dr **Branch Account (Personal A/c)** Cr

	A (Rs.)	B (Rs.)	C (Rs.)		A (Rs.)	B (Rs.)	C (Rs.)
To Opening Balances :				By Remittances :			
Stock	8,100	7,200	7,500	Cash Sales	21,300	18,750	19,500
Debtors	18,750	18,000	16,500	From Debtors	35,700	36,000	30,000
To Goods Sent to Branches	31,800	30,900	30,000	By Balance c/d (Stock + Debtors)	32,250	29,130	27,870
To Bank (Expenses) : Rent & Taxes	1,200	1,050	1,125				
Wages & Sundry Expenses	5,700	5,340	5,250				
To General P & L A/c (Profit transferred)	23,700	21,390	16,995				
	89,250	83,880	77,370		89,250	83,880	77,370

Dr. **Trading and Profit and Loss Account** Cr.

Particulars	A Rs.	B Rs.	C Rs.	Head office Rs.	Particulars	A Rs.	B Rs.	C Rs.	Head office Rs.
To Opening Stock	8,100	7,200	7,500	–	By Sales :				
To Goods Sent to Branches	31,800	30,900	30,000	–	Credit Sales (Less return)	40,200	38,640	34,260	–
To Wages	5,700	5,340	5,250		Cash Sales	21,300	18,750	19,500	–
To Gross Profit c/d	25,200	22,650	18,210	–	By Stock	9,300	8,700	7,200	–
	70,800	66,090	60,960	–		70,800	66,090	60,960	–
To Rent	1,200	1,050	1,125	–	By Gross Profit	25,200	22,650	18,210	–
To Allowances	75	60	90	–	By Branch N/p Transferred to H.O. A/c as per contra	–	–	–	62,085
To Bad Debts	225	150	–	–					
To Branch N/p Transferred to H.O. P & L A/c	23,700	21,390	16,995	–					
To H.O. Expenses				15,000					
To Head Office Net Profit				47,085					
	25,200	22,650	18,210	62,085		25,200	22,650	18,210	62,085

(C) Stock and Debtors System

This is another method of ascertaining the profit or loss made by the Branch. This method is useful only where the branch is instructed to sell the goods at the same price as already fixed by the Head office. Under this system, the Head office does not open a Branch Account, but it opens different accounts relating to various types of transactions in its books. Those various accounts are as follows :

(1) Branch Assets Account : A separate account is maintained for recording the transactions relating to each type of asset. Ex-Branch Debtors Account, Cash Account, Building Account, Furniture Account etc.

Branch Debtors Account is prepared to find out the closing balance of the Debtors.

Branch Cash Account is maintained for recording all cash translations of the Branch.

Fixed Assets account is maintained for recording the transactions relating to each type of fixed assets such as Building, Machinery etc.

(2) Branch Stock Account : This account is prepared to find out the shortage or surplus of stock at the Branch. It is just like Goods Account. This account is always prepared at invoice price.

(3) Branch Expenses Account : This account is prepared to show the summary of all the expenses incurred at the Branch. The Balance of this account is transferred to the second part of the Branch Adjustment Account.

(4) Branch Adjustment (P & L) Account : This account is just like trading and profit and loss account. It is divided into two parts. In the first part of this account all the loadings in the goods sent to the Branch, opening and closing stock of the Branch, and shortage or surplus of stock etc. are recorded. The balance being either gross profit or gross loss. The gross profit or gross loss is transferred to the second part of Branch Adjustment Account. All other expenses and losses are debited and all gains and incomes are credited to the second part of the Branch Adjustment Account. The balance being either net profit or net loss.

(5) Goods Sent to the Branch Account : This account is prepared to find out the net value of goods sent to the Branch. Goods sent to Branch, goods returned by the Branch and loading in the goods sent returned are recorded in this account. The balance of this account is transferred to the trading account.

Journal Entries

Under this system, the following journal entries are to be passed in the books of Head office :

(1) For goods sent to Branch.

Branch Stock Account	Dr.	With invoice price of goods sent.
To Goods Sent to Branch A/c		

(2) For goods returned by the Branch to the Head Office.

Good Sent to Branch Account	Dr.	With invoice price of goods returned.
To Branch Stock Account		

(3) For goods returned by Branch Debtors to the Branch.

Branch Stock Account	Dr.	With invoice price of goods returned.
To Branch Debtors' Account		

(4) For goods returned by Branch Debtors directly to the Head Office.

Goods Sent to Branch Account	Dr.	With invoice price of goods returned.
To Branch Debtors' Account		

(5) For cash sales at the Branch.

Branch Cash Account	Dr.	With amount of cash sales.
To Branch Stock Account		

(6) For credit sales at the Branch.

Branch Debtors' Account	Dr.	With amount of credit sales.
To Branch Stock Account		

(7) For cash received by Branch from Debtors.

Branch cash Account	Dr.	With amount of cash received.
To Branch Debtors' Account		

(8) For discount allowed, allowances and bad debts.

Branch Expenses Account	Dr.	With the total amount of discount, allowances etc.
To Branch Debtors' Account		

(9) For Branch expenses paid in cash.

Branch Expense Account	Dr.	With the total amount of such expenses.
To Branch Cash Account		

(10) For any surplus of goods in stock.

Branch Stock Account	Dr.	With invoice price of surplus stock.
To Branch Adjustment Account		

(11) For any deficit or shortage of goods in stock.

Branch Adjustment Account	Dr.	With invoice price of shortage in stock.
To Branch Stock Account		

(12) For closing Branch expenses.

Branch Adjustment Account	Dr.	With amount of closing Branch expenses.
To Branch Expenses Account.		

(13) For adjustment of excess price of opening stock.

Stock Reserve Account	Dr.	With amount of loading.
To Branch Adjustment A/c		

(14) For adjustment of excess price of closing stock.

Branch Adjustment Account	Dr.	With amount of loading.
To Stock Reserve Account		

(15) For adjustment of excess price of goods sent to Branch.

Goods Sent of Branch Account	Dr.	With amount of loading.
To Branch Adjustment A/c		

(16) For adjustment of excess price of goods returned by the Branch.

Branch Adjustment Account	Dr.	With amount of loading.
To Goods Sent to Branch A/c		

(17) For adjustment of excess price of surplus of stock.

Branch Stock Account	Dr.	With amount of loading.
To Branch Adjustment A/c		

(18) For adjustment of excess price of deficit of stock.

Branch Adjustment Account	Dr.	With amount of loading.
To Branch Stock Account		

(19) For transfer of profit or loss to general profit and loss account.

(i) If Profit – Branch Adjustment A/c	Dr.	With amount of net profit.
To General P & L A/c		
(ii) If Loss – General P & L Account	Dr.	With amount of net loss.
To Branch Adjustment A/c		

(20) For closing goods sent to Branch Account.

Goods Sent to Branch Account	Dr.	With amount of net balance.
To Trading Account		

Illustration 10

Sunder of Mumbai has a Branch at Kanpur under the supervision of 'X'. Goods are invoiced to the Branch at cost plus 50% under the strict instructions of selling goods only at invoice price. Goods are fully insured against the theft and fire. Following are the particulars about the branch transactions :

	Rs.		Rs.
Stock on 1-1-1990 (at cost price)	8,000	Cash received from Debtors	15,000
Debtors on 1-1-1990	5,000	Cash paid by Debtors directly to the Head office	8,000
Debtors on 31-12-1990	8,000	Direct expenses paid by Head office	250
Cash Sales	22,300	Indirect expenses paid by H.O.	4,500
Goods received from the Head office (at invoice price)	60,000	Stock on 31-12-1990 (at invoice price)	18,000
Loss by fire (at cost price)	4,000		

Calculate gross profit and net profit made by Branch by 'Stock and Debtors' system and open necessary accounts.

Solution :

Dr. **Branch Stock Account** Cr.

	Rs.			Rs.
To Balance b/d (at invoice price) (Rs. 8,000+50/100 of Rs. 8,000)	12,000	By Sales – Cash	22,300	
		Credit	26,000	48,300
To Goods Sent to Branch	60,000	By Loss by Fire (at invoice price) (Rs. 4,000 + 50/100 of 4,000)		6,000
To Surplus of Stock (Balancing figure)	300	By Balance b/d		18,000
	72,300			72,300

Dr. **Branch Debtors' Account** Cr.

	Rs.		Rs.
To Balance b/d	5,000	By Cash (Received)	15,000
To Credit Sales (Balancing figure)	26,000	By Cash (Cash paid by the debtors directly to H.O.)	8,000
		By Balance c/d	8,000
	31,000		31,000

Dr. **Branch Adjustment Account** Cr.

	Rs.		Rs.
To Loss by Fire (Loading)	2,000	By Stock Reserve Account (Loading in opening stock)	4,000
To Stock Reserve Account (Loading in closing stock)	6,000	By Goods Sent to Branch (Loading in goods sent)	20,000
To Direct Expenses	250	By Branch Stock Account (Loading in surplus stock)	100
To Gross Profit c/d	15,850		
	24,100		24,100
To Indirect Expenses	4,500	By Gross Profit b/d	15,850
To Net Profit (Transferred)	11,550	By Branch Stock Account : Surplus at cost	200
	16,050		16,050

Notes : (i) Gross profit and net profit of the Branch can be verified by preparing the simple trading and profit and loss account as below :

Dr. **Trading and Profit & Loss Account** Cr.

	Rs.			Rs.
To Opening Stock (at cost)	8,000	By Sales – Cash	22,300	
To Goods Sent to Branch (60,000–20,000 Loading)	40,000	Credit	26,000	48,300
To Direct Expenses	250	By Abnormal Loss by Fire (at cost)		4,000
To Abnormal Profit due to increase in stock at cost (300 – 100)	200	By Closing Stock (18,000 – 6,000 Loading)		12,000
To Gross Profit c/d	15,850			
	64,300			64,300
To Indirect Expenses	4,500	By Gross Profit		15,850
To Net Profit (Transferred)	11,550	By Surplus at cost		200
	16,050			16,050

(ii) Loss by fire has not been taken to Branch profit and loss account. This is made to know the correct profit of the Branch.

Illustration 11

Nanda Stores of Madurai had a Branch at Chennai to which the goods are supplied at selling price being 20% profit on sales. Branch was allowed to make sales only at invoice price except to the customers who purchased goods of Rs. 5,000 or more where goods can be sold at invoice price less trade discount of 3%. Expenses of the Branch are paid by the Head office. Calculate profit made by the Branch by "Stock and Debtor System" and open necessary accounts. Transactions during the year were as follows :

	Rs.		Rs.
Stock at Branch on 1-1-1990 (At invoice price)	32,000	Stock at Branch on 31-12-1990 (At invoice price)	4,000
Goods invoiced by the H.O.	60,000	Wages	2,000
Goods returned by the Branch to the Head office	2,400	Rent of shop	500
		Insurance	1,000
Sales : Cash 36,000		Manager salary	2,500
Credit 50,000	86,000	Cash received from Debtors	45,000
(Including sales to 'P' Rs. 6,000 who claimed trade discount of 3%)		Bad Debts	200
		Debtors on 31-12-1990	6,000
Goods returned to Branch by Customers other than 'P'	1,000	Depreciation on furniture charged to Branch	150

Solution :

Dr. **Branch Stock Account** Cr.

	Rs.			Rs.
To Balance b/d	32,000	By Sales : Cash	36,000	
To Goods Sent of Branch	60,000	Credit	50,000	86,000
To Branch Debtors' Account (Returns from debtors)	1,000	By Goods Sent to Branch		2,400
		By Branch Adjustment A/c : Trade discount at 3% on Rs. 6,000		180
		By Branch Adjustment A/c : Shortage in stock (Balancing figure)		420
		By Balance c/d		4,000
	93,000			93,000

Dr. **Branch Debtors Account** Cr.

	Rs.		Rs.
To Balance b/d (Balancing figure)	2,200	By Cash (Received)	45,000
		By Bad Debts	200
To Sales	50,000	By Branch Stock Account (Returns from Debtors)	1,000
		By Balance c/d	6,000
	52,200		52,200

Branch Adjustment Account

Dr.		Rs.	Cr.	Rs.
To Stock Reserve Account (Loading in closing stock)		800	By Stock Reserve Account (Loading in opening stock)	6,400
To Branch Stock Account (Loading in shortage stock)		84	By Goods Sent to Branch (Loading in goods sent)	12,000
To Goods Sent to Branch (Loading in returns)		480		
To Branch Stock Account : Trade discount		180		
To Wages		2,000		
To Gross Profit c/d		14,856		
		18,400		18,400
To Branch Expenses A/c :			By Gross Profit b/d	14,856
Rent	500			
Insurance	1,000			
Manager's Salary	2,500			
Bad Debts	200			
Depreciation	150	4,350		
To Branch Stock A/c (Cost of shortage stock)		336		
To Net Profit (Balance transferred)		10,170		
		14,856		14,856

Note : To know the real shortage of stock, trade discount has been added to the sales in the Branch Stock Account.

Illustration 12

Sunanda Mills Ltd., has two Branches at Navalgund and Nellikeri. Goods are invoiced to Branches at cost plus 50%. Branches remit all cash received to the Head Office and all the expenses are met by the Head office. From the following particulars prepare the necessary accounts and show the Profit on Stock and Debtors System :

Particulars	Navalgund	Nellikeri
Opening Stock (at invoice price)	9,300	15,600
Opening Debtors	6,800	8,700
Goods Sent to Branches (at cost price)	34,000	36,000
Sales : Cash	25,010	35,000
Credit	31,000	30,100

Cash Collected from debtors	30,400	29,800
Gods returned by debtors	1,200	1,500
Goods returned by branches to H.O.	1,500	—
Goods transferred from Nellikeri to Navalgund	2,100	2,100
Surplus in stock	—	300
Deficit in stock	450	—
Discount allowed	200	350
Expenses at Branches	5,400	6,700

(*Karnatak, B.Com., April, 1984*)

Solution :

Dr. **Branch Stock Account** Cr.

	Navalgund Rs.	Nellikeri Rs.		Navalgund Rs.	Nellikeri Rs.
To Balance b/d	9,300	15,600	By Sales – Cash	25,010	35,000
To Goods Sent to			Credit	31,000	30,100
Branch A/c (At invoice price)	51,000	54,000	By Goods Sent to Branch A/c (Returns)	1,500	—
To Branch Debtors A/c (Returns)	1,200	1,500	By Goods Sent to Branch A/c (Navalgund Branch)	—	2,100
To Goods Sent to Branch A/c (Goods	2,100	—	By Branch Adjustment A/c : Shortage	450	—
received from Nellikeri)			By Balance c/d	5,640	4,200
To Branch Adjustment A/c : Surplus	—	300	(Balancing figure)		
	63,600	71,400		63,600	71,400

Dr. **Branch Debtors' Account** Cr.

	Navalgund Rs.	Nellikeri Rs.		Navalgund Rs.	Nellikeri Rs.
To Balance b/d	6,800	8,700	By Cash (Received)	30,400	29,800
To Credit Sales	31,000	30,100	By Branch Stock A/c (Returns from Debtors)	1,200	1,500
			By Branch Expenses A/c (Discount allowed)	200	350
			By Balance c/d	6,000	7,150
	37,800	38,800		37,800	38,800

Dr. **Branch Expenses Account** Cr.

	Naval-gund Rs.	Nelli-keri Rs.		Naval-gund Rs.	Nelli-keri Rs.
To Branch Debtors A/c (Discount allowed)	200	350	By Branch Adjustment A/c (Balance transferred)	5,600	7,050
To Cash (Expenses)	5,400	6,700			
	5,600	7,050		5,600	7,050

Dr. **Branch Adjustment Account** Cr.

	Naval-gund Rs.	Nelli-keri Rs.		Naval-gund Rs.	Nelli-keri Rs.
To Stock Reserve A/c (Loading in closing stock)	1,880	1,400	By Stock Reserve A/c (Loading in opening stock)	3,100	5,200
To Branch Stock A/c (Loading in shortage)	150	—	By Goods Sent to Branch (Loading in goods		
To Goods Sent to Branch (Loading in returns)	500	—	Sent and Goods Transferred *i.e.*, 17,000 + 700,	17,700	
To Gross Profit c/d	18,270	21,200	18,000 – 700	—	17,300
			By Branch Stock A/c (Loading in surplus stock)	—	100
	20,800	22,600		20,800	22,600
To Branch Expense A/c (Expenses transferred)	5,600	7,050	By Gross Profit b/d	18,270	21,200
To Branch Stock A/c : Cost of shortage	300	—	By Branch Stock A/c : Cost of surplus	—	200
To Net Profit (Balance transferred)	12,370	14,350			
	18,270	21,400		18,270	21,400

Dr. **Goods Sent to Branch Account** Cr.

	Naval-gund Rs.	Nelli-keri Rs.		Naval-gund Rs.	Nelli-keri Rs.
To Branch Stock A/c (Returns to H.O.)	1,500	—	By Branch Stock A/c (Goods sent at invoice price)	51,000	54,000
To Branch Stock A/c (Goods transferred at invoice price)	—	2,100	By Branch Stock A/c (Goods transferred at invoice price)	2,100	—
To Branch Stock A/c (Loading on goods sent and goods transferred)	17,700	17,300	By Branch Stock A/c (Loading in goods returned)	500	—
To Trading Account (Balance transferred)	34,400	34,600			
	53,600	54,000		53,600	54,000

Illustration 13

A Company has a retail shop under the supervision of a Manager. The ratio of gross profit to selling price is constant at 25 per cent throughout the year to 31st Dec., 1965.

Branch Manager is entitled to a commission of 10 per cent of the profit earned by his branch, calculated before charging his commission but subject to a deduction from such commission equal to 25 per cent of any ascertained deficiency of branch stock. All goods were supplied to the branch by head office.

From the undermentioned figures, calculate the commission due to manager for the year to 31st Dec., 1965 :

	Rs.		Rs.
Stock at 1st Jan., 1965 at cost	37,368	Chargeable expenses	24,560
Goods sent to branch at cost	1,44,840	Stock at 31st Dec., 1965 on	
Sales	1,80,640	Selling Price	61,664
Manager's Commission paid on account	1,200		

(*I.C.W.A. Inter & B.Com., Madras, 1974*)

Solution :

Dr. **Branch Account** Cr.

	Rs.		Rs.
To Opening Stock at cost	37,368	By Sales	1,80,640
To Goods Sent at cost	1,44,840	By Closing Stock at cost (61,664–15,416 *i.e.*, 25% of gross profit included in closing stock)	46,248
To Expenses	24,560		
To Net Profit (Subject to Manager's Commission)	20,120		
	2,26,888		2,26,888

Calculation of Commission :

Commission of 10% of the profit before charging his commission is

	Rs. $20{,}120 \times \frac{10}{100}$ =	Rs. 2,012
Less : 25% of stock deficiency	Rs. $480 \times \frac{25}{100}$ =	Rs. 120
Commission for the year		Rs. 1,892
Less : Manager's commission paid on account		Rs. 1,200
	Balance due	Rs. 692

Stock deficiency is calculated by preparing the Branch Stock Account at selling price as follows :

Branch Stock Account

	Rs.		Rs.
To Opening Stock at selling price (37,368 + 1/3 of 37,368)	49,824	By Sales	1,80,640
To Goods Sent at selling price (1,44,840+1/3 of 1,44,840)	1,93,120	By Stock at selling price	61,664
		By Deficiency at selling price	640
	2,42,944		2,42,944

Note : (i) Deficiency at cost is Rs. 480 *i.e.*, 640 × 25/100.

(ii) 25% of selling price means ¼th of sales price or 1/3rd of cost price.

(D) Wholesale Branch System

Manufacturers may sell their goods through the wholesalers or through their retail branches. If the manufacturers sell their goods through their retail branches, they get the following benefits :

(i) They supply the right quality goods to the consumers at the most reasonable price. Hence, they attract consumers and increase the sales.

(ii) They make some profit which the wholesalers would have earned by selling the goods to the consumers. This is an additional profit which manufacturers earn due to branches. For example, if the cost price of an article is Rs. 100, the wholesale price is Rs. 150, retail price is Rs. 175 and the goods are sold to the consumers through wholesalers, the manufacturer earns only a profit of Rs. 50. Suppose, the goods are sold to the consumers through their retail Branches the manufacturer earns an additional profit of Rs. 25.

The profit of the Branch will be ascertained on the basis of invoice price. However, the Head office creates a stock Reserve for any unrealized profit in respect of goods lying unsold at invoice price. Such a system of ascertaining the profit or loss at the Branch is called Wholesale Branch System.

Illustration 14

M/s Surendra & Co., have their Head Office at Delhi and Branch at Kolkata. The goods are sent to Branch at 20% less than the list price (*i.e.*, catalogue price). Goods are sold to consumers at cost plus 100%. M/s Surendra & Co. also sells goods to their approved stockist at the same price at which they are selling to their Branch at Kolkata. From the following particulars, ascertain the profit made by the Branch as well as the Head office and show the provision for unrealised profit or stock at the Branch supplied by the Head office.

	Head Office Rs.	Branch Rs.
Opening stock (cost/invoice price)	80,000	32,000
Purchases during the year	3,00,000	—
Goods Sent to Branch (at invoice price)	48,000	—
Goods received from the Head office (at invoice price)	—	48,000
Goods sold to Approved Stockist	72,000	—
Goods sold to Consumers	60,000	40,000
Goods destroyed by accident (at invoice price)	—	1,000
Expenses	10,000	5,000

Solution :

Branch Trading and Profit & Loss Account

Dr. Cr.

	Rs.		Rs.
To Opening Stock	32,000	By Sales to Consumers	40,000
To Goods from Head office	48,000	By Goods Destroyed	1,000
To Gross Profit c/d	8,000	By Closing Stock	47,000
	88,000		88,000
To Loss of Goods Destroyed	1,000	By Gross Profit b/d	8,000
To Branch Expenses	5,000		
To Net Profit (Transferred to General P & L A/c)	2,000		
	8,000		8,000

General Trading and Profit & Loss Account (Head Office)

Dr. Cr.

	Rs.		Rs.
To Opening Stock	80,000	By Goods Sent to Branch	48,000
To Purchase	3,00,000	By Goods Sold to Stockists	72,000
To Gross Profit c/d	75,000	By Goods Sold to Consumers	60,000
		By Closing stock	2,75,000
	4,55,000		4,55,000
To Expenses	10,000	By Gross Profit b/d	75,000
To Stock Reserve on Closing Stock at Branch (47,000 × 100/160)	29,345	By Branch P & L A/c	2,000
To Net Profit (Transferred to Balance Sheet)	39,625	By Stock Reserve on Opening Stock at Branch (32,000 × 100/160)	2,000
	79,000		79,000

Working Notes :

(i) If the cost price is Rs. 100, list price will be Rs. 200 and invoice price will be Rs. 160 (200 – 40).

(ii) Closing stock of Head office and Branch is calculated as follows :

	Head Office	Branch
	Rs.	Rs.
Opening Stock (at invoice price)	80,000	32,000
Add : Purchases at cost	3,00,000	—
Add : Goods from Head office	—	48,000
	3,80,000	80,000
Less : Cost price of goods sent to Branch (48,000 × 100/160)	30,000	—
	3,50,000	80,000
Less : Cost price of goods sold to stockist (Rs. 72,000 × 100/160)	45,000	—
	3,05,000	80,000
Less : Cost price of goods sold to Consumers (invoice price in case of branch)		
(Rs. 60,000 × 100/200)	30,000	—
(Rs. 40,000 × 160/200)	—	32,000
	2,75,000	48,000
Less : Stock destroyed (at invoice price)	—	1,000
Closing stock	2,75,000	47,000

Illustration 15

Ashok Traders have their Head office at Bangalore and two Branches at Mysore and Madurai. Goods are purchased by the Branches and sold by them independently. The Mysore Branch makes at profit of 20% on sales and Madurai Branch 25% on sales. Goods are also supplied by one Branch to another at sales price (*i.e.*, at cost price to the receiving Branch). From the following particulars prepare trading accounts for the Branches after making reserve for unrealized profits.

	Mysore Branch	Madurai Branch
	Rs.	Rs.
Stock in the beginning	13,000	9,000
Purchases	55,000	60,000
Sales	75,000	80,000
Direct Expenses	3,000	2,500
Stock at the end	10,000	8,000

Other information :

(i) Opening stock of Branches at Mysore and Madurai includes goods of the value of Rs. 3,000 and Rs. 4,000 from Branch at Madurai and Branch at Mysore respectively at cost to the receiving Branch *i.e.*, at sales price of sending Branch.

(ii) Sales of Branch at Mysore includes transfer of goods to Madurai Branch at sales price Rs. 5,000. Similarly, sales of Madurai Branch includes transfer of goods to Mysore Branch Rs. 4,500.

(iii) Goods at the end at Mysore Branch includes goods received from Chennai Branch Rs. 2,000 and goods at the end at Madurai Branch includes Rs. 1,000 received from Mysore Branch.

Solution:

Dr. **Mysore Branch Trading Account** Cr.

	Rs.		Rs.
To Opening Stock (Including Rs. 3,000 from Madurai)	13,000	By Sales (Including transfer of goods Rs. 5,000 to Madurai)	75,000
To Purchases	55,000		
To Direct Expenses	3,000	By Stock at End (Including goods from Madurai Rs. 2,000)	10,000
To Gross Profit (Before making adjustment for unrealized profit)	14,000		
	85,000		85,000
To Stock Reserve for unrealized profit in closing stock at Madurai Branch (1,000 × 20/100)	200	By Gross Profit b/d	14,000
		By Stock Reserve for unrealised profit in opening stock at Madurai Branch (4,000×20/100)	800
To Gross Profit	14,600		
	14,800		14,800

Dr. **Madurai Branch Trading Account** Cr.

	Rs.		Rs.
To Opening Stock (Including Rs. 4,000 from Mysore)	9,000	By Sales (Including transfer of goods to Mysore Rs. 4,500)	80,000
To Purchases	60,000	By Stock at the End (Including goods from Mysore Rs. 1,000)	8,000
To Direct Expenses	2,500		
To Gross Profit (Before making adjustments for unrealized profit)	16,500		
	88,000		88,000

(*Contd.*)

Dr. **Madurai Branch Trading Account** (*Contd.*) Cr

	Rs.		Rs.
To Stock Reserve for unrealized profit in closing stock lying at Mysore Branch (2000×25/100)	500	By Gross Profit b/d	16,500
To Gross Profit	16,750	By Stock Reserve for unrealized profit in opening stock lying at Mysore Branch (3,000 × 25/100)	750
	17,250		17,250

Note : Profit at each Branch is to be ascertained after creating a stock reserve for the unrealized profit in respect of the stock which has been sold by it but lying unsold at the other Branch.

II. Independent Branches

Independent Branches are those which are free from the restrictions of Head office. They keep their own set of books separately and independently. They prepare trial balances and final accounts at the end of the trading period and send their copies to the Head office for their incorporation in the Head office Books. Independent Branches purchase goods also from the open market besides getting the goods from the Head office. They can even manufacture the goods and supply the goods to the Head office. Independent Branches need not remit all the cash received by them daily to the Head office. They are allowed to retain cash with themselves for their expenses but the excess cash may be remitted from time to time to the Head office as per the Head office instructions. Independent Branches open in their books Head office Account which is just like capital account of the branches. Similarly, the Head office opens in its books, Branch Account which is exactly in the reverse form of the Head office Account appearing in the Branch Books.

When the transactions are taken place between the Head office and the Independent Branch, the following journal entries are to be passed :

Entries to be passed in the Books of Head office :

(1) Goods supplied to Branch :	Branch A/c	Dr.
	To Goods Sent to Branch A/c	
(2) Cash sent to Branch :	Branch A/c	Dr.
	To Bank/Cash A/c	
(3) Goods returned by Branch :	Goods Sent to Branch A/c	Dr.
	To Branch A/c	
(4) Cash received from Branch :	Bank/Cash A/c	Dr.
	To Branch A/c	

Entries to be passed in the Books of Branch :

(1) Goods supplied by H.O. :	Goods Supplied by H.O. A/c	Dr.
	To Head Office A/c	
(2) Goods returned back to H.O. :	Head Office A/c	Dr.
	To Goods Returned to H.O. A/c	
(3) Goods received from H.O. :	Bank/Cash A/c	Dr.
	To Head Office A/c	
(4) Cash remitted to H.O. :	Head Office A/c	Dr.
	To Bank/Cash A/c	
(5) Goods supplied to H.O. : (by Branch)	Head Office A/c	Dr.
	To Goods Supplied to H.O. A/c	
(6) Purchases made at Branch :	Purchases A/c	Dr.
	To Cash/Creditors A/c	
(7) Sales made at Branch :	Cash/Debtors A/c	Dr.
	To Sales A/c	
(8) Branch expenses paid :	Expenses A/c	Dr.
	To Cash A/c	
(9) Stock of goods at Branch :	Stock A/c	Dr.
	To Trading A/c	

Depreciation on Branch Assets

Sometimes the Head office purchases assets like machinery, furniture etc., for the use of Branches. But the actual records of such assets are maintained in the books of Head office. As the assets are used by the Branches whereas accounts are kept by the Head office, the depreciation of such assets is to be recorded in the books of Head office and Branch as follows :

In the books of Head office		**In the Books of Branch**	
Branch Account	Dr.	Depreciation A/c	Dr.
To Branch Assets A/c		To Head Office A/c	

Expenses Incurred by Head office for Branches

If the Head office incurred expenses for all its Branches throughout the year, such expenses are to be charged proportionately to all the Branches at the end of the year. The entries for this will be as follows :

In the Books of Head office

(i) When the expenses are paid or incurred :

Expenses A/c Dr.
To Cash/Bank A/c

(ii) When the expenses are charged to Branch :

Branch A/c Dr.

To Expenses A/c

In the Books of Branch :

(i) When the expenses are charged by the Head Office :

Expenses A/c Dr.

To Head Office A/c

(ii) When the expenses transferred to P & L A/c :

P & L A/c Dr.

To Expenses A/c

Inter-Branch Transactions

With the instructions of the Head office one Branch sends goods or cash to another Branch. Such transactions are called as 'Inter Branch Transactions'. These transactions are not treated as transactions between the branches, but they are treated as transactions between Head office and Branch and they are recorded accordingly in the books of Branches. Entries for this are shown as below :

(i) In the Books of Head Office :

Receiving Branch A/c Dr.

To Sending Branch A/c

(ii) In the Books of Sending Branch :

Head Office A/c Dr.

To Goods Supplied A/c

(iii) In the Books of Receiving Branch :

Goods Received A/c Dr.

To Head Office A/c

Goods-in-transit and Cash-in-transit

Sometimes, goods or cash sent by the Head office may not be received by the Branch before the end of accounting year. Similarly, goods or cash sent by the Branches may not be received by the Head office before the end of accounting period. They will be received after the accounting year. This will be happened due to delay in transit. When the goods or cash remained in transit, they are called as 'goods-in-transit' and 'cash-in-transit'. If the goods or cash remained in transit on the closing date of accounts, there will be a difference of such amount between the balances of Head Office Account (in the books of Branch) and Branch account (in the books of Head Office).

Therefore, the following adjusting entry for reconciling the difference of balances should be passed either in the Head office Books or Branch Books, but not in both of them.

In the Books of Head Office :

(i)	For Goods-in-transit :	Goods-in-transit A/c	Dr.
		To Branch A/c	
(ii)	For Cash-in-transit :	Cash-in-transit A/c	Dr.
		To Branch A/c	

In the Books of Branch :

(i)	For Goods-in-transit :	Goods-in-transit A/c	Dr.
		To Head Office A/c	
(ii)	For Cash-in-transit :	Cash-in-transit A/c	Dr.
		To Head Office A/c	

Incorporation of Branch Trial Balance in the Head Office Books

At the end of the accounting year all independent Branches must submit a copy of trial balance to the Head office. Because all Branches whether dependent or independent, are responsible to the Head Office. After the receipt of copies of the trial balance from the independent branches, the Head Office will incorporate the same in its books and prepare the consolidated final accounts of the Head office and its Branches in the columnar form. The incorporation of Branch balances in the Head office book will be done by any of the below two methods.

(1) Detailed incorporation and (2) Abridged incorporation.

(1) *Detailed Incorporation*

Under this method, all items of trading and profit and loss account are incorporated in the books of Head office besides incorporating the Branch Assets and Liabilities. The following journal entries are to be passed in this connection.

(i) For incorporating debit items (*i.e.*, opening stock, net purchases and direct expenses) of Branch trading account :

Branch Trading Account	Dr.	With total of all debit items.
To Branch Account		

(ii) For incorporating credit items (*i.e.*, net sales and closing stock) of Branch trading account :

Branch Account	Dr.	With total of all credit items.
To Branch Trading Account		

(iii) For transfer of gross profit or gross loss of Branch trading account :

For transfer of gross profit :

Branch Trading Account	Dr.	With the amount of gross profit.
To Branch Account		

For transfer of gross loss :

Branch Account	Dr.	With the amount of gross loss.
To Branch Trading A/c		

(iv) For incorporating debit items (*i.e.*, expenses and losses) of Branch profit and loss account :

Branch Profit & Loss Account	Dr.	With total of all expenses and losses.
To Branch Account		

(v) For incorporating credit items (*i.e.*, incomes and gains) of Branch profit and loss account :

Branch Account	Dr.	With total of all incomes and gains.
To Branch Profit & Loss A/c		

(vi) For transfer of net profit or net loss of Branch profit and loss account :

For transfer of net profit :

Branch P & L A/c	Dr.	With the amount of net profit.
To Branch Account		

For transfer of net loss :

Branch Account	Dr.	With the amount of net loss.
To Branch P&L A/c		

(vii) For incorporating Branch assets :

Branch Assets Account	Dr.	With the amount of all assets.
To Branch Account		

(viii) For incorporating Branch liabilities :

Branch Account	Dr.	With the amount of all liabilities.
To Branch Liabilities A/c		

(2) *Abridged Incorporation*

Under this method Branch trading and profit and loss account is prepared by the Head office as a Memorandum Account. In this method the entries are passed only for incorporating the net profit or net loss and assets and liabilities of the Branch. They are as follows :

(*i*) *For incorporating Branch net profit :*

Branch Account	Dr.	With the amount of net profit.
To General Profit and Loss A/c		

Note : If there is net loss the reverse entry is passed.

(*ii*) *For incorporating Branch Assets :*

Branch Assets Account	Dr.	With the amount of each asset individually.
To Branch Account		

(*iii*) *For incorporating Branch Liabilities :*

Branch Account	Dr.	With the amount of each liabilities individually.
To Branch Liabilities Account		

Illustration 16

Show what entries would be passed by the H.O. to record the following transactions in their books. H.O. Accounts are closed every year on 31st December.

(i) Goods amounting to Rs. 6,000 transferred from 'X' Branch to 'Y' Branch under instructions from Head office.

(ii) Cash remitted by 'X' Branch Rs. 1,000 not received by the Head office till 31st December.

(iii) Goods supplied by Head office on 28th December worth Rs. 5,800 to its 'Y' Branch were received by the Branch later on 5th January.

(iv) Expenses paid by Head office on 28th December for its 'X' Branch Rs. 500 and for 'Y' Branch 800 not yet adjusted in the accounts.

(v) Goods sent by 'Y' Branch to 'X' Branch Rs. 800 are yet to be recorded.

(vi) 'Y' Branch collected Rs. 700 from a customer of Head office.

(vii) 'X' Branch paid Rs. 4,000 for a machine purchased by Head office for the use in Head office itself.

(viii) Stock stolen from the Head office to the 'X' Branch and charged to the 'X' Branch by the Head office but not credited to the Head Office in the 'X' Branch books as the Branch Manager declined to admit any liability Rs. 500 (not covered by insurance).

(ix) Provide depreciation at 8% on furniture when the furniture accounts are maintained by H.O.

Furniture at 'X' Branch	Rs. 4,000
Furniture at 'Y' Branch	Rs. 5,000

(x) The balance of 'X' Branch profit Rs. 3,000 is to be transferred to the H.O.

Solution :

In the Books of Head Office

Journal Entries

Sl. No.	Particulars		Dr. Rs.	Cr. Rs.
(i)	'Y' Branch Account	Dr.	6,000	
	To 'X' Branch Account			6,000
	(Being goods transferred under instructions from Head office)			
(ii)	Cash-in-transit Account	Dr.	1,000	
	To 'X' Branch Account			1,000
	(Being cash remitted to H.O. is in-transit)			
(iii)	Goods-in-transit Account	Dr.	5,800	
	To 'Y' Branch Account			5,800
	(Being goods supplied to 'Y' Branch are in-transit)			
(iv)	'X' Branch Account	Dr.	500	
	'Y' Branch Account	Dr.	800	
	To Expenses Account			1,300
	(Being expenses paid by H.O. for 'X' Branch Rs. 500 and 'Y' Branch Rs. 800 now being adjusted)			
(v)	'X' Branch Account	Dr.	800	
	To 'Y' Branch Account			800
	(Being goods received by 'X' Branch from 'Y' Branch on the implied instructions of H.O.)			
(vi)	'Y' Branch Account	Dr.	700	
	To Customer's Account			700
	(Being 'Y' Branch received cash from a customer of H.O.)			
(vii)	Machinery Account	Dr.	4,000	
	To 'X' Branch Account			4,000
	(Being 'X' Branch paid for the machinery of H.O.)			
(viii)	Profit & Loss Account	Dr.	500	
	To 'X' Branch Account			500
	(Being insured stock stolen on way to 'X' Branch)			

(Contd.)

Head office Journal Entries (*Contd.*)

Sl. No.	Particulars		Dr. Rs.	Cr. Rs.
(ix)	(i) 'X' Branch Account	Dr.	320	
	To Furniture Account			320
	(Being depreciation on furniture at 'X' Branch charged to 'X' Branch)			
	(ii) 'Y' Branch Account	Dr.	400	
	To Furniture Account			400
	(Being depreciation on furniture at 'Y' Branch charged to 'Y' Branch)			
(x)	'X' Branch Account	Dr.	3,000	
	To General Profit & Loss Account			3,000
	(Being 'X' Branch profit transferred to general profit & loss account)			

Illustration 17

A firm of engineers in Delhi, whose accounting year ends on 31st December, has two Branches — one at Agra and the other at Lucknow— at which a complete set of books is maintained.

On 31st Dec., 1987, the Agra and Lucknow Branch Accounts in Delhi books showed debit balances of Rs. 27,500 and Rs. 35,300 respectively before giving effect to the following transactions :

(a) Goods valued Rs. 2,500 were transferred from Lucknow to the Agra Branch under instructions from the Head office.

(b) A remittance of Rs. 3,500 made by the Agra Branch to the H.O. on 30th Dec., 1987, was received in Delhi on 2nd January following.

(c) The Agra Branch collected Rs. 1,500 from an Agra customer of the Head office.

(d) The Lucknow Branch paid Rs. 6,500 for some machinery purchased by the H.O. in Lucknow.

(e) For the year 1987 the Agra Branch showed a net loss of Rs. 2,500 and the Lucknow Branch a net profit of Rs. 4,500.

Make journal entries to record these matters in the Head office Books, and then write up the two Branch Accounts there in.

(*Agra, B.Com., 1948 & Vikram, B.Com., 1987*)

Solution :

Journal of Head office

Sl. No.	Particulars	Dr. Rs.	Cr. Rs.
(a)	Agra Branch Account Dr. To Lucknow Branch Account (Being goods transferred under instructions from Head office)	2,500	2,500
(b)	Cash-in-transit Account Dr. To Agra Branch Account (Being cash remitted to H.O. is in transit)	3,500	3,500
(c)	Agra Branch Account Dr. To Debtors' Account (Being collections made by Agra Branch from a H.O. customer)	1,500	1,500
(d)	Machinery Account Dr. To Lucknow Branch Account (Being machinery purchased by Branch for Head office)	6,500	6,500
(e)	(i) General P&L A/c Dr. To Agra Branch Account (Being loss incurred by Agra Branch)	2,500	2,500
	(ii) Lucknow Branch Account Dr. To General Profit & Loss A/c (Being profit made by Lucknow Branch)	4,500	4,500

Dr. **Agra Branch Account** Cr.

	Rs.		Rs.
To Balance b/d	27,500	By Cash-in-transit A/c	3,500
To Lucknow Branch A/c	2,500	By General P&L A/c	2,500
To Debtors A/c	1,500	By Balance c/d (Branch Assets)	25,500
	31,500		31,500

Dr. **Lucknow Branch Account** Cr.

	Rs.		Rs.
To Balance b/d	35,300	By Agra Branch A/c	2,500
To General P&L A/c	4,500	By Machinery A/c	6,500
		By Balance c/d (Branch assets)	30,800
	39,800		39,800

Illustration 18

The All India Traders Assembly Ltd., Delhi, has branches at Calcutta, Patna, Gauhati and Cuttack in the eastern zone. For efficient and speedy disposal of goods, these branches are given powers to enter into inter-branch transactions under advice to the Head office. Following are the inter-branch transactions for the month of April, 1979 :

Calcutta Branch :

(i) Sent goods to Patna Rs. 2,000, Gauhati Rs. 5,000 and Cuttack Rs. 9,000.

(ii) Drawn bills on Patna Rs. 1,000, Gauhati Rs. 3,000 and Cuttack Rs. 4,000.

(iii) Received goods from Patna Rs. 7,000, Gauhati Rs. 6,000 and Cuttack Rs. 15,000.

(iv) Bills accepted of Patna Rs. 2,000, Gauhati Rs. 3,000 and Cuttack Rs. 6,000.

Patna Branch (in addition to transactions as aforesaid) :

(i) Sent goods to Gauhati Rs. 15,000 and Cuttack Rs. 9,000.

(ii) Drawn bills on Gauhati Rs. 10,000 and Cuttack Rs. 5,000.

(iii) Received goods from Gauhati Rs. 6,000 and Cuttack Rs. 8,000.

(iv) Accepted bills drawn by Gauhati Rs. 3,000 and Cuttack Rs. 4,000.

Gauhati Branch (in addition to transactions as aforesaid) :

(i) Goods sent to Cuttack Rs. 6,000.

(ii) Bills drawn on Cuttack Rs. 4,000.

(iii) Goods received from Cuttack Rs. 8,000.

(iv) Bills accepted drawn by Cuttack Rs. 9,000.

Set out the journal entry that the Head office would pass on 30th April, 1979, showing the working out of the net figures in a tabular form.

(*C.A. Inter*)

Solution:

Journal of Head office

Date	Particulars		L.F.	Dr. Rs.	Cr. Rs.
30th April, 1979	Calcutta Branch Account	Dr.		9,000	
	To Patna Branch Account				6,000
	To Gauhati Branch Account				2,000
	To Cuttack Branch Account				1,000
	(Recording the result of Inter-branch transactions as per statement given below)				

Working Note :

Effect of Inter-Branch Transactions

	Calcutta		Patna		Gauhati		Cuttack	
	Dr. Rs.	Cr. Rs.	Dr. Rs.	Cr. Rs.	Dr. Rs.	Cr. Rs.	Dr. Rs.	Cr. Rs.
Calcutta Branch :								
(i)	—	16,000	2,000	—	5,000	—	9,000	—
(ii)	8,000	—	—	1,000	—	3,000	—	4,000
(iii)	28,000	—	—	7,000	—	6,000	—	15,000
(iv)	—	11,000	2,000	—	3,000	—	6,000	—
Patna Branch :								
(i)			—	24,000	15,000	—	9,000	—
(ii)			15,000	—	—	10,000	—	5,000
(iii)			14,000	—	—	6,000	—	8,000
(iv)			—	7,000	3,000	—	4,000	—
Gauhati Branch :								
(i)					—	6,000	6,000	—
(ii)					4,000	—	—	4,000
(iii)					8,000	—	—	8,000
(iv)					—	9,000	9,000	—
	36,000	27,000	33,000	39,000	38,000	40,000	43,000	44,000
		9,000	6,000		2,000		1,000	
		Dr.	Cr.		Cr.		Cr.	

Illustration 19

RG Ltd. of Bangalore has a Branch at Mysore which trades independently. The following is the summary of transactions of the Branch for the year ending 31st Dec., 1981.

	Rs.
Goods from Head office	16,000
Credit purchases	13,500
Cash purchases	4,500
Credit sales	33,000
Cash sales	27,000
Cash received from Debtors	28,000
Cash paid to Creditors	9,500
Expenses paid by Branch	10,000
Expenses of Branch paid by H.O.	3,000
Furniture purchased by Branch	1,000
Cash received from H.O.	2,000
Cash remitted to H.O.	28,000

Provide depreciation of furniture Rs. 100. Stock on 31-12-1981 Rs. 6,000. Prepare Branch Trading, P&L A/c, Balance Sheet as on 31-12-1981 and show Head Office Account.

(*Bangalore, B.Com., April, 1981*)

Solution :

In the Books of Mysore Branch

Dr. **Cash Account** Cr.

	Rs.		Rs.
To Cash Sales	27,000	By Cash Purchases	4,500
To Cash received from Debtors	28,000	By Sundry Creditors	9,500
To Cash received from H.O.	2,000	By Expenses	10,000
		By Furniture	1,000
		By Head Office A/c (Cash remitted)	28,000
		By Balance c/d (Balancing figure)	4,000
	57,000		57,000

Dr. **Debtors' Account** Cr.

	Rs.		Rs.
To Credit Sales	33,000	By Cash received from Debtors	28,000
		By Balance c/d (Balancing figure)	5,000
	33,000		33,000

Creditors' Account

Dr.	Rs.		Cr. Rs.
To Cash paid to Creditors	9,500	By Credit purchases	13,500
To Balance c/d (Balancing figure)	4,000		
	13,500		13,500

Branch Trading and P&L Account for the year ending 31st Dec., 1981

Dr.		Rs.	Cr.		Rs.
To Goods received from H.O.		16,000	By Sales :		
To Purchases :			Cash	27,000	
Cash	4,500		Credit	33,000	60,000
Credit	13,500	18,000	By Stock		6,000
To Gross Profit c/d		32,000			
		66,000			66,000
To Branch Expenses paid by Branch		10,000	By Gross Profit b/d		32,000
To Branch Expenses paid by H.O.		3,000			
To Depreciation on furniture		100			
To Head Office A/c (Net Profit transferred)		18,900			
		32,000			32,000

Balance Sheet as on 31-12-1981

Liabilities	Rs.	Assets		Rs.
Sundry Creditors	4,000	Cash		4,000
Head Office A/c	11,900	Debtors		5,000
		Stock		6,000
		Furniture	1,000	
		Less : Depreciation	100	900
	15,900			15,900

Head Office Account

Dr.	Rs.		Cr. Rs.
To Cash	28,000	By Goods received from H.O.	16,000
To Balance c/d (Balancing figure)	11,900	By Branch Expenses	3,000
		By Cash	2,000
		By P & L A/c (Net Profit transferred)	18,900
	39,900		39,900

Illustration 20

The following is the Trial Balance of Calcutta Branch as at 30th June, 1980 :

	Rs.	Rs.
Bombay Head Office	3,240	—
Stock, 1st July, 1980	6,000	—
Purchases	17,800	—
Goods received from H.O.	9,000	—
Sales	—	38,000
Goods supplied to H.O.	—	6,000
Salaries	1,500	—
Debtors	3,700	—
Creditors	—	1,850
Rent	960	—
Office Expenses	470	—
Cash in Hand and at Bank	1,780	—
Furniture	1,400	—
	45,850	45,850

Stock in hand was valued at Rs. 2,700.

The Branch Account in the Head office books on 30th June, 1980 stood at Rs. 460 (Debit Balance). On 28th June, the Head office forwarded goods to the value of Rs. 2,500 to the Branch where they were received on 3rd July. Similarly, a cash remittance of Rs. 1,200 by Branch on 29th June was received by the Head office on 1st July.

You are required to submit the journal entries necessary to incorporate the above figures showing the result of trading at Branch separately in the Head office books and to give the Calcutta Branch Account appearing finally in the Bombay Head office books.

(*B.Com., Agra, B.Com., Bangalore, Oct., 1982 & April, 1986*)

Solution :

Incorporation Entries, Head office Journal entries

Sl. No.	Particulars		L.F.	Dr. Rs.	Cr. Rs.
(i)	Goods-in-transit Account	Dr.		2,500	
	Cash-in-transit Account	Dr.		1,200	
	To Branch Account				3,700
	(Being the incorporation of items in transit)				
(ii)	Branch Trading Account	Dr.		32,800	
	To Branch Account				32,800
	(Being stock Rs. 6,000, purchases Rs. 17,800 and goods from H.O. Rs. 9,000 incorporated)				
(iii)	Branch Account	Dr.		46,700	
	To Branch Trading Account				46,700
	(Being sales Rs. 38,000, goods to H.O. Rs. 6,000 and stock at the end Rs. 2,700 incorporated)				
(iv)	Branch Trading Account	Dr.		13,900	
	To Branch P&L Account				13,900
	(Being incorporation of gross profit)				
(v)	Branch P&L Account	Dr.		2,930	
	To Branch Account				2,930
	(Being salaries 1,500, rent Rs. 960 and office expenses Rs. 470 incorporated)				
(vi)	Branch P& L Account	Dr.		10,970	
	To General P&L Account				10,970
	(Being net profit transferred to general P & L Account)				
(vii)	Branch Stock Account	Dr.		2,700	
	Branch Debtors' Account	Dr.		3,700	
	Branch Cash in Hand Account	Dr.		1,780	
	Branch Furniture Account	Dr.		1,400	
	To Branch Account				9,580
	(Being branch assets incorporated)				
(viii)	Branch Account	Dr.		1,850	
	To Branch Creditors' Account				1,850
	(Being branch creditors incorporated)				

Head Office Ledger
Branch Account

Dr. Cr.

	Rs.		Rs.
To Balance b/d	460	By Goods-in-transit	2,500
To Branch Trading A/c	46,700	By Cash-in-transit	1,200
To Branch Creditors	1,850	By Branch Trading A/c	32,800
		By Branch P&L A/c	2,930
		By Branch Assets	9,580
	49,010		49,010

Branch Trading and Profit & Loss Account
For the year ended 30th June, 1988

Dr. Cr.

		Rs.			Rs.
To Branch Account :			By Branch Account :		
Stock	6,000		Sales	38,000	
Purchases	17,800		Goods Supplied to H.O.	6,000	
Goods from H.O.	9,000	32,800	Closing Stock	2,700	46,700
To Gross Profit c/d		13,900			
		46,700			46,700
To Branch Account :			By Gross Profit b/d		13,900
Salaries	1,500				
Rent	960				
Office Expenses	470	2,930			
To Net Profit (Transferred to General P & L A/c)		10,970			
		13,900			13,900

Illustration 21

Bombay Head office has Branch at Bangalore. Goods are supplied to Branch but no charge is made between H.O. & Branch. The Branch Balance Sheet as on 31-12-1981 is as follows :

Balance Sheet as on 31-12-1981

Liabilities	Rs.	Assets	Rs.
Creditors	3,290	Sundry Debtors	46,700
Head Office A/c	44,720	Cash in Hand	50
		Cash at Bank	1,260
	48,010		48,010

The following transactions took place at the Branch till 30th June, 1982 :

	Rs.		Rs.
Sales	54,180	Creditors paid	3,800
Purchases	4,200	Cash paid to Bombay H.O.	29,560
Wages	5,700	Building extension paid to	
Salaries	560	the contractor	1,500
Fire insurance premium paid		Cash in Hand	60
(for one year)	480	Cash at Bank	1,450
Other expenses	200		
Cash collected from debtors	42,000		
Discount allowed	2,500		

Show the Head Office Account and the Balance Sheet as on 30-6-1982 in the Branch Books. Pass necessary journal entries.

(*Bangalore, B.Com., May, 1982*)

Solution :

Branch Books

Dr. **Cash Book** Cr

		Rs.			Rs.
To Balance b/d :			By Wages		5,700
in Hand	50		By Salaries		560
at Bank	1,260	1,310	By Building Account		1,500
To Sundry Debtors		42,000	By Fire Insurance		480
(Cash collected)			By Other Expenses		200
			By Creditors		3,800
			By Head Office Account		29,560
			By Balance c/d :		
			in Hand	60	
			at Bank	1,450	1,510
		43,310			43,310

Dr. **Sundry Debtors' Account** Cr.

	Rs.		Rs.
To Balance b/d	46,700	By Cash (Received)	42,000
To Sales	54,180	By Discount Allowed	2,500
		By Balance c/d	56,380
		(Balancing figure)	
	1,00,880		1,00,880

Sundry Creditors' Account

Dr.	Rs.		Cr. Rs.
To Cash (paid)	3,800	By Balance b/d	3,290
To Balance c/d (Balancing figure)	3,690	By Purchases	4,200
	7,490		7,490

Head Office Account

Dr.	Rs.		Cr. Rs.
To Building A/c	1,500	By Balance b/d	44,720
To Sundries	13,400	By Sales	54,180
To Cash A/c	29,560		
To Balance c/d	54,440		
	98,900		98,900

Note : In the absence of any information regarding opening stock, goods received from H.O. and closing stock, Trading and P&L A/c is not drawn, all the revenue items are transferred to H.O.

Balance Sheet as on 30th June, 1982

Liabilities	Rs.	Assets	Rs.
Head Office A/c	54,440	Cash in Hand	60
Creditors	3,690	Cash at Bank	1,450
		Debtors	56,380
		Prepaid Insurance	240
	58,130		58,130

Journal Entries

Sl. No.	Particulars		L.F.	Dr. Rs.	Cr. Rs.
1.	Head Office Account	Dr.		1,500	
	To Building Account				1,500
	(Being the transfer of building extension expenses)				
2.	Head Office Account	Dr.		13,400	
	To Purchases				4,200
	To Wages				5,700
	To Salaries				560
	To Others Expenses				200
	To Fire Insurance				240
	To Discount				2,500
	(Being transfer of debit items excluding prepaid insurance Rs. 240)				

(Contd.)

Journal Entries (*Contd.*)

3.	Sales Account Dr.	54,180	
	To Head Office Account		54,180
	(Being transfer of credit items)		

Illustration 22

From the following summaries of the weekly returns of a Branch, prepare Branch Final Accounts for the year ending 31-12-1980.

Cash Account of the Branch

		Rs.			Rs.
1-1-80	To Balance b/d	1,200	31-12-80	By Cash Purchases	4,360
31-12-80	To Cash Sales	4,13,680		By Wages	1,12,500
31-12-80	To Cash received from Debtors	12,350		By Expenses	2,320
				By Bank A/c	3,06,550
				By Balance c/d	1,500
		4,27,230			4,27,230

Dr. **Branch Debtors' Account** Cr.

		Rs.			Rs.
1-1-80	To Balance b/d	890	31-12-80	By Cash	10,000
31-12-80	To Sales	16,000		By Allowances	500
				By Balance c/d	6,390
		16,890			16,890

Branch current account in Head office books appears in a summarized form as follows :

			Rs.			Rs.
1-1-80	To Balance b/d :			1-1-80	By Balance of Rent & Taxes	4,340
	Cash	1,200				
	Debtors	890				
	Stock	16,380				
	Fittings	10,000	28,470			
31-12-80	To Goods		2,26,500	31-12-80	By Bank	3,06,550
	Cash –				By Balance c/d	60
	Rent & Taxes		20,200			
	Salaries		32,300			
	Sundry Expenses		2,480			
	Fittings		1,000			
			3,10,950			3,10,950

On 31-12-1980 stock at Branch was Rs. 20,400, liabilities for rent & taxes Rs. 6,320 and for salaries Rs. 1,000. Provide Rs. 1,100 for depreciation on fittings.

(*Calcutta, B.Com., 1969 & Bangalore, B.Com., Nov., 1981*)

Solution :

Branch Trading and P&L Account

Dr. **for the year ending 31st December, 1980** Cr.

		Rs.			Rs.
To Opening Stock		16,380	By Sales :		
To Goods received			Cash	4,13,680	
from Head Office		2,26,500	Credit	16,000	4,29,680
To Purchases		4,360	To Closing Stock		20,400
To Wages		1,12,500			
To Gross Profit c/d		90,340			
		4,50,080			4,50,080
To Rent & Taxes	20,200		By Gross Profit b/d		90,340
Less: Prepaid	4,340				
	15,860				
Add : Outstanding	6,320	22,180			
To Salaries	32,300				
Add : Outstanding	1,000	33,300			
To Allowance to Debtors		500			
To Sundry Expenses	2,480				
Add : Paid by Branch	2,320	4,800			
To Depreciation on Fittings		1,100			
To Net Profit (Balance of Profit transferred to H.O. A/c)		28,460			
		90,340			90,340

Balance Sheet as on 31st Dec., 1980

Liabilities		Rs.	Assets		Rs.
Outstanding Expenses :			Cash		1,500
Rent & Taxes	6,320		Debtors		6,390
Salaries	1,000	7,320	Stock		20,400
Head Office Account		30,870	Fittings	11,000	
			Less : Depreciation	1,100	9,900
		38,190			38,190

Dr. **Head Office Account** Cr.

	Rs.		Rs.
To Cash	3,06,550	By Balance b/d (28,470 – 4,340)	24,130
To Balance c/d	30,870	By Goods received from H.O.	2,26,500
		By Cash (20,200 + 32,300 + 2,480)	54,980
		By Fittings	1,000
		By Cash received from H.O. Debtors (12,350 – 10,000)	2,350
		By Branch P&L A/c	28,460
	3,37,420		3,37,420

Illustration 23

The Head office of a business and its Branch keep their own books and each prepares its own profit and loss account. The following are the balances appearing on the two sets of the books as on 31st December, 1989 after ascertainment of profits and after making all adjustments except those referred to bellow :

	Head Office		Branch	
	Dr. Rs.	Cr. Rs.	Dr. Rs.	Cr. Rs.
Capital	—	1,00,000	—	—
Fixed Assets	36,000	—	16,000	—
Stock	34,200	—	10,740	—
Debtors & Creditors	7,820	3,960	4,840	1,920
Cash	10,740	—	1,420	—
Profit & Loss A/c	—	14,660	—	3,060
Branch A/c	29,860	—	—	—
Head Office A/c	—	—	—	28,020
	1,18,620	1,18,620	33,000	33,000

Set out the Balance Sheet of the business as on 31st December, 1989 and the journal entries necessary (in both sets of books) to record the adjustments dealing with the following :

(a) On 31st December, the Branch had sent a cheque of Rs. 1,000 to the Head Office, not received by them nor credited to the Branch till next month.

(b) Goods valued at Rs. 440 had been forwarded by the Head office to the Branch and invoiced on 30th December but were not received by the Branch nor dealt with in their books till next month.

(c) It was agreed that the Branch should be charged with Rs. 300 for administrative service, rendered by the Head office during the year.

(d) Stock stolen from the Head office to the Branch and charged to the Branch by the Head office but not credited to the Head office in the Branch books as the Branch Manager declined to admit any liability, Rs. 400 (not covered by insurance).

(e) Depreciation of Branch assets of which accounts are maintained by Head office, not provided for Rs. 250.

(f) The balance of profit shown by the Branch is to be transferred to the Head office books.

(*Bangalore, April, 1992*)

Solution :

Head Office Journal

Sl. No.	Particulars		L.F.	Dr. Rs.	Cr. Rs.
1.	Cash-in-transit Account	Dr.		1,000	
	To Branch Account				1,000
	(Being cash-in-transit adjusted)				
2.	Goods-in-transit Account	Dr.		440	
	To Branch Account				440
	(Being goods-in-transit adjusted)				
3.	Branch Account	Dr.		300	
	To Profit & Loss A/c				300
	(Being charge made for administrative service to Branch)				
4.	Profit & Loss Account	Dr.		400	
	To Branch Account				400
	(Being stock stolen not admitted by Branch Manager now adjusted)				
5.	Branch Account	Dr.		250	
	To Branch Assets A/c				250
	(Being depreciation of branch assets maintained in H.O. Books now provided for)				
6.	Branch Account	Dr.		2,510	
	To General P&L A/c				2,510
	(Being branch profit adjusted)				

Branch Journal

Sl. No.	Particulars	L.F.	Dr. Rs.	Dr. Rs.
1.	Profit & Loss Account Dr.		300	
	To Head Office Account			300
	(Being charge for administrative services by H.O. adjusted)			
2.	Profit & Loss Account Dr.		250	
	To Head Office Account			250
	(Being depreciation of assets in Head Office books provided for)			
3.	Profit & Loss Account Dr.		2,510	
	To Head Office Account			2,510
	(Being profit adjusted)			

Balance Sheet as at 31st December, 1989

Liabilities		Rs.	Assets			Rs.
Capital		1,00,000	Fixed Assets :			
Creditors :			Head Office		36,000	
Head Office	3,960		Branch	16,000		
Branch	1,920	5,880	*Less :* Dep.	250	15,750	51,750
Profit & Loss A/c :			Stock:			
Head Office	14,560		Head Office		34,200	
Branch	2,510	17,070	Branch		10,740	
			In transit		440	45,380
			Debtors :			
			Head Office		7,820	
			Branch		4,840	12,660
			Cash :			
			Head Office		10,740	
			Branch		1,420	
			In transit		1,000	13,160
		1,22,950				1,22,950

Working Notes :

(1) Profit of Branch and Head office is ascertained by preparing P & L Account of Branch as well as Head office :

Branch P&L Account

Dr.	Rs.		Cr. Rs.
To Head Office Expenses A/c	300	By Profit (as given)	3,060
To Depreciation	250		
To Net Profit (Transferred to General P & L A/c)	2,510		
	3,060		3,060

General (H.O.) P&L Account

Dr.	Rs.		Cr. Rs.
To Branch Account (stock stolen)	400	By Profit (as given)	14,660
To Profit c/d	14,560	By Branch Account (Administrative services)	300
	14,960		14,960
To Net Profit (Transferred to Balance Sheet)	17,070	By Profit b/d	14,560
		By Branch A/c (Profit made by Branch)	2,510
	17,070		17,070

(ii) Branch account in the books of the Head office and Head office account in the books of the Branch will appear as follows :

Branch Account

(In the books of Head Office)

Dr.	Rs.		Cr. Rs.
To Balance b/d	29,860	By Goods-in-transit	440
To P&L A/c	300	By P&L A/c	400
To Branch Assets A/c	250	By Cash-in-transit	1,000
To General P&L A/c	2,510	By Balance c/d	31,080
	32,920		32,920

Head Office Account

(In the books of Branch)

Dr.	Rs.		Cr. Rs.
To Branch c/d	31,080	By Balance b/d	28,020
		By H.O. Expenses A/c	300
		By Depreciation	250
		By P&L A/c	2,510
	31,080		31,080

Illustration 24

The Bombay Head Office has a branch at Madras which maintains a complete set of account books. All purchases are made at Bombay and goods are invoiced to branch at selling price less 15%. The Branch manager is entitled to a commission at 1/3 of the net profit earned by the branch on the basis of invoice price. Trial Balance of the Head Office and the Branch as on 31st December, 1980 are given below :

Particulars	Head Office		Branch	
	Dr. Rs.	Cr. Rs.	Dr. Rs.	Cr. Rs.
Capital	—	9,420	—	—
Sundry Debtors	8,970	—	755	—
Sundry Creditors	—	2,460	—	615
Stock at the beginning of the year at cost : Head office	12,415	—	—	—
Branch	3,215			
Stock at the Branch at the beginning of year as invoiced	—	3,627	3,627	—
Purchases	30,725	—	—	—
Goods invoiced during the year	—	10,250	10,250	—
Salaries	3,528	—	1,468	—
Sundry expenses	1,617	—	229	—
Branch Adjustment A/c	2,323	—	—	—
Head Office Adjustment A/c	—	—	580	—
Cash in Hand and at Bank	2,480	—	326	—
Furniture	1,500	—	200	—
Sales	—	41,016	—	16,820
	66,773	66,773	17,435	17,435

The cost price of goods invoiced to Madras was Rs. 8,190. The Stock in the hand at the end of the year at Bombay was valued at Rs. 4,525 at cost and at Madras Rs. 1,416 at cost and Rs. 1,766 at invoice price. The difference between the adjustment accounts is due to a remittance in transit from the Branch to the Head Office.

Prepare the profit and loss account for the year ending 31st December, 1980 and the Balance sheet as at that date.

(*Adapted from C.A., & B.Com., Bangalore*)

Solution :

Memorandum Madras Branch Trading & Profit and Loss A/c

Dr. **(Invoice value)** Cr.

	Rs.		Rs.
To Opening Stock	3,627	By Sales	16,820
To Goods Received from H.O.	10,250	By Closing Stock	1,766
To Gross Profit c/d	4,709		
	18,586		18,586
To Salaries	1,468	By Gross Profit b/d	4,709
To Sundry Expenses	229		
To Manager's Commission (1/3 of 3012)	1,004		
To Net Profit	2,008		
	4,709		4,709

Trading and Profit and Loss Account for the year ending 31st Dec., 1980

Dr. Cr.

	Bombay Rs.	Madras Rs.		Bombay Rs.	Madras Rs.
To Opening Stock	12,415	3,215	By Sales	41,016	16,820
To Purchases	30,725	—	By Goods Sent to Branch	8,190	—
To Goods received from H.O.	—	8,190	By Closing Stock	4,527	1,416
To Gross Profit c/d	10,593	6,831			
	53,733	18,236		53,733	18,236
To Salaries	3,528	1,468	By Gross Profit b/d	10,593	6,831
To Sundry Expenses	1,617	229			
To Branch Manager's Commission		1,004			
To Net Profit c/d	5,448	4,130			
	10,593	6,831		10,593	6,831

Balance Sheet as on 31st December, 1980

Liabilities		Rs.	Assets		Rs.
Capital	9,420		Cash in Hand and at Bank :		
Add : Profit – H.O.	5,448		H.O.	2,480	
– Madras	4,130	18,998	Madras	326	2,806
Sundry Creditors :			Cash-in-transit		2,903
H.O.	2,460		Sundry Debtors :		
Madras	615	3,075	H.O.	8,970	
Outstanding Branch			Madras	755	9,725
Manager's Commission		1,004	Stock at cost :		
			H.O.	4,527	
			Madras	1,416	5,943
			Furniture :		
			H.O.	1,500	
			Madras	200	1,700
		23,077			23,077

Head Office Account

Dr. **(In the Books of Branch)** Cr.

	Rs.		Rs.
To Balance b/d	580	By Net Profit	4,130
To Balance c/d	6,453	By Cash-in-transit (2,323 + 580)	2,903
	7,033		7,033

Dr. **Madras Branch Account** Cr.

	Rs.		Rs.
To Balance b/d	2,323	By Balance c/d	6,453
To Net Profit	4,130		
	6,453		6,453

(III) Foreign Branches

When a branch is situated in a foreign country it is called a Foreign Branch. At the end of the accounting period, the Foreign Branch remits its Trial Balance in the foreign currency in which its transactions take place. On receipt of the Trial Balance from the Foreign Branch, the Head office convert the Branch Trial Balance from the foreign currency into the currency of that country where a Head office is situated in order to incorporate the Branch

Trial Balance in the books of Head office. Otherwise the accounting procedure itself is in no way different from that of independent branch.

Rules for Converting the Foreign Branch Trial Balance

The following rules will be adopted while converting the figures of foreign branch trial balance :

(a) When the rate of exchange between the two countries fairly constant or widely fluctuating, all the items of the trial balance will be converted at a fixed rate of exchange with the following exceptions :

(i) Remittance to H.O. will be taken at actual figure.

(ii) The H.O. account having a credit balance will be taken at a actual figure as shown by the branch account in the books of Head office having a debit balance.

(b) When the rate of exchange fluctuate frequently, the following rules will be followed for converting the foreign branch trial balance :

(i) Fixed assets should be converted at the rate of exchange prevailing on the day when these assets were purchased.

(ii) Fixed liabilities should be converted at the rate of exchange prevailing on the day when these liabilities were incurred.

(iii) Floating assets and liabilities should be converted at the rate of exchange prevailing on the closing day of the accounting period.

(iv) Remittances appearing in the Branch Trial Balance are converted at the figures at which they appear in the H.O. books.

(v) Revenue items will be converted at the average rate prevailing over the whole period except for the following :

(i) **Depreciation :** It should be converted at the same rate as that applicable to relative asset.

(ii) **Reserve for bad debts :** It should be converted at the same rate as that applicable to debts.

(iii) **Opening and closing stock :** Opening stock should be converted at the rate prevailing in the beginning of the year and closing stock should be converted at the rate prevailing at the end of the year, unless a fixed rate is adopted.

(vi) Head office account is converted at the same figure at which branch account appears in the H.O. Books.

After converting the branch trial balance, a new trial balance will be prepared. If there is any difference in the branch trial balance on account of conversion, it will be treated as loss or gain according to Dr. Balance or Cr. Balance and debit balance should be transferred to branch profit & loss account and credit balance should preferably be transferred to Exchange Fluctuation Reserve A/c instead of P&L A/c.

Illustration 25

A Trading Company has its Head office in London and a Branch in Bombay. The following is the Trial Balance of both the business on 31st December, 1981.

Trial Balance on 31st December

	London		Bombay	
	£	£	Rs.	Rs.
Stock, 1st Jan., 1981	16,000	—	1,28,700	—
Purchases and Sales	86,000	98,000	5,02,200	6,31,800
Expenses	6,000	—	1,05,300	—
Furniture	600	—	6,360	—
Sundry Debtors and Creditors	15,000	8,000	1,43,100	87,450
Bank	5,400	—	1,27,200	—
Share Capital :				
8,000 Shares of Rs. 5 each				
fully paid	—	40,000	—	—
Profit and Loss Account balance	—	1,000	—	—
Head Office Account	18,000	—	—	—
Bombay Branch Account	—	—	—	2,93,610
	1,47,000	1,47,000	10,12,860	10,12,860

The rate of exchange between Bombay and London may be taken at Rs. 15 to £ 1. Prepare the trading and profit and loss account and the balance sheet by the company as at 31st December, 1981, in sterling.

The closing stock were : London £ 12,500, Bombay Rs. 1,41,150.

(B.Com., Allahabad)

Solution :

Trial Balance of Bombay Branch as on 31st Dec., 1981
(As Converted into Sterling)

	Dr. £	Cr. £
Stock, 1st Jan., 1981	8,580	—
Purchases	33,480	—
Sales	—	42,120
Expenses	7,020	—

(Contd.)

Trial Balance of Bombay Branch as on 31st Dec., 1981 (*Contd.*)

	£	£
Furniture	424	–
Sundry Debtors	9,540	–
Sundry Creditors	–	5,830
Bank	8,480	
Head Office Account		18,000
Difference in Exchange Account		1,574
	67,524	67,524

Trading and Profit and Loss Account

Dr. **On 31st December, 1981** Cr.

	Head Office £	Bombay Branch £	Total £		Head Office £	Bombay Branch £	Total £
To Opening Stock	16,000	8,580	24,580	By Sales	98,000	42,120	1,40,120
To Purchases A/c	86,000	33,480	1,19,480	By Closing Stock	12,500	9,410	21,910
To Gross Profit c/d	8,500	9,470	17,970				
	1,10,500	51,530	1,62,030		1,10,500	51,530	1,62,030
To Expenses A/c	6,000	7,020	13,020	By Gross Profit b/d	8,500	9,470	17,970
To Net Profit	2,500	2,450	4,950				
	8,500	9,470	17,970		8,500	9,470	17,970

Balance Sheet as at 31st December, 1981

Liabilities	£	£	Assets	£	£
Share Capital :			Furniture :		
800 Shares of £ 5 each			Head Office	600	
fully paid		40,000	Bombay Branch	424	1,024
Sundry Creditors :			Sundry Debtors :		
Head Office	8,000		Head Office	15,000	
Bombay Branch	5,830	13,830	Bombay Branch	9,540	24,540
Profit & Loss A/c :			Stock :		
Balance b/d	1,000		Head Office	12,500	
Add : Net Profit	4,950	5,950	Bombay Branch	9,410	21,910
Reserve Account :			Bank :		
Difference in Exchange A/c		1,574	Head Office	5,400	
			Bombay Branch	8,480	13,880
		61,354			61,354

Illustration 26

Following are the Trial Balance of Bombay Head Office and New York Branch as on 31-12-1977 :

	Head Office		New York Branch	
	Dr. Rs.	Cr. Rs.	Dr. Dollars	Cr. Dollars
Capital Account	—	7,50,000		
Land and Building	1,50,000	—		
Goodwill	75,000	—		
Plant and Machinery	12,00,000	—	1,80,000	—
Furniture and Fittings	45,000	—	12,000	—
Stock 1-1-1977	5,10,000	—	84,000	—
Purchases	31,68,000	—	3,60,000	—
Goods from Head Office		—	1,20,000	—
Goods to New York Branch	—	11,78,000		
Sales	—	34,82,500		6,24,000
Salaries and Wages	1,44,000	—	12,000	—
Rent, Rates & Taxes	18,000	—	3,000	—
Insurance	10,500	—	1,500	—
Trade Expenses	27,000	—	3,000	—
Head Office				1,71,000
N.Y. Branch	12,33,500	—		
Sundry Debtors	3,30,000	—	36,000	—
Sundry Creditors	—	16,68,500	—	25,500
Cash Balance in Hand and with Banks	1,68,000	—	9,000	—
	70,79,000	70,79,000	8,20,500	8,20,500

(1) Stock as on 31-12-1977 was valued at :

Head Office	Rs. 4,38,000
N.Y. Branch	$ 78,000

(2) Depreciation on plant and machinery and furniture and fittings to be provided at 10% p.a.

(3) Rates of exchange were as follows :

(i) When plant & machinery and furniture & fixtures were purchased : $ 100 = Rs. 780.

(ii) On 1-1-1977 : $ 100 = Rs. 850.

(iii) On 1-12-1977 : $ 100 = Rs. 950.

(iv) Average rate for the year : $ 100 = Rs. 970.

You are required to prepare a combined columnar profit and loss account and balance sheet of the Head office and the branch.

(*C.A. Final, Old Scheme, Nov., 1978*)

Solution :

Branch Trial Balance as at 31st Dec., 1977

(As Converted into Rupees)

	Rate per $ 100	Dr. $	Cr. $	Rupees	Rupees
Plant and Machinery	780	1,80,000	—	14,04,000	—
Furniture and Fitting	780	12,000	—	93,600	—
Stock 1-1-1977	850	84,000	—	7,14,000	—
Purchases	970	3,60,000	—	34,92,000	—
Goods from H.O.	Actual	1,20,000	—	11,78,000	—
Sales	970		6,24,000		60,52,800
Salaries & Wages	970	12,000	—	1,16,400	—
Rent, Rates & Taxes	970	3,000	—	29,100	—
Insurance	970	1,500	—	14,550	—
Trade Expenses	970	3,000	—	29,100	—
Head Office	Actual	—	1,71,000	—	12,33,500
Sundry Creditors	950	—	25,500	—	2,42,250
Sundry Debtors	950	36,000	—	3,42,000	—
Cash Balance	950	9,000	—	85,500	—
Difference in Exchange				30,300	—
		8,20,500	8,20,500	75,28,550	75,28,550
	950	78,000		7,41,000	

Trading and Profit & Loss Account for the year ended 31st Dec., 1977

	Head Office Rs.	New York Branch Rs.		Head Office Rs.	New York Branch Rs.
To Opening Stock	5,10,000	7,14,000	By Sales	34,82,500	60,52,800
To Purchases	31,68,000	34,92,000	By Goods Sent to Branch	11,78,000	
To Goods from H.O.	–	11,78,000			
To Gross Profit c/d	14,20,500	14,09,800	By Closing Stock	4,38,000	7,41,000
	50,98,500	67,93,800		50,98,500	67,93,800
To Salaries & Wages	1,44,000	1,16,400	By Gross Profit b/d	14,20,500	14,09,800
To Rent, Rates & Taxes	18,000	29,100			
To Insurance	10,500	14,550			
To Trade Expenses	27,000	29,100			
To Depreciation :					
Plant & Machinery	1,20,000	1,40,400			
Furniture & Fittings	4,500	9,360			
To Difference in Exch.		30,300			
To Net Profit	10,96,500	10,40,590			
	14,20,500	14,09,800		14,20,500	14,09,800

Balance Sheet as on 31st Dec., 1977

Liabilities		Rs.	Assets		Rs.
Capital	7,50,000		Goodwill		75,000
Add : Profit of the year	21,37,090	28,87,090	Land & Building		1,50,000
Sundry Creditors :			Plant & Machinery :		
Head Office	16,68,500		Head Office	12,00,000	
Branch	2,42,250	19,10,750	Branch	14,04,000	
				26,04,000	
			Less : Depreciation	2,60,400	23,43,600
			Furniture & Fittings :		
			Head Office	45,000	
			Branch	93,600	
				1,38,600	
			Less : Depreciation	13,860	1,24,740
			Closing Stock :		
			Head Office	4,38,000	
			Branch	7,41,000	11,79,000
			Sundry Debtors :		
			Head Office	3,30,000	
			Branch	3,42,000	6,72,000
			Cash Balance :		
			Head Office	1,68,000	
			Branch	85,500	2,53,500
		47,97,840			47,97,840

EXAMINATION QUESTIONS

(A) Answer the following questions in not exceeding 4 lines each.

(*Each Carries 2 Marks*)

(1) What do you mean by branch?

(2) Give the classification of branches from accounting point of view. (*Karnataka, Oct., 1995*)

(3) What is debtor system? When is it used? (*M.K.U., Oct., 1992*)

(4) Where is stock and debtors system used? (*Shivaji, Oct., 1989*)

(5) What are independent branches?

(6) What journal entry would you pass in the books of the head office for depreciation of branch asset when shown in the books of the head office? (*Bangalore, June, 1981*)

(7) What is branch adjustment account in the context of accounts? (*Bangalore, Nov., 1981*)

(8) Pass the adjustment entry for the following transactions where H.O. dispatches goods at cost $33^1/_3$% profit :

(i) Opening stock of branch at invoice price of Rs. 4,000.

(ii) Goods sent to branch during the year at invoice price Rs. 4,000.

(9) Write a note on goods-in-transit and remittance in transit. (*Bangalore, Nov., 1983*)

(10) What do you mean by goods in transit? (*Bangalore, April, 1985 & KUD, April, 1997*)

(11) State the entry to be made to show remittances in transit in the books of H.O. When cash is sent by Branch to H.O. before the date of Balance Sheet but not received by H.O. on the date of Balance Sheet. (*Bangalore, Oct., 1985*)

(12) Give two examples of inter-branch transactions. (*Bangalore, April, 1986*)

(13) How do you record the inter-branch transactions? (*Madras, Oct., 1991*)

(14) What do you understand by inter-branch transactions? (*Karnataka, April, 1995*)

(15) What are inter-branch transactions? (*Karnataka, Oct., 1996*)

(16) How many types of branches are there? (*Kakatiya, April, 1993*)

(17) Differentiate branch accounts and departmental accounts.

(*Bharathidasan, April, 1993*)

(18) What is meant by invoice price method? Why is it followed?

(*Madurai Kamaraj, April, 1994*)

(19) What procedure would you follow for converting the trial balance of a foreign branch into home currency?

(*Cuttack, April, 1992*)

(20) Write the journal entry in the books of Head office for depreciation to be provided on branch fixed assets. Whose accounts are kept in H.O. books.

(*Karnataka, April, 1998*)

(B) Answer the following questions/problems :

(*Each Carries 8 Marks*)

(1) What is a branch? What are its objectives?

(2) What do you mean by stock and debtors system? What are its advantages?

(3) Explain the accounting treatment when the goods are invoiced from Head office to Branch at invoice price.

(4) Give the entries under stock and debtors system.

(5) Give the accounting treatment of the following :

(a) Goods in transit

(b) Cash in transit

(c) Depreciation when the assets are in the H.O. Books.

(*Bangalore, April, 1992*)

(6) What are the benefits by selling the goods through retail branches?

(*Alld., B.Com., 1987*)

(7) Write down the procedure of incorporating the branch trial balance in the H.O. Books.

(*Agra, Oct., 1979*)

(8) Give the rules for conversion of a branch trial balance in to that of H.O. currency, in the case of a foreign branch.

(*Gorakhpur, Oct., 1981*)

(9) From the following information prepare the branch account in the books of Head office. All the expenses are paid by the Head office and daily collections of branch are remitted to Head office.

	Rs.	Rs.
Stock on 1-1-1997		60,000
Petty cash on 1-1-1997		800
Goods sent to branch during the year		1,50,000
Cash sent to branch for :		
Salary	12,000	
Rent	3,000	
Petty Expenses	5,000	20,000
Cash received from branch		1,75,000
Goods returned by branch		6,000
Petty cash on 31-12-1997		2,000
Stock on 31-12-1997		70,000

Ans. : Profit Rs. 22,200; Branch A/c Total Rs. 2,53,000.

(10) Swastik Products Ltd. opened a branch at Belgaum on 1-12-1990. From the following particulars, prepare Branch A/c and find out profit or loss at Branch for the period ending 31-12-1990.

	Rs.	Rs.
Goods sent to Branch		40,000
Cash remittance to Branch for :		
Salaries	5,000	
Office Rent	1,200	
Office Expenses	800	7,000
Cash sales by Branch (Remitted to H.O.)		55,000
Stock on 31-12-1990		5,000

(*Karnataka, April, 1996*)

Ans. : Profit Rs. 13,000; Branch A/c Total Rs. 60,000.

(11) From the following information, prepare the branch account in the books of the H.O. for the year ending 31-12-92. All the expenses are to be paid by the Head office and the daily collections of the branch are remitted to the H.O.

	Rs.
Stock on 31-12-1992	1,25,000
Stock on 1-1-1992	75,000
Debtors on 1-1-1992	50,000
Debtors on 31-12-1992	70,000
Goods sent to branch	3,00,000
Cash sales remitted to H.O.	1,00,000

		Rs.
Cash collected from debtors & remitted to H.O.		1,40,000
Goods returned from branch		30,000
Cash sent to branch for :		
Salary	8,000	
Rent	2,000	10,000
Petty cash on 1-1-1992		100
Petty cash on 31-12-1992		100
Discount allowed to customers		5,000

(*Gulbarga, Oct., 1993 & KUD., April, 1997*)

Ans. : Profit Rs. 30,000; Branch A/c Total Rs. 4,65,100 and Credit Sales Rs. 1,65,000.

(12) The Union Stores Ltd. invoiced goods to its Surat Branch at cost. The branch maintained its sales ledger and remits all cash received daily to the H.O. The branch expenses are being paid by the H.O. by cheques.

From the following details relating to the branch, show the branch trading and P&L A/c in the books of H.O.

	Rs.
Debtors (1-1-1989)	13,100
Debtors (31-12-1989)	16,550
Stock (1-1-1989)	7,500
Stock (31-12-1989)	6,950
Goods received form H.O.	25,400
Goods returned to H.O.	350
Cash sales and credit sales	46,770
Allowances to customers	350
Cash received from debtors	24,600
Rent, rates, etc.	900
Wages and salaries	3,000
General trade expenses	650
Returns from customers	290
Discount allowed to customers	1,200
Bad debts	300

(*Gulbarga, Oct., 1990*)

Ans. : Gross profit Rs. 20,880; N.P. Rs. 14,480; Cash sales Rs. 16,580 (46,770 – 30,190).

(13) Bharat Traders opened a branch at Bellary on 1-1-1988. Goods are invoiced to branch at cost plus 20% which is the selling price. Following are the branch transactions during the year :

		Rs.
Goods supplied to the branch		45,000
Sales at branch :	Cash sales	13,000
	Credit sales	25,000
Cash received from debtors		18,600
Discount allowed		400
Cash sent to branch for expenses		5,000
Goods returned by branch		3,000
Closing stock at branch		8,400

Prepare the branch account in the books of H.O.

(*Gulbarga, Oct., 1989*)

Ans. : Profit Rs. 4,600; Branch A/c Total Rs. 56,500.

Note : 20% on cost is $16\frac{2}{3}$% on sales or 1/6 of selling price.

(14) Record the adjustment entries in the books of H.O. at Dharwad :

(a) Goods dispatched by Bijapur Branch to Belgaum Branch under intimation to H.O. Rs. 40,000.

(b) Cash remitted by Karwar Branch on 28-12-1994 but received by H.O. on 4-1-1995 Rs. 25,000.

(c) Audit fees Rs. 5,000 paid by H.O. is to be allocated equally to H.O. and three branches.

(d) H.O. received Rs. 9,000 from Karwar Branch customer and allowed him discount Rs. 100.

(*Karnatak, April, 1995*)

Hint : (a) Debit Belgaum Branch and credit Bijapur Branch Rs. 40,000.

(b) Debit cash in transit and credit Karwar Branch Rs. 25,000.

(c) Debit Each Branch Rs. 1,250 each and credit Audit fees Rs. 3,750.

(d) Debit cash and credit Karwar Branch Rs. 9,000.

(15) Pass adjustment entries in the H.O. books having independent branch (closing date 31st December) :

(i) Goods supplied by H.O. on 28th December, Rs. 15,000 reached Hubli branch on 4th January.

(ii) Cash remitted by Hareri branch on 29th December, Rs. 11,000 was received by H.O. on 3rd January.

(iii) Rs. 3,000 remitted by Hareri branch to Hubli branch under intimation to H.O.

(iv) Depreciation of Rs. 8,000 is provided on Hubli branch building whose account is kept in Head office. (*Karnatak, Oct., 1996*)

Hint : (i) Debit Goods in transit and credit Hubli Branch Rs. 15,000.
(ii) Debit Cash in transit and credit Hareri Branch Rs. 11,000.
(iii) Debit Hubli Branch and credit Hareri Branch Rs. 3,000.
(iv) Debit Hubli Branch and credit Branch Building Rs. 8,000.

(16) A trading company invoices goods at cost to its Trivandrum Branch. Expenses are met directly from Head Office, except petty cash expenses. Branch is advised to sell for cash only and deposit the day's sale proceeds in the Head Office Account. From the following, ascertain the profits of Trivandrum Branch through Debtors System :

	Rs.
Stock (January 1)	2,100
Petty cash (January 1)	50
Furniture (January 1)	250
Goods supplied from Head Office	7,800
Goods returned to Head Office	300
Cash sales	15,250
Stock (December 31)	1,950
Petty cash (December 31)	30
Furniture (December 31)	230
Salaries, wages, etc.	2,100
Rent	360

(*Kerala, April, 1992*)

Ans. : Branch profit Rs. 5,100.

(17) D. Chakraborty, Calcutta, has a branch at Bombay. Goods are supplied to the branch at cost. The expenses of the branch are paid from Calcutta and the Branch keeps a sales Journal and Debtors Ledger only. From the following information supplied by the branch, prepare Branch Account in the books of the Head Office :

	Rs.
Closing stock (1-4-1978)	24,000
Closing stock (31-3-1979)	18,000
Credit sales	41,000
Cash sales	17,500
Receipt from debtors	37,900
Sundry debtors on 31-3-1979	9,160
Goods received from Head Office	30,000
Goods received at H.O. on 31-3-1979	3,600
Expenses paid by H.O. for the branch	10,400

(*Bharathidasan, April, 1994*)

Ans. : Opening balance of branch debtors Rs. 6,060 & branch profit Rs. 15,700.

(18) A Head Office in Madras sends goods to its branch at Kerala. Prepare Branch Account to calculate profit.

	Rs.
Debtors on 1st July, 1985	12,000
Stock on 1st July, 1985	10,000
Goods sent to Branch	32,000
Cash sales	16,000
Cash received from Debtors	29,000
Goods returned to Head Office	1,920
Cheques sent to Branch for expenses	14,510
Stock on 31st December, 1985	12,000
Debtors on 31st December, 1985	22,500

(*Bharathiar, April, 1994*)

Ans. : Credit sales Rs. 39,500 and Branch profit Rs. 12,910.

(19) From the following particulars relating to Hyderabad Branch for the year ending 31st December, 1990, prepare Branch Account in the Head Office books.

	Rs.	Rs.
Stock at the Branch on 1-1-90		15,000
Debtors at the Branch on 1-1-90		30,000
Petty cash at the Branch on 1-1-90		300
Goods sent to Branch during 1990		2,52,000
Cash sales, 1990		60,000
Received from debtors, 1990		21,000
Credit sales during 1990		2,28,000
Cheques sent to Branch during 1990 :		
For salaries	9,000	
For rent and taxes	1,500	
For petty cash	1,100	11,600
Stock at the Branch on 31-12-1990		25,000
Petty cash, 31-12-1990		200
Goods returned by the Branch		2,000
Debtors on 31-12-1990		48,000

(*Madras, March, 1993*)

Ans. : On the basis of given credit sales, branch profit Rs. 34,300.

(20) Cochin Chemical company has a branch at Malapuram. Goods are supplied to branch at cost plus 25% by the Head Office at Cochin. From the following particulars, prepare a Branch Account in the Head Office books for the year ending 31st March, 1991 :

	Rs.
Goods supplied to Malapuram	75,000
Cash received from Debtors	50,000
Cash sales	20,000
Credit sales	70,000
Goods returned to Head Office	500
Sundry Debtors :	
1st April, 1990	10,000
31st March, 1991	30,000
Stock at Malapuram :	
1st April, 1990	12,000
31st March, 1991	20,000

(*Calicut, April, 1991*)

Ans. : Branch profit Rs. 36,800.

(21) The Bharat Stores, Agra, has a branch at Kanpur, goods are invoiced to the branch at selling price, being cost plus 25%. From the following details, prepare a Branch Account in the Head Office books :

	Rs.
Stock on 1st January, 1984	7,500
Stock on 31st December, 1984	9,000
Sundry Debtors on 1st January, 1984	4,200
Sundry Debtors on 31st December, 1984	5,400
Goods invoiced from Head Office	54,600
Rent, rates and taxes	2,400
Sundry expenses	480
Cash sales	32,400
Cash received from debtors	19,800
Wages paid	2,040
Wages still owing	200

(*Bharathiar, April, 1994*)

Ans. : Branch profit Rs. 5,800 and Credit sales Rs. 12,000.

(22) Pass the following Journal entries in the books of Head Office :

(a) When depreciation on branch furniture charged (Depreciation is Rs. 500).

(b) When branch office sent cash Rs. 5,000 to H.O. on 27-12-94 but H.O. received the same on 2-1-95.

(c) Dharwad branch sent goods worth of Rs. 3,000 to Hubli branch as per the instructions of H.O.

(d) H.O. sent goods to Belgaum branch Rs. 6,000 on 29-12-94 but branch received on 4-1-96. *(Bangalore, April, 1997)*

Hints : (a) Debit Branch A/c and credit Branch Furniture A/c.
(b) Debit Cash in transit A/c and credit Branch A/c.
(c) Debit Hubli Branch A/c and credit Dharwad Branch A/c.
(d) Debit Goods in transit A/c and credit Belgaum Branch A/c.

(C) Solve the following problems :

(Each Carries 16 Marks)

(I) Dependent Branch

(a) Debtors System : Cost price Method

(1) Hindustan Co. Ltd. invoices goods to its Belgaum Branch at cost. The branch sells the goods on credit as well as for cash. From the following details prepare the Branch Account, Branch Trading and Profit and Loss Account for the year ending 31-12-1980.

	Rs.	Rs.
Stock 1-1-80		12,500
Stock 31-12-80		14,500
Debtors 1-1-80		24,500
Debtors 31-12-80		36,200
Goods supplied to branch		45,400
Goods returned by branch		600
Petty cash 1-1-80		150
Petty cash 31-12-80		320
Cash remitted to branch for :		
Rent	1,200	
Salary	4,500	
Petty cash	1,000	6,700
Cash sales		32,800
Cash received from customers		32,600
Discount allowed to customers		1,500
Bad debts		400
Goods returned from customers		2,300

(Karnataka, Oct., 1982 & Mysore, April, 1979)

Ans. : G/P Rs. 36,200; N/P Rs. 27,770; Branch A/c Total Rs. 1,17,020; Credit Sales Rs. 48,500.

(2) The following are details of transactions of a branch :

	Rs.		Rs.
Goods sent to branch at cost	50,000	Credit sales	51,000
Goods returned from branch at cost	3,000	Closing stock with branch	17,000
		Branch debtors (closing balance)	7,700
Expenses paid by Head office	10,000	Discount allowed to customers by branch	1,800
Remittances received from branch	45,000	Received from debtors by the branch	42,500
Cash sales	2,500		

You are required to record the above transactions in the books of account of the Head office by adopting any one method of branch accounting best known to you.

(*Adapted from Part II, Indian Institute of Bankers, 1972*)

Ans. : Profit Rs. 11,700, Debtors in the beginning Rs. 1,000.

(3) A trading firm has a retail branch, which is supplied with goods from the Head office and which keeps its own sales ledgers and remits all cash received daily to the Head office, the branch expenses being paid by the Head office by weekly cheques.

From the following particulars draw up the Branch Account as it would appear in the books of the Head office for the six months ending 31st December, 1985.

	Rs.
Six months credit sales	2,485
Cash sales	1,460
Returns inwards	30
Cash received on ledger accounts	2,387
Debtors on 1st July, 1985	1,345
Stock on 1st July, 1985	840
Stock on 31st December, 1985	1,280
Goods received from Head office	2,276
Bad debts at Branch	65
Wages and sundry expenses	415
Rent, rates and taxes	402

(*Sagar, B.Com., 1966 & 1986*)

Ans. : Profit Rs. 1,197; Debtors at the end Rs. 1,348.

(4) The Poona Head office supplies to its Kolhapur Branch goods at cost but with definite instruction to sell the goods at a profit of 20% on selling price.

From the following details of the Kolhapur Branch, prepare Branch Account in the Head office books for the month of March, 1973.

	Rs.	Rs.
Stock on 28th Feb., 1973		36,000
Debtors on 28th Feb., 1973		60,000
Petty cash balance on 28th Feb., 1973		600
Goods received during the March, 1973 from H.O.		6,00,000
Remittance to H.O. during March, 1973 (including Rs. 1,20,000 for cash sales)		3,40,000
Amount received from H.O. (during March, 1973)		
For Salaries	18,000	
Rent & Insurance	3,000	
Petty cash	2,200	23,000
Stock on 31st March, 1973		60,000

The petty cash expenses for the month of March, 1973 amount to Rs. 2,400

(*Poona University, 1973*)

Ans. : Net Profit Rs. 1,20,600; Closing Branch Debtors Rs. 4,40,000.

Note : Calculation of total sales :

	Rs.
Opening stock	36,000
Add : Goods sent to branch (at cost)	6,00,000
	6,36,000
Less : Closing stock (at cost)	60,000
Cost of goods sold	5,76,000

Goods are sold at 20% profit on sales (*i.e.*, 5,76,000 × 100/80) = 7,20,000 selling price. Credit sales Rs. 6,00,000 (*i.e.*, total sales 7,20,000 – 1,20,000 cash sales).

(5) M/s. Mahajan Bros. invoiced goods to their various branches at cost. From the following details regarding South Coast branch prepare branch account to calculate profit :

	Rs.			Rs.
Debtors 31st December, 1985	2,000	Stock on 1st January, 1985		2,000
Goods sent to branch during 1985	7,000	Stock on 31 Dec., 1985		1,600
Goods returned by branch	800	Bad debts		70
Goods returned by Customers to Branch	150	Expenses paid by the Head office :		
		Rent from 1st January 1985 to 31st January 1986	1,300	
Cash sales	4,300			
Credit sales	6,000	Insurance to 31st Mar, 86	1,800	
Cash remitted to the Head office	11,300	Salaries and wages	2,800	5,900
Allowance to customers	40			

(*B.Com., Andhra, 1970 & 1985*)

Ans. : Net Loss Rs. 1,910.

Cost price and Invoice price Method

(6) X & Co. of Delhi have a branch at Madras. Goods are sent by the Head office at invoice price which is at the profit of 25% on cost price. All expenses of the branch are paid by the Head Office. From the following particulars, prepare branch account in the Head Office books.

(a) When goods are shown at cost price, and

(b) When goods are shown at invoice price.

	Rs.
Opening Balance :	
Stock at invoice price	11,000
Debtors	1,700
Petty cash	100
Goods sent to branch at invoice price	20,000
Expenses made by head office :	
Rent	600
Wages	200
Salary, etc.	900
Remittance made to Head office :	
Cash sales	2,650
Cash collected from Debtors	21,000
Goods returned by Branch at invoice price	400
Balance at the end :	
Stock at invoice price	13,000
Debtors at the end	2,000
Petty cash	25

[*B.Com.* (*Pass*), *Delhi, 1981 & K.U.D., April, 1992 Mod.*]

Ans. : (A) Net profit Rs. 8,095, (B) Net profit Rs. 8,095, Loading in opening stock Rs. 2,200, Loading in closing stock Rs. 2,600, Loading in goods sent Rs. 4,000, Loading in goods returned Rs. 80.

Invoice price Method

(7) A Calcutta Head office charges out goods supplied to its branch at cost plus 20% from the following particulars, prepare the branch Account.

	Rs.
Goods sent to Branch	1,05,936
Total sales	1,03,200
Cash sales	55,200
Cash received from Branch Debtors	44,000
Branch debtors at commencement	12,000
Branch stock at commencement	3,840
Branch stock at close of the period	6,720

(*Gorakhpur, B.Com., 1964*)

Ans. : Net profit Rs. 17,320; Loading in opening stock Rs. 640; Loading in goods sent Rs. 17,656; Loading in closing stock Rs. 1,120; Closing Debtors Rs. 17,656; Credit sales Rs. 48,000.

(8) The General Merchants Ltd., Kanpur, have a sales branch in Allahabad, and charge all goods sent to the branch at cost price plus $33^1/_3\%$ it is arranged that all cash received by the branch is to be paid daily to the Head Office Account in the Central Bank and the necessary advice sent to the Head Office. The branch is to effect very little credit sales. From the following particulars, prepare the necessary account in the Head Office Ledger showing the real profit of the branch for the year ending 31st December, 1965.

	Rs.
Stock on 1st January, 1965	12,000
Goods sent to branch less returns	80,000
Debtors on 1st January, 1965	1,500
Cash sent to the H.O. A/c in Bank	1,24,000
Rent, rate and taxes	3,200
Salaries, wages etc.	4,800
Debtors on 31st December, 1965	1,600
Stock on 31st December, 1965	14,800

(*Berhampur, B.Com., Hons., 1970; Magadh, M.Com., 1970; Allahabad, B.Com., 1946*)

Ans. : Net profit Rs. 58,200; Loading in Opening stock Rs. 3,000; Goods sent Rs. 20,000 and Closing stock Rs. 3,700.

(9) A Head Office in Bombay has a branch in Ahmedabad to which goods are invoiced by the Head Office at cost price plus 25%. All cash received by the branch is daily remitted to the Head office. All expenses are paid from Bombay. From the following particulars, show how the branch account will appear in the Head office books (Entries are to be made at invoice prices).

	Rs.	Rs.
Stock on 1st July, 1969 (at invoice prices)		12,500
Debtors on 1st July, 1969		12,000
Goods invoiced from Bombay		40,000
Remittance to Bombay :		
Cash sales	16,000	
Cash received from Drs.	29,500	45,500
Goods returned to H.O.		2,400
Cheques received from Bombay :		
Wages & Salaries	11,000	
Rent, rates, etc.	3,000	
Sundry Expenses	510	14,510

(*Contd.*)

Stock on 31st December, 1969	15,000
Debtors on 31st December, 1969	22,500

(*Patna, B.Com., 1958; Agra, B.Com., 1981 and Bangalore, Oct., 1995*)

Ans. : Net profit Rs. 6,390.

(10) B.K. Ltd., Hubli has a branch at Belgaum. Goods are invoiced to the branch at 20% on sales. The branch has been instructed to send all cash to the Head Office daily and all its expenses are paid by the Head Office.

The following is the summary of transactions at this branch for the year 1985 :

	Rs.	Rs.
Stock on 1-1-84 (invoice price)		30,000
Branch debtors on 1-1-84		18,000
Petty cash on 1-1-84		800
Goods sent to branch (at cost price)		1,28,000
Goods returned by branch (invoice price)		2,000
Goods returned by customers		480
Cash received from customers		60,000
Cash sales		1,00,000
Credit sales		60,000
Discount allowed to customers		60
Expenses paid by Head Office :		
Rent	2,400	
Salary	4,800	
Printing & Stationery	600	
Petty cash	1,200	9,000
Balance on 31-12-84 :		
Stock (invoice price)		28,000
Petty cash		600
Provision for doubtful debts		200

Prepare the Branch Account and Branch Debtors' Account in the Books of H.O.

(*Karnataka, B.Com., April, 1985, Bangalore, Oct., 1993*)

Ans. : Branch profit Rs. 22,060; Invoice price of goods supplied Rs. 1,60,000 (*i.e.,* 1,28,000 + 32,000); Loading on : Opening stock Rs. 6,000, Goods supplied Rs. 32,000, Goods returned Rs. 400 and Closing stock Rs. 5,600; Closing debtors Rs. 17,490; Branch A/c total Rs. 2,46,060.

(11) The Bharat Stores Ltd., Madras has a branch at Bellary. Goods are invoiced to the branch at selling price being cost plus 20% profit. The branch keeps its own sales ledger and deposits all cash received daily to the credit of Head Office Account opened in the State Bank of India. All the expenses are paid by cheques from the Head Office.

From the following particulars prepare the Branch Account and Branch Debtors Account in the books of the Head Office :

	Rs.
Stock on 1-1-81 (at invoice price)	12,000
Debtors on 1-1-81	40,000
Petty cash on 1-1-81	200
Goods invoiced from Head Office (at invoice price)	96,000
Expenses paid by cheques from Head Office :	
Rents & taxes	600
Sundry expenses	2,400
Cash sales for the year	60,000
Credit sales for the year	60,000
Cash collected from debtors	80,000
Bad debts for the year	4,000
Stock on 31-12-81 (at invoice price)	18,000
Petty cash on 31-12-81	50

(*Gulbarga, B.Com., April, 1982*)

Ans. : Branch profit Rs. 37,870; Loading on : Opening stock Rs. 2,000, Goods supplied Rs. 16,000 and Closing stock Rs. 3,000; Closing debtors Rs. 16,000; Branch A/c Total Rs. 1,92,050.

(12) The Calcutta Branch of Delhi Office keeps its own sales ledger and pays all cash receipts to the credit of Head Office Account in the Bank of India, Calcutta. All expenses are paid from Head office. The Head office supplied books to the branch at cost plus 20 per cent.

From the following details of the branch, prepare Calcutta Branch Account in the Delhi Head Office books for the year ended 31st December, 1971.

	Rs.
Stock on 1st January at invoice price	24,000
Stock on 31st December at invoice price	33,600
Debtors on 1st January, 1971	24,000
Cash sales	1,00,400
Credit sales	1,30,000

	Rs.
Cash and cheques received on Ledger Accounts in full satisfaction of Rs. 1,24,000	1,23,000
Goods supplied by Head Office at invoice price	2,40,000
Salaries	17,000
Rent	6,000
Other expenses	17,000

Returns from Branch debtors direct to Head office Rs. 2,400 (Head office invoice price being Rs. 1,920).

(*G.D.A. & I.A.S., 1965*)

Ans. : Net Loss Rs. 5,000; Loading on opening stock Rs. 4,000, Loading on goods sent Rs. 40,000; Loading on closing stock Rs. 5,600; Closing Debtors Rs. 27,600; Discount on Debtors Rs. 1,000.

(13) Sagar Traders of Sagar operate a branch at Mysore. Goods are invoiced to the branch at 20% profit on sale. Branch is advised to deposit cash everyday to the Head Office except petty cash which are met by the branch manager. From the following particulars prepare branch account to ascertain profit or loss of the branch :

	Rs.		Rs.
Stock 1st January, 1980	15,000	Expenses paid by Head Office :	
Petty cash 1st January, 1980	300	Rent	2,400
Debtors 1st January, 1980	8,500	Salary	4,200
Furniture 1st January, 1980	2,000	Furniture	1,600
Cash sales	56,000	Stock 31st Dec., 1980	12,000
Total sales	88,000	Bills receivable 31st Dec., 1980	2,000
Cash from debtors	28,500	Sale of Furniture on July 1, 1980	900
Goods to branch	80,000	(Book value of furniture on the	
Discount allowed	250	date of sale Rs. 950)	
Petty expenses	360		
Goods returned by branch	1,000		
Salary due 31st Dec., 1980	400		

It is required to write off furniture at 10% per annum on the opening balance.

(*B.Com., Mysore, April, 1982*)

Ans. : Profit Rs. 16,590; Loss on sale of furniture is not excluded.

(14) Akash Chappal Stores is having its branch at Jullundur. Goods are invoiced to the branch at 20% profit on sale. Branch has been instructed to send all cash daily to the Head office. All expenses are paid by the Head office except petty expenses which are met by the branch manager. From the following particulars prepare branch account in the books of Akash Chappal Stores, Kanpur.

	Rs.		Rs.
Stock on 1st January, 1978 (invoice price)	15,000	Discount allowed to debtors	300
		Expenses paid by the Head office :	
Sundry debtors on 1st Jan.	9,000	Rent	1,200
Cash in Hand on 1st Jan.	400	Salary	2,400
Office furniture on 1st January	1,200	Stationery and printing	300
Goods invoiced from the Head office (invoice price)	80,000	Petty expenses paid by Branch Manager	280
Goods returned to Head office	1,000	Depreciation is to be provided on branch furniture at 10% p.a.	
Goods returned by Debtors	480		
Cash received from Debtors	30,000	Stock on 31st December, 1978 at invoice price	14,000
Cash sales	50,000		
Credit sales	30,000		

(*B.Com., Panjab & Bombay*)

Ans. : Net profit Rs. 10,920; Loading on : Opening stock Rs. 3,000, Goods sent Rs. 15,800 and Closing stock Rs. 2,800; Balance of Debtors Account Rs. 8,220.

(15) Arunodaya Agencies opened a branch in Bangalore on 1st January, 1970. Goods were invoiced at selling price which is cost plus 25%. From the following particulars relating to the year 1970, you are required to prepare different accounts.

		Rs.	Rs.
Goods sent to Branch			3,00,000
Sales :	Cash	1,00,000	
	Credit	1,40,000	2,40,000
Goods returned by customers			3,000
Cash received from debtors			80,000
Discount allowed			1,000
Cash remitted to branch for :			
	Rent and rates	1,500	
	Salaries	6,000	
	Sundry expenses	1,000	8,500
Defective goods written off			1,000
Goods returned by Branch			12,000
Stock at the end			50,000

(*K.U. & P.U.*)

Ans. : Net profit Rs. 37,100; Loading on : Goods sent Rs. 60,000, Goods returned Rs. 2,400 and Closing stock Rs. 10,000; Balance of Debtors Account Rs. 56,000; Balance of Branch Stock A/c Rs. 50,000; Balance of Goods Sent to Branch A/c Rs. 2,29,600.

(b) Branch Trading and Profit & Loss Account

(16) A Calcutta Head Office charges our goods supplied to its Branch at cost plus 20%. From the following particulars prepare the Branch Trading A/c and the Branch Total Debtors' A/c as in the Head Office Books. Prepare also an account showing the actual Branch Profit :

	Rs.
Goods sent to Branch	1,05,936
Total sales	1,03,200
Cash sales	55,200
Cash received from Branch Debtors	44,000
Branch Debtors at commencement	22,000
Branch stock at commencement	3,840
Branch stock at close of the period	6,720

(*Patna, B.Com., 1959; Bombay, B.Com., 1928*)

Ans. : Gross profit Rs. 17,320; Closing Debtors Rs. 26,000; Branch profit Rs. 17,320; Loading on : Opening stock Rs. 640, Goods sent Rs. 17,656 and Closing stock Rs. 1,120.

(17) The Southern Confectionery Co. Ltd., Bangalore has a branch at Goa. Goods are invoiced to the Goa Branch at selling price being cost plus 25%.

The Goa Branch keeps its own sales ledger and transmits all cash received to Bangalore daily. All expenses are paid from Bangalore.

From the following details prepare a Profit and Loss A/c of the Goa Branch for the year 1967 :

	Rs.
Stock 1st Jan., 1967 (at invoice prices)	1,250
Stock 31st Dec., 1967 (at invoice prices)	1,500
Sundry Debtors, 1st Jan., 1967	700
Sundry Debtors, 31st Dec., 1967	900
Cash sales for the year	5,400
Credit sales for the year	3,500
Cash received for Ledger A/c	3,300
Goods invoiced from Bangalore	9,100

	Rs.
Rent & rates (paid from Bangalore)	400
Wages (paid from Bangalore)	340
Sundry expenses (paid from Bangalore)	80

(*Berhampur, B.Com., 1970, Patna, B.Com., 1985 & Chartered Accountant*)

Ans. : Gross profit Rs. 1,820; Net profit Rs. 1,000; Loading on : Opening stock Rs. 250, Goods received from H.O. Rs. 1,820 and Closing Stock Rs. 300.

(18) The Calcutta Paint Co. Ltd. has a branch at Kanpur. Goods are invoiced to the branch at the selling price, that being cost plus 25%. The branch sends all cash received to the Head office, all expenses being paid from Calcutta.

From the following particulars prepare a P&L A/c of the Kanpur Branch for the year ended 31st December, 1970 :

	Rs.
Invoice value of stock on 1st January, 1970	2,500
Invoice value of stock on 31st December, 1970	3,000
Sundry Debtors on 1st January, 1970	1,400
Sundry Debtors on 31st December, 1970	1,800
Ready money sales during the year	10,800
Sales on credit	7,000
Cash received on ledger accounts	6,600
Goods supplied from Head office	18,200
Wages	680
Rent and rates	800
Sundry expenses	160

(*Nagpur, B.Com., 1959; Sagar, B.Com., 1981*)

Ans. : Gross profit Rs. 3,640; Net profit Rs. 2,000; Loading on : Opening stock Rs. 500, Goods received from H.O. Rs. 3,640 and Closing stock Rs. 600.

(19) Shriram and Kishor Private Limited invoiced goods to Branch at cost plus 25% thereon. Both cash and credit sales are effected by the branch. Expenses are paid direct from the Head office. All cash received is remitted by the branch to its Head office. The following are the details of the transactions for the year ended 31st March, 1972.

	Rs.
Goods received from Head Office at invoice price	40,000
Returns to Head Office at invoice price	800
Stock on 1st April, 1971 at invoice price	8,000
Credit sales for the year	30,000
Cash sales for the year	18,700

	Rs.
Debtors as at 1st April, 1971	5,200
Cash received on ledger accounts	28,500
Discount allowed to customers	300
Bad debts written off	500
Returns from customers at selling price	700
Rent, rates etc.	60
Sundry expenses	300
Salaries and wages	1,200
Stock as on 31st March, 1972 at invoice price	6,000

Prepare Branch Account and Branch Trading and Profit and Loss Account in the books of Head Office from the above information.

(*Poona University, 1978 & 1983*)

Ans. : Branch profit Rs. 12,680; Closing debtors Rs. 5,200; Loading on : Opening stock Rs. 1,600, Goods sent Rs. 8,000, Goods returned Rs. 160 and Closing stock Rs. 1,200. Gross profit Rs. 15,040; N/P Rs. 12,680.

(20) A Delhi merchant has a Branch at Madras to which he charges out the goods at cost plus 25%. The Madras Branch keeps its own Sales Ledger and transmits all cash received to the Head Office everyday. All expenses are paid from the Head office. The transactions for the Branch were as follows :

	Rs.		Rs.
Stock (1-1-78)	11,000	Returns Inwards	500
Debtors (1-1-78)	100	Cheques sent to Branch :	
Petty cash	100	Rent	600
Cash sales	2,650	Wages	200
Goods sent to Branch	20,000	Salary and other expenses	900
Collection of ledger accounts	21,000	Stock (31-12-78)	13,000
Goods returned to H.O.	300	Debtors	2,000
Bad debts	300	Petty cash (31-12-78) including	
Allowances to Customers	250	miscellaneous income Rs. 25, not remitted	125

Prepare the Branch Trading and Profit and Loss Account and Branch Account for the year 31-12-1978.

(*B.Com., Mysore, April, 1969; B.Com., Panjab, 1979*)

Ans. : Gross profit Rs. 11,740; Net profit Rs. 9,715; Loading on : Opening stock Rs. 2,200, Goods sent Rs. 4,000, Goods returned Rs. 60 and Closing stock Rs. 2,600; Expenses debited to Branch A/c Rs. 1,700.

(21) Novelties Ltd. with its Head Office in Delhi invoiced goods to its branch at Bombay, at 20% less than the catalogue price which is cost plus 50% with instructions that cash sales were to be made at invoice price and credit sales at catalogue price less discount at 15% on prompt payment.

From the following particulars available from the branch, prepare the Branch Trading and Profit & Loss Account for the year ended 31st March, 1979 (showing adjustments) in the Head Office books so as to show the actual profit or loss on the Branch for the year.

	Rs.		Rs.
Stock on 1st April, 1978 (invoice price)	12,000	Discount allowed to Debtors	13,365
Debtors on 1st April, 1978	10,000	Expenses at the Branch	6,000
Goods received from Head office (invoice price)	1,32,000	Debtors on 31st March, 1979	11,000
Sales (cash)	46,000	Cash in Hand on 31st March, 1979	5,635
Cash realized from Debtors	85,635	Stock on 31st March, 1979 (invoice price)	15,000
Sales (credit)	1,00,000		
Remittance to Head Office	1,20,000		

It was further reported that a part of stock at the Branch was lost by the fire (not covered by insurance) during the year whose value is to be ascertained and a provision should be made for discount to be allowed to debtors as on 31st March, 1979 the basis of the year's trend of prompt payment.

(*CA Enter & GDA*)

Ans. : Gross profit Rs. 41,000; Net profit Rs. 17,798; Loading on : Opening stock Rs. 2,000 (*i.e.*, 1/6 of 12,000), Goods sent Rs. 22,000 and Closing stock Rs. 2,500. Stock destroyed by fire (at cost) Rs. 2,500 (*i.e.*, Rs. 3,000 – 1/6 of Rs. 3,000); Provision for discount Rs. 1,337 (*i.e.*, 15% of Rs. 8,910).

(c) Stock and Debtors System

(22) Using the Stock and Debtors System, find out the profit or loss made at the Bidar Branch for the year ending 31-12-79. Goods are invoiced to the branch at a profit of 20% on the invoice price :

	Rs.
Stock on 1-1-79 (at invoice price)	4,500
Debtors on 1-1-79	12,300
Goods sent to branch (at invoice price)	80,000
Cash sales	13,500
Credit sales	65,500

	Rs.
Cash received from debtors	53,000
Discount allowed to debtors	1,300
Cash sent to Branch for :	
Salary	12,000
Rent	10,000
Other expenses	2,500
Stock on 31-12-79 (at invoice price)	5,000

The difference in the stock represents shortage. Prepare the necessary ledger accounts.

(*Karnataka, non-Sem., Oct., 1980 & 1992*)

Ans. : Gross profit Rs. 15,800; Net loss Rs. 10,400; Closing debtors Rs. 23,500; Shortage Rs. 500 at invoice price.

(23) Poona Stores opened a branch in Bangalore to which goods are supplied at selling price, being 25% profit on sales.

From the following information prepare the necessary ledger accounts in the books of the Head Office under "Stock and Debtors System".

		Rs.
1.	Goods sent from Head Office at invoice price	1,68,000
2.	Goods returned from Branch to Head Office at invoice price	18,000
3.	Branch expenses paid by Head Office	10,000
4.	Expenses paid by the Branch	2,000
5.	Cash sales	80,000
6.	Credit sales	40,000
7.	Cash received by Branch from Branch Debtors	32,000
8.	Discount allowed to Branch Debtors	1,600
9.	Goods returned by customers	2,000
10.	Defective goods in bales written off	1,400
11.	Cash remitted by Branch to Head Office	1,10,000

(*Karnataka, Oct., 1981*)

Ans. : Gross profit Rs. 29,500 and Net profit Rs. 14,850; Closing stock Rs. 30,600; Closing debtors Rs. 4,400.

(24) Head Office Ltd. sent goods to its Branch office at selling price which is arrived at after adding 50% to cost price and all expenses are met by the Branch office. All collections by Branch are sent to bank in the account of Head Office.

The following particulars are available in respect of the year ended 31st March, 1979 :

	Rs.		Rs.
Stock as on 31st March, 1978 (at selling price)	45,000	Cash collections from debtors sent to Bank	7,750
Goods from Head office	1,51,500	Expenses	30,300
Cash paid into Bank	1,52,850	Deficiency in branch stock on actual stock-taking	300
Credit sales	6,750		
Debtors (on 31st March, 1978)	4,500		

You are required to draw up the Stock, Debtors and Branch Adjustment (profit and loss) Accounts of the Branch for the year ended 31st March, 1979.

(*CA. Final*)

Ans. : Net profit Rs. 22,700; Closing stock Rs. 36,600; Closing Debtors Rs. 3,500; Loading on : Opening stock Rs. 15,000, Goods sent Rs. 50,500 and Closing stock Rs. 12,200.

(25) Shrihas Ltd., Sholapur, a Trading Co. has a branch at Chiplum. All purchases are made by Head office and goods sent to the branch are invoiced at selling price, which is 20% above cost. Sales at the Branch are not credit terms. Branch expenses are paid by Head office and all cash received by the branch is remitted to H.O. All branch transactions are recorded in the H.O. books. Following information is given to you :

	Rs.
Branch stock (at cost to branch) on 1-1-1973	3,600
Branch debtors on 1-1-1973	2,575
Transactions during the year 1973 were :	
Goods sent to branch at invoice price	32,460
Returns from Branch to Head office at invoice price	642
Branch sales	33,780
Returns from customers to branch	354
Cash received from Branch Debtors	32,848
Discount allowed to Branch Debtors	1,415
Branch expenses paid	4,027

Branch stock at 31st December, 1973 (at invoice price) was Rs. 1,962 and expenses outstanding on that date were Rs. 50.

You are required to show Branch Stock A/c, Branch Stock Adjustment A/c, Goods Sent to Branch A/c, Branch Debtors A/c, Branch Expenses A/c and Branch P&L A/c in the ledger of Head office for the year ending 31st Dec., 1973.

(*Mysore University, Oct., 1970 Mod., Shivaji University, 1974*)

Ans. : Gross profit Rs. 5,571; Net profit Rs. 54; Shortage in stock Rs. 30; Closing debtors Rs. 1,738; Branch expenses Rs. 5,492; Loading on : Opening stock Rs. 600, Goods sent Rs. 5,410 and Closing stock Rs. 107. Loading in shortage Rs. 5.

(26) Dara Stores Ltd., with their Head office at Delhi, invoiced goods to its branch at Ghaziabad at 20% less than the list price which is cost plus 100% with instructions that cash sales were to be made at invoice price and credit sales at catalogue price (*i.e.*, list price).

From the following particulars available from the branch, prepare, branch stock account, branch adjustment account, branch profit and loss account and branch debtors account for the year ending 31st December, 19...

	Rs.		Rs.
Stock, on 1st January, 19... (invoice price)	6,000	Cash received from debtors	42,817
Debtors on 1st January, 19...	5,000	Expenses at branch	8,683
Goods received from Head office (invoice price)	66,000	Remittances to head office	60,000
Sales – Cash Rs. 23,000; Credit Rs. 50,000	73,000	Debtors on 31st Dec., 19...	12,183
		Stock on 31st December, 19... (invoice price)	8,800

[*Adapted from C.A.: Inter, B.Com.,* (*Hons*)*, Delhi, 1974, B.Com., Madras, April, 1984*]

Ans. : Gross profit Rs. 33,625; Net profit Rs. 24,817; Shortage in stock Rs. 200; Sale proceeds in excess of invoice price Rs. 10,000; Loading on : Opening stock Rs. 2,250 (*i.e.*, 6,000 × 60/160), Goods sent Rs. 24,750, Shortage Rs. 75 and Closing stock Rs. 3,300.

(27) Shri X has a retail branch at Allahabad. Goods are sent by the H.O. to the Branch marked at selling price which is cost plus 25%. All the expenses of the Branch are paid by the H.O. All cash collected by the Branch (from customers and from cash sales) is deposited to the credit of H.O.

From the following particulars of the Branch, prepare Branch Stock Account, Branch Debtors' Account, Branch Expenses Account and Branch Adjustment Account in the books of the Head Office.

	Rs.
Debtors on 1-1-1980	12,000
Debtors on 31-12-1980	14,000
Inventory with the Branch at invoice price :	
on 1-1-1980	16,000
on 31-12-1980	17,000
Cash sales during the year	60,000
Total amount deposited in the H.O. Account during the year	1,27,000
Return of goods to H.O. at invoice price	5,000
Salaries paid	6,000
Rent paid	4,000
Discount allowed to customers	2,000

	Rs.
Bad Debts written off	1,000
Spoilage	2,000

(*Calcutta, B.Com., Hons., 1981*)

Ans. : Gross profit Rs. 26,400; Net profit Rs. 11,800; Goods sent to branch Rs. 1,40,000; Credit sales Rs. 72,000; Branch expenses Rs. 13,000; Loading in : Opening stock Rs. 3,200, Goods sent Rs. 28,000, Goods returned Rs. 1,000, Spoilage Rs. 400 and Closing stock Rs. 3,400. Cash received from Debtors Rs. 67,000 (*i.e.*, 1,27,000 – 60,000).

(28) Sellwell Ltd. has two branches, in Cochin and Bangalore. During the year ended 31st March, 1976 goods have been invoiced to the Cochin branch at 20% above cost and to the Bangalore branch at 20% above cost. The branches do not maintain complete books of account but the following figures are available for the year ended on 31st March, 1976.

	Cochin Rs.	Bangalore Rs.
Opening stock at invoice price	10,000	10,000
Goods sent to Branch at cost	50,000	40,000
Amount remitted by branch	80,000	80,000
Amount remitted by Head office	15,000	15,000
Goods returned by branch at invoice price	3,000	–
Cash as on 1-4-1975	2,000	1,000
Cash as on 31-12-1976	1,000	500
Goods returned by customers at branch at selling price	5,000	4,000
Expenses at Branch in cash	9,000	3,000

All sales at the branches are for cash. During the year, Cochin Branch purchased fixed assets worth Rs. 4,000 and this amount is included in the figure of branch expenses. Cochin Branch transferred to the Bangalore Branch stock costing Rs. 5,000 during the year. The Bangalore Branch remitted Rs. 2,000 to the Cochin Branch also during the year. There was a closing stock of Rs. 24,000 valued at invoice price at the Cochin Branch. There was no closing stock at the Bangalore Branch. The Branch Stock Adjustment Account in the Head Office books showed the following position as on 1st April, 1975 :

For Cochin : Rs. 2,500 (Cr.)
For Bangalore : Rs. 2,000 (Cr.)

Prepare Branch Stock Account, Branch Stock Adjustment Account, Goods Sent to Branch Account, Branch Cash Account and Branch Profit and Loss Account in the Head Office books ignoring depreciation.

(*C.A., Inter, N.S., May, 1976*)

Ans. : Net profit : Cochin Rs. 36,000 and Bangalore Rs. 13,500; Branch sales : Cochin Rs. 76,000 and B'lore Rs. 73,500; Invoice price of goods sent : Cochin Rs. 60,000 and B'lore Rs. 50,000; Stock transferred by Cochin to B'lore at invoice price : Cochin Rs. 6,000 and B'lore Rs. 6,250.

(29) From the following particulars prepare a Branch Account showing the profit or loss from the branch :

	Rs.		Rs.
Opening stock at the branch	15,000	Expenses : Salaries	5,000
Goods sent at the branch	45,000	Other expenses	2,000
Sales	60,000		

Closing stock could not be ascertained but it is known that the branch usually sells at cost plus 20%. The Branch Manager is entitled to a commission of 5% on a profit of the branch before charging such commission.

(*C.A. Entrance*)

Ans. : Branch profit Rs. 2,850; Manager's Commission Rs. 150 (*i.e.*, 5% of Rs. 3,000); Closing stock Rs. 10,000 [*i.e.*, Rs. 60,000 *Less* cost of sales Rs. 50,000 (*i.e.*, Rs. 60,000 – 1/6 of Rs. 60,000)].

(d) Wholesales Branch System

(30) A Head Office sends goods to its branch at 20% less than the list price (*i.e.*, Catalogue price). Goods are sold to consumers at cost plus 100%. From the following particulars ascertain the profit made at the Head office and the Branch on the wholesale basis.

	Head Office Rs.	Branch Rs.
Purchases	2,00,000	–
Goods sent to branch (Invoice price)	80,000	–
Sales	1,70,000	80,000

Assume that Head office is selling goods to customers at catalogue price.

[*Bangalore, B.Com., 1985 and Delhi, B.Com. (Hons.), 1984*]

Ans. : Gross profit : Head office Rs. 1,15,000.
Net profit : Head office Rs. 1,09,000; and Branch Rs. 16,000.
Closing stock of Head Office Rs. 65,000 (2,00,000 – 1,35,000).
Closing stock of Branch Rs. 16,000 (80,000 – 64,000).

(31) A Head office invoices goods to its branch at 20% less than the list price. Customers are charged for goods sold to them at cost plus 100%. From the particulars given below prepare accounts for the year 1979 to show the profit made by the Head office and the branch.

(In case of branch on the wholesale basis)

	Head Office	Branch
	Rs.	Rs.
Opening stock at cost (invoice price in case of branch)	40,000	16,000
Purchases	4,00,000	–
Goods sent to branch (invoice price)	96,000	–
Sales	6,00,000	80,000
Expenses	86,000	4,000

(*Punjab, B.Com., Jan., 1979*)

Ans. : Gross profit : H.O. Rs. 3,36,000 and Branch Rs. 16,000; Net profit : H.O. Rs. 2,38,000 and Branch Rs. 12,000; Closing stock of H.O. Rs. 80,000 and Closing stock of Branch Rs. 48,000.

(32) The Mighty Bros. have their Head Office at Bombay and a Branch at Kanpur. The goods are sent to Branch at 20% less than the list price which is cost plus 100%.

From the following particulars, ascertain the profit made by the Branch as well as the Head office on wholesale basis :

	Head Office	Branch
	Rs.	Rs.
Opening stock (cost/invoice price)	20,000	10,000
Purchases	2,00,000	
Expenses	30,000	6,000
Goods destroyed by accident at invoice price		1,000
Sales at list price	1,70,000	80,000
Goods sent to the branch at invoice price	80,000	80,000

(*B.Com., Agra & C.A.*)

Ans. : Gross profit : H.O. Rs. 1,15,000 and Branch Rs. 16,000; Net profit : H.O. Rs. 88,375 and Branch Rs. 9,000; Closing stock : H.O. Rs. 85,000 (at cost) and Branch Rs. 25,000 (at invoice price). Stock Reserve for opening and closing stock Rs. 3,750 and Rs. 9,375 respectively.

(II) Independent Branch

(33) Give Journal entries for the following transactions in the books of Head Office. Head Office accounts are closed every year on 31st December :

(a) Cash remitted by X Branch Rs. 300 not received by the Head Office till 31st December;

(b) Goods sent by H.O. on 28th December worth Rs. 150 to its Y Branch not received by the Branch till 31st December.

(c) Expenses paid by H.O. on 28th December, for its X Branch Rs. 400 and for Y Branch Rs. 600 not yet adjusted in the accounts.

(d) Goods sent by X Branch to Y Branch Rs. 300 are yet to be recorded.

(e) X Branch collected Rs. 300 from a customer of Head Office.

(f) Y Branch paid Rs. 3,000 for a machine purchased by H.O. for the use in H.O. itself;

(g) H.O. expenses are to be allocated to X and Y Branches Rs. 3,000 and Rs. 2,500 respectively.

(h) Provide Depreciation at 10% on Furniture when the 'Furniture Accounts' are maintained by H.O.

Furniture at X Branch	Rs. 25,500
Furniture at Y Branch	Rs. 15,000

(*Karnataka University*)

(34) A Calcutta firm whose accounting year ends on 31st December has two branches— one at Agra and the other at Banaras. The Branches keep a complete set of books. On 31st December, 1970 the Agra and the Banaras branch's accounts in the Calcutta office books showed debit balance of Rs. 30,450 and Rs. 45,000 respectively before taking the following information into account :

(a) Goods valued Rs. 2,000 were transferred from Agra to Banaras under instructions from Head office.

(b) The Agra branch collected Rs. 2,500 from an Agra customer of the Head office.

(c) The Banaras Branch paid Rs. 5,000 for certain goods purchased by the Head office in Banaras.

(d) Rs. 5,000 remitted by the Agra Branch to Calcutta office on 29th December, 1970 was received on 3rd January following.

(e) The Banaras Branch received on behalf of the Head office Rs. 1,500 as dividend from a Banaras Company.

(f) For the year 1970 the Agra Branch showed a net loss of Rs. 1,250 and the Banaras branch a net profit of Rs. 5,400.

Pass journal entries to record these matters in the Head office books and write up the two branch accounts therein.

(*B.Com., Madras, April, 1976*)

(35) A Calcutta Head office passes one entry at the end of each month to adjust the position arising out of inter-branch transactions during the month. From the following inter-branch transactions in April 1969, make the entries in the books of Calcutta Head office :

(a) Delhi Branch

(i) Received goods from Nagpur branch Rs. 9,000 and Ahmedabad branch Rs. 6,000.

(ii) Sent goods to Ahmedabad branch Rs. 15,000 and Nagpur branch Rs. 12,000.

(iii) Received B/R from Ahmedabad branch Rs. 9,000.

(iv) Sent acceptances to Nagpur branch Rs. 6,000 and Ahmedabad branch Rs. 3,000.

(b) Kanpur Branch [Apart from (a) above]

(i) Received goods from Nagpur branch Rs. 15,000 and Delhi branch Rs. 6,000.

(ii) Cash sent to Nagpur branch Rs. 3,000 and Delhi branch Rs. 6,000.

(c) Nagpur Branch [Apart from (a) and (b) above]

(i) Sent goods to Ahmedabad branch Rs. 9,000

(ii) Received B/R from Ahmedabad branch Rs. 9,000

(iii) Received cash from Ahmedabad branch Rs. 5,000

(*I.C.W.A. Inter, 1969*)

Ans. : Kanpur Branch A/c Dr. Rs. 12,000
Nagpur Branch A/c Dr. Rs. 2,000
To Delhi Branch A/c Rs. 12,000
To Ahmedabad Branch A/c Rs. 2,000

(36) A limited company having its Head Office in Bombay receives the following trial balance from its Bangalore Branch :

Debit	Rs.	Credit	Rs.
Opening stock	21,800	Head Office Account	21,000
Purchases	42,300	Sundry Creditors	5,600
Wages	10,200	Discount Earned	300
Salaries	6,300	Sales	81,000
General Expenses	8,300		
Sundry Debtors	18,200		
Cash at Bank	800		
	1,07,900		1,07,900

The Closing stock at the Branch was Rs. 19,700. In the Head office books the branch account shows debit balance of Rs. 26,500. It is noted that the goods and cash sent by Head Office had not yet reached to the tune of Rs. 1,000 and Rs. 4,500 respectively. Head Office Expenses of Rs. 3,100 is chargeable to the Branch Account. Branch assets whose accounts are kept in the Head Office books were to be depreciated by Rs. 3,600.

Incorporate the Branch figures in the Head Office books giving journal entries and also prepare the branch account.

(*Karnataka, Oct., 1983*)

Ans. : G.P. Rs. 26,400; N.P. Rs. 5,400; Branch Account total Rs. 1,39,800. Goods-in-transit Rs. 1,000 and Cash-in-transit Rs. 4,500.

(37) On 31st December, 1966, the Trial Balance of the Gorakhpur Branch stood as follows :

	Rs.		Rs.
Stock on 1st Jan., 1963	6,000	Delhi Office Account	11,000
Furniture	2,400	Sales	22,800
Debtors	5,600	Sundry Creditors	200
Goods Received from Delhi Office	16,000		
Salaries, Rent & Expenses	2,200		
Cash in Hand	1,800		
	34,000		34,000

Stock on 31st December, 1966, Rs. 4,600.

Find out the Gorakhpur Branch profit, and draft Journal entries incorporating the Gorakhpur branch assets and liabilities in the Delhi office books. Prepare also the Gorakhpur Branch account in the Delhi Office Ledger.

(*Gorakhpur, B.Com., 1967*)

Ans. : Gross profit Rs. 5,400; Net profit Rs. 3,200.

(38) A firm has its Head office at Delhi and a branch at Nagpur. From the following particulars, prepare the combined Balance sheet and Nagpur Branch Account in the books of Delhi Office.

Particulars	Head Office Rs.	Branch Rs.
Capital	20,000	
Profit & Loss Account (1-4-82)	2,715	—
Current year's profit	8,415	3,484
Creditors on open accounts	5,930	—
Creditors for expenses	390	—
Goods from Head office	—	7,000
Cash received from branch	9,987	—
Head office account (1-4-82)	—	7,298
	47,437	17,782
Premises	8,000	4,000
Fixtures	800	400

(*Contd.*)

	Rs.	Rs.
Stock-in-trade (31-3-83)	9,000	1,800
Trade debtors	8,000	650
Branch Account (1-4-82)	7,298	–
Goods sent to Branch	7,200	–
Cash remitted to head office	–	10,287
Cash at bank	7,139	645
	47,437	17,782

(Gulbarga, April, 1984 Mod.)

Ans. : Balance Sheet total Rs. 40,934. Branch Account total Rs. 17,982. Cash-in-transit Rs. 300 and Goods-in-transit Rs. 200 are to be adjusted to reconcile the balance.

(39) A Ltd. Company, Bombay has a branch in Poona. The following are the ledger balances of the branch as on 31-12-1958 :

	Rs.		Rs.
Purchases	4,500	Interest (Cr.)	1,250
Sales	15,000	Goods from H.O.	7,000
Creditors	5,600	Sundry Expenses	200
Machinery	10,000	H.O. Current A/c	11,000
Stock	7,500		
Debtors	2,000		
Bank	1,650		

Stock on 31-12-1958 Rs. 3,500.

On enquiry you are told that :

(1) The Head office sent goods to branch of Rs. 500 on 30-12-1958 but the branch received them on 4-1-1959.

(2) The branch furniture stood in H.O. books at Rs. 400.

(3) In Head office books the Branch Current A/c had a balance of Rs. 11,500.

Give the final account of the Branch after depreciating branch furnitures and machinery by 5%. Also give Branch Current A/c in the H.O. books.

(Poona University, 1962; Shivaji University, 1971)

Ans. : Gross profit Rs. 7,000; Net profit Rs. 30; Balance sheet Total Rs. 16,650. Branch Current Account Total Rs. 36,870.

(40) The following are the trial balances of a Head office and its Branch as on 30-6-1957 :

	Head Office Rs.	Branch Office Rs.		Head Office Rs.	Branch Office Rs.
Debtors	2,500	1,200	Capital	27,000	—
Branch :			Creditors	3,000	2,000
Current A/c	2,900	—	Discount	1,400	300
Purchases	36,000	12,000	Goods sent to		
Furniture : H.O.	1,200	—	Br. A/c	14,000	—
Branch	500	—	Salary	35,000	29,000
Stock	11,500	4,500	H.O. Current A/c	—	2,600
Bank	21,600	1,600			
Rent	1,000	300			
Salary	3,200	600			
Goods from H.O.	–	13,700			
	80,400	33,900		80,400	33,900

The closing stock was at the Head office Rs. 18,000 and at Branch Rs. 8,000, you are told that on 30-6-57 the Head office sent goods to Branch Rs. 300 which the branch received on 4-7-57.

Prepare the Trading Account and Profit and Loss A/c of the Head Office and the branch in the columnar form for the year ended 30-6-57 after charging depreciation on furniture at H.O. and at branch at 5% and give the combined Balance Sheet as on that date.

Also give the branch current account after incorporating the branch figures in it. The journal entries for incorporation are not to be given.

(*Poona University, April, 1961*)

Ans. : Gross profit : H.O. Rs. 19,500 and Branch Rs. 6,800.
Net profit : H.O. Rs. 16,640 and Branch Rs. 6,175.

Balance Sheet total Rs. 54,815.

(41) From the following information, show :

(a) The journal entries to incorporate the trial balance of the branch in the Head office books, and

(b) The branch current account after incorporation of the branch data.

Poona branch trial balance as at December 31, 1972 is as under :

	Rs.		Rs.
Purchases	17,350	Sales	38,200
Goods from H.O.	8,100	H.O. Current account	7,560
Selling expenses	4,260	Creditors	2,340
Administrative expenses	2,040		
Sundry expenses	1,380		
Petty cash	50		
Cash at Bank	1,050		
Debtors	6,400		
Stock on 1st July, 1972	7,270		
	48,100		48,100

Stock on hand at the branch on December 31, 1972 Rs. 8,200. Poona branch current account in the Head office books showed a balance of Rs. 8,980 by the closing date. A provision for doubtful debts is to be raised, calculated at 1½% of debtors accounts.

(*B.Com., Osmania, 1973*)

Ans. : Gross profit Rs. 13,680; Net profit Rs. 5,904. Goods-in-transit Rs. 880. Branch current account total Rs. 57,276.

(42) The following position is shown by the books of a Bombay business and its two branches as on 31st December, 1986.

Bombay Balance Sheet

Liabilities	Rs.	Assets	Rs.
Capital	25,000	Plant and Machinery	12,000
Creditors	3,000	Stock	6,900
'A' Branch Current Account	1,500	Debtors	6,500
Profit and Loss Account	7,000	'B' Branch Current Account	1,100
		Cash	10,000
	36,500		36,500

'A' Branch Balance Sheet

Liabilities	Rs.	Assets	Rs.
Creditors	3,900	H.O. Current Account	2,400
		Stock	600
		Debtors	700
		Cash	200
	3,900		3,900

'B' Branch Balance Sheet

Liabilities	Rs.	Assets	Rs.
H.O. Current Account	300	Stock	1,800
Creditors	4,000	Debtors	2,200
		Cash	300
	4,300		4,300

Upon investigation it was found that the following transactions had taken place on 31st December, 1986 :

(a) Bombay Office forwarded goods to the value of Rs. 500 to Branch 'A' and Rs. 600 to Branch 'B' which were not received by them until 3rd January, 1987.

(b) Branch 'A' remitted Rs. 400 cash to Bombay office which was received by it on 2nd January, 1987.

(c) Branch 'A' returned Rs. 200 goods to Bombay office which were received by it on 3rd January, 1987.

You are required to pass journal entries in the books of Head Office and prepare a consolidated balance sheet of the whole business thereafter.

(*Karnataka University*)

Ans. : 'A' Branch Current A/c total Rs. 2,400; 'B' Branch Current A/c total Rs. 1,100. Combined Balance Sheet total Rs. 42,900.

(43) A Limited Company with its Head Office at Delhi has a branch office in Kanpur which obtains supplies partly from Head office at cost and partly from outside suppliers. The Branch keeps a separate set of books. On the 30th June, 1987, the following trial balance was extracted.

	Head Office		Branch Office	
	Dr. (Rs.)	Cr. (Rs.)	Dr. (Rs.)	Cr. (Rs.)
Share Capital	—	30,000	—	—
Fixed Assets	16,000	—	8,000	—
Profit & Loss Account on 1-7-86	—	4,000	—	—
Opening stock at cost	14,000	—	1,900	—
Debtors and Creditors	17,000	10,000	1,500	2,050
Cash	3,000	—	1,000	—
Purchases and sales	1,20,000	1,40,000	6,750	20,500
Sundry expenses	15,000	—	2,250	—
Goods from Head Office to Branch	—	12,000	11,500	—
Current Account	11,000	—	—	10,350
Total	1,96,000	1,96,000	32,900	32,900

The difference between the balance on the Head Office and branch current account is due to goods and cash being in transit at the close of the year. Fixed assets are to be depreciated at 10 per cent. Stocks on 30th June, 1987 were : Head Office Rs. 10,000 and Branch Rs. 2,100.

Prepare the company's profit and loss account for the year ended 30th June, 1987 and its balance sheet on the same date.

(Vikram, B.Com., 1988, and Agra, B.Com.)

Ans. : Gross profit : Branch Rs. 2,450 and H.O. Rs. 28,000; Net profit– Head office Rs. 11,400; Net loss– Branch Rs. 600. Balance Sheet total Rs. 56,850.

(44) Burjoriji and Chhaganlal are partners sharing profits and losses in the proportion of 2/3rd and 1/3rd respectively. Burjoriji managed the Bombay office and chhaganlal managed the Kanpur office. On 31st December, 1978, the Trial Balance stood as follows :

Bombay Office		Kanpur Office	
	Rs.		Rs.
Stock 1st January	1,08,000	Stock on 1 January	78,000
Kanpur Office (Dr.)	45,000	Bombay Office (Cr)	36,000
Burjoriji's Capital	2,04,000	Chhaganlal's Capital	48,000
Purchases	1,92,000	Book Debts	30,000
Sales	3,12,000	Purchases	1,02,000
Plant at Bombay	72,000	Sales	1,44,000
Plant at Kanpur	48,000	Creditors	12,000
Book Debts	45,000	Wages	24,000
Creditors	42,000	Carriage and cartage	2,400
Wages	36,000	Cash in Hand	3,600
Carriage and Cartage	5,400	Stock on 31st Dec.	85,200
Cash in Hand	6,600		
Stock on 31st December	1,00,800		

Interest on capital is to be allowed at 5% and depreciation at 5% is to be charged on plants.

Pass the necessary Journal Entries in the books of both offices (except those relating to trading and profit and loss accounts) and prepare separately the Final Accounts and the Balance Sheets of the Bombay and Kanpur offices.

(Adapted from G.D.A.)

Ans. : In the books of Bombay : Gross profit Rs. 71,400, Net profit Rs. 57,600, Kanpur Office Account total Rs. 59,400, Balance Sheet total Rs. 3,06,600.

In the books of Kanpur : Gross profit Rs. 22,800; Net profit Rs. 18,000; Bombay Office Account total Rs. 59,400; Balance Sheet total Rs. 1,27,800.

(45) Universal Ltd. has its H.O. in Calcutta and a Branch in Bombay which keeps its own books. Summarised Trial Balances at 31st December, 1978 are given below. The Bombay profit for 1978 has not been incorporated in the H.O. books.

Calcutta :

	Dr. Rs.	Cr. Rs.
Capital	—	1,00,000
Fixed Assets	1,40,000	
Current Assets & Liabilities	88,000	49,000
Profit & Loss A/c :		
Balance 1st Jan., 1978	—	67,000
Calcutta profit for 1978	—	54,000
Bombay Branch A/c, 1st Jan., 1978	66,400	—
Remittances from Branch	—	30,000
Goods Sent to Branch (at cost)	5,600	
	3,00,000	3,00,000

Bombay :

	Dr. Rs.	Cr. Rs.
Fixed Assets	36,500	—
Current Assets & Liabilities	31,800	17,300
Head Office A/c 1st Jan., 1978	—	66,400
Remittances to H.O.	32,000	—
Goods from H.O.	—	5,150
Profit & Loss A/c, 1978	—	11,450
	1,00,300	1,00,300

The Branch remitted Rs. 2,000 cash to H.O. on 30th Dec., 1978 and H.O. sent goods to the Branch of Rs. 450 (at cost) on the same day. Write up the Branch A/c in H.O. Ledger, the H.O. A/c in Branch Ledger. You are required to prepare a summarized B/S the for entire business.

(*Calcutta, B.Com., 1969 & Poona, B.Com., 1989*)

Ans. : Closing of Branch A/c and H.O. A/c Rs. 53,000; Balance Sheet total Rs. 2,98,750.

(46) M/s Ram Chand & Co. of Hyderabad, have a branch in Delhi. The Delhi branch deals not only in the goods from the Head office but also buys some auxiliary goods and deals in them. They however, do not prepare any profit and loss account but submit all the accounts to the Head office at the end of the year and open them afresh on the basis of the advice from their Head office. The fixed assets accounts are also maintained at the Head office.

The goods from the Head office are invoiced at selling prices to give a profit of 20% on the sale price. The goods sent from the branch to the Head office are at cost. From the following particulars prepare the branch account, branch trading and profit and loss account and branch assets accounts in Head office books.

Trial Balance of Delhi Branch as on 31-12-1964

Debits	Rs.	Credits	Rs.
Head office		Sales	1,00,000
(Opening balance 1-1-64)	15,000	Goods to Head office	3,000
Goods from Head office	50,000	Head office current account	15,000
Purchases	20,000	Sundry creditors	3,000
Opening stock (H.O. Goods at invoice prices)	4,000		
Opening stock of other goods	500		
Salaries	7,000		
Rent	3,000		
Office expenditure	2,000		
Cash in Hand	500		
Cash at bank	4,000		
Sundry debtors	15,000		
	1,21,000		1,21,000

The branch balances as on 1st January, 1964 were as under :

Furniture Rs. 5,000; Sundry debtors Rs. 9,500; Cash Rs. 1,000; Creditors Rs. 30,000; Stock (H.O. Goods at invoice prices) Rs. 4,000; Other goods Rs. 500.

The closing stock at branch of the Head office goods at invoice prices is Rs. 3,000 and that of purchased goods at cost is Rs. 1,000. Depreciation is to be provided at 10 per cent on branch assets.

[*C.A. (Final), May, 1965; B.Com., Madras, April, 1977*]

Ans. : Gross profit Rs. 42,700; Net profit Rs. 30,200; Loading on : Opening stock Rs. 800, Goods sent Rs. 10,000 and Closing stock Rs. 600; Head office current account total Rs. 50,000.

(47) Goods sent to a Branch were charged by the Head office at cost plus 10 per cent. Head office makes a uniform gross profit of $33^1/_3$% on selling price on all its other sales. The Branch sells goods at a uniform gross profit to Branch of 25% on selling price.

The following transactions have taken place during the year ended on 31st March, 1977.

(1) Head office purchases amounted to Rs. 14,64,000, purchases returns were Rs. 61,650 and discount allowed by suppliers amounted to Rs. 30,090.

(2) Sales by Head office amounted Rs. 10,80,000. Goods sent to Branch were Rs. 5,44,500 (at invoice price), discount allowed to customers amounted to Rs. 9,180.

(3) Goods sent to Branch for Rs. 66,000 in March, 1977 were not received at the Branch until April, 1977.

(4) Branch purchased goods locally for Rs. 1,87,500, discount allowed by suppliers amounted Rs. 4,875.

(5) Overhead expenses of Head office were Rs. 2,80,260 and of Branch Rs. 80,475.

(6) Sales by the Branch amounted Rs. 7,20,000, discount allowed to customers amounted to Rs. 5,640 and cost of goods lost-in-transit was Rs. 8,010.

(7) Branch stock as on 31st March, 1977 included stock invoiced by Head office at Rs. 1,15,500.

You are required to prepare Columnar Trading and Profit and Loss Account of Head office and the Branch for the year ended 31st March, 1977.

(*C.A. Final O.S., May, 1977*)

Ans. : Gross profit : H.O. Rs. 4,03,500 and Branch Rs. 1,80,000. Net profit: H.O. Rs. 1,33,650 and Branch Rs. 90,750. Closing stock at H.O. Rs. 2,47,350; Closing stock at Branch Rs. 1,17,990; Stock reserve at Branch Rs. 10,500 (*i.e.*, 1/11 of 1,15,500).

(48) XY & Co. commenced business on 1-1-1977 with Head office at Calicut and a Branch at Tiruchur. All goods were purchased by Head office and normally packed immediately but on 31-12-1977, goods costing Rs. 5,000 remained unpacked.

Only packed goods were sent to the Branch which were charged at selling price less 10%.

Following information is furnished to you as on 31st Dec., 1977 from the Head office and Branch office books :

	Head Office	Branch Office
	Rs.	Rs.
Capital Account	40,000	–
Drawings by proprietor	10,000	–
Purchases	4,00,000	–
Packing materials bought	6,000	–
Sales	3,20,000	1,00,000

(*Contd*)

	Rs.	Rs.
Dispatch of goods to Branch	1,13,400	
Selling expenses	16,000	800
Clerk's salary, wages etc.	20,000	3,000
Sundry Debtors	28,000	4,200
Sundry Creditors	26,600	5,000
Current Accounts :		
Head Office (Credit balance)		12,000
Branch Office (Debit balance)	19,000	
Bank balances	1,000	
Goods received from Head Office		1,08,000

You are further informed that :

(a) Sales by Head Office were at a uniform gross profit, after charging packing materials of 20% on the fixed selling price.

(b) Sales at Branch were at fixed selling price.

(c) Goods invoiced and dispatched by Head Office to Branch in December, 1977 for Rs. 5,400 were received in the Branch only on 10th January, 1978.

(d) Stock of packing materials on hand as on 31st December, 1977 was valued at Rs. 1,000.

(e) Remittance of Rs. 1,600 from the Branch to the Head Office was in transit on 31-12-77.

(f) Rs. 2,000 worth of stock at selling price was damaged at the Branch. For valuing stock, this was reduced by Rs. 1,090 below the invoice cost to the Branch. It was decided that the Head Office and the Branch would share equally the loss occasioned by this and also the deficit in stock, ascertained on actual stock-taking at the Branch of goods at selling price of Rs. 500.

Prepare the profit and loss accounts of the Tiruchur and Calicut offices and also a Balance sheet as at 31-12-77 of the business.

(*C.A. Inter, New Scheme, November, 1978*)

Ans. : Gross profit : H.O. Rs. 76,600 and Branch Rs. 10,000.
Net profit : H.O. Rs. 37,480 and Branch Rs. 5,430.
Balance Sheet total Rs. 1,04,510.

Hints : (i) Stock Reserve Rs. 2,350 (*i.e.*, 10/90 of Rs. 21,150).

(ii) Gross profit made by H.O. : 20% of sales

of Rs. 3,20,000	64,000
10/90 of Goods sent to Branch	12,600
	76,600

(III) Foreign Branch

(49) The firm "Hasi Khusi & Co." with its H.O. in Calcutta has a branch in London.

At the end of each year (December 31) a Trial Balance sent by the Branch in sterling currency is converted into rupee currency at the Head Office.

The following Trial Balance for the year has been compiled at the Branch as on December 31, 1988 :

	£	S	d	£	S	d
Bills Receivable	1,953	1	8			
Sundry Debtors	3,890	16	8			
Sundry Creditors				977	10	0
Purchases	11,000	0	0			
Sales				18,333	6	8
Furnitures & Fixture (Jan., 1)	1,000	0	0			
-Do- (Purchased 10th May)	175	0	0			
Stock (Jan., 1)	1,837	10	10			
Establishment charges	3,208	6	8			
Rent, rates & taxes	366	13	4			
Sundry Office Expenses	1,378	0	0			
Depreciation on Furniture & fixtures	128	6	8			
Remittances to H.O.	1,468	10	6			
Head Office Account	—	—	—	7,859	2	2
Cash in Hand and at Bank	766	13	4	—	—	—
	27,169	18	10	27,169	18	10

The stock in hand on December 31, 1988 was £ 2,108-6-8.

The rates of exchange were :

From December 31, 1987 to June 30, 1988 – 1s 9d to the rupee.

From July 1st, 1988 to December 31, 1988 – 1s 11d to the rupee.

In the Calcutta Books, the balance of the London Branch Account and of the remittances from London Branch Account appear as Rs. 84,148 and Rs. 15,009 respectively.

The original Furniture and Fixtures were bought when the rate of exchange was 1s 8d to the rupee. Convert the above Trial Balance into rupee currency.

(Calcutta, B.Com.)

Ans. : Average rate of exchange = $\frac{\text{1s 9d + 1s 11d}}{2}$ = *i.e.*, 1s 10d.

Difference in Exchange Cr. Rs. 41. Closing stock amount to Rs. 22,000.

(50) On 31st December, 1990, the following balance appeared in the books of Calcutta Branch of an English firm having its office in London :

	Rs.	Rs.
Stock on 1st Jan., 1990	12,600	—
Purchases and sales	75,000	1,12,500
Debtors and creditors	39,000	26,000
Bills receivable and payable	10,400	9,100
Salaries and wages	4,800	—
Rent, rates and taxes	5,100	—
Furniture	4,910	—
Cash at Bank	28,990	
London Account	—	33,200
	1,80,800	1,80,800

Stock on 31st December, 1990 was Rs. 32,500.

Branch account in the London books showed a debit balance of £ 2,680 on 31st December, 1990 and furniture appeared in the Head office books at £ 350.

The rate of exchange on 31-12-1989 was Rs. 14 and on 31-12-1990 Rs. 13. The average rate for the year 1990 was Rs. 12.

Prepare in the Head office books, the profit and loss account and the balance sheet of the branch. (*B.Com., Agra & Bangalore*)

Ans. : Difference in exchange £ 400 (Dr.). Closing stock amounted to £ 2,500; Gross profit £ 4,725, Net Profit £ 3,900, B/s total £ 9,280.

Note : If the difference in exchange is taken into P & L A/c, the profit would be £ 3,500 and balance sheet total would be £ 8,880.

(51) Convert the following trial balance as on 31st December, 1989, of the Calcutta Branch which has got its Head office in London :

	Rs.	Rs.
Stock in Hand	12,600	—
Purchases	75,000	—
Sales		1,12,500
Sundry Drs.	27,000	—
Sundry Crs.		18,000
Bills Receivable	7,200	—
Bills Payable		6,300
Wages & Salaries	4,800	—
Rent, rates & taxes	3,600	—
Sundry Charges	1,500	—
Fixtures & Furniture	5,000	—
Cash at Bank	33,300	—
Land on A/c	—	33,200
	1,70,000	1,70,000

Stock on 31st December, 1969, was Rs. 22,500. Calcutta Branch (Dr. Balance) in London Books was £ 2,880. Fixtures and furniture appeared in London Books at £ 350.

The rate of exchange on 31st December, 1968 was Rs. 14 and on 31st December, 1969 Rs. 9. The average rate for the year 1969 was Rs. 12.

Prepare also the P & L A/c and Balance Sheet of the Calcutta Branch in Sterling, showing how would you deal with the difference in exchange.

(Bombay, B.Com.)

Ans. : Difference in exchange Cr. £ 870.
Closing stock £ 2,500; Gross profit £ 4,725;
Net profit £ 3,900 and B/S Total £ 10,350.

Additional Problems

(52) The Bellary Head Office has branch at Hospet. From the following trial balance of the branch and the other information given, prepare the branch trading and profit and loss account and the balance sheet.

Trial Balance as at.....

Name of the Accounts	Debit Rs.	Credit Rs.
Opening Stock	5,000	–
Furniture	500	–
Goods from Head Office	26,000	–
Purchases	4,500	–
Returns Inwards from Customers	500	–
Salaries	3,000	–
General expenses	500	–
Rent	300	–
Bad debts	100	–
Carriage	100	–
Sundry Debtors	5,000	–
Bank Balance	1,500	–
Allowances to Customers	100	–
Bills Receivable	1,000	–
Sales	–	44,000
Returns to Head Office	–	200
Sundry Creditors	–	2,900
Head Office Account	–	1,000
	48,100	48,100

Other information :

(1) It was found that the cash remittance of Rs. 500 by the Head office was not received by the Head office before the end of the accounting period.

(2) 10% depreciation on the asset worth Rs. 5,000 purchased by the Head office was to be provided for.

(3) The stock of unsold goods at the branch was valued at Rs. 4,000.

(*Gulbarga, Oct., 1986*)

Ans. : Gross Profit Rs. 12,100 & Net Profit Rs. 7,600.
H.O. A/c balance Rs. 9,600 & B/s Total Rs. 12,500.

(53) The following are the ledger balances of a Head Office and its independent Branch as on 31-12-1991.

Sl. No.	Particulars	H.O.	Branch
1.	Capital	60,000	—
2.	Profit & Loss Account (1-1-1991) Cr.	5,000	2,000
3.	Buildings	20,000	5,000
4.	Furniture	14,000	2,000
5.	Fixtures	1,500	500
6.	Profit for the year	10,000	4,000
7.	Creditors for goods	5,000	1,000
8.	Creditors for rent and taxes	1,000	500
9.	Closing stock	12,500	5,500
10.	Debtors	15,000	5,000
11.	Goods sent to branch	12,000	—
12.	Goods received from Head Office	—	10,000
13.	Cash remitted to Head Office by Branch	6,000	7,000
14.	Cash at bank	2,000	2,500
15.	Head Office account	—	10,000
16.	Branch account	10,000	—

Prepare the branch account in the books of Head office and the combined balance sheet of the Head office and branch as on 31-12-1991.

(*Karnataka, Oct., 1993*)

Ans. : Branch Account Total Rs. 29,500;
Balance Sheet Total 88,500.

Hint : Cash-in-transit Rs. 1,000 and Goods-in-transit Rs. 2,000.

(54) From the following particulars as shown by the books of a branch prepare the branch account, cash account, branch debtors' and creditors' account.

	Rs.
Balance as on 1-1-1990 :	
Petty cash balance	2,300
Opening stock at invoice price	50,000
Sundry debtors at branch	24,000
Sundry creditors at branch	11,200
Furniture at branch	28,000
Transactions for the year ending 31-12-1990 :	
Goods sent to branch	4,04,000
Cash sales at branch	5,80,000
Credit sales at branch	95,000
Allowances to debtors	1,500
Cash received from customers	80,000
Bad debts written off	1,200
Cash purchases by branch	40,500
Credit purchases by branch	99,800
Cash remittances by Head office :	
Rent	2,800
Salaries	12,000
Insurance	960
Petty expenses	480
Balance as on 31-12-1990 :	
Closing stock at cost	30,000
Closing balance of creditors	23,000
Closing petty cash	2,300

Other information :

Goods are sent to branch at 20% profit on sale price, Depreciate furniture at 10% per annum. *(Karnataka, April, 1993)*

Ans. : Net profit 1,79,760; Branch account total Rs. 7,27,300.
Closing debtors Rs. 36,300 and Cash remitted to H.O. Rs. 5,31,500.
Cash paid to Creditors Rs. 88,000 and Cash A/c total Rs. 6,60,000.
Loading on : Opening stock Rs. 10,000 and Goods sent Rs. 80,800.

Note : (1) Branch account is debited with Rs. 28,000 and credited with Rs. 25,200 (28,000 – 2,800) on account of Furniture.

(2) Opening stock and Goods sent are at invoice price but Closing stock is at cost price.

(3) Branch account is debited with closing creditors of Rs. 23,000 and credited with opening creditors of Rs. 11,200.

(55) From the following particulars prepare the necessary ledger accounts in the books of Head office under Stock & Debtors System. The Head office supplied goods to branch at cost 25% :

	Rs.	Rs.
Stock on 1-1-1987 at invoice price		5,000
Debtors on 1-1-1987		3,500
Goods sent to branch at invoice price		16,000
Expenses paid by the Head office for :		
Salary	800	
Rent	300	
Other expenses	400	1,500
Cash remitted by branch :		
Cash Sales	2,600	
Cash collected from debtors	10,000	12,600
Total sales		19,000
Discount allowed to debtors		200
Goods returned by customers		400
Stock on 31-12-1987 at invoice price		3,000

(*Gulbarga, Oct., 1995*)

Ans. : Gross profit Rs. 3,720 and Net profit Rs. 2,500.
Closing Debtors Rs. 9,300 and Branch expenses Rs. 1,700.

Notes : (i) 25% or ¼ on cost is 20% or 1/5 on invoice price.
(ii) Difference of Rs. 600 in Branch Stock A/c is surplus in stock at invoice price.

(56) A Head Office at Bombay has branch at Calcutta. The company closes its accounts on 31st December each year. What adjustment entries are required to be passed in the books of both the Head Office and the Calcutta Branch in regard to the following :

(i) A remittance of Rs. 5,000 by the Calcutta Branch on 22-12-1987 is received by the Head Office on 5-1-1988.

(ii) Goods worth Rs. 10,000 sent by Head Office on 20-12-1987 reaches the Branch on 6-1-1988.

(iii) Depreciation at 10% p.a. is to be provided on machinery at Calcutta costing Rs. 70,000 the account of which is in the books of Head Office.

(iv) The Calcutta Branch paid Rs. 1,000 dividend to the local shareholder on behalf of the Head Office.

(*Bangalore, April, 1991*)

Hint : In the books of H.O. : Debit Dividend A/c and credit Calcutta Branch A/c.
In the book of Branch : Debit H.O. A/c and credit Bank A/c.

(57) The Calcutta Head Office usually sends goods to its Bombay Branch at cost price plus 25%. Further, wherever required, the branch purchases goods independently. From the following details, prepare the Bombay Branch Account in the Head Office books.

		Rs.
(a)	Petty cash balance on 1-1-91	2,000
(b)	Petty cash balance on 31-12-91	2,000
(c)	Stock on hand on 1-1-91:	
	Goods received from Head Office	6,400
	Goods purchased from outside	1,600
(d)	Goods sent to the branch	68,000
(e)	Cash sales	13,000
(f)	Credit sales	1,19,000
(g)	Credit purchases	15,200
(h)	Collections from debtors	1,12,200
(i)	Debtors as on 1-1-91	8,200
(j)	Debtors as on 31-12-91	11,200
(k)	Office expenses (cash sent from H.O.)	30,000
(l)	Stock on hand on 31-12-91:	
	Goods received from H.O.	6,000
	Goods purchased from outside	2,000
(m)	Amount paid to creditors (out of collections made)	14,800
(n)	Creditors as on 1-1-91	800
(o)	Creditors as on 31-12-91	1,200

(*Bangalore, October, 1992*)

Ans. : Net profit Rs. 28,680; Loading in opening stock Rs. 1,280; Loading in goods sent Rs. 13,600 and Loading in closing stock Rs. 1,200.

Notes : (i) Cash remitted is Rs. 1,10,400 (*i.e.*, 13,000 + 97,400 *i.e.*, 1,12,200 less payment to creditors Rs. 14,800).

(ii) Credit sales and credit purchases do not appear in the Branch Account.

(58) Write journal entries in the books of Head Office and the Branch as on 31-12-1992.

(a) The Head Office had sent goods on 28-12-92 worth Rs. 10,000 to the Branch, which received these goods on 3-1-1993.

(b) On 27-12-1992, the Branch had remitted Rs. 750 to the Head Office which received this amount on 1-1-1993.

(c) Depreciation on Branch Assets was Rs. 4,000. The account of these assets was kept in the books of the Head Office.

(d) A clerk of the Branch had rendered services worth Rs. 600 in the Head Office (His salary was paid by the Branch).

(Bangalore, April, 1993)

Hint : In the books of Head office : Debit Clerk Salaries A/c and credit Branch A/c.
In the books of Branch : Debit Head Office A/c and credit Bank Account.

(59) The Bangalore Trading Company invoiced goods to its Branch at cost. The following is the summary of transactions entered into at the Branch during the year ended 31st December, 1990 :

	Rs.
Stock on 1st January	7,000
Debtors on 1st January	12,600
Petty cash on 1st January	200
Goods sent from H.O.	26,000
Goods returned to H.O.	1,000
Cash sales	17,500
Credit sales	28,400
Allowances to customers	200
Discount to customers	1,400
Bad debts	600
Goods returned by customers	500
Salaries and wages	6,200
Rent and rates	1,200
Sundry expenses	800
Cash received from debtors	28,500
Stock on 31st December, 1990	6,500
Debtors on 31st December, 1990	9,800
Petty cash on 31st December, 1990	100

Prepare Memorandum Branch Trading and Profit and Loss Account and show the profit made by the branch.

(Bangalore, Oct., 1994)

Ans. : Gross profit Rs. 19,900 and Net profit Rs. 9,400 and Branch Account Total Rs. 63,400.

Notes : (i) Actual petty cash expenses debited to P & L A/c is Rs. 100 (200 – 100).

(ii) Opening petty cash of Rs. 200 should be debited and closing petty cash of Rs. 100 should be credited to Branch A/c. But, actual petty cash expenses of Rs. 100 should not appear in the Branch Account.

(60) The following is the trial balance of Kumta Branch as on 31-3-1995 :

Debit Balance	Rs.	Credit Balance	Rs.
Head Office Account	3,240	Sales	38,000
Stock (on 1-4-1994)	6,000	Goods supplied to	
Purchases	17,800	Head Office	6,000
Goods received from		Creditors	1,850
Head Office	9,000		
Salaries	1,500		
Debtors	3,700		
Rent	960		
Office expenses	470		
Cash	1,780		
Furniture	1,400		
	45,850		45,850

(a) Branch Stock on 31-3-1995 Rs. 2,700.

(b) Branch Account (in Head Office books) Rs. 460 (Dr.).

(c) Cash-in-transit Rs. 3,700.

(d) Depreciate furniture at Rs. 5%.

Give the adjustment and incorporation entries in the books of Head Office.

(*Karnataka, April, 1996*)

Ans. : Gross profit Rs. 13,900; Net profit Rs. 10,900.

Branch A/c total in the H.O. books Rs. 49,010.

Balance Sheet total Rs. 13,210.

(61) (a) What are the different types of branches that Head Office can open? Explain them briefly.

(b) From the following Trial Balance of Belgaum Branch, pass incorporation entries in the books of Bangalore Head Office and prepare Belgaum Branch Account.

Trial Balance as on 31-12-97

	Dr. Rs.		Cr. Rs.
Opening Stock (1-1-97)	2,000	Head Office Account (1-1-97)	17,400
Salaries	5,000	Sales	36,000
Sundry Debtors	20,000	Sundry Creditors	2,000
Cash	2,000	Commission	600
Purchases	4,000		
Goods from Head Office	20,000		
Rent	1,500		
Discount	900		
Stationery	600		
	56,000		56,000

Closing stock as on 31-12-97 Rs. 13,000.

(*Karnataka, April, 1998*)

Ans. : Gross profit Rs. 23,000, Net profit Rs. 15,600 and Branch Account Total Rs. 69,000 (Debit side 17,400 + 49,000 + 600 + 2,000 and credit side 26,000 + 8,000 + 35,000).

12

DEPARTMENTAL ACCOUNTS

Meaning

When a trader deals in different kinds of commodities or services, he normally divides his stores into a number of departments or divisions under one roof and one management. Such divisions or sections are known as 'Departments'. These departments rendering different types of services in the same building or under one roof. Departmental stores are the best example of such departments. Departmental stores are having separate departments for selling of medicines, stationery, textiles, provisions etc. Each department is separately managed and all the departments are managed by the General Manager who frames the common policy for the various departments of a business concern.

When there are a number of departments under one roof and one management, it is essential to prepare a separate trading and profit and loss accounts for each department in addition to final accounts for the business as a whole. Such accounts are called "departmental accounts". These accounts are to be prepared to know the trading result of each department individually. If only a combined profit and loss account is prepared for the business as a whole, the profit or loss of each department cannot be known. Hence, a separate accounts are to be prepared to compare the results of one department with those of other departments.

Objectives

Following are the main objectives or advantages of departmental accounts :

(1) They help the business to compare the trading results of one department with that of another.

(2) They help the proprietor in formulating the policy to expand the business on profitable lines.

(3) They help to take necessary steps to improve the department, which is under loss.

(4) They help to give an additional reward to the departmental manager on the basis of the profits of his department.

Methods of Departmental Accounts

There are two methods of recording departmental transactions. They are as follows :

(i) Keeping the accounts of each department independently and assuming each department to be a separate unit. But at the end of the accounting year, the result of all departments will be combined to know the trading result of the business concern as a whole.

(ii) Keeping the accounts of all the departments together in a tabular or columnar form.

Accounting Procedure

Under departmental accounts, the subsidiary books are kept on columnar basis. For example, if a business concern has three departments A, B & C, the subsidiary books such as Purchases Book, Sales Book, Purchase Returns Book, Sales Returns Book etc. should have a separate columns for each of the departments. Ledger accounts are also kept in a columnar form to know the position of each department separately. With the help of department-wise details, the Departmental Trading and Profit and Loss Account will be prepared in the columnar form.

Allocation of Expenses

There are certain indirect expenses which are common to all the departments and may not be recorded separately for each department. Such common expenses should be allocated according to the ratio given in the problem. If the ratio is not given, then the expenses will be allocated on the basis of the following procedure :

Indirect Expenses	Basis of Allocation
1. Purchases expenses such as carriage inwards, freight duty, octroi etc.	1. On the basis of net purchases (*i.e.*, after deducting returns, if any) (Inter-departmental purchases should be ignored).
2. Selling expenses such as advertisement, discount allowed, commission, bad debts, sales tax, carriage outwards etc.	2. On the basis of net sale (*i.e.*, after deducting returns, if any) (Inter-departmental sales should be ignored).
3. Building expenses such as rent, rates and taxes, fire insurance, depreciation, repairs etc.	3. On the basis of space occupied by each department.
4. Labour welfare expenses such as canteen, recreation etc.	4. On the basis of worker employed by each department.

Indirect Expenses	Basis of Allocation
5. Machinery expenses such as repairs, depreciation etc.	5. On the basis of cost price of machine or cost of repairs to machines.
6. Power, lighting, heating, electricity etc.	6. On the basis of meter reading or points or space occupied by each department.
7. Works Manager's salary.	7. On the basis time spent in the work of each department.
8. Salary or wages of staff appointed.	8. On the basis of number of employees appointed in each department.
9. Insurance of goods, godown rent etc. related to closing stock.	9. On the basis of ratio of closing stock of the each department.
10. All other expenses.	10. On the basis of sales ratio or specific ratio given.

Note : There are certain common indirect expenses like Bank interest, Accountancy charges, Audit fees etc., which cannot be allocated to any department on any one of the above basis. Such expenses should directly debited to the general profit and loss account . Alternatively, they should be allocated equally to the departments.

Allocation of Common Incomes

Commission earned is related to the sales. Hence, it is allocated in the ratio of net sales. Similarly, discount earned is concerned to the purchases. Hence, it is allocated in the ratio of net purchases. Other incomes such as interest on investment, interest from Bank etc., should be apportioned according to the ratio given in the problem and in the absence of which they should be allocated equally to the departments.

Inter-departmental Transfers

Supplying goods from one department to another department is called inter-departmental transfer or inter-departmental transaction. Such transfers should be treated as 'Sales' for the department which makes transfer and 'Purchases' for the department which receives the goods. Usually, transfer of goods is made at cost price. When the goods are transferred at invoice price or selling price a reserve should be made on the closing stock of such goods equal to the amount of profit involved therein. Similarly, if one department renders service to the another department, similar adjustment will be made. Transfer of goods from one department to another department will have no effect on net sales or net purchases for allocation purpose.

Illustration 1

From the following Balances extracted from the books of B.N. Pal, prepare departmental Trading Account and Profit and Loss Account for the year ended 31st October, 1978 and Balance Sheet as on that date.

	Rs.	Rs.
Capital	—	50,000
Land and Building	12,500	—
Furniture Department A	2,500	—
Opening Stock Department A	3,000	—
Opening Stock Department B	4,000	—
Purchases Department A	1,00,000	—
Purchases Department B	1,50,000	—
Sales Department A	—	2,00,000
Sales Department B	—	3,00,000
Audit Fees	5,000	—
Electricity	10,000	—
Salary	50,000	—
Carriage Inward	5,000	—
Rent	40,000	—
Sundry Debtors	20,000	—
Sundry Creditors	—	10,000
Drawings	28,000	—
Cash at Bank	1,00,000	—
Sales Commission	30,000	—
	5,60,000	5,60,000

Additional information :

(1) Depreciated Land and Building by 5% and Furniture by 10% p.a.

(2) Staff is employed in the ratio of 2 : 1.

(3) Area occupied by each Department is equal.

(4) Electricity consumed is in the ratio of 1 : 2.

(5) Closing Stock Department A Rs. 13,000 and that of Department B Rs. 26,000.

(6) Audit fees be apportioned on the basis of turnover.

(B.Com., K.U.D., Gulbarga & Shivaji)

Solution :

Departmental Trading and Profit and Loss Account
For the year ended 31st October, 1978

	Dept. A Rs.	Dept. B Rs.		Dept. A Rs.	Dept. B Rs.
To Opening Stock	3,000	4,000	By Sales	2,00,000	3,00,000
To Purchases	1,00,000	1,50,000	By Closing Stock	13,000	26,000
To Carriage Inward (Purchases 2 : 3)	2,000	3,000			
To Gross Profit c/d	1,08,000	1,69,000			
	2,13,000	3,26,000		2,13,000	3,26,000
To Salaries (2 : 1)	33,333	16,667	By Gross Profit b/d	1,08,000	1,69,000
To Rent (Area-equal)	20,000	20,000			
To Electricity (1 : 2)	3,333	6,667			
To Audit Fees (Sales 2 : 3)	2,000	3,000			
To Dep. : on Building (Area -equal) on	313	312			
Furniture	250	—			
To Sales Commission (Sales 2 : 3)	12,000	18,000			
To Net Profit	36,771	1,04,354			
	1,08,000	1,69,000		1,08,000	1,69,000

Balance Sheet as on 31st October, 1978

Liabilities	Rs.	Rs.	Assets	Rs.	Rs.
Capital	50,000		Land & Building	12,500	
Add : Net Profit			*Less* : Dept. (313 + 312)	625	11,875
Dept. A	36,771		Furniture	2,500	
Dept. B	1,04,354		*Less* : Dept.	250	2,250
	1,91,125		Stock : Dept. A	13,000	
Less : Drawings	28,000	1,63,125	Dept. B	26,000	39,000
Sundry Creditors		10,000	Sundry Debtors		20,000
			Cash and Bank		1,00,000
		1,73,125			1,73,125

Illustration 2

The directors of Departmental Stores Limited wish to ascertain, approximately, the net profit of the 'A', 'B' and 'C' departments separately for the quarter ended March 31, 1972. It is found impracticable actually to take stock on that date but an adequate system of departmental accounting is in use and the normal rates of gross profit, for the departments concerned, are 40%, 30% and 20% on turnover, respectively. Indirect expenses are charged in proportion to departmental turnover.

Following are the figures for each department :

	A	B	C
Stock on 1-1-1972	30,000	35,000	15,000
Purchases to March 31, 1972	35,000	37,000	23,500
Sale to March 31,1972	60,000	50,000	30,000
Direct Expenses	10,100	7,250	3,550

Total indirect expenses for the period (including those relating to other departments) were Rs. 21,000 on total sales Rs. 4,20,000.

Prepare a statement showing gross profit, net profit after making reserve for stock at 10% in respect of each department.

(B.Com., Meerut, 1973; Sagar, 1956; Allahabad, 1966; Kar., April, 1988 modified and Berhampur, 1970)

Solution :

Departmental Trading and Profit and Loss Account

Dr. **For the year ended 31st March, 1972** Cr.

	A Rs.	B Rs.	C Rs.		A Rs.	B Rs.	C Rs.
To Opening Stock	30,000	35,000	15,000	By Sales	60,000	50,000	30,000
To Purchases	35,000	37,500	23,500	By Closing Stock	39,100	44,750	18,050
To Direct Expenses	10,100	7,250	3,550	(Balance figure)			
To Gross Profit c/d	24,000	15,000	6,000				
	99,100	94,750	48,050		99,100	94,750	48,050
To Indirect Expenses (5% on Sales)	3,000	2,500	1,500	By Gross Profit b/d	24,000	15,000	6,000
To Stock Reserve (10 % of Stock)	3,910	4,475	1,805				
To Net Profit	17,090	8,025	2,695				
	24,000	15,000	6,000		24,000	15,000	6,000

Working Note :

Percentage of Indirect Expenses to Sales is calculated as follows :

$$\frac{21,000}{4,20,000} \times 100 = 5\%$$

Illustration 3

The following purchases were made by a business house having three departments :

Department A 1,000 units
Department B 2,000 units } at total cost of Rs. 1,00,000
Department C 2,400 units

Opening stock were :

Department A 120 units; Department B 80 units and Department C 152 units. The sales were :

Department A 1,020 units at Rs. 20 each
Department B 1,920 units at Rs. 22.50 each
Department C 2,496 units at Rs. 25 each.

The rate of gross profit is the same in each case. Prepare Departmental Trading Account.

(B.Com., Calcutta, 1978, Institute of Company Secretary Inter, 1972 and Bangalore, Oct., 1991)

Solution :

To find out the rate of Gross Profit, it is assumed that all units purchased have been sold away.

Sales : Dept. A 1,000 units at Rs. 20 each	20,000
Dept. B 2,000 units at Rs. 22.50 each	45,000
Dept. C 2,400 units at Rs. 25 each	60,000
Total Sales	1,25,000
Less : Total Cost of purchases	1,00,000
Gross Profit	25,000

Percentage of gross profit will be $\frac{25,000 \times 100}{1,25,000} = 20\%$

Now we can find out the cost price of units purchased for each department.

	Selling Price	Gross Profit	Cost Price
Department 'A'	Rs. 20.00	Rs. 4.00	Rs. 16
Department 'B'	Rs. 20.50	Rs. 4.50	Rs. 18
Department 'C'	Rs. 25.00	Rs. 5.00	Rs. 20

Gross profit is calculated 20% of selling price and cost price is ascertained by deducting the gross profit in the selling price.

Units of closing stock of each department is calculated as follows :

	Opening Stock + Purchases – Sales = Units of closing stock
Department A	120 units + 1,000 units – 1,020 units = 100 units
Department B	80 units + 2,000 units – 1,920 units = 160 units
Department C	152 units + 2,400 units – 1,496 units = 1056 units.

Now departmental trading account will be prepared as follows :

Dr. **Departmental Trading Account** Cr.

	Dept. A Rs.	Dept. B Rs.	Dept. C Rs.		Dept. A Rs.	Dept. B Rs.	Dept. C Rs.
To Opening Stock (Units × Cost Price)	1,920	1,440	3,040	By Sales (Units × Selling Price)	20,400	43,200	62,400
To Purchases (Units × Cost Price)	16,000	36,000	48,000	By Closing Stock (Units × Cost Price)	1,600	2,880	1,120
To Gross Profit c/d	4,080	8,640	12,480				
	22,000	46,080	63,520		22,000	46,080	63,520

Illustration 4

From the undermentioned information and instructions, prepare departmental trading and profit and loss account in columnar form of the three departments of the Outfitters Ltd.

	Tailoring	Ladies	Outfitting
Stock January 1, 1978	41,280	33,975	93,721
Stock Dec. 31, 1978	32,840	43,828	81,626
Purchases for the year	2,10,342	75,296	1,39,109
Returns (Purchases)	14,382	5,629	1,823
Sales for the year	4,00,173	1,54,085	3,62,189
Returns (Sales)	Nil	3,259	11,217
Wages	72,823	30,084	24,613

Goods were transferred as follows (all at cost) :

Tailoring to ladies wear, Rs. 389 and to outfitting Rs. 6,679; Ladies wear to tailoring Rs. 5,315; outfitting to tailoring Rs. 4,271 and to ladies wear Rs. 5,801.

Apportion equally : stationery Rs. 921; postage Rs. 663; general charges Rs. 39,627; insurance Rs. 1,785 and depreciation Rs. 5,460.

Allocate the following further expenditure as you think best and append notes stating the basis selected for each item :

Establishment Rs. 63,395; bad debts Rs. 19,823; advertising Rs. 7,293 and income tax, Rs. 11,028.

Rent and taxes Rs. 45,437 is to be splitted up in proportion to space occupied *i.e.*, tailoring 4, ladies wear 2, outfitting 3, other space 2.

Approximate apportionment is all that is necessary; charge any old balance to outfitting department.

(*B.Com., Bangalore, 1979; Allahabad, 1960 and Bangalore, May, 1993*)

Solution :

Trading and Profit and Loss Account

Dr. **For the year ended 31st December, 1978** Cr.

	Tailoring Rs.	Ladies Rs.	Outfitting Rs.		Tailoring Rs.	Ladies Wear Rs.	Outfitting Rs.
To Opening Stock	41,280	33,975	93,721	By Sales	4,00,173	1,54,085	3,62,189
To Purchases	2,10,342	75,296	1,39,109	By Purchases returns	14,382	5,629	1,823
To Sales Returns	—	3,259	11,217				
To Wages	72,823	30,084	24,613	By Transfer to Ladies Wear	389	—	5,801
To Transfer from Tailoring	—	389	6,679	By Transfer to Outfitting	6,679	—	—
To Transfer from Ladies Wear	5,315	—	—	By Transfer to Tailoring	—	5,315	4,271
To Transfer from Outfitting	4,271	5,801	—	By Closing Stock	32,840	43,828	81,626
To Gross Profit c/d	1,20,432	60,053	1,80,371				
	4,54,463	2,08,857	4,55,710		4,54,463	2,08,857	4,55,710
To Stationery (Equally)	307	307	307	By Gross Profit b/d	1,20,432	60,053	1,80,371
To Postage (Equally)	221	221	221				
To General Charges (Equally)	13,209	13,209	13,209				
To Insurance (Equally)	595	595	595				
To Depreciation (Equally)	1,820	1,820	1,820				
To Establishment (8 : 3 : 7)	28,176	10,565	24,654				
To Bad Debts (8 : 3 : 7)	8,810	3,304	7,709				
To Advertising (8 : 3 : 7)	3,242	1,215	2,836				
To Rent and Taxes (4 : 2 : 3)	16,523	8,261	12,392				
To Rent and Taxes (other space–equally)	2,753	2,754	2,754				
To Net Profit (before tax)	44,776	17,802	1,13,874				
	1,20,432	60,053	1,80,371		1,20,432	60,053	1,80,371
To Income Tax (45 : 18 : 114)	2,804	1,122	7,102	By Net Profit before tax	44,776	17,802	1,13,874
To Net Profit	41,972	16,680	1,06,772				
	44,776	17,802	1,13,874		44,776	17,802	1,13,874

Notes : (1) Establishment, bad debts and advertising have been divided in the net sales ratio *i.e.*, 4,00,173 : 1,50,826 : 3,50,972 or 8 : 3 : 7.

(2) Rent and taxes amounted to Rs. 45,437 is apportioned as follows:

Tailoring		Ladies Wear		Outfitting		Other Space
4	:	2	:	3	:	2
16,523		8,261		12,392		8,261

Rent and taxes (other space) amounted to Rs. 8,261 is apportioned equally.

(3) Income tax is apportioned in the ratio of profit before tax *i.e.,* 44,776 : 17,802 : 1,13,874 or 45 : 18 : 114.

Illustration 5

A concern has two departments X and Y. From the following particulars prepare a consolidated trading account for the year ending December 31, 1988.

	X	Y
	Rs.	Rs.
Opening Stock at Cost	20,000	12,000
Purchases	92,000	68,000
Carriage	2,000	2,000
Wages	12,000	8,000
Sales	1,40,000	1,12,000
Purchased goods transferred :		
by 'X' to 'Y'	—	8,000
by 'Y' to 'X'	10,000	—
Finished goods transferred :		
by 'Y' to 'X'	35,000	
by 'X' to 'Y'	—	40,000
Returns of finished goods :		
by 'Y' to 'X'	10,000	—
by 'X' to 'Y'	—	7,000
Closing Stock :		
(i) Purchased goods	4,500	6,000
(ii) Finished goods	24,000	14,000

You are informed that purchased goods have been transferred at their respective departmental purchase cost and finished goods at departmental market price and that 25% of the finished stock (closing) at each department represented goods received from other department.

(*Mangalore, B.Com., Oct., 1984; B.Com., Dibrugarh, Meerut and Bangalore, April, 1994*

Solution :

Dr. **Trading Account for the year ending 31st Dec., 1988** Cr.

	X Rs.	Y Rs.	Total Rs.		X Rs.	Y Rs.	Total Rs.
To Opening Stock	20,000	12,000	32,000	By Sales	1,40,000	1,12,000	2,52,000
To Purchases	92,000	68,000	1,60,000	By Transfer of			—
To Carriage	2,000	2,000	4,000	purchased goods	8,000	10,000	—
To Wages	12,000	8,000	20,000	By Transfer of			
To Transfer of				finished goods	40,000	35,000	—
purchased goods	10,000	8,000	—	By Returns of			
To Transfer of				finished stock	7,000	10,000	—
finished goods	35,000	40,000	—				
To Returns of				By Closing stock :			
finished goods	10,000	7,000	—	Purchased goods	4,500	6,000	10,500
To Gross Profit c/d	42,500	42,000	84,500	Finished goods	24,000	14,000	38,000
	2,23,500	1,87,000	3,00,500		2,23,500	1,87,000	3,00,500
To Stock Reserve	875	1,800	2,675	By Gross Profit b/d	42,500	42,000	84,500
To Net Profit	41,625	40,200	81,825				
	42,500	42,000	84,500		42,500	42,000	84,500

Working Notes :

(1) Stock Reserve for 'X' Department

$$= \frac{\text{Gross Profit}}{\text{Sales + Transfer of finished goods to 'Y' – Returns of finished goods from 'Y'}} \times 25\% \text{ of finished goods of 'Y'}$$

$$= \frac{42{,}500}{1{,}40{,}000 + 40{,}000 - 10{,}000} \times 25\% \text{ of Rs. } 14{,}000$$

$$= \frac{42{,}500}{1{,}70{,}000} \times 3{,}500 = \text{Rs. } 875$$

(2) Stock Reserve for 'Y' Department

$$= \frac{\text{Gross Profit}}{\text{Sales + Transfer of finished goods to 'X' – Returns of finished goods from 'X'}} \times 25\% \text{ of finished goods of 'X'}$$

$$= \frac{42{,}000}{1{,}12{,}000 + 35{,}000 - 7{,}000} \times 25\% \text{ of Rs. } 24{,}000$$

$$= \frac{42{,}000}{1{,}40{,}000} \times 6{,}000 = \text{Rs. } 1{,}800.$$

Illustration 6

From the following balance, prepare Departmental Trading and Profit and Loss Account for the year ended 31st March, 1981 and Balance Sheet as at that date.

		Rs.		Rs.
Stock 1-4-1981	Dept. A	17,000	Discount Allowed	2,220
	Dept. B	14,500	Discount Received	650
Purchases	Dept. A	35,400	Advertising	3,680
	Dept. B	30,200	Carriage Inwards	2,340
Sales	Dept. A	60,800	Furniture and Fittings	3,000
	Dept. B	51,250	Plant & Machinery	21,000
Wages	Dept. A	8,200	Sundry Debtors	6,060
	Dept. B	2,700	Sundry Creditors	18,600
Rent, Rates, Taxes and Insurance		9,390	A's Capital A/c	47,660
Sundry Expenses		3,600	A's Drawings A/c	4,500
Salaries		3,000	Cash in Hand	170
Light and Heating		2,100	Cash at Bank	9,900

The following information is also provided :

(a) Internal transfer of goods from Dept. A to Dept. B Rs. 420.

(b) The items rent, rates, taxes and insurance, sundry expenses, lighting and heating, salaries and carriage inwards to be apportioned 2/3 to Dept. A and 1/3 to Dept. B.

(c) Advertising to be apportioned equally.

(d) Discounts allowed and received are apportioned on basis of departmental sales and purchases (excluding transfers).

(e) Depreciation at 10% p.a. on furniture and fittings and on plant and machinery. This is to be charged 3/4 to Dept. A and ¼ to Dept. B.

(f) Services rendered by Dept. B to Dept. A are not included in wages Rs. 500.

(g) Stock as at 31st March, 1981: A Dept. Rs. 16,740 and B Dept. Rs. 12,050.

(h) Fixed assets remain uncharged during the year.

(B.Com., Bombay, 1984; Madras, 1987; Mysore, March, 1966 and 1993 Mod.)

Solution :

Departmental Trading and Profit and Loss Account

Dr. **For the year ended 31st March , 1981** Cr.

	A Rs.	B Rs.		A Rs.	B Rs.
To Opening Stock	17,000	14,500	By Sales	60,800	51,250
To Purchases	35,400	30,200	By Transfer to 'B'	420	—
To Wages	8,200	2,700	By Closing Stock	16,740	12,050
To Transfer from 'A'	—	420			
To Carriage Inwards	1,560	780			
To Gross Profit c/d	15,800	14,700			
	77,960	63,300		77,960	63,300
To Rent, Rates etc.	6,260	3,130	By Gross Profit b/d	15,800	14,700
To Sundry Expenses	2,400	1,200	By Discount	350	300
To Salaries	2,000	1,000	(35,400 : 30,200)		
To Lighting & Heating	1,400	700	By Service Rendered	—	500
To Discount Allowed	1,205	1,015	By Net Loss	1,255	—
(60,800 : 51,200)					
To Advertising	1,840	1,840			
To Depreciation :					
Furniture & Fittings	225	75			
Plant & Machinery	1,575	525			
To Service Rendered	500	—			
To Net Profit	—	6,015			
	17,405	15,500		17,405	15,500

Balance Sheet as on 31st March, 1981

Liabilities		Rs.	Assets		Rs.
A's Capital	47,660		Plant and Machinery	21,000	
Less : A's Drawings	4,500		*Less :* Depreciation	2,100	18,900
	43,160		Furniture & Fittings	3,000	
Less : Loss of A Dept.	1,255		*Less :* Depreciation	300	2,700
	41,905		Sundry Debtors		6,060
Add : Profit of B Dept.	6,015	47,920	Cash in Hand		170
Creditors		18,600	Cash at Bank		9,900
			Stock : Department A	16,740	
			Department B	12,050	28,790
		66,520			66,520

Illustration 7

A departmental store has two Departments Dept. A and Dept. B. It was arranged that Dept. 'B' has to receive its requirements from Dept. 'A' at its usual selling price which includes 20% profits. Following are the figures relating to the year ending 31-3-1979.

	Dept. A Rs.	Dept. B Rs.
Stock on 1-4-1978	20,000	—
Purchases from outside	50,000	10,000
Sales	50,000	35,000
Salary	6,000	2,000
Goods supplied by Dept. 'A' to Dept. 'B'	15,000	—
Stock on 31-3-1979	25,000	3,000

Other expenses are :

Rent Rs. 3,000

General Expenses Rs. 1,000

Area occupied Dept. A 2/3 and Dept. B 1/3

It has been estimated that stock held by Dept. 'B' consists of goods supplied by Dept. 'A' to the extent 2/3.

Prepare departmental and Common Trading Profit and Loss Account for the year ending 31-3-1979. *(B.Com., K.U.D., 1977)*

Solution :

Departmental Trading and Profit and Loss Account
Dr. **For the year ended 31st March, 1979** Cr.

	A Rs.	B Rs.		A Rs.	B Rs.
To Opening Stock	20,000	—	By Sales	50,000	35,000
To Purchases	50,000	10,000	By Transfer to B	15,000	—
To Transfer from 'A'	—	15,000	By Closing Stock	25,000	3,000
To Gross Profit c/d	20,000	13,000			
	90,000	38,000		90,000	38,000
To Rent (2 : 1)	2,000	1,000	By Gross Profit b/d	20,000	13,000
To Gen. Expenses (10 : 7 Sales ratio)	588	412			
To Salary	6,000	2,000			
To Profit	11,412	9,588			
	20,000	13,000		20,000	13,000
To Stock Reserve [20% on 2,000 (2/3 of 3,000)]	—	400	By Profit (Dept. A & B) (11,410 + 9,590)	—	21,000
To Net Profit	—	20,600			
	—	21,000		—	21,000

Illustration 8

A firm has two departments—Sawmill and Furniture. Furniture is made with wood supplied by the Sawmill department at its usual selling price. From the following figures prepare Departmental Trading and Profit and Loss Account for the year ended 1978.

	Sawmill Rs.	Furniture Rs.
Opening Stock—1st Jan., 1978	1,50,000	25,000
Sales	11,00,000	2,25,000
Purchases	10,00,000	7,500
Supply to Furniture Dept.	1,50,000	—
Selling Expenses	10,000	3,000
Wages	—	30,000
Stock—31st Dec., 1978	1,00,000	30,000

The value of stocks in Furniture Department consist of 75% wood and 25% other expenses. The Sawmill Department earned gross profit at 15% in 1977. General expenses of business as a whole came to Rs. 55,000.

(*Mangalore, B.Com., Oct., 1985 & Calcutta, B.Com., Adv. Acct. Hons.,1980*)

Solution :

Departmental Trading and Profit and Loss Account

Dr. **For the year ended 31st December, 1978** Cr.

	Sawmill Rs.	Furniture Rs.		Sawmill Rs.	Furniture Rs.
To Opening Stock	1,50,000	25,000	By Sales	11,00,000	2,25,000
To Purchases	10,00,000	7,500	By Transfer to Furniture	1,50,000	—
To Wages	—	30,000	By Closing Stock	1,00,000	30,000
To Transfer from Sawmill	—	1,50,000			
To Gross Profit c/d	2,00,000	42,500			
	13,50,000	2,55,000		13,50,000	2,55,000
To Selling Expenses	10,000	3,000	By Gross Profit b/d	2,00,000	42,500
To Profit	1,90,000	39,500		—	—
	2,00,000	42,500		2,00,000	42,500

General Profit and Loss Account

Dr **For the year ended 31st Dec., 1978** Cr.

	Rs.			Rs.
To General Expenses	55,000	By Departmental Profits :		
To Stock Reserve	787	Sawmill	1,90,000	
To Net profit	1,73,713	Furniture	39,500	2,29,500
	2,29,500			2,29,500

Working Notes :

Stock Reserve is calculated as follows :

Rate of gross profit on sales $\frac{2,00,000}{12,50,000} \times 100 = 16\%$

(in Sawmill Department)

Sales amounted to Rs. 12,50,000 includes the amount of transfer to furniture department.

Share of wood in opening stock of furniture = 75% of Rs. 25,000 = Rs. 18,750

Share of wood in closing stock of furniture = 75% of Rs. 30,000 = Rs. 22,500

Reserve required for unrealized profit on closing stock = 16% of Rs. 22,500 = Rs. 3,600

Less : Reserve already made on opening stock at 15% of Rs. 18,750 = 2,813

Additional reserve to be made Rs. 787

Illustration 9

M/s Highway Garage consists of three departments— spares, service and repairs; each department being managed by a departmental manager whose commission was respectively 5%, 10% and 10% of the respective departmental profit, subject, however, to a minimum of Rs. 3,000 in each case. Inter-departmental transfers take place at a 'loaded' price as follows :

From Spares to Service 5% above cost

From Spare to Repairs 10% above cost

From Repairs to Service 10% above cost

In respect of the year ended on March 31st, 1978, the firm had already prepared and closed the Departmental Trading and Profit and Loss Account. Subsequently, it was discovered that the closing stock of departments had included inter-departmentally transferred goods at loaded price instead of the correct cost price. From the following information, prepare a statement recomputing the department profit or loss.

	Spares Rs.	Service Rs.	Repairs Rs.
Final Net Profit/Loss	19,000 (Loss)	25,200 (Profit)	36,000 (Profit)
Inter-departmental transfer included at "Loaded" price in the departmental stocks	—	32,500 (10,500 from spares and 22,000 from repairs)	2,100 (from spares)

(*B.Com., Madurai and C.A., Inter*)

Solution :

In the Books of Messrs. Highway Garage
Statement Recomputing Departmental Profit and Loss
For the year ended 31st March, 1978

Particulars	Spares Rs.	Service Rs.	Repairs Rs.
Gross Net Profit/ Loss	(–)19,000	25,200	36,000
Add : Back Commission of Departmental Manager			
(i) Minimum (due to loss)	(+)3,000	—	—
(ii) 1/9 of 25,200 = 2,800			
∴ Minimum Rs. 3,000	—	3,000	—
(iii) 1/9 of 36,000	—	—	4,000
	(–)16,000	28,200	40,000
Less : Adjustment of unrealized profit included in stock wrongly valued at loaded price			
(i) 5/105 of 10,500	(–) 500	—	—
(ii) 10/110 of 22,000	—	—	2,000
(iii) 10/110 of 2,100	(–)191	—	—
Adjusted Profit/Loss	(-)16,691	28,200	38,000
Less : Commission to Dept. Manager			
(i) Minimum	(-)3,000	—	—
(ii) Minimum	—	3,000	—
(iii) 10%	—	—	3,800
Real Net Profit/Loss	(–)19,691	25,200	34,200

Illustration 10

From the following balances of Ravi, prepare departmental Trading Account and Profit and Loss Account for the year ended 31st December, 1980 after adjusting the unrealized profit if any :

	Dept. A Rs.	Dept. B Rs.
Opening Stock	25,000	20,000
Purchases	4,50,000	7,78,000
Sales	6,40,000	9,60,000

General expenses incurred for both the departments were Rs. 75,000.

Other informations :

(a) Closing Stock of Dept. A Rs. 27,000 (including goods received from Dept. B for Rs. 9,000 at cost).

(b) Closing Stock of Dept. B Rs. 30,000 (including goods received from Dept. A for Rs. 8,000 at cost price).

(c) Opening Stock of Dept. A and B included goods of the value of Rs. 3,000 and Rs. 2,000 received from Dept. B and Dept. A respectively at cost price.

(d) The gross profit is uniform from year to year.

(*Bangalore, B.Com., 1987 & Mysore, B.Com., Oct., 1981*)

Solution :

Departmental Trading and Profit and Loss Account of Ravi
For the year ended 31st October, 1980

	Dept. A Rs.	Dept. B Rs.		Dept. A Rs.	Dept. B Rs.
To Opening Stock	25,000	20,000	By Sales	6,40,000	9,60,000
To Purchases	4,50,000	7,78,000	By Closing Stock	27,000	30,000
To Gross Profit c/d	1,92,000	1,92,000			
	6,67,000	9,90,000		6,67,000	9,90,000
To General Expenses (Sales ratio 2 : 3)	30,000	45,000	By Gross Profit b/d	1,92,000	1,92,000
To Profit (Transferred to General P& L A/c)	1,62,000	1,47,000			
	1,92,000	1,92,000		1,92,000	1,92,000

General Profit and Loss Account

Dr. **For the year ended 31st Dec., 1980** Cr.

	Rs.	Rs.		Rs.	Rs.
To Stock Reserve required :			By Departmental Profits :		
Additional stock in Dept. A			Dept. A	1,62,000	
received from Dept. B :			Dept. B	1,47,000	3,09,000
Closing Stock	9,000				
Less : Opening stock	3,000				
20% of	6,000	1,200			
To Stock in Dept. B					
received from Dept. A :					
Closing Stock	8,000				
Less : Opening Stock	2,000				
30% of	6,000	1,800			
To Net Profit		3,06,000			
		3,09,000			3,09,000

Working Notes :

(1) Stock of Department 'A' will be adjusted according to the rate applicable to Dept. B. This is :

$$\frac{1{,}92{,}000 \text{ (G/P)}}{9{,}60{,}000 \text{ (Sales)}} \times 100 = 20\%.$$

(2) Stock of Department 'B' will be adjusted according to the rate applicable to Dept. 'A'. This is :

$$\frac{1{,}92{,}000 \text{ (G/P)}}{6{,}40{,}000 \text{ (Sales)}} \times 100 = 30\%.$$

EXAMINATION QUESTIONS

(A) Answer the following questions in not exceeding 4 lines each :

(*Each Carries two Marks*)

(1) What do you mean by departments?

(2) What are departmental accounts?

(3) What do you mean by inter-departmental transfer?

(4) Mention the two objectives of departmental accounts.

(5) What are the objects of preparing the departmental accounts?

(*Kar., April, 1995*)

(6) How do you allocate the following expenses in departmental accounts?

(a) Discount received
(b) Audit fees.

(*Kar., Oct., 1995*)

(7) How do you record inter-departmental transfer of cash?

(*Kar., April, 1996*)

(8) How do you allocate the advertisement expenses in case of a departmental organization?

(*Kar., Oct., 1996*)

(9) How do you allocate the Works Manager's salary in departmental accounts?

(10) How do you allocate the labour welfare expenses in case of departmental accounts?

(11) What do you mean by inter-departmental transactions?

(*Kar., April, 1997*)

(12) How do you allocate the following expenses in departmental account:

(a) Insurance Premium on Stocks
(b) Lighting Bills.

(*Kar., April, 1998*)

(B) Answer the following question/problems :

(*Each Carries eight Marks*)

(1) What are the objects and advantages of preparing the departmental accounts?

(2) How would you allocate the various types of expenses to various departments?

(3) Explain the basis of allocation of common expenses among different departments.

(M.K.U., Oct., 1989)

(4) How would you allocate the following indirect expenses among the different departments of a departmental organisation :

(a) Depreciation (b) Insurance
(c) Lighting (d) Advertisement and
(e) Rent?

(Madras, April, 1992)

(5) How do you allocate the following expenses in departmental accounts:

(a) Salaries (b) Lighting
(c) Discount allowed (d) Rent and taxes, and
(e) Canteen expenses?

(Mysore, April, 1989)

(6) How do you allocate the following expenses between the different departments of a departmental organization :

(a) Advertisement (b) Lighting
(c) Carriage inwards (d) Discount allowed and
(e) Canteen expenses?

(Mysore, April, 1992)

(7) How do you allocate the following expenses :

(a) Director's fees (b) Canteen expenses
(c) Debt collection charges and (d) Salaries of travelling sales representatives?

(Mangalore, April, 1993)

(8) The business is carried on in three separate departments. Indirect expenses are to be apportioned in the ratio of 3:2:1 to A, B and C respectively. From the following particulars prepare the Columnar Trading and Profit and Loss Accounts of the three departments.

Particulars	A	B	C
Opening Stock	1,800	500	100
Closing Stock	2,000	500	300
Sales	11,000	5,600	4,900
Wages	2,700	1,300	900
Purchases	4,000	1,500	1,200
Salaries	900	600	400

Rent and taxes Rs. 1,200; Insurance Rs. 480; Postage Rs. 150; Bad debts : A Rs. 270, B Rs. 140 and C Rs. 220; Depreciation Rs. 600 and Printing Rs. 300.

(*Gulbarga, April, 1989*)

Ans. : Gross Profit : A Rs. 4,500; B Rs. 2,800 and C Rs. 3,000.
Net Profit : A Rs. 1,965; B Rs. 1,150 and C Rs. 1,925.

(9) The following data is obtained for the departments of a retail shop for the year ending 31st March, 1991.

	Dept. A	Dept. B
Sales	3,00,000	1,80,000
Gross Profit	90,000	54,000
Net Profit	60,000	—
Net Loss	—	16,000
Purchases	1,80,000	1,08,000

From the study of the above data, find the following :

(a) Percentage of gross profit on sales.

(b) Administrative and selling expenses of departments.

(c) Percentage of net profit on sales.

(*Adapted from My. U., B.Com.*)

Ans. : Percentage of G/P on Sales : A 30% and B 30%.
Administrative and Selling Expenses : A Rs. 30,000 and B Rs. 70,000.
Percentage of N/P on Sales : A 20% and B $8^{8}/_{9}$%.

(10) From the following information prepare the departmental trading and profit and loss account for the year ending 31-3-90.

Particulars	Dept. X	Dept. Y	Total
Opening Stock	10,000	16,000	26,000
Purchases	40,000	32,000	72,000
Wages	6,000	4,000	10,000
Sales	90,000	60,000	1,50,000
Office Salaries	—	—	48,000
Office Rent	—	—	32,000
Discount Allowed	—	—	8,800
Discount Earned	—	—	2,880
Stock of Goods on 31-3-1990	34,000	28,000	62,000

Other informations :

(a) Office staff appointed : X 10 men and Y 5 men.

(b) Area occupied : X 100 sq. ft. and Y 60 sq. ft.

(c) Depreciation on furniture of Rs. 12,000 at 10% and on machinery of Rs. 80,000 at 5% to be distributed equally between the two departments.

(d) Inter-departmental transactions: 'X' to 'Y' Rs. 16,000 is not included in the above transactions. This should be excluded for calculation of ratio.

(*Karnataka, Oct., 1992 & April, 1998*)

Ans. : Gross Profit : 'X' Rs. 84,000 and 'Y' Rs. 20,000.

Net Profit : 'X' Rs. 25,720 and Net Loss : 'Y' Rs. 12,840.

Note : Discount allowed is allocated in the net sales ratio *i.e.*, 3 : 2 and discount earned is allocated in the net purchases ratio *i.e.*, 5 : 4.

(11) A departmental stores request you to prepare its columnar trading and profit and loss account. It is not possible to ascertain the value of closing stock but the stores charges gross profit uniformly at 40% and 30% to departments X and Y respectively.

The following are the details :

	X Dept.	Y Dept.
Opening stock	30,000	28,000
Sales	1,40,000	1,20,000
Purchases	90,000	72,000
Office expenses	18,300	28,400
Selling expenses	10,400	9,200

Ans. : Gross Profit : X Rs. 56,000 (40% of 1,40,000)

Y Rs. 36,000 (30% of 1,20,000)

Net Profit : X Rs. 24,780 and Net Loss : Y Rs. 2,720

Closing Stock : X Rs. 36,000 and Y Rs. 16,000.

Note : Stock reserve at 7% of stock : 'X' Rs. 2,520 and Rs. 1,120 is debited to P&L A/c of the respective departments.

(C) Solve the following problems :

(*Each Carries 16 Marks*)

(1) From the following information prepare the departmental trading and profit and loss account for the year ending 31-12-81.

		Rs.
Opening stock	Dept. A	11,800
Opening stock	Dept. B	14,200
Purchases	Dept. A	75,900
Purchases	Dept. B	50,000
Sales	Dept. A	1,00,000
Sales	Dept. B	80,000
Purchases returns	Dept. A	900
Wages	Dept. A	9,000
Wages	Dept. B	8,000
Carriage inwards		2,500
Rent and rates		6,000
Salaries		11,600
Advertising		8,100
General expenses		5,400
Discount allowed		4,500
Discount earned		1,500
Insurance premium		600

The following additional information is also available :

(1) The departments A and B have occupied space in the ratio of 2 : 1.

(2) The closing stock of Dept. A was Rs. 21,000 and B Rs. 15,000.

(3) Salaries to be allocated equally between the departments A and B.

(Karnataka, Oct., 1982)

Ans. : Gross Profit : Dept. 'A' Rs. 23,700; Dept. 'B' Rs. 21,800
Net Profit : Dept. 'A' Rs. 4,450 ; Dept. 'B' Rs. 6,350.

Note : Advertising general expenses and discount allowed are allocated in the sales ratio (5 : 4). Carriage inwards and discount earned are allocated in the purchases ratio (3 : 2). Rent and rates are allocated in the ratio of space occupied (2 : 1). Insurance premium is allocated in the closing stock ratio (7 : 5), assuming that it is on the insurance of stock of goods.

(2) From the following particulars prepare the departmental trading and profit and loss account for the year ending 31-12-82 and balance sheet as on that date.

Trial Balance as on 31-12-1982

S. No.	Name of the Accounts	Dr. Rs.	Cr. Rs.
(1)	Plant	43,700	—
(2)	Purchases : Department A	19,574	—
	Department B	14,846	—
(3)	Wages : Department A	3,846	—
	Department B	1,946	—
(4)	Insurance (25% prepaid)	368	—
(5)	Carts and Motors	7,500	—
(6)	Sundry Expenses	2,850	—
(7)	Discount	516	—
(8)	Sales : Department A	—	53,000
	Department B	—	26,500
(9)	Bills Payable	—	341
(10)	Opening Stock : Department A	7,261	—
	Department B	6,947	—
(11)	Vehicle Expenses	360	—
(12)	Sundry Debtors	22,030	—
(13)	Sundry Creditors	—	6,620
(14)	Bad Debts	720	—
(15)	Postage	846	—
(16)	Carriage	1,500	—
(17)	Salaries	7,500	—
(18)	Capital Account	—	60,000
(19)	Provision for Doubtful Debts	—	720
(20)	Furniture	1,055	—
(21)	Stationery	3,216	—
(22)	Cash in Hand	600	—
		1,47,181	1,47,181

Apportion the expenses between the departments in their respective turnover. Depreciate plant and carts and motors at 10% each, furniture by Rs. 280. Stock on 31-12-82 was : Dept. A Rs. 9,432 and Dept. B Rs. 7,846.

(*Karnataka, Oct., 1984*)

Ans. : Gross Profit : Dept. 'A' Rs. 30,751; Dept. 'B' Rs. 10,107; Net profit : Dept. 'A' Rs. 16,295; Dept. 'B' Rs. 2,879; Balance Shcet Total Rs. 86,135.

Note : Provision for doubtful debts appearing in the trial balance is to be shown as deduction from the debtors in the balance sheet. Because there is no information in the problem regarding the creation of new provision. Hence, it is continued. All expense: are allocated in the sales ratio (*i.e.*, 2 : 1).

(3) You are given below the trial balance of Mr. Sadananda for the year ending 31-3-1979.

	Dr. Rs.	Cr. Rs.
Capital on 1-4-78	—	50,000
Drawings	10,200	—
Opening Stock : Radios	45,000	—
Watches	21,000	—
Sales : Radio	—	2,94,000
Watches	—	1,46,000
Purchases : Radios	2,25,000	—
Watches	1,15,000	—
Salaries	12,600	—
Publicity Expenses	9,000	—
Rent, Rates & Taxes	3,000	—
Commission	10,800	—
Miscellaneous Expenses	5,100	—
Furniture & Fixtures	12,300	—
Sundry Debtors	16,800	—
6% Government of India Loan	10,000	—
Sundry Creditors	—	8,800
Interest on Government Loan	—	600
Provision for Bad Debts	—	900
Cash in Hand	4,500	—
	5,00,300	5,00,300

Prepare the departmental trading and profit and loss account for the year ended 31-3-79 after considering the following :

(1) Stock on 31-3-79 : Radios Rs. 30,000 and Watches Rs. 24,000.

(2) Rs. 1,200 is to be written off from sundry debtors as bad debts and a provision for doubtful debts has to be increased thereafter to 10% or the outstanding debts.

(3) Outstanding expenses on 31-3-79 are : Publicity Rs. 1,500; Salaries Rs. 1,200 and Commission Rs. 1,800.

(4) Provide depreciation at 10% on furniture and fixtures.

(5) Revenue items are to be allocated in the ratio of 2:1 between Radio and Watches Department.

(*Karnataka, April, 1981 & 1982 Mod.*)

Ans. : Gross Profit : Radios Rs. 54,000; Watches Rs. 34,000; Net Profit : Radios Rs. 22,340; Watches Rs. 18,170.

Note : All the incomes and expenses have been allocated in the given ratio *i.e.*, 2 : 1.

(4) Trading and profit and loss account of Machine Tools Ltd., for the six months ending 31-12-78 is presented to you in the following manner :

	Rs.		Rs.
To Purchases :		By Sales :	
Machine Tools A	2,81,400	Machine Tools A	3,00,000
Loose Tools B	1,81,200	Loose Tools B	2,00,000
Watches C	1,28,800	Watches C	50,000
To Salaries & Wages	96,000	By Closing Stock :	
To Rent	21,600	Machine Tools A	1,20,200
To Sundry Expenses	22,000	Loose Tools B	40,600
To Net Profit	69,000	Watches C	89,200
	8,00,000		8,00,000

Prepare the departmental trading and profit and loss account for each of the three departments wherein machine tools, loose tools and watches are sold respectively. The following further information is available :

(1) Machine tools and loose tools are sold in the machine shop itself and the watches are sold in the show room.

(2) Salaries and wages comprise as follows :

Machine Shop ¾ and Show Room ¼. It was decided to allocate machine shop salaries and wages in the ratio of 2 : 1 between the two departments, *viz.*, Machine Tools and Loose Tools respectively.

(3) The rent of the Show Room is Rs. 1,200 p.m. The rent of Machine Shop is to be divided equally between Machine Tools and Loose Tools departments.

(4) Sundry expenses are to be allocated on the basis of the turnover of the respective departments.

(*Karnataka, Oct., 1979, Non-Sem.*)

Ans. : Gross Profit : Dept. 'A' Rs. 1,38,800; Dept. 'B' Rs. 59,400 and Dept. 'C' Rs. 10,400;

Net Profit : Dept. 'A' Rs. 71,600; Dept. 'B' Rs. 20,200 and Dept. 'C' Rs. 20,800.

Note : Allocation of Salaries & Wages : For Machine Shop Rs. 72,000 (Dept. 'A' Rs. 48,000 and Dept. 'B' Rs. 24,000) and for Show Room Rs. 24,000 (Dept. 'C' Rs. 24,000 *i.e.*, 96,000 × ¼). Allocation of Rent : For Show Room Rs. 7,200 (Dept. 'C' Rs. 1,200 × 6) and for the Machine Shop Rs. 14,400 (Dept. 'A' Rs. 7,200 and Dept.'B' Rs. 7,200). Sundry Expenses are allocated in the sales ratio (*i.e.*, 6 : 4 : 1).

(5) From the following information prepare the departmental trading and profit and loss account for the year ending 31-12-83.

		Rs.
Opening Stock	Dept. A	2,50,000
Opening Stock	Dept. B	4,00,000
Purchases	Dept. A	10,00,000
Purchases	Dept. B	8,00,000
Wages	Dept. A	1,50,000
Wages	Dept. B	1,00,000
Office Salaries		12,00,000
Office Rent		8,00,000
Discount Allowed		2,20,000
Discount Earned		72,000
Sales	Dept. A	22,50,000
Sales	Dept. B	15,00,000

Other informations :

(a) Stock of goods on 31-12-1983 : Dept. A Rs. 8,50,000 and Dept. B Rs. 7,00,000.

(b) Office staff appointed : Dept. 'A' 10 persons and Dept. 'B' 5 persons.

(c) Area occupied : Dept. 'A' 1000 sq. ft., and Dept. 'B' 600 sq. ft.

(d) Depreciation on furniture worth Rs. 3,00,000 at 10% and plant worth Rs. 20,00,000 at 5% to be distributed between the two departments equally.

(e) Inter-departmental transactions : Dept. 'A' to Dept. 'B' Rs. 4,00,000 which is not included in the above information.

(f) Exclude the Inter-departmental transactions for calculation of the ratios.

(*Gulbarga, Oct., 1984, 1987 & April, 1992 Mod.; Karnataka, April, 1986 Mod. & Bangalore, April, 1995*)

Ans. : Gross Profit : Dept. 'A' Rs. 21,00,000; Dept. 'B' Rs. 5,00,000 ; Net Profit : Dept. 'A' Rs. 7,01,500; Net Loss : Dept. 'B' Rs. 2,62,500.

Note : Allocation— Salary 10 : 5 (*i.e.*, Staff appointed); Rent 5 : 3 (*i.e.*, Area occupied); Discount allowed 3 : 2 (*i.e.*, Sales); Discount earned 5 : 4 (*i.e.*, Purchases).

(6) A business is carried on in three separate departments. Expenses not directly chargeable to any department are apportioned one half to A; three-tenths to B and one-fifth to C. From the following particulars, prepare Trading and Profit and Loss Accounts of three departments (in columnar form).

Particulars	A	B	C	Total
Opening Stock	1,782	560	125	2,467
Closing Stock	1,936	471	316	2,723
Outside Purchases	4,041	1,537	1,256	6,834
Outside Sales	11,174	5,613	4,851	21,638
Salaries	945	572	416	1,933
Bad Debts	276	143	224	643
Wages	2,740	1,328	915	4,983
Management Salaries				1,200
Rent, Rates, Taxes				1,460
Insurance				210
Expenses of Van etc.				870
Postage and Telegrams				110
Sundry Expenses				530
Depreciation Written off				740
Stationery and Printing				260
Advertising				450

Inter-departmental Sales :

A to B— Rs. 904 and A to C— Rs. 482
B to A—Rs. 1,126 and B to C—Rs. 219
C to A—Rs. 348 and C to B—Rs. 100

(*Bombay University & Mangalore University*)

Ans. : Gross Profit : Dept. 'A' Rs. 4,459; Dept 'B' Rs. 3,000 and 'C' Rs. 2,618; Net Profit : Dept. 'A' Rs. 323; 'B' Rs. 536 and 'C'Rs. 812.

Note : Inter-department Sales : Dept. 'A' Rs. 1,386; 'B' Rs.1,345 & 'C' Rs. 448; Inter-department Purchases : Dept. 'A' Rs. 1,474; 'B' Rs. 1,004 & 'C' Rs. 701.
Indirect expenses are allocated in the ratio of 5 : 3 : 2.

(7) A firm had two departments—cloth and readymade clothes. Cloth were made by firm itself out of cloth supplied by the cloth department at its usual selling price, which is 20% above the cost. From the following figures prepare departmental Trading and Profit and Loss account for the year 1985.

	Cloth Department Rs.	Readymade Clothes Dept. Rs.
Opening Stock on 1st Jan., 1985	3,00,000	48,000
Purchases	20,00,000	15,000
Sales	22,00,000	5,00,000
Transfer to Readymade Clothes Department	3,60,000	—
Stock on 31st Dec., 1985	2,00,000	60,000
Expenses of Manufacturing and Selling	20,000	6,000

During the year the firm has incurred the following expenses :

General Expenses	Rs. 1,35,000
Building Rent	Rs. 2,400

Divide the General Expenses on the basis of turnover and charge rent in the ratio of 2 : 1 to the Cloth and Readymade Clothes department respectively.

(K.U., April, 1989 & Bombay, B.Com)

Ans . : Gross Profit : Dept. 'A' Rs. 4,40,000; Dept. 'B' Rs. 1,31,000; Net Profit : Dept 'A' Rs. 3,28,400; Dept. 'B' Rs. 1,05,200.

Note : Stock Reserve Rs. 1,200 and sales ratio 22 : 5.

(8) Jule, the proprietor of a departmental store, decided to calculate separate profit for his first two departments X and Y for the month ending 31st January, 1989. Stock on 31st January could not be valued for certain unavoidable reasons but his rates of gross profit (calculated without reference to direct expenses) on sales for the two departments are 40 per cent and 30 per cent.

The following figures are given :

	Dept. X Rs.	Dept. Y Rs.
Stock on 1 Jan., 1989	9,000	8,400
Sales	42,000	36,000
Purchases	27,000	21,600
Direct Expenses	5,490	8,520

Indirect expenses for the whole business (containing five departments) are Rs. 10,800 which are to be charged in proportion to departmental sales, except as to one-sixth, which is to be divided equally. Sales for remaining three departments were Rs. 1,02,000.

Prepare a statement showing profit for the two departments.

(*Adapted from B.Com., Bangalore*)

Ans. : Gross Profit : Dept. 'X' Rs. 16,800; Dept. 'Y' Rs. 10,800; Closing Stock: Dept. 'X' Rs.10,800; Dept. 'Y' Rs. 4,800; Net Profit : Dept. 'X' Rs. 8,850; Dept. 'Y' Rs. 120.

Note : Allocation of Indirect Expenses :

(1) 1/6th to be charged equally for five Depts. Rs. 1,800
For each department is 1,800/5 Rs. 360

(2) Remaining Rs. 9,000 is allocated to X Dept. Rs. 2,100 (42,000/1,80,000); 'Y' Dept. Rs. 1,800 (36,000/1,80,000); & Other three Depts. Rs. 5,100 (1,02,000/1,80,000).

(9) Complex Limited had three departments A, B and C. The following information is provided.

	A	B	C
	Rs.	Rs.	Rs.
Opening Stock	3,000	4,000	6,000
Direct Material	8,000	12,000	—
Wages	5,000	10,000	—
Closing Stock	4,000	14,000	8,000
Sales	—	—	34,000

Stocks of each department are valued at cost to the department concerned. Stocks of A department are transferred to B at a margin of 50% above departmental cost. Stocks of B department are transferred to C department at a margin of 10% above departmental cost.

Other expenses were :

	Rs.
Salaries	2,000
Printing and Stationery	1,000
Rent	6,000
Interest Paid	4,000
Depreciation	3,000

Allocate expenses in the ratio of departmental gross profit. Opening figure of reserves for unrealized profit and departmental stocks were :

Department B Rs. 1,000
Department C Rs. 2,000

Prepare departmental trading and profit and loss account.

[*C.A.* (*Inter*), *Nov., 1984*]

Ans. : Gross Profit : Dept 'A' Rs. 6,000 ; Dept. 'B' Rs. 3,000 & Dept. 'C' Rs. 3,000; Net Loss Rs. 4,918; Internal transfer to Dept.'B' Rs. 18,000 and to Dept. 'C' Rs. 33,000; Reserve for unrealized profit on closing stock Rs. 3,918 and opening reserve for unrealized profit on stock Rs. 3,000

(10) A firm had two departments, cloth and readymade clothes. The readymade clothes were made by the firm itself out of cloth supplied by the cloth department at its usual selling price. From the following figures, prepare Departmental Trading and Profit and Loss Account for the year 1984.

	Cloth Department Rs.	Readymade Clothes Dept. Rs.
Opening stock on 1-1-1984	3,00,000	50,000
Purchases	20,00,000	15,000
Sales	22,00,000	4,50,000
Transfer to Readymade Clothes		
Department : Expenses—Manufacturing	—	60,000
Selling	20,000	6,000
Stock on 31-12-1984	2,00,000	60,000

The stock in the readymade clothes department may be considered as consisting of 75% cloth and 25% other expenses. The cloth department earned gross profit at the rate of 15% in 1983. General expenses of the business as a whole came to Rs. 1,10,000.

(*Adapted from Mangalore University, Oct., 1985 & B.Com., Bharatidasan, April, 1981*)

Ans. : Gross Profit : Cloth Dept. Rs. 4,00,000 and Readymade Clothes Dept. Rs. 85,000. Net Profit : Cloth Dept. Rs. 3,80,000 and Readymade Clothes Dept. Rs. 79,000.

(11) The Directors of Departmental Stores Ltd. wish to ascertain approximately, the net profits of the departments 'A', 'B' and 'C', separately for the four months ended April 30th, 1983. It is found impracticable actually to take stock on that date but an adequate system of departmental accounting is in use and the normal rates of gross profit for the departments concerned are 40%, 30% and 20% on turnover respectively. Indirect expenses are charged in proportion to Departmental turnover.

The following are the figures for the each Department :

Particulars	A	B	C	Total
Stock (1-1-1973)	6,000	7,000	3,000	16,000
Purchases for four months	7,000	6,500	4,700	18,300
Sales for four months	12,000	10,000	6,000	28,000
Direct expenses	2,020	1,450	710	4,180

The total indirect expenses for period (including those relating to other departments) were Rs. 4,200 on total sales of Rs. 84,000.

Prepare Departmental Trading and Profit and Loss Accounts (for the Directors) making a Stock Reserve of 10% for each department, on the estimated value on April 30th.

(*Adapted from C.A. & K.U.D., April, 1994*)

Ans. : Gross Profit : Dept. 'A' Rs. 4,800; 'B' Rs. 3,000 and 'C' Rs. 1,200; Net Profit : Dept. 'A' Rs. 1,600; 'B' Rs. 400 & 'C' Rs. 100; Closing Stock : Dept. 'A' 5,800; 'B' Rs. 6,500 & 'C' Rs. 2,900; Indirect Expenses : Dept. 'A' Rs. 600; 'B' Rs. 500 & 'C' Rs. 300; Stock Reserve : Dept. 'A' Rs. 580; 'B' Rs. 650 & 'C' Rs. 290.

(12) The following balances were extracted from the books of Vijay Shankar. You are required to prepare departmental trading account and profit and loss account for the year ended 31st December, 1989, after adjusting the unrealized department profit if any :

	Dept. A Rs.	Dept. B Rs.
Opening Stock	50,000	40,000
Purchases	6,50,000	9,10,000
Sales	10,00,000	15,00,000

General expenses incurred for both the departments were Rs. 1,25,000 and you are also supplied with the following information : (a) Closing Stock of Department A Rs. 1,00,000 including goods from Department B for Rs. 2,00,000 including goods from Department A for Rs. 30,000 at cost to Department B. (b) Opening stock of Department A and Department B include goods of the value of Rs. 10,000 and Rs. 15,000 taken from Department B and Department A respectively at cost to transferee departments. (c) The goods profit is uniform from year to year.

(*Institute of Company Secretaries, Final, 1971 and B.Sc., Madras, April, 1984*)

Ans. : Gross Profit : Dept. 'A' Rs. 4,00,000 & Dept. 'B' Rs. 7,50,000; Net Profit Rs. 10,14,000; Stock Reserve : Dept. 'A' Rs. 5,000 (*i.e.*, 50% of 20,000 – 10,000) and Dept. 'B' Rs. 6,000 (*i.e.*, 40% of Rs. 30,000 – 15,000).

(13) From the following particulars prepare the departmental trading and profit and loss account for the year ending 31-12-1980.

Trial balance as on 31-12-1980

S. No.	Name of the Accounts		Dr. Rs.	Cr. Rs.
(1)	Plant		40,700	—
(2)	Purchases :	Department A	19,500	—
		Department B	14,800	—
(3)	Wages :	Department A	3,800	—
		Department B	1,900	—
(4)	Insurance		400	—
(5)	Motor Vehicles		10,000	—
(6)	Sundry expenses		2,800	—
(7)	Discount		500	—
(8)	Sales :	Department A	—	55,000
		Department B	—	50,000
(9)	Bills Payable		—	1,000
(10)	Sundry Creditors		—	8,000
(11)	Opening Stock :	Department A	8,000	—
		Department B	7,000	—
(12)	Vehicle Expenses		400	—
(13)	Sundry Debtors		20,000	—
(14)	Bad Debts		700	—
(15)	Postage & Telegrams		800	—
(16)	Carriage on Sales		2,000	—
(17)	Salaries		8,000	—
(18)	Furniture		2,000	—
(19)	Stationery		4,000	—
(20)	Capital		—	60,000
(21)	Cash in Hand		6,700	—
(22)	Land & Building		20,000	—
			1,74,000	1,74,000

Apportion all the revenue expenses equally between both the departments. Depreciate plant at 10% and furniture by 5%. Stock on 31-12-1980 was : Department A Rs. 9,000 and Department B Rs. 7,000.

(*Karnataka, April, 1991*)

Ans. : Gross Profit : Dept. A—Rs. 32,700, Dept. B—Rs. 33,300; Net Profit : Dept. A—Rs. 20,815; Dept. B—Rs. 21,415; Balance Sheet Total Rs. 1,11,230.

(14) From the following particulars prepare the accounts to disclose the total and individual profits of the two departments A and B of Bangalore:

Debit Balance		Rs.	Credit Balances		Rs.
Opening Stock :	A	1,52,000	Sales :	A	10,00,000
	B	1,08,000		B	8,00,000
Purchases :	A	7,51,000	Discount Earned		14,300
	B	6,98,000			
Carriage Inwards		28,600			
Salaries :	A	90,000			
	B	85,000			
General Salaries		1,16,000			
Rent and Rates		60,000			
Advertising		81,000			
General Expenses		54,000			
Discount Allowed		18,000			
Accounting Charges		5,000			

The following additional information is available :

(a) Goods transferred from department A to B Rs. 50,000. This has not been recorded.

(b) General Salaries are to be allocated equally.

(c) The departments A and B have occupied the space in the ratio of 3:2.

(d) Closing Stock was : Department A Rs. 1,78,000 and Department B Rs. 1,50,000.

(*Gulbarga, Oct., 1992*)

Ans. : Gross Profit : A Rs. 3,10,177 and B Rs. 80,223; Net Profit : A Rs. 46,089 and Net Loss : B Rs. 1,50,389.

Hint : (1) Ratio and Allocation : General salaries 1 : 1; rent and rates 3 : 2; advertising general expenses and discount allowed 5 : 4; accounting charges 1 : 1; carriage inwards : A Rs. 14,823 and B Rs. 13,777; discount earned : A Rs. 7,412 and B Rs. 6,888.

(2) Inter-departmental transfers Rs. 50,000 are debited to B and credited to A.

(15) From the following information prepare the departmental trading and profit and loss account (in columnar form) for the year ending 30-9-1991.

	P Rs.	Q Rs.	R Rs.
(1) Department-wise :			
Stock on 1-10-1990	17,000	14,500	6,800
Stock on 30-9-91	16,740	12,050	13,000
Purchases	35,000	30,000	25,000
Sales	60,000	50,000	40,000
(2) Common for departments :			
Salaries			10,500
Rent			9,000
Discount allowed			2,400
Discount earned			3,600
Carriage inwards			10,800
Manager's salary			15,000

Inter-departmental transfer of goods : P to Q Rs. 4,800. P to R Rs. 1,400 and Q to R Rs. 3,200.

Cost of service rendered by department : P to R Rs. 1,600.

(3) Other informations :

(a) Departments P & R are on the first floor occupying equal area and department R is on the ground floor.

(b) Salaries are for ground floor 1/3 and for first floor 2/3.

(c) Number of employees in the first floor P : 4 and Q : 3.

(d) The rent of department R is Rs. 400 per month.

(*Karnataka, Oct., 1993*)

Ans.: Gross Profit : P – Rs. 26,740; Q – Rs. 12,350 & R – Rs. 13,600; Net Profit : P – Rs. 17,680 & Q – Rs. 2,650; Net Loss : R – Rs. 940.

Hint : (1) Ratio and Allocation : Purchases ratio : 7 : 6 : 5; Sales ratio 6 : 5 : 4; Manager's Salary 1 : 1 : 1; Staff salary : P – Rs. 4,000 & Q – Rs. 3,000 Rent : P – Rs. 2,100 and Q – Rs. 2,100.

(2) Inter-departmental transfer of goods: Debit to Q – Rs. 4,800 and to R – Rs. 1,400 + 3,200; Credit to P – Rs. 4,800 +1,400 and to Q – Rs. 3,200.

(3) Service rendered is debited to R and credited to P – Rs. 1,600 in the profit and loss account.

(16) You are given below the trial balance of Mr. Gururaj as at 31-3-1993.

Name of Accounts		Dr.	Cr.
Capital on 1-4-1992		—	1,00,000
Drawings		20,400	—
Opening Stock :	Radios	90,000	—
	Watches	42,000	—
Sales :	Radios	—	5,88,000
	Watches	—	2,92,000
Purchases :	Radios	4,50,000	—
	Watches	2,30,000	—
Salaries		25,200	—
Publicity Expenses		18,000	—
Rent, Rates & Taxes		6,000	—
Commission		21,600	—
Miscellaneous Expenses		10,200	—
Furniture		24,600	—
Sundry Debtors		33,600	—
6% Government of India Loan		20,000	—
Sundry Creditors		—	17,600
Interest on Government Loan		—	1,200
Provision for Bad Debts		—	1,800
Cash on Hand		9,000	—
		10,00,600	10,00,600

Prepare the trading and profit and loss account for the year ended 31-3-1993 after considering the following :

(1) Stock on 31-3-1993 : Radios Rs. 60,000 and Watches Rs. 48,000.

(2) Rs. 2,400 is to be written off from debtors as bad debts and a provision for doubtful debts has to be made at 10% on the debtors.

(3) Outstanding expenses on 31-3-1993 are : Publicity Rs. 3,000, Salaries Rs. 2,400 and Commission Rs. 3,600.

(4) Provide depreciation at 10% on furniture.

(5) Revenue items are to be allocated in the ratio of 2 : 1 between Radios and Watches departments.

(*Gulbarga, Oct., 1994*)

Ans. : Gross Profit : Radios Rs.1,08,000 and Watches Rs. 68,000, Net Profit : Radios Rs. 44,680 and Watches Rs. 36,340.

(17) Wholesales Traders Ltd. Deals in 3 departments of merchandise. The balances of accounts as at 31-12-1990 are as follows :

	Rs.		Rs.
Share Capital :		Salaries	54,000
50,000 Shares of Rs.10 each	5,00,000	Carriage	12,600
6% Debentures	3,00,000	Travelling expenses	6,300
Stock 1-1-1990		Advertisement	8,100
Dept. I	70,000	Printing and stationery	13,500
Dept. II	40,000	Rates and taxes	1,800
Dept. III	60,000	General charges	36,900
Purchases :		Debenture interest up to	
Dept. I	14,10,000	30-6-1990	9,000
Dept. II	7,00,000	Sundry creditors	1,01,000
Dept. III	10,50,000	Bills receivable	2,80,000
Sales :		Sundry debtors	2,66,000
Dept. I	18,60,000	Bills payable	30,000
Dept. II	9,15,000	General reserve	1,45,000
Dept. III	13,80,000	Goodwill	90,000
Wages :		Land and buildings	1,80,000
Dept. I	2,80,000	Profit and Loss	
Dept. II	1,30,000	Accounts (Cr.)	24,000
Dept. III	2,10,000		
Motor Lorries	1,30,000		
Furniture and Fixtures	72,000		
Bank	1,44,800		

Adjustments :

Bad Debts Rs. 2,000, Bills Receivable—Bad Rs. 1,600. Closing Stock : Dept. I —Rs. 60,000, Dept. II —Rs. 50,000, Dept. III —Rs. 65,000.

Depreciate Land and Building by 2½%; Furniture and Fixtures by 10%; Motor Lorries by 25%. Allocate depreciation on motor lorries in the ratio of 2 : 1 : 1 and the other expenses in the ratio of the total of opening stock and purchases of each department.

Prepare the departmental Profit and Loss Account in a columnar form for the year ended 31st December, 1990 and the Balance Sheet on that date in the prescribed form.

(Bangalore, Oct., 1991)

Ans. : Gross Profit : Dept. I – Rs. 1,54,400; Dept. II – Rs. 92,200 and Dept. III – Rs. 1,20,800;

Net Profit : Dept. I – Rs. 69,750; Dept. II – Rs. 49,875 and Dept. III – Rs. 61,375.

Notes : (i) Other expenses (*i.e.*, other than depreciation on motor lorries) are allocated in the ratio of 4 : 2 : 3 (*i.e.*, 14,80,000 : 7,40,000 : 11,10,000).

(ii) Debenture interest including outstanding debenture interest is Rs. 18,000 (9,000 + 9,000).

(18) A departmental stores and two departments A and B. Usually, B Dept. secures the required goods from A Dept. at selling price. The following details are given on 31-3-1991.

	Dept. A Rs.	Dept. B Rs.
Stock on 1-4-1990	20,000	—
Purchases from outside	50,000	10,000
Sales	50,000	35,000
Salaries, etc.	6,000	2,000
Goods supplied by Dept. A to Dept. B	15,000	—
Stock on 31-3-1991	25,000	3,000

Other expenses were : rent Rs. 3,000 and general expenses Rs. 1,000

Space occupied : A Dept.—2/3 and B Dept.—1/3

Number of workers : Dept. A—20 men and Dept. B—14 men.

Use the basis of number of workers for distribution of general expenses. It is estimated that 2/3 of the closing stock of Dept. B is a part of the goods received from Dept. A.

From the above particulars, prepare the Departmental Trading and Profit and Loss Account and the General Profit and Loss Account.

(*Bangalore, Oct., 1992*)

Ans. : Gross Profit : Dept. A Rs. 20,000 and Dept. B Rs. 13,000.
Net Profit carried to General Profit and Loss Account :
Dept. A Rs. 11,412 and Dept. B Rs. 9,588.

Stock reserve Rs. 800 $\left(3{,}000 \times \frac{2}{3} = 2{,}000;\ 2{,}000 \times \frac{40}{100}\right)$

Gross Rate 40% (100 × 20,000/50,000) and Final Net Profit Rs. 20,200.

Note : Rent is allocated in the ratio of space occupied (2 : 1) and general expenses are allocated in the ratio of number of workers (10 : 7).

(19) A firm has two departments A and B. During the trading period ending 31-3-1995, the requisite figures were as follows :

Particulars	Dept. A Rs.	Dept. B Rs.	Total Rs.
Opening stock	5,000	7,000	12,000
Purchases	42,000	52,000	94,000
Sales	80,000	93,000	1,73,000
Purchases returns	2,000	2,000	4,000
Sales returns	2,000	2,000	4,000
Closing stock	6,000	8,000	14,000
Carriage inwards	—	—	4,500
Wages	5,000	6,000	11,000
Discount received	—	—	1,800
Carriage outwards	—	—	1,300
Salaries	10,000	13,000	23,000
General salaries	—	—	13,000
Rent, rates, taxes	—	—	5,000
Discount allowed	—	—	1,300
Sundry expenses	—	—	2,600

Prepare Trading and Profit and Loss A/c in tabular form assuming that :

(1) Rent, rates and taxes are pertaining to business premises which are occupied by the two departments equally.

(2) Depreciation at 10% is to be charged on machinery costing Rs. 60,000 which is used by the two departments in 2 : 1 ratio.

(*Bangalore, Oct., 1995*)

Ans. : Gross Profit : Dept. A – Rs. 32,000 and Dept. B – Rs. 33,500.
Net Profit : Dept. A – Rs. 7,900 and Dept. B – Rs. 7,200.

Notes : (i) Carriage inwards and discount received are apportioned in the net purchases ratio of 4 : 5.

(ii) General salaries, sundry expenses, carriage outwards and discount allowed are apportioned in the net sales ratio of 6 : 7.

(20) The following particulars are taken from the books of a departmental Stores:

Particulars	Dept. A Rs.	Dept. B Rs.	Dept. C Rs.
Purchases	1,00,000	1,50,000	4,00,000
Returns outwards	10,000	5,000	15,000
Sales	3,05,000	6,10,000	9,15,000
Returns inwards	5,000	10,000	15,000
Wages	20,000	30,000	40,000
Opening stock	25,000	35,000	5,000
Closing stock	40,000	25,000	20,000

(a) Inter-departmental transfers :

From A to B Rs. 5,000 and C Rs. 10,000

From B to A Rs. 2,500 and C Rs. 5,000

From C to A Rs. 3,500 and B Rs. 4,500.

(b) The following expenses are to be allocated equally :

Telephone Rs. 1,500, Insurance Rs. 3,000 and Salaries Rs. 4,500.

(c) Rent Rs. 12,000 to be divided among the departments A, B and C in the ratio of 1 : 1 : 2.

(d) Other expenses :

Discount Rs. 9,000, Bad debts Rs. 6,000, Income tax Rs. 30,000 and legal charges Rs. 10,000. Income tax and legal expenses cannot conveniently be allocated.

Prepare the Columnar Trading and Profit and Loss Account.

(*Karnataka, April, 1996*)

Ans. : Gross Profit : A – Rs. 2,14,000; B – Rs. 4,13,000 and C – Rs. 4,83,000.

Net Profit : A – Rs. 2,05,500; B – Rs. 4,02,000 and C – Rs. 4,66,500.

13

COMPANY ACCOUNTS–I

(Redemption of Preference Shares and Issue of Bonus Shares)

Redemption of Preference Shares

Meaning : The process of repayment of redeemable preference shares to the preference shareholders either at the option of the company or after the expiry of the stipulated period is called 'redemption of preference shares'. According to Section 80 of the Indian Companies Act, 1956, those preference shares which can be redeemed after a specified period or at the discretion of the company are called 'redeemable preference shares'.

Legal Provisions : When the Company has issued the redeemable preference shares, they are to be redeemed after the expiry of a fixed period of time. However, these shares are to be redeemed subject to the following conditions laid down by the Companies Act :

(1) Such shares cannot be redeemed unless they are fully paid up. In other words, partly paid preference shares cannot be redeemed, only fully paid up preference shares are to be redeemed.

(2) Such shares can be redeemed at par or at a premium, but not at a discount.

(3) Such shares can be redeemed (i) out of profits available for dividends and/or (ii) out of proceeds of fresh issue of equity or preference shares (but not out of debentures).

(4) Such shares can also be redeemed partly out of divisible profits and partly by the proceeds of fresh issue of shares.

(5) If such shares are redeemed out of divisible profits, a sum equal to the face value or nominal value of such shares must be transferred to 'Capital Redemption Reserve Account'.

(6) If such shares are redeemed at a premium, such premium is adjusted against either Profit and Loss Account or Shares Premium Account as the case may be.

(7) The Capital Redemption Reserve Account can only be utilised for the purpose of issuing fully paid bonus shares (partly paid bonus shares cannot be made out of Capital Redemption Reserve A/c).

(8) Such shares must be redeemed within one month from the date of issue of fresh shares, otherwise the new issue will be subject to capital duty.

(9) Particulars of shares redeemed must be notified to the Registrar within one month thereafter.

(10) It must be remembered that the redemption of preference shares shall not be considered as a reduction of its authorised share capital.

If any officer of the company failed to comply the provisions of this section, will be furnished with a fine which may be extended up to Rs. 1,000.

Sometimes, some of the assets of the company may be sold to raise the funds for the purpose of redemption of preference shares. When the assets are sold at the time of redemption of preferance shares and if there is any profit or loss on the sale of such assets, it should be transferred to the Profit and Loss Account and after the transfer such profit or loss to the Profit and Loss Account, the balance remained in the Profit and Loss Account should be considered as the divisible profit.

Sometimes, some fresh issue of debentures is made at the time of redemption of preference shares, but the proceeds of such fresh issue of debentures are not taken into account for the purpose of determining the amount of transfer to be made from the divisible profits to the capital redemption reserve. However, an entry should be passed in the books of the company for the fresh issue of debentures made.

Accounting Entries

Following are the journal entries to be passed in connection with the redemption of preference shares.

(1) Entries for the fresh issue of shares (whether equity or preference) :

(a) If the fresh issue of shares is made at par :

Bank Account	Dr.	With the amount received
To Equity/Pref. Share Capital A/c		

(b) If the fresh (i.e., new) issue of shares is made at a premium :

Bank Account	Dr.	With the amount received
To Equity/Pref. Share Capital A/c		With nominal value
To Share Premium A/c		With amount of premium

(c) If the fresh issue of shares is made at a discount :

Bank Account	Dr.	With the amount received
Share Discount Account	Dr.	With the amount of discount
To Equity/Pref. Share Capital A/c		With nominal value

(2) Entries for the fresh (i.e., new) issue of debentures :

(a) If the fresh issue of debentures is made at par :

Bank Account	Dr.	With the amount received
To Debentures' A/c		

(b) If the fresh issue of debentures is made at a premium :

Bank Account	Dr.	With the amount received
To Debentures' A/c		With nominal value
To Debentures' Premium A/c		With the amount of premium

(c) If the fresh issue of debentures is made at a discount :

Bank Account	Dr.	With the amount received
Debentures' Discount Account	Dr.	With the amount of discount
To Debentures' A/c		With nominal value

(3) Entries for the sale of any asset :

(a) If the assets are sold at cost price or book value :

Bank Account	Dr.	With the amount received on sale
To Respective Assets A/c		

(b) If the asset is sold at a profit :

Bank Account	Dr.	With the amount realised
To Respective Asset A/c		With cost price of an asset
To Profit and Loss A/c		With the amount of profit

(c) If the asset is sold at a loss :

Bank Account	Dr.	With the amount received
Profit and Loss A/c.	Dr.	With the amount of loss
To Respective Asset A/c		With cost price of an asset

(4) Entry for the transfer of divisible profits to the Capital Redemption Reserve Account :

If the redeemable preference shares are redeemed out of divisible profits, an amount equal to the nominal value of shares so redeemed should be transferred from any of the divisible profits to the capital redemption reserve account. The entry for the transfer of divisible profits to the capital redemption reserve account will be :

Any of the Divisible Profits A/c	Dr.	With the total amount of
Or Profit and Loss Account	Dr.	redeemable Pref. shares
Or General Reserve Account	Dr.	With nominal value
Or Any Revenue Reserve A/c	Dr.	With premium amount
To Capital Redemption Reserve A/c		
To Share Premium Account (if Any)		

(5) Entries for redemption of preference shares at par and at a premium out of divisible profits or fresh issue of shares (whether equity or preference) :

(a) When the redeemable preference shares are redeemed at par :

(i) *Entry for the transfer of Redeemable Pref. Share Capital to Redeemable Pref. Shareholders' Account :*

Redeemable Pref. Share Capital A/c	Dr.	With the amount equal
To Redeemable Pref. Shareholders' A/c		to the nominal value

(ii) *Entry for the actual payment of the Redeemable Preference Shareholders :*

Redeemable Pref. Shareholders' A/c	Dr.	With the amount paid
To Bank or Cash A/c		to shareholders

If the redeemable preference share capital is paid directly to the shareholders, only the following one entry is to be passed instead of the above two entries [(*i.e.*, (i) & (ii)].

Redeemable Pref. Share Capital A/c	Dr.	With the amount paid
To Bank or Cash A/c		to shareholders

(b) When the Redeemable Preference Shares are redeemed at a premium :

(i) *Entry for the transfer of Redeemable Pref. Share Capital to Redeemable Pref. Shareholders' Account :*

Redeemable Pref. Share Capital A/c	Dr.	With nominal value
Premium on Redemption Pref. Shares' A/c	Dr.	With the amount of premium
To Redeemable Pref. Shareholders' A/c		With the amount paid

(ii) *Entry for the payment of Redeemable Preference Shareholders :*

Redeemable Pref. Shareholders' A/c	Dr.	With the amount paid
To Bank or Cash A/c		to shareholders

If the redeemable preference share capital is paid directly to the shareholders, only the following one entry is to be passed instead of the above two entries [*i.e.*, (i) and (ii)].

Redeemable Pref. Shareholders' A/c	Dr.	With the amount paid
To Bank A/c		to shareholders

(6) Entry for the adjustment of premium payable on redemption of preference shares (if any):

Share Premium A/c	Dr.	With the amount of
Or Profit and Loss A/c	Dr.	premium payable on
To Premium on Redemption of Pref. Shares' A/c		redemption.

(7) Entry for the issue of bonus shares out of Capital Redemption Reserve :

(a) *Entry for the issue of bonus shares :*

Capital Redemption Reserve A/c Dr. } With the amount of bonus
To Bonus to Shareholders' A/c } shares issued

(b) *Entry for transferring the bonus account :*

Bonus to Shareholders' A/c Dr. } With the amount of bonus
To Share Capital Account } share issued

Illustration 1

X Co. Ltd. has 1,000 redeemable preference shares of Rs. 100 each fully paid. The shares have now become ready for redemption. It is decided that the whole amount will be redeemed out of fresh issue of equal amount of equity shares of Rs. 10 each.

Show the necessary journal entries, if all the shares are redeemed (a) at par and (b) at 5% premium.

Solution :

Journal Entries

S. No.	Particulars	L.F.	Dr. Rs.	Cr. Rs.
(a)	**If the shares are redeemed at par :**			
1.	Bank Account Dr.		1,00,000	
	To Equity Share Capital A/c			1,00,000
	(Being the issue of 10,000 equity shares of Rs. 10 each for cash)			
2.	Redeemable Pref. Share Capital A/c Dr.		1,00,000	
	To Redeemable Pref. Shareholders' A/c			1,00,000
	(Being the amount payable to the preference shareholders on redemption)			
3.	Redeemable Pref. Shareholders' A/c Dr.		1,00,000	
	To Bank Account			1,00,000
	(Being the amount paid to shareholders)			
(b)	**If the shares are redeemed at a premium:**			
1.	Bank Account Dr.		1,00,000	
	To Equity Share Capital A/c			1,00,000
	(Being the issue of 10,000 equity shares of Rs. 10 each for cash)			

(Contd.)

Journal Entries (*Contd.*)

2.	Redeemable Pref. Share Capital A/c Dr. Premium on redemption of Pref. Shares' A/c Dr. To Redeemable Pref. Shareholders' A/c (Being the amount payable to the shareholders)		1,00,000 5,000	1,05,000
3.	Profit and Loss Account Dr. To Premium on Redemp. of Pref. Shares' A/c (Being the transfer of requisite amount from P & L A/c to provide premium of 5%)		5,000	5,000
4.	Redeemable Pref. Shareholders' A/c Dr. To Bank Account (Being the amount paid to pref. shareholders on redemption)		1,05,000	1,05,000

Illustration 2

Shrinivas Motor Ltd. issued 3,000, 8% redeemable preference shares of Rs. 10 each, all of which were taken up and fully paid. The company decided to redeem the shares out of accumulated profits. Record the necessary journal entries in the books of the company, if all the shares are redeemed, at par and at a premium of 5%.

Solution :

Journal Entries

Sl. No.	Particulars	L.F.	Dr. Rs.	Cr. Rs.
(a)	**If the shares are redeemed at par :**			
1.	Profit and Loss Account Dr. To Capital Redemption Reserve A/c (Being the transfer of requisite amount from P & L A/c to reserve)		30,000	30,000
2.	8% Redeemable Pref. Share Capital A/c Dr. To Redeemable Pref. Shareholders' A/c (Being the amount payable to the preference shareholders on redemption)		30,000	30,000
3.	Redeemable Pref. Shareholders' A/c Dr. To Bank Account (Being the amount paid to the pref. shareholders)		30,000	30,000

(*Contd.*)

Journal Entries (*Contd.*)

(b)	**If the shares are redeemed at premium :**			
1.	Profit and Loss Account Dr.		31,500	
	To Premium on Redemption of Pref. Shares' A/c			1,500
	To Capital Redemption Reserve A/c			30,000
	(Being the transfer of requisite amount from P & L A/c to reserve account to provide 5% Premium and nominal value of shares)			
2.	8% Redeemable Pref. Share Capital A/c Dr.		30,000	
	Premium on Redemption of Pref. Shares' A/c Dr.		1,500	
	To Redeemable Pref. Shareholders' A/c			31,500
	(Being the amount payable to the pref. shareholders on redemption)			
3.	Redeemable Pref. Shareholders' A/c Dr.		31,500	
	To Bank Account			31,500
	(Being the amount paid to pref. shareholders)			

Illustration 3

The following balances are appearing in the Ledger of the Company on 31st December, 1995.

Share Capital : Equity shares (fully paid up)	3,50,000
Preference shares (fully paid)	1,25,000
Share Premium Account	20,000
General Reserve	80,000
Profit and Loss Account (Cr. Balance)	45,000

The company is decided to redeem the preference shares at a premium of 4% out of its general reserve and undistributed profit.

Pass the journal entries relating to the redemption of preference shares.

Solution :

Journal Entries

S.No.	Particulars	LF	Dr. Rs.	Cr. Rs.
1.	Preference Share Capital Account Dr.		1,25,000	
	Premium on Redemption of Pref. Shares A/c Dr.		5,000	
	To Preference Shareholders' Account			1,30,000
	(Being amount due to the preference shareholders on redemption at a premium of 4%)			
2.	Share Premium Account Dr.		5,000	
	To Premium on Redemption of Pref. Shares A/c			5,000
	(Being the transfer of the requisite amount from share premium account to provide 4% premium)			
3.	General Reserve Account Dr.		80,000	
	Profit and Loss Account Dr.		45,000	
	To Capital Redemption Reserve A/c			1,25,000
	(Being the transfer of the requisite amount to capital redemption reserve account)			
4.	Preference Shareholders' Account Dr.		1,30,000	
	To Bank Account			1,30,000
	(Being the amount paid to the pref. shareholders)			

Illustration 4

The under noted balances were extracted from the ledger of Zee Ltd. :

		Rs.
(1)	100 Redeemable Cumulative Preference Shares :	
	10,000 Shares of Rs. 100 each, fully called up	10,00,000
	Less : Calls unpaid at Rs. 25 per share	5,000
	Amount paid up	9,95,000
(2)	Share Premium Account	1,40,000
(3)	Development Rebate Reserve	5,00,000
(4)	General Reserve	3,40,000
(5)	Proposed Dividend since sanctioned on cumulative preference shares	78,400

The directors redeemed the preference shares at a premium of 10% and for that purpose, made a fresh issue of equity shares of Rs. 10 each at par for such amount as necessary for the purpose after utilising the available source to the maximum extent and satisfying the amount of preference dividend. Rs. 2,00,000 of the development rebate reserve is free for distribution as dividend.

Give journal entries for recording the above transactions.

(B.Com., Bangalore & I.C.W.A., Dec., 1984)

Solution :

In the Books of Zee Ltd.
Journal Entries

S. No.	Particulars	LF	Dr. Rs.	Cr. Rs.
1.	Bank Account Dr.		4,60,000	
	To Equity Share Capital Account			4,60,000
	(Being 46,000 equity shares of Rs. 10 each are issued for cash for the purpose of redemption)			
2.	Development Rebate Reserve A/c Dr.		2,00,000	
	General Reserve Account Dr.		3,40,000	
	To Capital Redemption Reserve A/c			5,40,000
	(Being the transfer of the requisite amount to capital redemption reserve account)			
3.	10% Redeemable Pref. Share Capital A/c Dr.		9,80,000	
	Premium on Redemption of Pref. Shares A/c Dr.		98,000	
	To Redeemable Pref. Shareholders' A/c			10,78,000
	(Being the amount payable to the redeemable pref. shareholders)			
4.	Share Premium Account Dr.		98,000	
	To Premium on Redemption of Pref. Shares A/c			98,000
	(Being the transfer of the requisite amount from share premium account to provide 10% premium)			
5.	Redeemable Pref. Shareholders' A/c Dr.		10,78,000	
	To Bank or Cash Account			10,78,000
	(Being the amount paid to shareholders)			
6.	Proposed Dividend Dr.		78,400	
	To Bank Account			78,400
	(Being the proposed pref. dividend paid)			

Working Notes :

(1) As per the Section 80 of the Companies Act, 1956, only fully paid up pref. shares are to be redeemed. Therefore, 200 $\left(\frac{5,000}{25}\right)$ partly paid preference shares cannot be redeemed. Therefore, payment to redeemable pref. shareholders is arrived as below :

9,800 (10,000 – 200) Pref. Shares of Rs. 100 each	Rs. 9,80,000
Premium on such Redeemable Pref. Shares	Rs. 98,000
	Rs. 10,78,000

(2) Issue of fresh equity shares :

	Rs.
Total funds required for the nominal value of Cumulative Pref. Shares (10,000 × 100)	10,00,000
Less : Capital Redemption Reserve A/c	5,40,000
Issue of fresh of shares for redemption	4,60,000

Illustration 5

A company has 8,000 redeemable preference shares of Rs. 100 each fully paid. The company decides to redeem the shares on Sept. 30, 1991, at a premium of 7%. The company has sufficient profits but in order to augment liquid funds the following issues are made.

(1) 3,000, 6% debentures of Rs. 100 each at Rs. 106.

(2) 2,000, equity shares of Rs. 100 each at Rs. 111.

The issues were fully subscribed and all the amounts were received. The redemption was duly carried out. Give journal entries.

(*B.Com., M.K.U., April, 1983*)

Solution :

Journal Entries

S.No.	Particulars	L.F.	Dr. Rs.	Cr. Rs.
1.	Bank Account Dr.		3,18,000	
	To 6% Debentures' Account			3,00,000
	To Debenture Premium Account			18,000
	(Being the issue of 3,000 6% debentures at a premium)			
2.	Bank Account Dr.		2,22,000	
	To Equity Share Capital Account			2,00,000
	To Share Premium Account			22,000
	(Being 2,000 shares of Rs. 100 each issued at a premium)			
3.	Share Premium Account Dr.		22,000	
	Profit and Loss Account Dr.		34,000	
	To Premium on Redemption of Pref. Shares' A/c			56,000
	(Being the share premium and accumulated profit utilised for the redemption of pref. shares)			
4.	Profit and Loss Account Dr.		6,00,000	
	To Capital Redemption Reserve A/c			6,00,000
	(Being the amount not covered by the fresh issue of shares for redemption purpose transferred to the capital redemption reserve a/c)			

Contd.

Journal Entries (*Contd.*)

5.	Redeemable Pref. Share Capital A/c Dr. Premium on Redemp. of Pref. Shares' A/c Dr. To Redeemable Pref. Shareholders' A/c (Being the amount due to the Shareholders on redemption)		8,00,000 56,000	 8,56,000
6.	Redeemable Pref. Shareholders' A/c Dr. To Bank Account (Being the amount paid to the Shareholders)		8,56,000	 8,56,000

Notes :

(1) Only the proceeds of fresh issue of shares should be taken into account for the purpose of redemption and not the proceeds of fresh issue of debentures.

(2) The Amount required for the redemption of pref. shares is arrived as follows :

	Rs.
(i) Total nominal value of shares to be redeemed	8,00,000
(ii) Premium on redemption of shares	56,000
	8,56,000

(3) The amount of profit transferred to capital redemption reserve is given as below:

	Rs.
Nominal value of the pref. shares to be redeemed	8,00,000
Less : Redemption covered by the proceeds of fresh issue of equity shares (only the face value of shares issued)	2,00,000
Balance of redemption to be met out of divisible profits	6,00,000

(4) The amount required for the payment of premium on redemption of shares is arrived as below :

	Rs.
(i) Share premium from fresh issue of shares	22,000
(ii) Adjustments from Profit and Loss Account	34,000
	56,000

(5) The amount of premium on the issue of shares should be used for the payment of premium on redemption of preference shares.

Illustration 6

On Jan. 1, 1985, Shibpur Motor Ltd. issued 3,000 7% redeemable preference shares of Rs. 10 each, all of which were taken up and fully paid. The shares were issued on condition that the same at any time after March 31, 1990, could be redeemed at a premium of Rs. 4 per share.

On June 30, 1992, the company decided to redeem the shares. For the purpose it issued 1,800 6% preference shares of Rs. 10 each at a premium of Re. 1 per share on July 15, 1992. The shares were subscribed and paid for by July 31, 1992. The 7% redeemable preference shares were redeemed on the same date.

The company had a balance of Rs. 28,000 in its Profit and Loss Account. On 1-9-1992, the company decided to issue 5,000 fully paid bonus shares of Rs. 10 each for allotment to equity shareholders in the ratio of one equity share for every four shares held. It had also a Reserve of Rs. 1,10,000.

Record the necessary journal entries in the books the company.

(B.Com., C.U. and I.C.W.A., Dec., 1982)

Solution :

Journal Entries

Date	Particulars	L.F.	Dr. Rs.	Cr. Rs.
1992	Bank Account Dr.		19,800	
July 31	To 6% Preference Share Capital A/c			18,000
	To Share Premium Account			1,800
	(Being 1,800 Pref. Shares are issued at a premium for the purpose of redemption)			
" "	7% Redeemable Pref. Share Capital A/c Dr.		30,000	
	Premium on Redemption of Pref. Shares' A/c Dr.		12,000	
	To Redeemable Pref. Shareholders A/c			42,000
	(Being the amount due to redeemable preference shareholders)			
" "	Share Premium Account Dr.		1,800	
	Profit and Loss Account Dr.		10,200	
	To Premium on Redemp. of Pref. Shares' A/c			12,000
	(Being the premium on redemption is adjusted against Share premium account and P & L A/c)			
" "	Profit and Loss Account Dr.		12,000	
	To Capital Redemption Reserve A/c			12,000
	(Being the transfer of requisite amount from P&L A/c to capital redemption reserve account)			
" "	Redeemable Pref. Shareholders' A/c Dr.		42,000	
	To Bank Account			42,000
	(Being the amount paid to shareholders)			

Contd.

Journal Entries (*Contd.*)

Sept. 1	Capital Redemption Reserve A/c Dr.		12,000	
	Profit and Loss (balance) A/c Dr.		5,800	
	(28,000 – 12,000 = 16,000 – 10,200)			
	General Reserve A/c (Required amount) Dr.		32,200	
	To Bonus to Shareholders' A/c			50,000
	(Being the bonus shares declared as per Board's Resolution dated....)			
" "	Bonus to Shareholders' Account Dr.		50,000	
	To Equity Share Capital A/c.			50,000
	(Being the bonus shares are allotted)			

Illustration 7

P.P. Ltd. has an authorised share capital of Rs. 10 lakhs. Its summarised balance sheet as on 31st December, 1994 is as under :

Liabilities		Rs.	Assets		Rs.
Share Capital :			Fixed Assets :		
Issued and fully paid :			Plant and		
15,000, 5% Redeemable Pref.			Machinery	4,00,000	
Shares of Rs. 10 each	1,50,000		Furniture	42,000	
30,000 Equity Shares			Vehicles	48,000	4,90,000
of Rs. 10 each	3,00,000	4,50,000	Investments		1,00,000
Share Premium		1,35,000	Current Assets :		
General Reserve		1,60,000	Stocks	2,10,000	
Profit and Loss A/c		55,000	Debtors	1,10,000	
Sundry Creditors		2,00,000	Balance at Bank	90,000	4,10,000
		10,00,000			10,00,000

On January 1, 1985, the company decided to redeem the whole of the preference share capital at a premium of 5%. For this purpose, it is decided to sell the investments realising Rs. 97,500.

Only July 1, 1985 the company issued equity bonus shares, fully paid, in the ratio of one for every equity share held on that date.

Draft the journal entries to record the above transactions and draw up the Balance Sheet of the Company after incorporating these entries.

(*B.Com., Bangalore, Oct., 1980 and Nov., 1983 mod.*)

Solution :

Journal Entries

Date	Particulars		L.F.	Dr. Rs.	Cr. Rs.
1985	Bank Account	Dr.		97,500	
Jan. 1	Profit and Loss Account	Dr.		2,500	
	To Investment Account				1,00,000
	(Being the investment sold at Rs. 97,500 and loss debited to P & L A/c)				
" "	Preference Share Capital A/c	Dr.		1,50,000	
	Premium on Redemption of Pref. Shares' A/c	Dr.		7,500	
	To Pref. Shareholders' Account				1,57,500
	(Being the amount payable on shareholders on redemption)				
" "	Share Premium Account	Dr.		7,500	
	To Premium on Redemp. of Pref. Shares' A/c				7,500
	(Being the premium on redemption provided out of share premium)				
" "	General Reserve Account	Dr.		1,50,000	
	To Capital Redemption Reserve A/c				1,50,000
	(Being the capital redemption reserve is created out of general reserve for the purpose of redemption)				
" "	Redeemable Pref. Shareholders' A/c	Dr.		1,57,500	
	To Bank Account				1,57,500
	(Being the amount paid to shareholders)				
July 1	Capital Redemption Reserve A/c	Dr.		1,50,000	
	Share Premium Account	Dr.		1,27,500	
	General Reserve A/c	Dr.		10,000	
	Profit and Loss Account	Dr.		12,500	
	To Bonus to Shareholders' A/c				3,00,000
	(Being the issue of bonus shares in the ratio of 1 : 4 out of capital redemption account, share premium, general reserve and balance out of P & L A/c)				
" "	Bonus to Shareholders' Account	Dr.		3,00,000	
	To Equity Share Capital A/c				3,00,000
	(Being the bonus shares are allotted)				

Balance Sheet of P.P. Ltd. as on July 1, 1985

Liabilities	Rs.	Assets	Rs.
Share Capital :		**Fixed Assets :**	
Authorised Capital :		Plant and Machinery	4,00,000
1,00,000 Shares of Rs. 10 each	10,00,000	Furniture	42,000
Issued, Subscribed, Called up		Vehicles	48,000
and Paid up : 60,000 Equity		**Current Assets :**	
shares of Rs. 10 each fully		Debtors	1,10,000
paid up (out of above 30,000 shares have been issued as bonus shares out of capital redemption reserve Rs. 1,50,000, share premium Rs. 1,27,500, general reserve Rs. 10,000 and P & L A/c Rs. 12,500)	6,00,000	Stock	2,10,000
		Bank (90,000+97,500–1,57,500)	30,000
Reserve & Surplus :			
Profit and Loss A/c (55,000-2,500=52,500-12,500)	40,000		
Current Liabilities & Provisions:			
Sundry Creditors	2,00,000		
	8,40,000		8,40,000

Illustration 8

J Ltd. decided to redeem their preference shares as on March 31, 1985. On which date their position was as under :

Liabilities	Rs.	Assets	Rs.
Share Capital :		Cash at Bank	1,40,000
4,000 Equity Shares of Rs. 100 each	4,00,000	Other assets	8,60,000
4,000 Red. Pref. Shares of Rs. 50 each Rs. 25 per share paid up	1,00,000		
2,000 Red. Pref. Shares of Rs. 100 each fully paid	2,00,000		
Reserve and Surplus :			
Share Premium	20,000		
Capital Reserve	80,000		
Dividend Equalisation Reserve	1,10,000		
Sundry Liabilities	90,000		
	10,00,000		10,00,000

The redemption was to be at a premium of 5%. To enable the redemption to be carried out, the company decides to issue, after carrying out the necessary formalities required under law, sufficient number of new equity shares at a discount of 10%. The redemption is duly carried out.

Show the journal entries relating to the redemption and new issue and also show the balance sheet after redemption.

(B.Com., Mysore and C.A. Adapted)

Solution :

In the Books of J Ltd.
Journal Entries

Date	Particulars		L.F.	Dr. Rs.	Cr. Rs.
1985	Bank Account	Dr.		90,000	
Mar. 31	Discount on Issue of Shares' A/c	Dr.		10,000	
	To Equity Share Capital A/c				1,00,000
	(Being 1,000 equity shares are issued at a discount for cash for the purpose of redemption)				
" "	Red. Preference Share Capital A/c	Dr.		2,00,000	
	Premium on Redemption of Pref. Shares' A/c	Dr.		10,000	
	To Pref. Shareholders' Account				2,10,000
	(Being the amount payable to the preference shareholders)				
" "	Dividend Equalisation Reserve A/c	Dr.		1,10,000	
	To Capital Redemption Reserve A/c				1,10,000
	(Being the requisite amount taken from dividend equalisation reserve for the redemption of Pref. Shares)				
" "	Share Premium Account	Dr.		10,000	
	To Discount on Issue of Shares' A/c				10,000
	(Being the discount on issue if shares are written off against share premium account)				
" "	Redeemable Pref. Shareholders' A/c	Dr.		2,10,000	
	To Bank Account				2,10,000
	(Being amount paid to pref. shareholders)				

Balance Sheet. as at 31st March, 1985

Liabilities	Rs.	Assets	Rs.
Share Capital :		Sundry Assets	8,60,000
5,000 Equity Shares of Rs. 100 fully each paid	5,00,000	Cash at Bank (1,40,000 + 90,000–2,10,000)	20,000
4,000 Redeemable Pref. Shares of Rs. 50 each Rs. 25 paid	1,00,000		
Reserve & Surplus :			
Capital Redemption Reserve	1,10,000		
Capital Reserve	80,000		
Current Liabilities and Provisions :			
Sundry Liabilities	90,000		
	8,80,000		8,80,000

Working Notes :

(1) Capital reserve is not allowed to be utilised for redemption.

(2) As per Section 80, Pref. Shares cannot be redeemed until and unless they are fully paid up. Therefore, 4,000 Pref. Shares (which are partly paid) cannot be redeemed.

(3) 2,000 Pref. Shares (which are fully paid) are to be redeemed. For this purpose, dividend equalisation reserve should be utilised fully *i.e.*, Rs. 1,10,000. The balance amount i.e., Rs. 90,000 (2,00,000 – 1,10,000) will be covered by the fresh issue of equity shares. Since the equity shares are issued at a discount of 10%, the nominal value of equity shares to be issued will be arrived as below :

Net amount to be received	Discount on Issue of Shares	Nominal Value of Equity Shares to be issued
Rs. 90	Rs. 10	Rs. 100
Rs. 90,000	Rs. 10,000	Rs. 1,00,000 $\left(100 \times \frac{90,000}{90}\right)$

Illustration 9

The summarised Balance Sheet of Sterling Ltd. as on 31-12-1994 was as follows :

Liabilities	Rs.	Assets	Rs.
Share Capital :		Sundry Assets	34,00,000
Issued and Paid up :		Cash	6,00,000
10,000 8% Redeemable Pref. Shares of Rs. 100 each	10,00,000		
1,00,000 Equity Shares of Rs. 10 each	10,00,000		
General Reserve	2,00,000		
Capital Reserve	5,00,000		
Profit & Loss Account	9,50,000		
Creditors	3,50,000		
	40,00,000		40,00,000

The preference shares were redeemable on 31-3-1995 at a premium of 25%, for the purpose, the company decided to issue 50,000 equity shares of Rs. 10 each at a premium of Rs. 4 per share payable in full on 15-3-1995.

- Show the necessary ledger accounts.

(*C.U., B.Com. (Hons.) & I.C.W.A.— Adapted*)

Solution :

Dr. **8% Redeemable Preference Share Capital A/c** Cr.

	Rs.		Rs.
To Red. Pref. Shareholders' A/c	10,00,000	By Balance b/d	10,00,000
	10,00,000		10,00,000

Dr. **Redeemable Preference Shareholders' A/c** Cr.

	Rs.		Rs.
To Bank Account	12,50,000	By Red. Pref. Share Capital A/c	10,00,000
		By Premium on Redemption of Pref. Shares' A/c	2,50,000
	12,50,000		12,50,000

Dr. **Equity Share Capital A/c** Cr.

	Rs.		Rs.
To Balance b/d	15,00,000	By Balance b/d	10,00,000
		By Bank (Fresh issue) A/c	5,00,000
	15,00,000		15,00,000
		By Balance b/d	15,00,000

Dr. **Premium on Redemption of Preference Shares A/c** Cr.

	Rs.		Rs.
To Red. Pref. Shareholders' A/c	2,50,000	By Share Premium A/c	2,00,000
		By Profit and Loss A/c	50,000
	2,50,000		2,50,000

Dr. **Share Premium Account** Cr.

	Rs.		Rs.
To Premium on Redemption of Pref. Shares' A/c	2,00,000	By Bank Account	2,00,000
	2,00,000		2,00,000

Dr. **Profit and Loss Account** Cr.

	Rs.		Rs.
To Premium on Redemption of Pref. Shares' A/c	50,000	By Balance b/d	9,50,000
To Capital Redemption Reserve A/c	5,00,000		
To Balance c/d	4,00,000		
	9,50,000		9,50,000

Illustration 10

The Balance Sheet of Gay Ltd. as at 31st December 1990 was as follows :

Liabilities	Rs.	Assets	Rs.
Share Capital :		Fixed Assets	8,00,000
(Shares of Rs. 100 each fully paid)		Invesments	1,00,000
		Cash	2,00,000
Equity	5,00,000	Other Current Assets	5,00,000
7% Redeemable Preference	3,00,000		
Shares Premium	50,000		
Capital Reserve	1,00,000		
Revenue Reserve	2,00,000		
6% Debentures	3,00,000		
Creditors	1,50,000		
	16,00,000		16,00,000

Both the Redeemable Preference Shares and Debentures were due for redemption on January 1, 1991. Gay Ltd. took the following steps in this respect :

1. It issued 2,000 equity shares of Rs. 100 each at a premium of 10%, the shares were fully subscribed and paid for.
2. It sold the investments for Rs. 90,000.
3. It arranged a bank overdraft to the extent necessary.

The redemption was duly carried out. Prepare the Balance Sheet of the company immediately afterwards.

(*B.Com., C.U. and B.U.*)

Solution :

Balance Sheet of Gay Ltd. as on 1st Jan., 1991

Liabilities	Rs.	Assets	Rs.
Share Capital :		**Fixed Assets**	8,00,000
7,000 (5,000 + 2,000) Equity Shares at Rs. 100 each fully called up and paid up	7,00,000	**Current Assets :** Other Current Assets	5,00,000
Reserve and Surplus :			
Capital Reserve	1,00,000		
Capital Redemption Reserve	1,00,000		
Share Premium (50,000 + 20,000)	70,000		
Revenue Reserve (2,00,000 – 1,10,000)	90,000		
Current Liabilities :			
Creditors	1,50,000		
Bank Overdraft	90,000		
	13,00,000		13,00,000

Working Notes :

(1) The amount of Bank Overdraft is arrived as below :

	Rs.	Rs.
Amount needed for the redemption of shares and debentures (Rs. 3,00,000 + Rs. 3,00,000)		6,00,000
Less : Amount available :	Rs.	
(i) Cash in Hand	2,00,000	
(ii) Amount received on issue of equity shares	2,20,000	
(iii) Amount received on sale of investments	90,000	5,10,000
Amount required to be raised through Bank overdraft		90,000

(2) The amount of revenue reserve is arrived as below :

		Rs.
Existing balance of revenue reserve		2,00,000
Less : (i) Loss on sale of investments	10,000	
(ii) Transfer to Capital Redemption Reserve for redemption of Pref. Shares	1,00,000	1,10,000
Balance of revenue reserve		90,000

Equation for determining the minimum number of shares to be issued for redemption

If the fresh issue of shares for the redemption is not given in the problem, but states that the minimum possible issue of shares is to be made to meet the redemption, the minimum issue of shares will be arrived by applying the following equation :

Redeemable Pref. Shares + Premium on Redemption	=	Premium in the Balance Sheet	+	Divisible Profit in the Balance Sheet	+	Fresh Issue (say x)	+	Premium on Fresh Issue

The above equation is applicable only when the premium on redemption is more or equal to the premium available in the Balance Sheet plus premium to be received on fresh issue of shares. It is clear from the following example.

Example :

500 Redeemable preference shares of Rs. 100 each.

The redeemable preference shares are to be redeemed at 10% premium.

Share premium available in the Balance Sheet Rs. 2,500.

Profit available for dividend Rs. 25,000.

Fresh issue of shares is to be made at 10% premium.

Calculate the minimum issue to be made.

Solution :

Equation for determining the fresh issue :

Redeemable Pref. Shares + Premium on Redemption	=	Premium Appearing in the Balance Sheet	+	Divisible Profit Available in the Balance Sheet	+	Fresh Issue (say x)	+	Premium on Fresh Issue of Shares

$$50{,}000 + 5{,}000 = 2{,}500 + 25{,}000 + x + 10\% \text{ of } x$$

$$55{,}000 = 27{,}500 + x + \frac{1}{10}x$$

$$x + \frac{1}{10}x = 55{,}000 - 27{,}500$$

$$x + \frac{1}{10}x = 27{,}500$$

$$10x + x = 2{,}75{,}000$$

$$11x = 2{,}75{,}000$$

$$x = 25{,}000$$

$\therefore$ The fresh issue of shares is to be made for Rs. 25,000.

Verification :

		Rs.
Amount to be transferred to the Capital Redemption Reserve A/c (Face value of Red. Pref. Shares – Fresh issue) (*i.e.*, Rs. 50,000 – Rs. 25,000)		25,000
Premium on Red. of Pref. Shares (*i.e.*, 10% on Rs. 50,000)		5,000
Premium appearing in the Balance Sheet	Rs. 2,500	
Premium on fresh issue of shares *i.e.*, 10% on Rs. 25,000	2,500	5,000
Uncovered Premium to be met out of divisible profits		Nil

In this case the entire profit available for dividend Rs. 25,000 is available for the redemption of preference shares. Therefore, for the balance of Rs. 25,000 (50,000 – 25,000), the fresh issue is to be made to redeem the preference shares.

Suppose, the premium on the redemption of preference shares is less than the premium available in the Balance Sheet plus the premium to be received on the fresh issue of shares, the above equation is not applied because, if the premium appearing in the Balance Sheet and premium on the fresh issue of shares is more than the premium required on redemption, the fresh issue does not represent the minimum issue.

Continuing the above example, let us assume that the fresh issue being made at a premium of 25% and all other information remain the same.

$$50{,}000 + 5{,}000 = 2{,}500 + 25{,}000 + x + 25\% \text{ of } x$$

$$55{,}000 = 2{,}500 + 25{,}000 + x\ \frac{1}{4}\ x$$

$$x + \frac{1}{4}x = 55{,}000 - 27{,}500$$

$$x + \frac{1}{4}x = 27{,}500$$

$$4x + x = 1{,}10{,}000$$

$$5x = 1{,}10{,}000$$

$$x = 22{,}000$$

∴ The fresh issue of shares is to be made for Rs. 22,000.

Verification :

Amount to be transferred to the Capital Redemption Reserve Account is (*i.e.*, 50,000 – 22,000)		= 28,500
Premium on Redemption of Pref. Shares (10% of Rs. 50,000)=		5,000
Premium appearing in the Balance Sheet	2,500	
Premium on fresh issue *i.e.*, 25% of Rs. 22,000	5,500 =	8,000

In this case the amount to be transferred to the Capital Redemption Reserve Account is Rs. 28,500, but the amount available for dividend is Rs. 25,000 only. Therefore, the application of the equation is not required for arriving the minimum issue. In this case, the minimum issue should be made at least equal to Rs. 25,000.

Issue of Bonus Shares/Capitalisation of Profits

Meaning : Bonus shares are those shares which are allotted to the existing equity shareholders without receiving any consideration from them in the form of cash or kind. A company can pay the dividend in cash to its shareholders only when it has more funds, but it cannot pay the dividend in cash to its shareholders due to shortage of funds. In such case, the company issues new shares to the existing shareholders instead of paying the dividend in cash. Such shares are known as 'Bonus Shares'. These shares are issued to capitalise profits of the company. The company issues the bonus shares out of accumulated profits and reserve. Since the profit or reserve is being capitalised, it is also called capitalisation of profit or reserve. Bonus shares are issued to the existing shareholders in proportion to their shareholding and dividend rights. If the bonus shares are offered to the existing shareholders, it does not affect company's working capital position. In order to avoid the outflow of cash from the business and at the same time to satisfy the shareholders, the company will issue the bonus shares to the equity shareholders. Sanction of controller of capital issues is necessary for the issue of bonus shares. The Govt. of India has prescribed certain guidelines for the issue of bonus shares. The sanction of 'Controller of Capital Issues' will be obtained only if these guidelines have been followed.

Guidelines for the Issue of Bonus Shares

The Capital Issue Control Act, 1947, gives the following important guidelines for the issue of issue of bonus shares, effective from August, 1981.

(1) The Articles of Association of the Company permit the issue of bonus shares.

(2) Free reserves created out of real profits and share premium collected in cash can be utilised for the purpose of issuing bonus shares.

(3) Reserve created by the revaluation of fixed assets are not permitted to utilise for the purpose.

(4) Development Rebate Reserve or Investment Allowance Reserve may be considered as free reserve for the purpose of calculation of residual reserve.

(5) The residual reserves after bonus issue should be at least 40% of the increased paid up capital.

(6) 30% of the average profits (before tax but after providing preference dividend) for the previous three years should at least yield a dividend of 10% of the expanded equity capital.

(7) Capital Redemption Reserve, if any, for the computation of said 40% of the residual reserve, is not to be taken into consideration.

(8) Bonus shares are not permitted unless the partly paid shares are made fully paid.

(9) Declaration of bonus issue in lieu of dividends is not allowed.

(10) The Controller of Capital Issues has consented to the issue of bonus shares.

Sources of Bonus Shares

Bonus Shares can be issued out of the followings :

(1) Capital Redemption Reserve

(2) Share Premium

(3) Capital Profits and Reserves

(4) General Reserve

(5) Balance in the Profit and Loss Account

(6) Any other reserves accumulated out of profits.

It should be remembered that Capital Redemption Reserve and Share Premium will be utilised only for issuing fully paid bonus shares and not for making partly paid up shares into fully paid shares.

Right Shares or Right Issue

Whenever a company proposed to increase its subscribed capital, it is the legal obligation of the company to first offer the shares to the existing equity shareholders on pro-rata basis. This is known as Rights Issue. Such shares when allotted to the shareholders are called as 'Right Shares'.

As per the Companies Act, 1956 Section 81(1) 'right shares are those shares which are issued after the original issue of shares, but having an inherent right of the existing shareholders to subscribed to these shares in proportion to their holding'.

If the existing shareholders do not accept the offer within a period of 15 days or more, then, these shares can also be issued to the new members. Usually, these shares are issued to the existing shareholders at a concessional rate, which is less than the market price. Suppose, a company offers to its shareholders the right to buy one equity share of Rs. 50 each at Rs. 55 for every five equity shares of Rs. 50 each held, and if the market price of one equity is Rs. 70, then, the value of the right will be arrived as follows :

	Rs.
Market price of 5 equity shares (5 × 70)	= 350
Add : Issue price of 1 new equity share	= 55
Total price of 6 shares	405
Value of one share *i.e.*, 405/6	= 67.50

The value of right = Rs. 70 – Rs. 67.50 = Rs. 2.50.

Accounting Entries

The following journal entries are to be passed for the issue of bonus shares :

(A) When the bonus is utilised for making partly paid shares into fully paid :

(1) Entry for transfer of profit or reserve to Bonus Account :

Profit and Loss A/c	Dr.	With the total Amount of of bonus
General Reserve A/c	Dr.	
Capital Reserve A/c	Dr.	
To Bonus to Shareholders' A/c		

(2) Entry for transfer of share call money to Share Capital A/c :

Share Final Call A/c	Dr.	With the amount of call money
To Share Capital A/c		

(3) Entry for transfer of total amount of bonus to Call A/c :

Bonus to Shareholders' A/c	Dr.	With total amount of bonus
To Share Final Call A/c		

(B) When the payment of bonus is made by the issue of fully paid bonus shares :

(1) Entry for transfer of profit or reserve to Bonus Account :

Profit and Loss A/c	Dr.	With the total amount of nominal value of shares
General Reserve A/c	Dr.	
Share Premium A/c	Dr.	
Capital Reserve A/c	Dr.	
Capital Redemption Reserve A/c	Dr.	
To Bonus to Shareholders' A/c		

(2) Entry for transfer of nominal value to Share Capital and Share Premium Account :

Bonus to Shareholders' A/c	Dr.	With total amount of bonus
To Share Capital A/c		With total amount of nominal value
To Share Premium A/c (if any)		With total amount of Premium

Illustration 1

A limited company declared a bonus of Rs. 5,00,000 out of its reserve fund. This bonus is to be utilised as follows :

(a) To pay Rs. 1,00,000 in cash.

(b) To issue 20,000 equity shares of Rs. 10 each as fully paid bonus shares.

(c) To utilise the balance of bonus towards the final call of Rs. 2 per share on 1,00,000 equity shares of Rs. 10 each which are partly paid up.

Pass the necessary journal entries to give effect to the above.

(Gulbarga, Oct., 1982)

Solution :

Journal Entries

Sl. No.	Particulars	L.F.	Dr. Rs.	Cr. Rs.
1.	Reserve Fund Account Dr.		5,00,000	
	To Bonus to Shareholders' Account			5,00,000
	(Being amount transferred for bonus payable to shareholders)			
2.	Share Final Call Account Dr.		2,00,000	
	To Equity Share Capital Account			2,00,000
	(Being transfer of share final call money to equity share capital account)			
3.	Bonus to Shareholders' Account Dr.		5,00,000	
	To Bank or Cash A/c			1,00,000
	To Share Final Call Account			2,00,000
	To Equity Share Capital Account			2,00,000
	(Being bonus paid in cash Rs. 1,00,000, bonus utilised for issue of 20,000 fully paid shares of Rs. 10 each and the balance adjusted against call money on 1,00,000 shares of Rs. 2 each)			

Illustration 2

Journalise the following transactions.

A company having an issued capital of Rs. 15,00,000 in shares of Rs. 20 each, on which Rs. 15 per share is paid up. It decides to declare a bonus out of profit and capital reserve at the rate of $33^1/_3$% on the paid up capital with the object of making the shares fully paid. For this purpose it used the entire amount of Rs. 3,00,000 from capital reserve account and the balance from the net profits.

(Gulbarga, April, 1983)

Solution :

Journal Entries

Sl. No.	Particulars		L.F.	Dr. Rs.	Cr. Rs.
1.	General Reserve Account	Dr.		3,00,000	
	Profit and Loss Account	Dr.		75,000	
	To Bonus to Shareholders' Account				3,75,000
	(Being bonus declared Rs. 3,00,000 out of general reserve and balance from profits)				
2.	Share Call Account	Dr.		3,75,000	
	To Share Capital Account				3,75,000
	(Being transfer of call money on 75,000 shares of Rs. 5 per share)				
3.	Bonus to Shareholders' Account	Dr.		3,75,000	
	To Share Capital Account				3,75,000
	(Being bonus utilised for call money)				

Working Notes :

Calculation of bonus declared : Rs.

Number of shares issued $\left(\frac{15,00,000}{20}\right)$ = 75,000

Paid up Capital (75,000 shares of Rs. 15 each) = 11,25,000

Bonus declared $33\frac{1}{3}$ % or $\frac{1}{3}$ of Rs. 11,25,000 = 3,75,000

Illustration 3

Pure Company Ltd. has accumulated large profits in the Reserve Account and the Board of Directors decide to utilise a part of this reserve in order to make the capital properly representative of the financial position.

The paid up share capital is Rs. 10,00,000 consisting of 90,000 Equity Shares of Rs. 10 each fully paid up and 20,000 Equity Shares (face value Rs. 10 each), Rs. 5 per share paid up. The directors decide to issue one bonus shares at a premium of Rs. 10 for every fully paid shares held and to make the partly paid shares fully paid.

Give the necessary journal entries.

(Bangalore, B.Com., April, 1988 and I.C.W.A., Dec., 1981)

Solution :

In the books of the Company
Journal Entries

Sl.No.	Particulars	L.F.	Dr. Rs.	Cr. Rs.
1.	General Reserve Account Dr.		18,00,000	
	To Bonus to Shareholders' Account			18,00,000
	(Being bonus declared out of general reserve)			
2.	Bonus to Shareholders' Account Dr.		18,00,000	
	To Equity Share Capital Account			9,00,000
	To Share Premium Account			9,00,000
	(Being 90,000 equity shares of Rs. 10 each at a premium of Rs. 10 each are issued by way of bonus shares in the ratio of one for every one share held)			
3.	Share Final Call Account Dr.		1,00,000	
	To Share Capital Account			1,00,000
	(Being the share final call money of 20,000 equity shares of Rs. 5 each transferred to share capital account)			
4.	General Reserve Account Dr.		1,00,000	
	To Bonus to Shareholders' Account			1,00,000
	(Being bonus declared out of general reserve)			
5.	Bonus to Shareholders' Account Dr.		1,00,000	
	To Share Final Call Account			1,00,000
	(Being bonus utilised for the payment of final call of Rs. 5 per share on 20,000 shares)			

Illustration 4

The following are extracts from the Balance Sheet of A Ltd. as on December 31, 1988 :

	Rs.
Authorised Capital :	
10,000 Equity Shares of Rs. 10 each	1,00,000
Issued and Subscribed Capital :	
5,000 Equity Shares of Rs. 10 each fully paid up	50,000
Reserve Fund	35,000
Profit and Loss Account	10,000

A resolution was passed to issue 1,000 bonus shares of Rs. 10 each by providing Rs. 5,000 out of the P & L A/c and balance out of the Reserve Fund.

Set out Journal Entries to give effect to the resolution and show how they would affect the Balance Sheet. *(A.C.S., June, 1979 and 1984)*

Solution :

Journal Entries

Sl. No.	Particulars		L.F.	Dr. Rs.	Cr. Rs.
1.	Profit and Loss Account	Dr.		5,000	
	Reserve Fund Account	Dr.		5,000	
	To Bonus to Shareholders' Account				10,000
	(Being bonus declared Rs. 5,000 out of P&L A/c and balance from reserve fund)				
2.	Bonus to Shareholders' Account	Dr.		10,000	
	To Share Capital Account				10,000
	(Being issue of 1,000 bonus share of Rs. 10 each)				

Balance Sheet of A Ltd. as on 31st Dec., 1988

Liabilities	Rs.	Assets	Rs.
Share Capital :		Fixed Assets	—
Authorised : 10,000 Equity Share of Rs. 10 each	1,00,000		
Issued and Subscribed Capital :		Current Assets	—
6,000 Equity Shares of Rs. 10 each fully paid (Out of these, 1,000 shares have been issued as fully paid bonus shares)	60,000		
Reserve Fund	30,000		
Profit and Loss Account	5,000		

Illustration 5

The following is the Balance Sheet of X Ltd. as on 31-12-1985.

Liabilities	Rs.	Assets	Rs.
Share Capital :		Land and Building	3,00,000
10,000 shares of Rs. 100 each Rs. 75 paid	7,50,000	Stock	5,00,000
		Machinery	4,00,000
Share Premium	1,00,000	Sundry Debtors	2,75,000
General Reserve	1,50,000	Bank	25,000
Profit and Loss Account	2,00,000		
Sundry Creditors	3,00,000		
	15,00,000		15,00,000

On the above date the company decided to capitalise its reserves and profits by issuing bonus to shareholders as follows :

(1) To make their partly paid shares fully paid; and

(2) To issue one fully paid bonus share of Rs. 100 for every ten shares already held in the company.

For this purpose the company decided to utilise the entire amount of share premium and general reserve and use the Profit and Loss Account balance of the required extent.

Pass the journal entries and redraft the balance sheet of the company.

(*Karnataka, Oct., 1985 and Gulbarga, April, 1991*)

Solution :

Journal Entries

Sl. No.	Particulars		L.F.	Dr. Rs.	Cr. Rs.
1.	Share Premium Account	Dr.		1,00,000	
	General Reserve Account	Dr.		1,50,000	
	Profit and Loss Account	Dr.		1,00,000	
	To Bonus to Shareholders' Account				3,50,000
	(Being bonus declared out of share premium and general reserve and balance out of profit)				
2.	Share Call Account	Dr.		2,50,000	
	To Share Capital Account				2,50,000
	(Being share call money transferred to shares capital a/c)				
3.	Bonus to Shareholders' Account	Dr.		3,50,000	
	To Share Call Account				2,50,000
	To Share Capital Account				1,00,000
	(Bonus utilised in payment of calls amount and issued 1,000 fully paid bonus shares of Rs. 100 each)				

X's Balance Sheet

Liabilities	Rs.	Assets	Rs.
Share Capital :		Land and Building	3,00,000
11,000 Shares of Rs. 100 each		Stock	5,00,000
fully paid	11,00,000	Machinery	4,00,000
(Of the above, 1,000 shares of		Sundry Debtors	2,75,000
Rs. 10 each are issued as fully		Bank	25,000
paid bonus shares)			
Profit and Loss Account	1,00,000		
Sundry Creditors	3,00,000		
	15,00,000		15,00,000

Illustration 6

The Balance Sheet of COSMOS Ltd. on 31st Dec., 1994, was as follows:

Liabilities	Rs.	Assets	Rs.
4,000 Equity Shares of Rs. 100 each Rs. 80 paid	3,20,000	Sundry Assets	10,00,000
Share Premium Account	60,000		
Capital Redemption Reserve Account	70,000		
General Reserve	1,00,000		
Profit and Loss Account	3,00,000		
Sundry Creditors	1,50,000		
	10,00,000		10,00,000

The directors recommended the following with a view to capitalising whole of Share Premium Account, Capital Redemption Reserve Account, General Reserve and 50,000 out of Profit and Loss Account :

(a) The existing shares be made fully paid without the shareholders having to pay anything.

(b) Each shareholder to be given fully paid bonus shares at a premium of 25% for the remaining amount in proportion to his holding.

Assuming that the scheme is accepted and that all formalities are gone through, give journal entries and also show in what proportion bonus shares will be distribution among shareholders.

(B.Com., Osmania, Oct., 1981 and I.C.W.A., June, 1985 old)

Solution :

In the books of COSMOS Ltd.
Journal Entries

Date	Particulars	L.F.	Dr. Rs.	Cr. Rs.
1994 Dec. 31	Share Final Call Account Dr.		80,000	
	To Equity Share Capital Account			80,000
	(Being final call of Rs. 20 per share made on 4,000 shares)			
" "	General Reserve Account Dr.		80,000	
	To Bonus to Shareholders' Account			80,000
	(Being bonus shares declared out of general reserve)			
" "	Bonus to Shareholders' Account Dr.		80,000	
	To Share Final Call Account			80,000
	(Being bonus utilised for the payment of final call)			

Contd.

In the books of COSMOS Ltd.
Journal Entries (*Contd.*)

Date	Particulars		L.F.	Dr.	Cr.
Dec. 31	Share Premium Account	Dr.		60,000	
	Capital Redemption Account	Dr.		70,000	
	General Reserve Account (1,00,000–80,000)	Dr.		20,000	
	Profit and Loss Account	Dr.		50,000	
	To Bonus to Shareholders' Account				2,00,000
	(Being bonus declared out of share premium, capital redem., general reserve and P & L A/c)				
" "	Bonus to Shareholders' Account	Dr.		2,00,000	
	To Equity Share Capital Account				1,60,000
	To Share Premium Account				40,000
	(Being 1,600 equity shares of Rs. 10 each are issued by way of bonus at a premium of 25%, 2 shares are issued for every 5 shares)				

Working Notes :

(i) Premium on bonus shares is arrived as below :

$$\text{Rs. } 2,00,000 \times \frac{225}{125} = \text{Rs. } 40,000$$

Therefore, face value of equity shares will be Rs. 1,60,000 (*i.e.*, Rs. 2,00,000 – Rs. 40,000)

(ii) Proportion of shares is arrived as below :
1,600 bonus shares are issued for 4,000 shares. Therefore, the proportion of shares issued will be – 1,600 : 4,000. Ratio = 2 : 5.

COSMOS Ltd. Balance Sheet as on 31st Dec., 1994

Liabilities	Rs.	Assets	Rs.
Share Capital :			
5,600 Equity Shares of Rs. 100 each fully paid	5,60,000	Sundry Assets	10,00,000
(Of the above, 1,600 shares of Rs. 100 each are issued as fully paid bonus shares)			
Share Premium A/c	40,000		
Profit and Loss Account (3,00,000 – 50,000)	2,50,000		
Sundry Creditors	1,50,000		
	10,00,000		10,00,000

EXAMINATION QUESTIONS

(A) Answer the following questions in not exceeding 4 lines each :

(*Each Carries two Marks*)

(1) What are redeemable preference shares? (*Kar., Oct., 1996*)

(2) Give the journal entry for the fresh issue of shares at a discount.

(3) Give the journal entry to redeem the redeemable preference shares at a premium?

(*Bangalore, Oct., 1991*)

(4) Mention the entry for the adjustment of premium payable on redemption of preference shares.

(5) What are bonus shares ?

(6) Give the entry for transfer of total amount of bonus to call account.

(7) Pass the entry for transfer of profit or reserve to bonus account.

(8) What is 'Right Issue' ? (*M.K.U., Oct.,1992*)

(9) What are right shares? (*Panjab, April, 1991*)

(10) What do you mean by Capital Redemption Reserve?

(*Karnataka, Oct., 1995*)

(11) Distinguish between shares and debentures? (*Kar., April, 1997*)

Hints : (i) Shares are part of the capital and debentures are part of the loan of the company.

(ii) Dividends are payable on shares out of profit only, but interest on debentures must be paid whether there are profits or not.

(iii) Rate of dividends is varying, but rate of interest is fixed.

(iv) Shareholders have voting power, but debentureholders do not have voting right.

(12) State three conditions for redemption of preference shares.

(*Karnataka, April, 1998*)

(B) Answer the following questions/problems :

(*Each Carries eight Marks*)

(1) Mention the important legal provisions relating to redemption of preference shares.

(*Bangalore, Nov., 1981*)

(2) Give the equation for determining the minimum number of shares to be issued for redemption.

(*Bangalore, Oct., 1989*)

(3) Give the meaning and method of capitalization of reserve in a company.

(*Bangalore, April, 1984*)

(4) Mention the guidelines for the issue of bonus shares.

(5) What are the sources of bonus shares ?

(6) Journalise the following in the books of Honest Co. Ltd., at the time of issue and redemption.

(i) 1,500 7% preference shares of Rs. 100 each issued at a discount of 5% and redeemable at par after 5 years.

(ii) 2,500 7% preference shares of Rs. 100 each issued at a discount of 5% and redeemable at a premium of 5% after 10 years.

(*Karnataka, April, 1979*)

Notes :

(A) Entry for the issue of 7% preference shares :

			Rs.	Rs.
(i)	Bank A/c	Dr.	1,42,500	—
	Discount on Issue of Shares' A/c	Dr.	7,500	—
	To Preference Share Capital A/c		—	1,50,000
(ii)	Bank A/c.	Dr.	2,37,500	—
	Discount on Issue of Shares' A/c	Dr.	12,500	—
	To Preference Share Capital A/c		—	2,50,000

(B) Cash paid on redemption of shares Rs. 2,62,500 (2,50,000 + 12,500).

(7) The following balances are appearing in the ledger of a company as on 31-12-1980 :

	Rs.
Equity Shares (fully paid up)	6,00,000
Redeemable Preference Shares (fully paid up)	3,00,000
General Reserve	2,00,000
Profit and Loss Account (Cr. Balance)	1,25,000
Share Premium Account	50,000

The company decided to redeem the preference shares out of general reserve and undistributed profits.

Give journal entries relating to the redemption of preference shares.

(*Karnataka, Oct., 1981*)

Note : Entry for the transfer of the required amount from general reserve and P & L A/c to capital redemption reserve :

General Reserve A/c	Dr.	2,00,000	
Profit and Loss Account.	Dr.	1,00,000	
To Capital Redemption Reserve A/c			3,00,000

(8) A company has 4,000 6% redeemable preference shares of Rs. 100 each fully paid. The company decides to redeem the shares on Dec. 31, 1981 at a premium of 5%. The company makes the following issue :

(a) 1,000 equity shares of Rs. 100 each at premium of 100%

(b) 1,000 6% debentures of Rs. 100 each.

The issue was fully subscribed and all the amounts were received. The redemption was duly carried out. The company has sufficient profits. Give journal entries for recording the above transactions.

(*C.A.I.I.B., Dec., 1990*)

Note : Entry for the transfer of profit to capital redemption reserve account :

Profit and Loss Account	Dr.	3,00,000	
To Capital Redemption Reserve A/c			3,00,000

(Nominal value Rs. 4,00,000—Fresh issue Rs. 1,00,000)

(9) Journalise the following transactions in the books of Mysore Ltd.

Declared a bonus of Rs. 2,40,000 to the shareholders out of general reserve. This bonus is paid by the issue of 20,000 equity shares of Rs. 10 each as fully paid up bonus shares at premium of Rs. 2 per share.

(*Gulbarga, Oct., 1982*)

(10) X Ltd. has resolved to utilise Rs. 3,00,000 out of the General reserve balance to declare a bonus to the shareholders by paying the final call of Rs. 3 on 1,00,000 equity shares of 10 each. Along with this, the company further decided to utilise the balance of the share premium account to issue fully paid-up bonus shares in the ratio of one equity share for every five equity shares held.

Show journal entries in the books of 'X' Ltd.

(*A.C.S., June, 1980 and M.K.U., M.Com., Nov., 1988*)

Note : Bonus shares issued 2,000 of Rs. 10 each.

(11) Automobiles Co. Ltd., has the following items in its balance sheet :

(i) 1,00,000 Equity shares of Rs. 50 each, Rs. 40 paid up

(ii) General Reserve Rs. 10,50,000

(iii) Share Premium Rs. 5,00,000

(iv) Capital Reserve Rs. 7,00,000

The company decided to :

(a) Capitalise its general reserve to convert the existing partly paid shares into fully paid up shares.

(b) Issue bonus shares of Rs. 10 each as fully paid at a premium of 25%, utilizing share premium and capital reserve fully. Pass the journal entries for the above. (*Karnataka, April, 1988*)

Note : Bonus shares issued 19,200 of Rs. 50 each at 25% premium (*i.e.*, share capital Rs. 9,60,000 and share premium Rs. 2,40,000).

(12) Swastik Ltd., issued 5,000 6% redeemable preference shares of Rs. 100 each. It redeemed 1,000 preference shares at 10% premium. It had general reserve of Rs. 30,000 and credit balance to P & L A/c Rs. 40,000. The balance amount required was raised by issuing equity shares of Rs. 10 each at par.

Pass the journal entries in the books of the company.

(Karnataka, April, 1995)

Notes : (i) Profit Rs. 40,000 and Reserve Rs. 30,000 are transferred to capital redemption fund Rs. 60,000 and premium Rs. 10,000.

(ii) 4,000 equity shares of Rs. 10 each are issued for the balance required for redemption.

(13) A company has 2,000, 11% preference shares of Rs. 100 each fully paid. It decides to redeem the same out of profit. Pass the journal entries if the shares are redeemed (1) At par value; and (2) At 10% premium.

(14) The following balances are appearing in the ledger of the company as on 31-12-1997 :

Share Capital :	Rs.
Equity Shares (fully paid up)	3,00,000
Preference Shares (fully paid up)	
(Redeemable at 10% premium)	2,00,000
General Reserve	1,50,000
Profit and Loss Account (Cr. Balance)	1,00,000
Share Premium Account	30,000

The company decided to redeem the Preference Shares fully out of General Reserve to the extent of full amount and balance from Profit and Loss Account.

Give the journal entries relating to the redemption of Preference Shares.

(Karnataka, April, 1998)

Hint : Entry for the transfer of the required amount from general reserve and profit and loss account to capital redemption reserve : Debit General Reserve A/c (1,50,000) and P & L A/c (50,000) and Credit Capital Redemption Reserve A/c.

(C) Solve the following Problems :

(Each Carries 16 Marks)

(1) The following balances were extracted from the books of a limited company as on 31-3-92 :

		Rs.
(a)	2,000 8% Redeemable preference shares of Rs. 100 each fully called	2,00,000
	Less : Calls in arrears at Rs. 20 per share on 200 shares	4,000
	Paid up amount	1,96,000
(b)	General reserve	90,000
(c)	Capital reserve	10,000

The preference shares were redeemed on this day at a premium of Rs. 5 per share. The company issued further equity shares of Rs. 100 each at 10% premium, which were necessary for the purpose of redemption. These shares were fully subscribed and paid up.

Pass the journal entries to record the issue of equity shares and redemption of Preference Shares.

(*Karnataka, Oct., 1993*)

Hints : (i) Payments to redeemable preference shareholders Rs. 1,89,000 (1,80,000 + 9,000)

(ii) Issue of fresh equity shares for redemption :

Total funds required for the nominal value Rs.	1,80,000
Less : Funds available *i.e.*, general reserve	90,000
Issue of fresh equity shares	90,000

Equity share premium of Rs. 9,000 (*i.e.*, 10% of 90,000) is adjusted against premium (Rs. 9,000) on redemption of preference shares.

(iii) Number of pref. shares redeemed is equal to 1,800 (*i.e.*, 2,000 –200), because only fully paid shares are to be redeemed.

(2) The following is the balance sheet of a limited company as on 31st Dec., 1981 :

Liabilities	Rs.	Assets	Rs.
6% Redeemable Pre. Shares :		Sundry Assets	3,10,000
1,000 Shares of Rs. 100 each	1,00,000	Cash at Bank	1,40,000
Equity Shares :			
2,000 Equity Shares of Rs. 100 each	2,00,000		
Sundry Creditors	30,000		
Profit and Loss A/c	1,20,000		
	4,50,000		4,50,000

The company resolved to redeem its preference share capital at a premium of 2% out of profits.

Pass the necessary Journal Entries and show the important Ledger Accounts and the Company's Balance Sheet after the completion of redemption.

(*Adapted from Mysore, B.Com., Sept., 1969*)

Ans. : Balance Sheet Total Rs. 3,48,000; Balance of P& L A/c Rs. 18,000.

Notes : (i) Amount debited to P & L A/c. Rs. 1,02,000 *i.e.*, Rs. 2,000 premium on redemption of Pref. Shares and Rs. 1,00,000 Capital redemption reserve.

(ii) Balance of cash Rs. 38,000 (1,40,000 – 1,02,000).

(3) The following is Balance Sheet of Dhanvanti Ltd. as on 31-12-1990 :

Liabilities		Rs.	Assets	Rs.
Share Capital :			Sundry Assets	6,10,000
5,000 Equity Shares of Rs. 100 each fully paid		5,00,000	Cash at Bank	4,40,000
2,000 Red. Pref. Shares of Rs. 100 each fully called	2,00,000			
Less : Calls unpaid (Rs. 20 per share)	2,000	1,98,000		
1,000 7% Redeemable Preference Shares of Rs. 100 each Rs. 60 per share paid		60,000		
Profit & Loss Account		2,40,000		
Creditors		52,000		
		10,50,000		10,50,000

On the above date the preference shares are redeemed to the extent possible at a premium of 5%. Give Journal Entries and also show the amended balance sheet.

(*Karnataka, April, 1983*)

Ans. : Balance Sheet Total Rs. 8,50,500; Balance of Profit Rs. 40,500.

Notes : (i) The amount debited to P & L A/c Rs. 1,99,500 *i.e.*, Rs. 9,500 premium on redemption of Pref. Shares and Rs. 1,90,000 capital redemption reserve.

(ii) Balance of cash Rs. 2,40,500 (*i.e.*, 4,40,000 – 1,99,500).

(iii) Number of Pref. Shares redeemed = 1,900 (2,000 – 100 *i.e.*, 2,000/20).

(4) The following is the summarized Balance Sheet of a company as on April 30, 1979 :

Liabilities	Rs.	Assets	Rs.
Issued, Subscribed and Paid up Capital :		Sundry Assets	18,00,000
		Cash at Bank	6,60,000
4,000, 8% redeemable pref. shares of Rs. 100 each fully called up and paid up	4,00,000		
3,000, 9% Redeemable pref. shares of Rs. 100 each, Rs. 80 paid-up	2,40,000		
1,00,000 Equity shares of Rs. 10 each fully called up and paid up	10,00,000		
Share Premium A/c	50,000		
Revenue Reserve	5,00,000		
Current Liabilities	2,70,000		
	24,60,000		24,60,000

It was decided to redeem both the classes of preference shares on June 30, at a premium of 5%. In May 1979, the company issued for cash as many equity shares of Rs. 10 each as were necessary to provide for redemption of both classes of preference shares, which could not otherwise redeemed. The issue was fully subscribed and all the monies were received.

Give the Journal Entries in the books of the company and draw up the amended Balance Sheet.

(A.C.S., Dec., 1979)

Ans. : Balance Sheet Total Rs. 19,85,000; Cash at Bank Rs. 1,85,000 (*i.e.*, 6,60,000 + 60,000 + 2,00,000 – 7,35,000).

Hints : (i) Amount received on calls Rs. 60,000 (*i.e.*, 3,000 shares of Rs. 20 each)

(ii) Balance of Share Premium A/c Rs. 15,000 (*i.e.*, Rs. 50,000 – 35,000 premium)

(iii) Amount received on the fresh issue of shares Rs. 2,00,000.

(5) Spot Light Limited, has issued Share Capital of 60,000, 8% Redeemable Cumulative Preference Shares of Rs. 20 each and 4,00,000, Equity Shares of Rs. 10 each. The preference shares are redeemable at a premium of 5% on 1st January, 1981.

As at 31st Dec., 1980, the company's Balance Sheet showed the following position :

Liabilities	Rs.	Assets	Rs.
Issued Share Capital :		Plant and Machinery	25,00,000
60,000, 8% redeemable		Furniture and Fixture	9,00,000
Cumulative Preference Shares		Stock	15,00,000
of Rs. 10 each fully paid	12,00,000	Debtors	14,00,000
4,00,000 Equity Shares of		Investments	3,50,000
Rs. 10 each fully paid	40,00,000	Balance at Bank	3,50,000
Profit and Loss A/c	7,00,000		
Sundry Creditors	11,00,000		
	70,00,000		70,00,000

In order to facilitate the redemption of preference shares it was decided :

(a) to sell the Investments for Rs. 3,00,000.

(b) to finance part of the redemption from company funds subjected to leaving of balance of profit and loss account of Rs. 2,00,000.

(c) to issue sufficient Equity Shares of Rs. 10 each at a premium of Rs. 2 per share to raise the balance of funds required.

The preference shares were redeemed on due date and equity shares were fully subscribed.

You are required to prepare :

(i) Journal Entries to record the above transactions.

(ii) A Memorandum Balance Sheet as on completion of redemption.

(I.C.W.A., June, 1981)

Ans. : Balance Sheet Total Rs. 65,90,000; Cash at Bank Rs. 2,90,000 (*i.e.*, 3,50,000 + 3,00,000 + 7,50,000 + 1,50,000 – 12,60,000).

Hints : (1) The amount of fresh issue of equity shares is arrived as below :

Total fund required for nominal value	12,00,000
Less : Funds available from Profit and Loss A/c (*i.e.,* 7,00,000–50,000 Loss on sale of investment = 6,50,000 – 2,00,000 minimum balance to be retained on Profit and Loss A/c)	4,50,000
Total amount to be required	7,50,000

$$\therefore \text{ No. of shares to be issued} = \frac{7{,}50{,}000}{10} = 75{,}000$$

(2) Shares Premium A/c balance Rs. 90,000
[*i.e.*, Rs. 1,50,000 (75,000 × 2) – 60,000]

(6) The following is the balance sheet of X Co. Ltd. as on 31-12-1994.

Liabilities		Rs.	Assets	Rs.
Share Capital :			Cash at Bank	1,50,000
2,000 Equity Shares of			Sundry Assets	3,50,000
Rs. 100 each fully paid		2,00,000		
1,000 Redeemable Pref.				
Shares of Rs. 100 each				
fully called	1,00,000			
Less : Calls unpaid				
Rs. 20 per share	1,000	99,000		
Profit and Loss A/c		1,50,000		
Sundry Creditors		51,000		
		5,00,000		5,00,000

On the above date, the preference shares were redeemed to the possible extent at a premium of 10%.

Pass the journal entries and show the amended balance sheet.

(*Karnataka, Oct., 1995*)

Ans. : Balance of Profit Rs. 45,500 (1,50,000 – 95,000 = 55,000 – 9,500); Capital Redemption Reserve Rs. 95,000 an Balance Sheet Total Rs. 3,95,500.

Note : 950 shares are fully paid. Hence they are redeemed. But, partly paid 50 shares are not redeemed.

Problems on Issue of Bonus Shares

(7) The extracts are given from the draft Balance Sheet of Bharat Gears Ltd., as on 31st December, 1984 :

	Rs.
Authorised Capital :	
20,000 Equity Shares of Rs. 10 each	2,00,000
Issued and Subscribed Capital :	
7,000 Equity Shares of Rs. 10 each, fully called up	70,000
Reserve Fund	36,000
Profit and Loss Account	29,000

The board of directors pass a resolution to capitalise a part of existing reserves and profits by issuing bonus shares. One bonus share is being issued for every 4 equity shares held at present. For this purpose, Rs. 10,000 are to provide out of reserve fund and the balance out of the Profit and Loss Account.

Set out Journal Entries to give effect to the resolution and show how they would affect the Balance Sheet of the company.

(*B.Com., Panjab*)

Note : Bonus shares issued 1,750 of Rs. 10 each; Balance of Reserve fund Rs. 26,000 and Profit and Loss A/c Rs. 21,500.

(8) H Ltd. has the capital consisting of 10,000 equity shares of Rs. 100 each Rs. 75 per share paid up.

The company has a share premium account of Rs. 1,00,000, general reserve of Rs. 1,50,000 and profit and loss account credit balance Rs. 2,00,000.

On 31-12-1991 the company decided to capitalise its premium, reserve and profit by declaring bonus to the shareholders to be utilised as follows :

(a) To make the partly paid shares as fully paid up.

(b) To issue one fully paid bonus shares of Rs. 100 each for every 10 shares already held in the company.

For the above purpose the company decided to utilise the entire amount of share premium and general reserve and to utilise the profit and loss account balance only to the required extent.

Pass the necessary journal entries in the books of the company.

(*Gulbarga, Oct., 1993 and Karnataka, Oct., 1994*)

Note : Total bonus declared Rs. 3,50,000 of which Rs. 2,50,000 is utilised for adjusting against final call and 1,00,000 is utilised for issuing 1,000 bonus shares of Rs. 100 each.

(9) A company has accumulated large profits in the reserve account and directors decided to utilise a part of this in order to make the capital property representative of the financial position.

The paid up share capital is Rs. 10,00,000 consisting of 90,000. Equity Shares of Rs. 10 each fully paid and 20,000 equity shares (face value Rs. 10 each) Rs. 5 per share paid up. The directors decided to issue one bonus share at a premium of Rs. 10 for every fully paid share held and to make the partly paid shares fully paid. At the date of the allotment of bonus shares, the market value of the equity share stands at Rs. 33.

Give necessary journal entries in respect of the above transactions.

(*B.Com., Panjab*)

Note : Bonus Shares issued 1,10,000 of Rs. 10 each at a premium Rs. 10.

(10) The balance sheet of Tungabhadra Ltd. as on 31-12-1984 was as follows :

Liabilities	Rs.	Assets	Rs.
Share Capital :		Goodwill	2,00,000
4,000 Shares of		Plant and Machinery	2,50,000
Rs. 100 each	4,00,000	Land and Buildings	1,75,000
Share Premium	1,00,000	Investments	1,25,000
General Reserve	2,00,000	Sundry Debtors	1,50,000
Profit and Loss A/c	1,60,000	Cash at Bank	40,000
Sundry Creditors	90,000	Cash in Hand	10,000
	9,50,000		9,50,000

The company decided to issue bonus shares at the rate of '3' shares for every '4' shares held by utilizing the shares premium, Rs. 1,20,000 out of general reserve and the balance out of profit and loss account.

Give the journal entries to give effect of the above and prepare amended balance sheet.

(*Gulbarga, April, 1985*)

Ans. : Bonus declared Rs. 3,00,000. Balance of profit Rs. 80,000 and Balance Sheet Total Rs. 9,50,000.

(11) The following balance sheet shows the position of Mick Cements Ltd. as on 31-12-1985 :

Liabilities	Rs.	Assets	Rs.
10,000 Shares of Rs. 100		Sundry Assets	20,50,000
each Rs. 75 paid	7,50,000		
General Reserve	4,00,000		
Profit and Loss A/c	3,00,000		
Share Premium	2,00,000		
Sundry Creditors	4,00,000		
	20,50,000		20,50,000

The company decided to make the shares fully paid out of profit and loss account. Further they decided to issue one fully paid up bonus share for every two shares held. For this purpose the share premium account was to be used fully and then the general reserve.

Pass the journal entries in the books of the company and prepare a fresh balance sheet after making the above agreements.

(*Gulbarga, Oct., 1988*)

Ans. : Bonus share issued 5,000 of Rs. 100 each; Profit utilised Rs. 2,50,000; Balance Sheet Total Rs. 20,50,000.

(12) The following is the balance sheet of a limited company as on 31-3-1993 :

Liabilities	Rs.	Assets	Rs.
Share Capital :		Goodwill	50,000
2,000 Equity Shares of		Buildings	80,000
Rs. 100 each Rs. 70		Machinery	40,000
paid up	1,40,000	Furniture	24,000
Share Premium	60,000	Stock	56,000
General Reserve	30,000	Debtors	60,000
Profit and Loss A/c	50,000	Cash at Bank	10,000
Sundry Creditors	40,000		
	3,20,000		3,20,000

On the above date the company decided to capitalise its reserve and profits by declaring bonus to be utilised as follows :

(a) To make partly paid shares as fully paid shares.

(b) To issue 3 fully paid bonus shares of Rs. 10 each for every 10 shares already held in the company.

For the above purpose the company decided to utilise the entire amount of share premium and general reserve and the balance out of Profit and Loss Account.

Pass the journal entries and prepare the amended balance sheet of the company.

(*Gulbarga, Oct., 1994*)

Ans. : Bonus declared Rs. 1,20,000 (60,000 + 30,000 + 30,000); Balance Sheet Total Rs. 3,20,000 (2,60,000 + 20,000 + 40,000).

(13) The following balance sheet of Happy Coments Ltd. as on 31-12-1995 :

Liabilities	Rs.	Assets	Rs.
Share Capital :		Buildings	5,00,000
5,000 Shares of Rs. 100		Machinery	2,00,000
each Rs. 75 per share paid	3,75,000	Stock	2,00,000
General Reserve	2,00,000	Bank	1,25,000
Profit and Loss A/c	1,50,000		
Share Premium	1,00,000		
Sundry Creditors	2,00,000		
	10,25,000		10,25,000

The company decided to make the shares fully paid out of profit and loss account. Further they decided to issue one fully paid bonus share for every two shares already held. For this purpose the share premium was to be utilised fully and the balance out of general reserve.

Pass the journal entries in the books of the company and prepare the fresh balance sheet.

(*Gulbarga, April, 1996*)

Ans. : Bonus shares issued Rs. 2,50,000; Profit utilised Rs. 1,25,000 (5,000 × 25); Balance Sheet Total Rs. 10,25,000 (Share Capital Rs. 7,50,000).

14

COMPANY ACCOUNTS–II

(Redemption of Debentures)

Meaning : Redemption of debentures means repayment of debentures issued by a company. In other words, it refers to discharge the liability in respect of debentures issued. Debentures can be redeemed at the expiry of the specified period or even before that. The amount to be paid on redemption of debentures is determined by the terms and conditions and also the circumstances of the redemption. If the debentures are redeemed either at the expiry of specified period or in annual instalments, the redemption will be made at par or at a premium. But if the debentures are redeemed at any time before the expiry of a specified period by purchasing the own debentures in the open market, the redemption may be made at par or at a discount or at a premium.

Sources of the Redemption of Debentures

Debentures can be redeemed out of :

(1) Profits

(2) Capital *i.e.*, working capital

(3) Funds raised by the issue of new shares or debentures.

(4) Funds raised by the disposal of some of the fixed assets.

(5) Sale proceeds of debenture redemption fund investments.

(6) Amount of insurance policy taken for his purpose.

Debentures can also be redeemed by the issue of new shares or debentures in exchange for the existing debentures.

Methods of Redemption of Debentures

The following are the main methods of redeeming the debentures :

(1) Redemption of debentures at or within the specified period as per the terms of issue.

(2) Redemption of debentures by annual drawings.

(3) Redemption of debentures by conversion.

(4) Redemption of debentures by purchase of own debentures in the open market.

The above methods are discussed in detail as below :

(1) Redemption of debentures at the expiry of the specified period or at any time within the specified period

Under this method, the entire amount is paid to the debentureholders at the expiry of the specified period or at the option of the company, at any time within the specified period under the terms of issue. The amount may be paid either the face value or at more than or less than the face value of the debentures. The entire amount of debenture is paid in one lump sum either (a) out of working capital (*i.e.*, general cash), (b) out of profits, (c) out of proceeds of the fresh issue of shares or debentures, (d) out of sale proceeds of some fixed assets, (e) out of sinking fund created for the purpose, or (f) out of insurance policy amount created for the purpose.

(A) Redemption of debentures out of capital

Under this method, the entire amount of debentures is paid in lump sum out of the working capital (i.e., general cash) either at or within the specified period. The following Journal entries are to be passed in this case :

(a) When the debentures are redeemed at par :

(i) *If the debentures become due :*

Debentures' Account	Dr.	With nominal or face value of debentures to be redeemed
To Debentureholders' A/c *or* Debenture Redemption A/c		

(ii) *If the debentures are redeemed :*

Debentureholders' Account *or* Debenture Redemption A/c	Dr.	With the amount paid to debentureholders
To Bank Account		

(b) When the debentures are redeemed at a discount :

(i) *If the debentures become due :*

Debentures' Account	Dr.	With nominal value
To Debentureholders' A/c *or* Debenture Redemption A/c		With the amount payable
To Profit on Redemption of Debentures' A/c		With the amount of discount

(ii) *If the debentures are redeemed :*

Debentureholders' Account *or*	Dr.	With the amount paid to debentureholders
Debenture Redemption A/c	Dr.	
To Bank Account		

(c) When the debentures are redeemed at a premium :

(i) *If the debentures become due :*

Debenture Account	Dr.	With nominal value
Premium on Redemption of Debenture Account	Dr.	With the amount of premium
To Debentureholders' A/c *or* Debenture Redemption A/c		With the amount payable

(ii) *If the debentures are redeemed :*

Debentureholders' Account *or* Debenture Redemption A/c	Dr.	With the amount paid to the debentureholders
To Bank Account		

Note : The profit made on the redemption of debentures is a capital profit. Hence, it has to be transferred to Capital Reserve Account with the help of the following entry :

Profit on Redemption of Debentures' Account	Dr.	With the amount of profit on redemption of debentures
To Capital Reserve A/c		

Hint : If the debentures to be redeemed are transferred to the debentureholders' account, debentureholders' account is to be credited. Similarly, if the debentures to be redeemed are transferred to the debenture redemption account, then, debenture redemption account is to be credited.

Illustration 1

On 1st January, 1993, the Chetana Ltd., issued 3,000 6% Debentures of Rs. 100 each at a discount of 10% and these Debentures were redeemed at a premium of 5% at the end of three years out of capital. Give the necessary entries.

Solution :

In the books of Chetana Ltd.
Journal Entries

Date	Particulars		L.F.	Dr. Rs.	Cr. Rs.
1993	Bank Account	Dr.		2,70,000	
Jan. 1	Loss on Issue of Debentures' A/c	Dr.		45,000	
	To Debentures' Account				3,00,000
	To Premium on Redem. of Debentures' A/c				15,000
	(Being 3,000 debentures of Rs. 100 each issued at a discount of 10% but repayable at a premium of 5%)				

(Contd.)

Journal Entries *(Contd.)*

Dec. 31	Profit and Loss Account Dr.		15,000	
	To Loss on Issue of Debentures A/c			15,000
	(Being 1/3rd of loss on issue of debentures written off in 1993 transferred to Profit and Loss A/c)			
1994	Profit and Loss Account Dr.		15,000	
Dec. 31	To Loss on Issue of Debentures' A/c			15,000
	(Being 1/3rd of loss on issue of debentures written off in 1994 transferred to Profit and Loss A/c)			
1995	Profit and Loss Account Dr.		15,000	
Dec. 31	To Loss on Issue of Debentures' A/c			15,000
	(Being 1/3rd of loss on issue of debentures written off in 1995 transferred to Profit and Loss A/c)			
1995	Debentures Account Dr.		3,00,000	
Dec. 31	Premium on Redem. of Debenture A/c Dr.		15,000	
	To Debentureholders' Account			3,15,000
	(Being the transfer of the amount due on debentures' redeemable at a premium of 5%)			
1995	Debentureholders' Account Dr.		3,15,000	
Dec. 31	To Bank Account			3,15,000
	(Being the amount paid to debentureholders)			

(B) Redemption of Debentures out of Profits

Under the method, the entire amount of debenture is paid to the debentureholders in lump sum out of the accumulated profits either at or within the specified period. The accounting entries to be passed, in this case, will be the same as those passed in the case of redemption of debentures out of capital. But, when the debentures are redeemed at or within specified period out of profits, an amount equal to the face value or nominal value of debentures redeemed is to be transferred from profit to general reserve account. Therefore, one more journal entry is required to be passed as below :

Profit and Loss Appropriation A/c Dr. To General Reserve Account	With the amount of profit transferred togeneral reserve

Illustration 2

On 1-1-1993 a Limited Company issued debentures of the face value of Rs. 5,00,000 at par repayable at par at the end of four years out of profit. Show the necessary journal entries.

Solution :

In the books of the Company Ltd.
Journal Entries

Date	Particular	L.F.	Dr. Rs.	Cr. Rs.
1993	Bank Account Dr.		5,00,000	
Jan. 1	To Debentures' Account			5,00,000
	(Being the debentures issued at par)			
1996	Debentures' Account Dr.		5,00,000	
Dec. 31	To Debentureholders' A/c			5,00,000
	(Being the transfer of the amount due on debentures redeemable to Debentureholders' A/c)			
1996	Debentureholders' A/c Dr.		5,00,000	
Dec. 31	To Bank Account			5,00,000
	(Being payment made to debentureholders)			
1996	Profit and Loss Appropriation A/c Dr.		5,00,000	
Dec. 31	To General Reserve Account			5,00,000
	(Being an amount equal to the nominal value of the debentures redeemed is transferred from Profit and Loss Appropriation A/c to General Reserve Account)			

(C) Redemption of debentures out of proceeds of fresh issue of shares or debentures

Under this method, cash is paid to the debentureholders at or within the specified period out of the proceeds of the fresh issue of shares or debentures made for the purpose of redemption of debentures. The journal entries to be passed in this case are given below:

(a) Entries for the fresh issue of shares or debentures :

(i) *If the fresh shares or debentures are issued at par :*

Bank Account	Dr.	With amount received on the issue of fresh shares or debentures
To Share Capital A/c or		
To Debentures' A/c		

(ii) *If the fresh shares or debentures are issued at a discount :*

Bank Account	Dr.	With actual amount received
Discount on Issue of Shares' A/c *or*		
Discount on Issue of Debentures' A/c	Dr.	With the amount of discount allowed
To Share Capital A/c *or* Debentures' A/c		With the nominal value of fresh issue

(iii) *If the fresh shares or debentures are issued at a premium :*

Bank Account	Dr	With total amount received
To Share Capital A/c *or* Debentures' Account		With the nominal value of fresh issue
To Share Premium A/c *or* Debentures Premium A/c		With the amount of Premium

(b) Entries for the redemption of debentures :

The journal entries to be passed in this case, will be the same as those passed in the case of redemption of debentures out of capital.

Illustration 3

On 1-1-1993, the Moon Ltd., issued 6,000 8% debentures of Rs. 100 each at par repayable at par at the end of the four years or at any time within the maturity. On 31st December, 1996, the company issued 6,000 equity shares of Rs. 100 each at a premium of 5% for the purpose of redemption of debentures. All the shares were duly subscribed and fully paid and debentures were redeemed.

Show the necessary journal entries and ledger accounts for four years.

Solution :

In the Books of Moon Ltd.

Journal Entries

Date	Particulars	L.F.	Dr. Rs.	Cr. Rs.
1993	Bank Account Dr.		6,00,000	
Jan. 1	To Debentures' Account			6,00,000
	(Being the debentures issued at par)			
1996	Bank Account Dr.		6,30,000	
Dec. 31	To Equity Share Capital A/c			6,00,000
	To Share Premium A/c			30,000
	(Being equity shares are issued at a premium)			
1996	Debentures' Account Dr.		6,00,000	
Dec. 31	To Debentureholders' A/c			6,00,000
	(Being transfer of debentures to be redeemed to debentureholders' account)			
1996	Debentureholders' Account Dr.		6,00,000	
Dec. 31	To Bank Account			6,00,000
	(Being amount paid to debentureholders)			

Ledger Accounts :

Dr. **Debentures Accounts** Cr.

		Rs.			Rs.
1993 Dec. 31	To Balance c/d	6,00,000	1993 Jan. 1	By Bank A/c	6,00,000
		6,00,000			6,00,000
1994 Dec. 31	To Balance c/d	6,00,000	1994 Jan. 1	By Balance b/d	6,00,000
		6,00,000			6,00,000
1995 Dec. 31	To Balance c/d	6,00,000	1995 Jan. 1	By Balance b/d	6,00,000
		6,00,000			6,00,000
1996 Dec. 31	To Debenture-holders' A/c	6,00,000	1996 Jan. 1	By Balance b/d	6,00,000
		6,00,000			6,00,000

Dr. **Debentureholders' Account** Cr.

		Rs.			Rs.
1996 Dec. 31	To Bank A/c	6,00,000	1996 Dec. 31	By Debentures A/c	6,00,000
		6,00,000			6,00,000

(D) Redemption of debentures out of the sale proceeds of some fixed assets

Under this method, the entire cash of debentures is paid to the debentureholders either at or within the specified period out of the sale proceeds of some fixed assets. The following entries are to be passed in this case :

(a) Entries of the sale of fixed assets :

(i) *If the fixed asset is sold at the book value :*

Bank Account	Dr.	With the amount of sale proceeds received
To Concerned Fixed Asset		

(ii) *If the fixed asset is sold at a profit :*

Bank Account	Dr.	With the amount received
To Concerned Fixed Asset		With the book value
To Profit and Loss Account		With the amount of profit

(iii) *If the fixed asset is sold at a loss :*

Bank Account	Dr.	With the amount received
Profit and Loss Account	Dr.	With the amount of loss
To Concerned Fixed Asset A/c		With the book value

(b) Entries for the redemption of debentures :

The journal entries to be passed in this case, will be same as those passed in the case of redemption of debentures out of capital.

Illustration 4

On 1-1-1990, Not-So-Well Ltd., issued 2,500 debentures of Rs. 100 each at par redeemable at par at the end of the five years. On 31-12-1994, the company sold the plant of Rs. 3,00,000 for Rs. 3,10,000 and the debentures were redeemed with the sale proceeds of the plant.

Show the journal entries.

Solution :

Not-So-Well Ltd.
Journal Entries

Date	Particulars	L.F.	Dr. Rs.	Cr. Rs.
1990 Jan. 1	Bank Account Dr. To Debentures' Account (Being debentures are issued at par)		2,50,000	2,50,000
1994 Dec. 31	Bank Account Dr. To Plant Account To Profit and Loss A/c (*i.e.*, Profit on sale of plant *i.e.*, 3,20,000 – 3,00,000) (Being plant sold at a profit)		3,20,000	3,00,000 20,000
1994 Dec. 31	Debentures' Account Dr. To Debentureholders' A/c (Being transfer of debentures to be redeemed to debentureholders' account)		2,50,000	2,50,000
1994 Dec. 31	Debentureholders' Account Dr. To Bank Account (Being cash paid to debentureholders)		2,50,000	2,50,000

(E) Redemption of Debentures out of Sinking Fund

Sinking fund or Debenture Redemption Fund is created by setting aside a certain fixed amount out of profit at the end of every year. The money so set aside is invested outside the business in gilt-edge securities. The interest earned on such securities is also reinvested in the outside securities along with the annual fixed amount provided. The investments in the outside securities and the interest received on the investments are to be credited to the Sinking Fund Account or Debenture Redemption Fund Account till the debentures are to be redeemed. When debentures become due for redemption, the securities or sinking fund investments are disposed of and the proceeds are utilised for the purpose of redemption on debentures. The profit or loss on sale of such securities or investments being transferred to Sinking Fund Account. If any balance is left in the Sinking Fund Account after the redemption of debentures, the same (i.e., profit) is to be transferred to General Reserve Account. The annual investment or instalment amount is calculated with the help of Sinking Fund Table.

Journal Entries :

The entries to be passed at the various stages are given below :

(a) At the end of the first year :

(*1*) *For the amount set aside every year :*

Profit and Loss Appropriation A/c To Sinking Fund A/c *or* Debenture Redemption Fund A/c	Dr.	With the amount set aside out of profits

(*2*) *For investing the amount set aside in securities :*

Sinking Fund Investment A/c *or* Debenture Redemption Fund Investment A/c To Bank or Cash Account	Dr.	With the actual amount invested in securities

(b) At the end of second and subsequent year :

(*1*) *For interest received on previous year's or years' investments :*

Bank Account To Interest on Sinking Fund Investment A/c	Dr.	With the amount of interest received on investments

(*2*) *For interest transferred to sinking fund :*

Interest on Sinking Fund Investment A/c To Sinking Fund Account	Dr.	With the amount of interest received

(*3*) *For the annual amount set aside:*

Profit & Loss Appropriation A/c To Sinking Fund A/c	Dr.	With the amount set aside out of profit

(*4*) *For investing the amount set aside plus interest in securities :*

Sinking Fund Investment A/c To Bank or Cash A/c	Dr.	With the amount set aside plus interest

(c) At the end of last year in which redemption is carried out :

(*1*) *For interest received on previous year's investments :*

Bank Account To Interest on Sinking Fund Investment Account	Dr.	With the amount of interest received on investments

(2) *For interest transferred to sinking fund :*

Interest on Sinking Fund Investment A/c	Dr.	With the amount
To Sinking Fund Account		of interest received

(3) *For the annual amount set aside :*

Profit & Loss Appropriation A/c	Dr.	With the amount
To Sinking Fund A/c		set aside

(4) *For investment sold and realised :*

Bank or Cash Account	Dr.	With sale proceeds
To Sinking Fund Investment A/c		of investments

(5) *For transferring the profits or losses on sale of investments :*

(i) *If there is a profit on sale of investments :*

Sinking Fund Investment A/c	Dr.	With the amount of
To Sinking Fund Account		profit

(ii) *If there is a loss on sale of investments :*

Sinking Fund Account	Dr.	With the amount of
To Sinking Fund Investment A/c		loss

(6) *For redeeming or paying off the debentures :*

(i) *If debentures are redeemed at par :*

Debentures' Account	Dr.	With the nominal
To Bank or Cash Account		value of debentures

(ii) *If debentures are redeemed at a discount :*

Debentures' Account	Dr.	With the nominal value
To Bank or Cash Account		With actual cash paid
To Profit on Sinking Fund A/c		With the amount of discount

(iii) *If debentures are redeemed at a Premium :*

Debentures' Account	Dr.	With the nominal value
Premium on Redemption of Debentures' A/c	Dr.	With the amount of premium
To Bank Account		With actual cash paid

Note : The premium on Redemption of Debentures is closed by transferring to Share Premium A/c or Sinking Fund A/c.

(7) *For transferring the balance of sinking fund account to general reserve :*

Sinking Fund Account	Dr.	With the amount of
To General Reserve Account		balance

(8) *For payment made to debentureholders :*

Debentureholders' Account	Dr.	With the amount paid
To Bank or Cash A/c		

Illustration 5

On January 1, 1995, R Ltd., issued 3,500 5% debentures of Rs. 10 each repayable at par at the end of the 4 years. It was decided to create a sinking fund for redemption of the debentures and invest the amount of fund in 4% Government Securities.

The Sinking Fund Table shows that an investment of Re. 0.235490 annually over 4 years fetches Re. 1 at 4% compound interest.

Show the necessary ledger accounts for 4 years.

Solution :

In the books of R. Ltd.

Dr. **5% Debentures' Accounts** Cr.

		Rs.			Rs.
31-12-95	To Balance c/d	35,000	1-1-95	By Bank A/c	35,000
		35,000			35,000
31-12-96	To Balance c/d	35,000	1-1-96	By Balance b/d	35,000
		35,000			35,000
31-12-97	To Balance c/d	35,000	1-1-97	By Balance b/d	35,000
		35,000			35,000
31-12-98	To Bank	35,000	1-1-98	By Balance b/d	35,000
		35,000			35,000

Dr. **Debenture Sinking Fund Account** Cr.

		Rs.			Rs.
31-12-95	To Balance c/d	8,242.15	31-12-95	By P & L Appropriation A/c	8,242.15
		8,242.15			8,242.15
31-12-96	To Balance c/d	16,813.99	1-1-96	By Balance b/d	8,242.15
			31-12-96	By Interest on Sinking Fund Investment A/c	329.69
			31-12-96	By P&L Appropriation A/c	8,242.15
		16,813.99			16,813.99
31-12-97	To Balance c/d	25,728.70	1-1-97	By Balance b/d	16,813.99
			31-12-97	By Interest on Sinking Fund Investment A/c	672.56
			31-12-97	By P&L Appropriation A/c	8,242.15
		25,728.70			25,728.70
31-12-98	To General Reserve (Balancing Figure transferred)	35,000.00	1-1-98	By Balance b/d	25,728.70
			31-12-98	By Interest on Sinking Fund Investment A/c	1,029.15
			31-12-98	By P&L Appropriation A/c	8,242.15
		35,000.00			35,000.00

Dr. **Debenture Sinking Fund Investment Account** Cr.

		Rs.			Rs.
31-12-95	To Bank (Instalment)	8,242.15	31-12-95	By Balance c/d	8,242.15
		8,242.15			8,242.15
1-1-96	To Balance b/d	8,242.15	31-12-96	By Balance c/d	16,813.99
31-12-96	To Bank (Interest)	329.69			
31-12-96	To Bank (Instalment)	8,242.15			
		16,813.99			16,813.99
1-1-97	To Balance b/d	16,813.99	31-12-97	By Balance c/d	25,728.70
31-12-97	To Bank (Interest)	672.56			
31-12-97	To Bank (Instalment)	8,242.15			
		25,728.70			25,728.70
1-1-98	To Balance b/d	25,728.70	31-12-98	By Bank (sold)	25,728.70
		25,728.70			25,728.70

Dr. **Interest on Sinking Fund Investment Account** Cr.

		Rs.			Rs.
31-12-96	To Sinking Fund	329.69	31-12-96	By Bank	329.69
		329.69			329.69
31-12-97	To Sinking Fund	672.56	31-12-97	By Bank	672.56
		672.56			672.56
31-12-98	To Sinking Fund	1,029.15	31-12-98	By Bank	1,029.15
		1,029.15			1,029.15

Working Notes :

(1) **Calculation of annual instalment amount :** To raise Re. 1 at 4% interest for four years, the amount required to set aside every year is Re. 0.235490. Therefore, to raise Rs. 35,000 for the redemption of debentures, the amount required to be set aside every year is Rs. 8,242.15 (i.e., 0.235490 × 35,000).

(2) The amount of investment sold is given in the problem, hence, it is assumed that they are sold at book value.

(3) The investments should not be made in the last year as they are to be sold in that year.

Illustration 6

On 1st January 1995, A Ltd. issued debentures for Rs. 50,000 redeemable at a premium of 10% at the end of 3 years. It has been decided to establish a sinking fund for the purpose, the investments being expected to realise 5% interest net. Annual instalment to provide Re. 1 at the end of 3 years at 5% compound interest is Re. 0.317209.

On December 31, 1997, the balance at Bank was Rs. 25,000 and the investments realised Rs. 35,000. The debentures were paid off.

Give journal entries and show ledger accounts.

Solution :

In the book of A Ltd.
Journal Entries

Date	Particular	L.F.	Dr. Rs.	Cr. Rs.
1990 Jan. 1	Bank Account Dr. Loss on Issue of Debentures' A/c Dr. To Debentures' Account To Premium on Redemption of Debentures' A/c (Being the issue of 50,000 debentures at par and repayable at a premium of 10%)		50,000 5,000	 50,000 5,000
Dec. 31	Profit & Loss Appropriation A/c Dr. To Sinking Fund Account (Being the amount set aside for the redemption of debentures 0.317209 × 55,000 = 17,446.50)		17,446.50	 17,446.50
Dec. 31	Sinking Fund Investment A/c Dr. To Bank Account (Being the amount of investment made)		17,446.50	 17,446.50
1996 Dec. 31	Bank Account Dr. To Interest on Sinking Fund Investment A/c (Being interest received at 5% on investments)		872.33	 872.33
1996 Dec. 31	Interest on Sinking Fund Investment A/c Dr. To Sinking Fund Account (Being interest transferred to sinking fund a/c)		872.33	 872.33
1996 Dec. 31	Profit & Loss Appropriation A/c Dr. To Sinking Fund Account (Being the amount set aside for the redemption of debentures)		17,446.50	 17,446.50
1996 Dec. 31	Sinking Fund Investment A/c Dr. To Bank Account (Being the annual instalment plus interest 17,446.50 + 872.32 invested)		18,318.82	 18,318.82
1997 Dec. 31	Bank Account Dr. To Interest on Sinking Fund Investment A/c (Being the interest received on investment at 5%)		1,788.27	 1,788.27

(Contd.)

Journal Entries (*Contd.*)

Date	Particulars		L.F.	Dr.	Cr.
1997 Dec. 31	Interest on Sinking Fund Investment A/c	Dr.		1,788.27	
	To Sinking Fund Account				1,788.27
	(Being interest transferred to sinking fund a/c)				
1997 Dec. 31	Profit & Loss Appropriation A/c	Dr.		17,446.50	
	To Sinking Fund Account				17,446.50
	(Being the amount set aside for the redemption)				
1997 Dec. 31	Bank Account	Dr.		35,000	
	To Sinking Fund Investment A/c				35,000
	(Being the investments sold)				
1997 Dec. 31	Sinking Fund Account	Dr.		765.33	
	To Sinking Fund Investment A/c				765.33
	(Being the loss on sale of investments transferred)				
1997 Dec. 31	Debentures' Account	Dr.		50,000	
	Premium on Redem. of Debentures' A/c	Dr.		5,000	
	To Bank Account				55,000
	(Being redemption of debentures at a premium)				
1997 Dec. 31	Sinking Fund Account	Dr.		5,000	
	To Loss on Issue of Debentures' A/c				5,000
	(Being the loss on issue of debentures written off against sinking fund account)				
1997 Dec. 31	Sinking Fund Account	Dr.		49,234.67	
	To General Reserve Account				49,234.67
	(Being the balance of sinking fund account transferred to general reserve on redemption of debentures)				

Ledger Accounts :

Dr. **Debentures' Account** Cr.

		Rs.			Rs.
31-12-95	To Balance c/d	50,000	1-1-95	By Balance b/d	50,000
		50,000			50,000
31-12-96	To Balance c/d	50,000	1-1-96	By Balance b/d	50,000
		50,000			50,000
31-12-97	To Bank	50,000	1-1-97	By Balance b/d	50,000
		50,000			50,000

Dr. **Premium on Redemption of Debentures' Account** Cr.

		Rs.			Rs.
31-12-95	To Balance c/d	5,000	1-1-95	By Loss on Issue of Debentures' A/c	5,000
		5,000			5,000
31-12-96	To Balance c/d	5,000	1-1-96	By Balance b/d	5,000
		5,000			5,000
31-12-97	To Bank	5,000	1-1-97	By Balance b/d	5,000
		5,000			5,000

Dr. **Sinking Fund Account** Cr.

		Rs.			Rs.
31-12-95	To Balance c/d	17,446.50	31-12-95	By P&L Appropriation A/c	17,446.50
		17,446.50			17,446.50
31-12-96	To Balance c/d	35,765.33	1-1-96	By Balance b/d	17,446.50
			31-12-96	By Interest on Sinking Fund Investment A/c	872.33
			31-12-96	By P&L Appropriation A/c	17,446.50
		35,765.33			35,765.33
31-12-97	To Sinking Fund Investment A/c (transfer)	765.33	1-1-97	By Balance b/d	35,765.33
31-12-97	To Loss on Issue	5,000.00	31-12-96	By Interest on Sinking Fund Investment A/c	1,788.27
31-12-97	To General Reserve	49,234.67		By P&L Appropriation A/c	17,446.40
		55,000.00			55,000.00

Dr. **Sinking Fund Investment Account** Cr.

		Rs.			Rs.
31-12-95	To Bank (Instalment)	17,446.50	31-12-95	By Balance c/d	17,446.50
		17,446.50			17,446.50
1-1-96	To Balance b/d	17,446.50	31-12-96	By Balance c/d	35,765.33
31-12-96	To Bank (Interest)	872.33			
31-12-96	To Bank (Instalment)	17,446.50			
		35,765.33			35,765.33
1-1-97	To Balance b/d	35,765.33	31-12-97	By Bank (Sale Proceeds)	35,000.00
				By Sinking Fund A/c (Loss transferred)	765.33
		35,765.33			35,765.33

Dr. **Interest on Sinking Fund Investment Account** Cr.

		Rs.			Rs.
31-12-96	To Sinking Fund A/c	872.33	31-12-96	By Bank	872.33
		872.33			872.33
31-12-97	To Sinking Fund A/c	1,788.27	31-12-97	By Bank	1,788.27
		1,788.27			1,788.27

Dr. **Bank Account** Cr.

		Rs.			Rs.
31-12-97	To Balance b/d	25,000	31-12-97	By Debentures	50,000
31-12-97	To Sinking Fund (Investment)	35,000		By Premium on Debentures	5,000
				By Balance c/d	5,000
		60,000			60,000

Note : The difference of 10 paise is adjusted in the last instalment.

Illustration 7

A Company has Rs. 60,000 6% debentures outstanding on 1-1-1990. On that date the Debenture Redemption Fund Account stood at Rs. 50,000 represented by Rs. 59,000, 3% Government of India Loan. The annual Instalment added to the debenture redemption fund is Rs. 8,230.

On 31-12-1990 the balance at bank (after interest on investments had been received) was Rs. 15,640. On that date the investments were sold at 83% net and the debentures were paid off.

Show the necessary ledger accounts for the year 1990.

(*Karnataka, Oct., 1983 & Mysore, Oct., 1969*)

Solution :

Dr. **Debenture Redemption Fund Account** Cr.

		Rs.			Rs.
31-12-90	To Debenture Redemption Fund Investment A/c (transfer)	1,030	1-1-90	By Balance b/d	50,000
			31-12-90	By Interest on Debenture Redemption Fund Investment A/c	1,770
31-12-90	To General Reserve (balance transferred)	58,970	31-12-90	By P&L Appropriation A/c	8,230
		60,000			60,000

Dr. Debenture Redemption Fund Investments Account Cr.

		Rs.			Rs.
1-1-90	To Balance c/d (face value Rs. 59,000)	50,000	31-12-90	By Bank $\left(59,000 \times \frac{83}{100}\right)$ (sale proceeds)	48,970
			31-12-90	By Debenture Redemption Fund A/c (Loss transferred)	1,030
		50,000			50,000

Dr. Bank Account Cr.

		Rs.			Rs.
31-12-90	To Balance b/d	15,640	31-12-90	By 6% Debentures	59,000
31-12-90	To Debenture Redemption Fund Investments (Sale proceeds)	48,970	31-12-90	By Balance c/d	5,610
		64,610			64,610

Notes : (i) It is assumed that interest on debentures has already been paid.

(ii) The balance of debenture redemption fund investment account should also be Rs. 50,000 *i.e.*, equal to the amount of fund.

Illustration 8

The Electronics Co. Ltd., had issued 9% debentures of Rs. 6,00,000, they were redeemable at 5% premium on 31-12-1986. On that date the following accounts showed the balances as below :

		Rs.
(1)	Debentures Redemption Account	6,50,000
(2)	Debentures Redemption Fund Investment Account (in 5% Government Bonds 1985 of the face value of Rs. 5,55,000)	5,43,000
(3)	Bank Account	5,70,000
(4)	Premium on Redemption of Debentures Account	30,000

On 31-12-1986, the investments were sold at 101% and all the debentures were duly redeemed.

Show the concerned accounts in the books of the company for the redemption of debentures.

(*Karnataka, Oct., 1988*)

Solution :

Dr. **9% Debentures' Account** Cr.

		Rs.			Rs.
31-12-86	To Bank (paid)	6,30,000	31-12-86	By Balance b/d	6,00,000
				By Premium on Redemption of Debentures	30,000
		6,30,000			6,30,000

Dr. **Premium on Redemption of Debentures' Account** Cr.

		Rs.			Rs.
31-12-86	To 9% Debentures (transferred)	30,000	31-12-86	By Balance b/d	30,000
		30,000			30,000

Dr. **Debenture Redemption Fund Account** Cr.

		Rs.			Rs.
31-12-86	To General Reserve (balance transferred)	6,67,550	31-12-86	By Balance b/d	6,50,000
			31-12-86	By Debenture Redemption Fund Investment A/c (transfer)	17,550
		6,67,550			6,67,550

Dr. **Debenture Redemption Fund Investment Account** Cr.

		Rs.			Rs.
31-12-86	To Balance b/d (face value Rs. 5,55,000)	5,43,000	31-12-86	By Bank (sale proceeds) $\left(i.e.,\ 5{,}55{,}000 \times \frac{101}{100}\right)$	5,60,550
31-12-86	To Debenture Redemption Fund A/c (transfer)	17,550			
		5,60,550			5,60,550

Dr. **Bank Account** Cr.

		Rs.			Rs.
31-12-86	To Balance b/d	5,70,000	31-12-86	By 9% Debentures	6,30,000
31-12-86	To Debenture Redemption Fund Investments (sale proceeds)	5,60,550	31-12-86	By Balance c/d	5,00,550
		11,30,550			11,30,550

Illustration 9

From the following balances of Sangameshwar Co. Ltd. as on 31-3-1982, write up the ledger accounts concerned :

	Rs.
11% Debentures	20,00,000
Debenture Redemption Fund	20,84,000
Debenture Redemption Investment	20,84,000

On 30-6-1982 the investments were sold for Rs. 22,70,400 and the debentures were paid off at 102% together with accrued interest which had been paid up to 31-3-1982.

(*Gulbarga, April, 1983*)

Solution :

Dr. **11% Debentures' Account** Cr.

		Rs.			Rs.
30-6-82	To Bank (paid)	20,40,000	1-4-82	By Balance b/d	20,00,000
				By Premium on Redemption of Debentures	40,000
		20,40,000			20,40,000

Dr. **Premium on Redemption of Debentures' Account** Cr.

		Rs.			Rs.
30-6-82	To 11% Debentures	40,000	30-6-82	By Debenture Redemption Fund A/c (adjusted)	40,000
		40,000			40,000

Dr. **Interest on Debentures' Account** Cr.

		Rs.			Rs.
30-6-82	To Bank (paid)	55,000	30-6-82	By Profit and Loss A/c	55,000
		55,000			55,000

Dr. **Debenture Redemption Fund Account** Cr.

		Rs.			Rs.
30-6-82	To Premium on Redemption of Debentures A/c (adjusted)	40,000	1-4-82	By Balance b/d	20,84,000
	To General Reserve (balance transferred)	22,30,400	30-6-82	By Debenture Redemption Fund Investments A/c (transfer)	1,86,400
		22,70,400			22,70,400

Dr. **Debenture Redemption Fund Investment Account** Cr.

		Rs.			Rs.
1-4-82	To Balance b/d	20,84,000	30-6-82	By Bank (sale proceeds)	22,70,400
30-6-82	To Debenture Redemption Fund A/c (profit transferred)	1,86,400			
		22,70,400			22,70,400

Illustration 10

The Debenture Redemption Fund Account of a limited company stood at Rs. 1,60,000 represented by Rs. 2,00,000 (nominal value) investments.

The debentures stood at Rs. 5,00,000 and the company sold Rs. 24,000 investments (nominal value) at Rs. 85 for the purpose of redeeming Rs. 20,000 debentures at Rs. 102.

Show the necessary ledger accounts (ignore interest).

(*Karnataka, Oct., 1981*)

Solution :

Dr. **Debenture Redemption Fund Account** Cr.

	Rs.		Rs.
To Premium on Redemption of Debentures (2% of 20,000)	400	By Balance b/d	1,60,000
To General Reserve (transferred)	20,000	By Debenture Redemption Fund Investment A/c (transfer)	1,200
To Balance c/d	1,40,800		
	1,61,200		1,61,200
		By Balance b/d	1,40,800

Dr. **Debenture Redemption Fund Investment Account** Cr.

	Rs.		Rs.
To Balance b/d (face value Rs. 2,00,000)	1,60,000	By Bank (24,000 × 85/100) (sale proceeds)	20,400
To Debenture Redemption Fund A/c (profit transferred)	1,200	By Balance c/d (face value Rs. 1,76,000 *i.e.*, 2,00,000 – 24,000) $\left(\frac{1,60,000 \times 1,76,000}{2,00,000}\right)$ = 1,40,800	1,40,800
	1,61,200		1,61,200
To Balance b/d	1,40,800		

Dr. **Debentures' Account** Cr.

	Rs.		Rs.
To Bank (i.e., 20,000 + 400 premium)	20,400	By Balance b/d	5,00,000
		By Premium on Redemption of Debentures (transfer)	400
To Balance c/d	4,80,000		
	5,00,400		5,00,400
		By Balance b/d	4,80,000

Note : Profit on sale of investments has been arrived as below :

Amount realised from sale of investments	Rs. 20,400
Less : Purchase price of investments sold	Rs. 19,200
Profit on sale of investments	Rs. 1,200

Purchase price of investments sold is calculated as below :

Investments of the nominal value of Rs. 2,00,000 were purchased for Rs. 1,60,000. Therefore, investments of the nominal value of Rs. 24,000 were purchased for

$$\left(\frac{1,60,000 \times 24,000}{2,00,000}\right) = \text{Rs. } 19,200$$

Illustration 11

A company had Rs. 4,00,000 6% debentures outstanding on 1-1-1990 redeemable at a premium of 2 ½% on 31-12-1990. On 30-6-1990, the company purchased their own debentures of the face value of Rs. 1,00,000 at 99% and immediately cancelled them. On 1-1-1990, the sinking fund for redemption of debentures as well as the corresponding investments showed a balance of Rs. 3,50,000 each. The investments were realised at a discount of 10% and the debentures were redeemed.

Show the Sinking Fund Account, Sinking Fund Investment Account and 6% Debenture Account for 1990. Ignore interest and taxes.

(C.U., B.Com. Hons.)

Solution :

In the Books of the Company

Dr. **6% Debentures' Account** Cr.

		Rs.			Rs.
30-6-90	To Bank (Purchase and cancellation of 1,00,000 Debentures at 99%)	99,000	1-1-90	By Balance b/d	4,00,000
	To Sinking Fund A/c (Profit on cancellation)	1,000	31-12-90	By Premium on Redemption of Debentures (2 ½% on 3,00,000)	7,500
31-12-90	To Bank	3,07,500			
		4,07,500			4,07,500

Dr. **Sinking Fund Account** Cr.

		Rs.			Rs.
31-12-90	To Premium on Redemption of Debentures	7,500	1-1-90	By Balance b/d	3,50,000
31-12-90	To Sinking Fund Investment A/c (Loss on sale)	35,000	30-6-90	By 6% Debentures' A/c (Profit on cancellation)	1,000
31-12-90	To General Reserve (Transferred)	3,08,500			
		3,51,000			3,51,000

Dr. **Sinking Fund Investment Account** Cr.

		Rs.			Rs.
1-1-90	To Balance b/d	3,50,000	31-12-90	By Bank (Sales proceeds)	3,15,000
				By Sinking Fund A/c (Loss on sale)	35,000
		3,50,000			3,50,000

(F) Redemption of Debentures out of Insurance Policy Account

Under this method, an insurance policy is taken for an amount equal to the amount of debentures to be redeemed at the expiry of a specified period. A fixed amount of premium is paid at the beginning of every year to the insurance company and in its turn, the insurance company returns the policy amount at the expiry of the period and the amount will be utilised for redemption of debentures.

This method is similar to Sinking Fund Method. However, the points of difference between the two methods are : (1) Appropriation and the investments are made at the end of the year under sinking fund method, but under the policy method, premium is paid at the beginning of every year and the appropriation is made at the end of each year. (2) Under the policy method, investments are not made in any outside securities as in case of sinking fund method, but the insurance policy is taken out for the amount necessary for the redemption of debentures. (3) Interest is calculated and credited every year under sinking fund method, whereas under policy method, interest is not calculated and credited every year but interest is calculated in total i.e., the difference between the policy amount and premiums paid will be considered as interest at the time of realising the policy amount.

Accounting Entries

The following entries are to be passed under this method :

(1) At the beginning of every year (including last year) :

Entry for the payment of annual premium will be :

Debenture Redemption Fund Policy A/c Dr. } With the amount of
To Bank Account } premium paid

(2) At the end of every year (including last year) :

Entry for the transfer of an amount equal to the premium paid will be :

Profit and Loss Appropriation A/c Dr.		With the amount of
To Debenture Redemption Fund A/c		premium appropriated

(3) At the end of the last year :

In addition to the above two entries the following further entries are to be passes at the end of the last year :

(*a*) *Entry for the receipt of policy amount from the Insurance Co. :*

Bank Account Dr.	With the amount of
To Debenture Redemption Fund Policy A/c	of policy received

(*b*) *Entry for the transfer of profit (interest i.e., difference between the policy amount and premium paid) on policy account :*

Debenture Redemption Fund Policy A/c Dr.	With the amount
To Debenture Redemption Fund A/c	of interest accrued

(*c*) *Entry for the payment of debentures :*

Debenture Account Dr.	With the amount
To Bank Account	paid on redemption

(*d*) *Entry for the transfer of fund account balance to general reserve :*

Debenture Redemption Fund A/c Dr.	With credit balance
To General Reserve Account	of fund a/c

Illustration 12

On 1-1-1994 X Ltd., issued 5,000, 12% debentures of Rs. 100 each repayable at the end of three years at par. The terms of issue included that the company must provide a sinking fund for redemption of debentures on 31-12-1996. The Board of Directors decided to take out an insurance policy to provide the necessary cash. Premium of Rs. 1,37,325 was paid every year and an interest of 10% p.a. at compound rate was expected. Policy amount was received at the expiry of three years and the debentures were redeemed. Show the ledger accounts.

Solution :

Dr. **12% Debentures' Account** Cr.

		Rs.			Rs.
31-12-94	To Balance c/d	5,00,000	1-1-94	By Bank	5,00,000
		5,00,000			5,00,000
31-12-95	To Balance c/d	5,00,000	1-1-95	By Balance b/d	5,00,000
		5,00,000			5,00,000
31-12-96	To Bank	5,00,000	1-1-96	By Balance b/d	5,00,000
		5,00,000			5,00,000

Dr. **Debenture Redemption Fund Account** Cr.

		Rs.			Rs.
31-12-94	To Balance c/d	1,51,057	31-12-94	By P&L Appropriation A/c	1,37,325
				By Debenture Redemption Policy A/c (Int.)	13,732
		1,51,057			1,51,057
31-12-95	To Balance c/d	3,17,220	1-1-95	By Balance b/d	1,51,057
			31-12-95	By P & L Appro. A/c	1,37,325
			31-12-95	By Debenture Redemption Policy A/c (Int.)	28,838
		3,17,220			3,17,220
31-12-96	To General Reserve	5,00,000	1-1-96	By Balance b/d	3,17,220
			31-12-96	By P&L Appropriation A/c	1,37,325
			31-12-96	By Debenture Redemption Policy A/c (Int.)	45,455
		5,00,000			5,00,000

Dr. **Debenture Redemption Policy Account** Cr.

		Rs.			Rs.
1-1-94	To Bank (Premium)	1,37,325	31-12-94	By Balance c/d	1,51,057
31-12-94	To Debenture Redemption Fund A/c (Interest)	13,732			
		1,51,057			1,51,057
1-1-95	To Balance b/d	1,51,037	31-12-95	By Balance c/d	3,17,220
1-1-95	To Bank (Premium)	1,37,325			
31-12-95	To Debenture Redemption Fund A/c (Interest on Rs. 1,51,057+1,37,325)	28,838			
		3,17,220			3,17,220
1-1-96	To Balance b/d	3,17,220	31-12-96	By Bank (Policy amount realised)	5,00,000
1-1-96	To Bank (Premium)	1,37,325			
31-12-96	To Debenture Redemption Fund A/c (Interest on Rs. 3,17,220+1,37,325)	45,455			
		5,00,000			5,00,000

Note : If interest is not considered every year, at the end of the third year the surplus will be Rs. 88,025 (*i.e.*, 13,732 + 28,838 + 45,455) in the policy a/c.

Illustration 13

On 1-1-1994 P Ltd. issued 1,00,000 debentures at par repayable at a premium of 10% after three years on 31st December, 1996. For the redemption of these debentures, company took an insurance policy to provide the necessary cash. The annual premium is Rs. 34,551.

Give the necessary ledger accounts, relating to the issue and redemption of debentures.

Solution :

Dr. **Debentures' Account** Cr.

		Rs.			Rs.
31-12-96	To Bank A/c	1,00,000	1-1-94	By Bank A/c	1,00,000
		1,00,000			1,00,000

Dr. **Premium on Redemption of Debentures' Account** Cr.

		Rs.			Rs.
31-12-94	To Bank A/c	10,000	31-12-96	By Sinking Fund A/c	10,000
		10,000			10,000

Dr. **Debenture Redemption Fund Account** Cr.

		Rs.			Rs.
31-12-94	To Balance c/d	34,551	31-12-94	By P & L Appropriation A/c	34,551
		34,551			34,551
31-12-95	To Balance c/d	69,102	1-1-95	By Balance b/d	34,551
			31-12-95	By P & L Appropriation A/c	34,551
		69,102			69,102
31-12-96	To Premium on Redem. of Debentures A/c (1,00,000 × 10/100)	10,000	1-1-96	By Balance b/d	69,102
			31-12-96	By P&L App. A/c	34,551
31-12-96	To General Reserve A/c (Transfer)	1,00,000	31-12-96	By Debenture Redemption Fund Policy A/c (Accrued interest)	6,347
		1,10,000			1,10,000

Dr. **Debenture Redemption Policy Account** Cr.

		Rs.			Rs.
1-1-94	To Bank (Premium)	34,551	31-12-94	By Balance c/d	34,551
		34,551			34,551
1-1-95	To Balance b/d	34,551	31-12-95	By Balance c/d	69,102
1-1-95	To Bank A/c (Premium)	34,551			
		69,102			69,102
1-1-96	To Balance b/d	69,102	31-12-96	By Bank (Policy amount realised)	1,10,000
1-1-96	To Bank A/c (Premium)	34,551			
31-12-96	To Debenture Redemption Fund A/c (Accrued interest balancing figure)	6,347			
		1,10,000			1,10,000

Note : Compound interest will be 3% p.a.

(2) Redemption of Debentures by Annual Drawings

Under this method, a certain portion of total debentures is redeemed at the end of every year or any other fixed period and gradually all the debentures are redeemed within specified period. The debentures that are to be redeemed every year are decided by drawing lots out of the total debentures to be redeemed. The amount of debentures to be redeemed by having a draw of lottery may be equal or varying. Under this method, slips of debentures to be redeemed are put in a drum and are mixed up and the required slips are to be taken out of drum at random. Those debentures whose slips drawn out of the drum are redeemed during that year either at par or at a premium. Redemption by annual drawings may be carried out either out of working capital or out of profits.

(A) Redemption by annual drawing out of capital

The entries to be passed for redemption, in this case, will be the same as those passed in the case of redemption of debentures at the expiry of the specified period out of capital, stated earlier.

Illustration 14

On 1st January, 1994 Z Co. Ltd. issued Rs. 2,00,000 6% debentures at a discount of 10% repayable at par by annual drawings out of capital as shown below :

On 31-12-1994 Debentures of Rs. 50,000
On 31-12-1995 Debentures of Rs. 75,000
On 31-12-1996 Debentures of Rs. 75,000

Give the necessary journal entries for the above period assuming that interest is payable every year on 31st December.

Solution : **In the books of Z Co. Ltd.**

Journal Entries

Date	Particulars	L.F.	Dr. Rs.	Cr. Rs.
1994	Bank Account (2,00,000 – 20,000) Dr.		1,80,000	
Jan. 1	Discount on Issue of Debentures A/c Dr.		20,000	
	To Debentures Account			2,00,000
	(Being the debentures issued at a discount)			
Dec. 31	Profit and Loss A/c (20,000 × 2/8) Dr.		5,000	
	To Discount on Issue of Debentures A/c			5,000
	(Being 3/6th of discount on issue of debentures written off transferred to P & L A/c)			
Dec. 31	Interest on Debentures' Account Dr.		12,000	
	To Bank Account			12,000
	(Being the payment of interest at 6% on Rs. 2,00,000)			*(Contd.)*

Journal Entries (*Contd.*)

Date	Particulars		L.F.	Dr.	Cr.
Dec. 31	Debentures' Account	Dr.		50,000	
	To Debentureholders' Account				50,000
	(Being the debentures transferred to debenture-holders' account)				
Dec. 31	Debentureholders' Account	Dr.		50,000	
	To Bank Account				50,000
	(Being the payment made to debentureholders)				
1995 Dec. 31	Profit and Loss A/c (20,000 × 3/8)	Dr.		7,500	
	To Discount on Issue of Debentures' A/c				7,500
	(Being 2/6th of discount on written off transferred to P&L A/c)				
Dec. 31	Interest on Debentures' Account	Dr.		9,000	
	To Bank Account				9,000
	(Being the payment of interest at 6% on Rs. 1,50,000)				
Dec. 31	Debentures' Account	Dr.		75,000	
	To Debentureholders' Account				75,000
	(Being the debentures transferred to debenture-holders' account)				
Dec. 31	Debentureholders' Account	Dr.		75000	
	To Bank Account				75,000
	(Being the payment made to debentureholders)				
1996 Dec. 31	Profit and Loss A/c (20,000 × 3/8)	Dr.		7,500	
	To Discount on Issue of Debentures' A/c				7,500
	(Being 1/6th of discount on issue of debentures written off transferred to P&L A/c)				
Dec. 31	Interest on Debentures' Account	Dr.		4,500	
	To Bank Account				4,500
	(Being the payment of interest at 6% on Rs. 75,000)				
Dec. 31	Debentures' Account	Dr.		75,000	
	To Debentureholders' Account				75,000
	(Being the debentures to be redeemed transferred to debentureholders' account)				
Dec. 31	Debentureholders' Account	Dr.		75,000	
	To Bank Account				75,000
	(Being the payment made to debentureholders)				

Note : The loss on issue of debentures is written off over three years in the ratio of 2 : 3 : 3 (*i.e.*, 50,000 : 75,000 : 75,000)

(B) Redemption by annual drawings out of profits

The entries to be passed for redemption, in this case, will be the same as those passed in case of redemption of debentures at or within the specified period out of profits, stated earlier.

Illustration 15

On 1-1-1994 S Co. Ltd. issued Rs. 4,50,000 debentures at par repayable at a premium of 8% in 3 years by annual equal instalments out of profits.

(a) Give the journal entries for the first year.

(b) Show the necessary ledger accounts till the date of redemption.

Solution :

In the books of S Co. Ltd.

Journal Entries

Date	Particulars		L.F.	Dr. Rs.	Cr. Rs.
1994	Bank Account	Dr.		4,50,000	
Jan. 1	Loss on Issue of Debentures' Account	Dr.		36,000	
	To Debentures' Account				4,50,000
	To Premium on Redem. of Debentures' A/c				36,000
	(Being issue of debentures at par repayable at a premium of 8%)				
Dec. 31	Profit and Loss Account	Dr.		18,000	
	To Loss on Issue of Debentures' A/c				18,000
	(Being 3/6th of loss on issue of debentures written off transferred to P & L A/c)				
Dec. 31	Debentures' Account	Dr.		1,50,000	
	Premium on Redem. of Debentures' A/c	Dr.		12,000	
	To Bank Account				1,62,000
	(Being the debentures are paid directly with proportionate premium)				
Dec. 31	Profit and Loss Appropriation Account	Dr.		1,50,000	
	To General Reserve Account				1,50,000
	(Being the nominal value of debentures redeemed out of profits transferred from P & L Appropriation A/c to General Reserve A/c)				

Note : Except first entry, all the remaining entries will be continued in the subsequent years.

Debentures' Account

Dr.					Cr.
		Rs.			Rs.
31-12-94	To Bank A/c	1,50,000	1-1-94	By Bank A/c	4,50,000
31-12-94	To Balance c/d	3,00,000			
		4,50,000			4,50,000
31-12-95	To Bank A/c	1,50,000	1-1-95	By Balance b/d	3,00,000
31-12-95	To Balance c/d	1,50,000			
		3,00,000			3,00,000
31-12-96	To Bank A/c	1,50,000	1-1-96	By Balance b/d	1,50,000
		1,50,000			1,50,000

Note : Debentures are paid directly without transferring them to the debentureholders' account.

Premium on Redemption of Debentures' Account

Dr.					Cr.
		Rs.			Rs.
31-12-94	To Bank A/c	12,000	1-1-94	By Loss on Issue of Debentures' A/c	36,000
31-12-94	To Balance c/d	24,000			
		36,000			36,000
31-12-95	To Bank A/c	12,000	1-1-95	By Balance b/d	24,000
31-12-95	To Balance c/d	12,000			
		24,000			24,000
31-12-96	To Bank Account	12,000	1-1-96	By Balance b/d	12,000
		12,000			12,000

Loss on Issue of Debentures' Account

Dr.					Cr.
		Rs.			Rs.
1-1-94	To Premium on Redemption of Debentures' A/c	36,000	31-12-94	By Profit and Loss A/c	18,000
			31-12-94	By Balance c/d	18,000
		36,000			36,000
1-1-95	To Balance b/d	18,000	31-12-95	By P & L A/c (36,000 × 2/6)	12,000
			31-12-95	By Balance c/d	6,000
		18,000			18,000
1-1-96	To Balance b/d	6,000	31-12-96	By P & L A/c (36,000 × 1/6)	6,000
		6,000			6,000

Note : The loss on issue of debentures is written off over three years in the ratio of 3 : 2 : 1 (*i.e.*, 4,50,000 : 3,00,000 : 1,50,000).

(3) Redemption of Debentures by Conversion

Conversion means exchange of old debentures for new debentures or new shares. Under this method, old debentures are to be redeemed by the issue of new debentures or new shares, but not by the payment of cash. Therefore, the company need not raise any funds for the redemption of debentures under this method. Usually, the company will exchange the new debentures of lower rate of interest for the old debentures carrying higher rate of interest and thereby, reduces the amount of interest payable on debentures in future. When the new shares are issued for redemption of old debentures, then, the debentureholders get an opportunity to become the shareholders or owners of the company. Usually, this conversion is not made at a discount on the market price but at a premium on the face value of debentures or shares.

The following journal entries are to be passed for the redemption of debentures by conversion.

(a) If the new debentures/shares are issued at par :

Debentures' Account	Dr.	With the nominal value of debentures converted
To New Debentures' A/c *or* Share Capital Account		

(b) If the new debentures/shares are issued at a discount :

Debentures' Account	Dr.	With the nominal value of debentures
Discount on Issue of Debentures/ Shares A/c	Dr.	With the amount of discount
To New Debentures' A/c *or* Share Capital A/c		With the total of above two items

(c) If the new debentures/shares are issued at a premium :

Debentures' Account	Dr.	With the nominal value of debentures
To New Debentures' A/c *or* Share Capital A/c		With the nominal value of new debentures/shares
To Debenture/Share Premium A/c		With the amount of premium

Illustration 16

On 1st January, 1992 the Nagpur Chemical Works Ltd. issued 16,000 5% debentures of Rs. 100 each at Rs. 95 each. Debentureholders had an option to convert their holdings into 6% preferences shares of Rs. 100 each at a premium of Rs. 25 per share. On 31st December, 1992, one year's interest had accrued on these debentures which was not paid. A holder of 100 debentures notified his intention to convert his holding into 6% preference shares.

Journalise the above transactions and draw the Company's Balance Sheet as at 31st December, 1992.

(*B.Com., Nagpur, Oct., 1992*)

Solution :

In the books of the Nagpur Chemical Works Ltd.
Journal Entries

Date	Particulars		L.F.	Dr. Rs.	Cr. Rs.
1992 Jan. 1	Bank or Cash A/c	Dr.		15,20,000	
	Discount on Issue of Debentures' A/c	Dr.		80,000	
	To 5% Debentures' Account				16,00,000
	(Being 16,000, 5% debentures are issued at Rs. 95 each)				
Dec. 31	Interest on Debentures' Account	Dr.		80,000	
	To Sundry Debentureholders' A/c				80,000
	(Being interest due on debentures)				
Dec. 31	5% Debentures' Account	Dr.		1,00,000	
	To 6% Preference Share Capital A/c				80,000
	To Shares Premium Account				20,000
	(Conversion of 1000 debentures to 800, 6% Preference Shares of Rs. 100 each at a premium of Rs. 25 per share)				
Dec. 31	Sundry Debentureholders' A/c	Dr.		5,000	
	To Bank or Cash Account				5,000
	(Being interest paid on 100, 5% debentures on conversion)				

Balance Sheet as on 31st December, 1992

Liabilities	Rs.	Assets	Rs.
Share Capital :		Bank or Cash	15,15,000
800, 6% Preference		(15,20,000 – 5,000)	
shares of 100 each	80,000	Discount on Issue of	
15,000, 5% Debentures		Debentures	80,000
of Rs. 100 each	15,00,000	Profit and Loss A/c	80,000
Sundry Debentureholders	75,000		
Share Premium	20,000		
	16,75,000		16,75,000

Illustration 17

On 10th January, 1993 X Ltd. issued 10,000 6% debentures of Rs. 100 each redeemable at par after 15 years. The terms of issue, however, provided that the debentures could be redeemed by giving 6 months' notice at any time after 5 years at a premium of 4% either by payment in cash or by allotment of preference shares and/or other debentures according to the option of the debentureholders.

On 10th April, 1993, the company informed the debentureholders to redeem the debentures on 1st October, 1993, either by payment in cash or by allotment of 8% preference shares of Rs. 100 each at Rs. 130 per share or 7% 2nd debentures of Rs. 100 each at Rs. 96 per debenture.

Holders of 4,000 debentures accepted the offer of the preference shares, holders of 4,800 debentures accepted the offer of 7% 2nd debentures and the rest demanded cash.

Give Journal Entries recording the above redemption.

(I.C.W.A. Adapted)

Solution :

In the books of X Ltd.
Journal Entries

Date	Particulars	L.F.	Dr. Rs.	Cr. Rs.
1993	6% Debentures' Account $\left(\frac{4,00,000 \times 104}{100}\right)$ Dr.		4,16,000	
Oct., 1	To 8% Preference Share Capital A/c $\left(\frac{4,16,000 \times 100}{130}\right)$			3,20,000
	To Share Premium A/c $\left(\frac{4,16,000 \times 30}{130}\right)$			96,000
	(Being the 4,000 debentureholders are allotted 8% preference shares of Rs. 100 each at a premium of Rs. 30 per share)			
Oct. 1	6% Debentures Account $\left(\frac{4,80,000 \times 104}{100}\right)$ Dr.		4,99,200	
	Discount on Issue of Debentures A/c Dr. $\left(\frac{4,99,200 \times 4}{96}\right)$		20,800	
	To 7% 2nd Debentures' Account			5,20,000
	(Being the 4,000 debentureholders are allotted 7% 2nd debentures of Rs. 100 each at a discount of 4%)			*(Contd)*

Journal Entries *(Contd.)*

Oct. 1	6% Debentures' Account $\left(\frac{1,00,000 \times 104}{100}\right)$ Dr.		1,24,800	
	To Bank Account			1,24,800
	(Being the amount paid for 1,200 debentures in cash)			
Oct. 1	Share Premium Account Dr.		60,800	
	To Premium on Redemption of Debentures' A/c			40,000
	To Discount on Issue of Debentures' A/c			20,800
	(Being the premium on redemption of debentures and discount on issue of debentures are written off)			
Oct. 1	Profit and Loss Appropriation Account Dr.		1,20,000	
	To General Reserve Account			1,20,000
	(Being the transfer of an equal amount of nominal value of debentures (1,200 × 100) redeemed in cash)			

(4) Redemption of Debentures by Purchase of Own Debentures in the Open Market

Under this method, a company purchases its own debentures which have already been issued to the public. Usually, the company purchases its own debentures in the open market i.e., in the stock exchange when the ruling price is low. The debentures may be purchased by the company out of profits or out of debenture redemption fund i.e., sinking fund. The purpose of purchasing its own debentures in the open market may before cancellation or for re-issue or for investments.

Under this method, the following points are worth nothing while passing the accounting entries.

(a) Purchases of debentures at par, at a discount or at a premium :

Under the method also, the debentures are to be purchased at par, at a discount or at a premium depending upon the price prevailing in the stock exchange.

(i) *Purchase of debentures at par i.e., at their face value :*

When a company purchases its own debentures having a paid up value of Rs. 40,000 for Rs. 40,000, it is said to be purchases of debentures at par. The journal entry for this will be :

Debentures Account	Dr.	40,000	
To Bank Account			40,000

(ii) *Purchase of debentures at a discount i.e., at a lower value than their face value :*

When a company purchases its own debentures of the value of Rs. 40,000 at Rs. 39,000, it is said to be purchase of debentures at a discount. The entry for this will be :

Debentures' Account	Dr.	40,000	
To Bank Account			39,000
To Profit on Redemption/Cancellation of Debentures' A/c			1,000

(iii) *Purchase of debentures at a premium i.e., at a price higher than the face value :*

When a company purchases its own debentures of the value of Rs. 40,000 at Rs. 41,000, it is said to be purchase of debentures at a premium. The entry for this will be :

Debentures' Account	Dr.	40,000	
Loss on Redemption/Cancellation of Debentures' A/c	Dr.	1,000	
To Bank Account			41,000

Notes : (i) Profit on redemption/cancellation of debentures is a capital profit. Hence, it should be transferred to Capital Reserve Account if there is no sinking fund. When there is a sinking fund it should be transferred to Sinking Fund Account.

(ii) Loss on redemption/cancellation of debentures is a capital loss. Hence, it should be written off either from Profit and Loss A/c or any other capital profit.

(b) Purchase of debentures for cancellation :

Usually, the debentures are to be purchased for cancellation. When the debentures are purchased for cancellation, the debenture account should be debited with the paid up value of debentures purchased. An amount equal to the paid up value or nominal value of debentures cancelled should be transferred out of profits or out of sinking fund created for this purpose. The amount paid by way of interest should be debited to the interest account. The profit on cancellation of debentures should be transferred to capital reserve (if there is no sinking fund) or sinking fund (if there is a sinking fund) and loss on cancellation of debentures should be written of either from Profit and Loss A/c or any other capital profit.

(c) Purchase of debentures as an investment :

Some times, the companies purchase their own debentures as an investment to save the amount of interest payable to debentureholders. When a company purchases its own debentures as an investment, a separate account called "Investment in Own Debentures Account" or simply "Own Debenture Account" is opened in the books. This account will be debited by the actual amount paid for the debentures purchased. These debentures are to be shown as investment in the assets side of the Balance Sheet. When these debentures are sold and cancelled in future, the profit or loss on such sale and cancellation will be transferred to General Reserve Account.

(d) Purchase of debentures before the date of payment of interest :

When the own debentures are purchased by the company exactly on the due date *i.e.*, the date when payment of interest becomes due, the full amount of interest will be paid to the debentureholders as usual. Suppose, a company purchases its own 8% 3,000 debentures of Rs. 100 each at Rs. 95 on 1-10-1994. The date of payment of interest being 30th June and 31st December. In this case, the company purchases its own debentures exactly on the due date *i.e.*, on 31st December. Therefore, the full amount of interest i.e., Rs. 12,000 from 1st July to 31st December, will be paid to the debenture-holders as usual.

But if the own debentures are purchased before the due date of interest, the question arises whether the purchase price includes until the date of purchase or not. Therefore, it is necessary to note whether the price paid by the company is quoted as "Cum-interest" or "Ex-interest".

Cum-Interest or Cum-Dividend : If the price paid for the debentures includes the interest until the date of purchase, the same is known as 'Cum-interest or Cum-dividend'. Suppose, a company purchases its own 8% 3,000 debentures of 100 each at Rs. 95 cum-interest on 1-10-1994. The date of payment of interest is 30th June and 31st December every year. In this case, the entry for the purchase of own debentures will be :

(a) *If the own debentures are purchased for cancellation :*

8% Debentures' Account	Dr.	3,00,000	
Interest on Debentures' A/c (for 3 months) (*i.e.*, from 1st July to 30th Sept., 1994)	Dr.	8,000	
To Bank Account (3,000 × 95)			2,85,000
To Profit on Redemption of Debentures' A/c			23,000
(Being 3,000 debentures purchased at 95 cum-interest and cancelled immediately)			

(b) *If the own debentures are purchased for investment :*

Own Debentures' Account	Dr.	2,77,000	
Interest on Debentures' A/c	Dr.	8,000	
To Bank Account			2,85,000
(Being the price paid for the purchase of debentures)			

Note : When the debentures purchased for investment, the question of profit or loss on redemption of debentures does not arise, because, the debentures purchased are not cancelled.

Ex-Interest or Ex-Dividend : If the price paid for the debentures does not include the interest until the date of purchase, the same is known as 'Ex-interest or Ex-dividend'. The interest for the expired period is to be paid to the holders separately in addition to the price paid for the debentures. Suppose, in the above example, if the purchase price of the debentures is 95 Ex-interest, apart from this, the company has to pay the accrued interest of Rs. 8,000 to the holders of the debentures on the date of purchase. In this case, the entry will be :

(*a*) *If the own debentures are purchased for cancellation :*

8% Debentures' Account	Dr.	3,00,000	
Interest on Debentures' A/c	Dr.	8,000	
(3 months *i.e.*, from 1-7-94 to 1-10-94)			
To Bank A/c (2,85,000 + 8,000)			2,93,000
To Profit on Redemption of Debentures' A/c			15,000
(Being 3,000 debentures purchased at 95 Ex-interest and cancelled immediately)			

(*b*) *If the own debentures are purchased for investment :*

Own Debentures' Account	Dr.	2,85,000	
Interest on Debentures' A/c	Dr.	8,000	
To Bank Account			2,93,000
(Being the price paid for the purchase of debentures)			

Note : Here also, the question of profit or loss on redemption does not arise, as the debentures are purchased for investment and not for cancellation.

Tutorial Note : If it is not clear whether the price quoted is cum-interest or ex-interest, the price quoted should always be taken as an ex-interest price.

Illustration 18

On 1st January, 1995 Importers Ltd. issued 2,000 8% debentures at Rs. 100 each at par.

(i) On 1st January, 1997 the company purchased its own 1,000 debentures at Rs. 105 each in the open market and cancelled them immediately.

(ii) On 1st January, 1998 the company purchased debentures of the face value of Rs. 1,00,000 for Rs. 1,98,500 in the open market, held them as an investments for one year and then cancelled them.

Pass the journal entries in the books of the company. Ignore debenture interest and interest on own debentures.

Solution :

In the books of Importers Ltd.

Journal Entries

Date	Particulars	L.F.	Dr. Rs.	Cr. Rs.
1995 Jan. 1	Bank Account Dr. To 8% Debentures' Account (Being 2,000 8% debentures are issued at Rs. 100 each)		2,00,000	2,00,000
1997 Jan. 1	(i) 8% Debentures' Account Dr. Loss on Redemption/Cancellation of Debentures' A/c Dr. To Bank Account (Being purchase of 1,000 8% debentures at Rs. 105 in the open market)		1,00,000 5,000	1,05,000
Jan. 1	Profit and Loss Account *or* Share Premium A/c Dr. To Loss on Redemption/Cancellation on Debentures Account (Being the loss on redemption of debentures written off from P&L A/c or Share Premium Account)		5,000	5,000
1998 Jan. 1	(ii) Own Debentures' Account Dr. To Bank (Being purchase of debentures of the value of Rs. 1,00,000 for Rs. 1,98,500)		1,98,500	1,98,500
1999 Jan. 1	8% Debentures' Account Dr. To Own Debentures' Account To Profit on Cancellation of Own Debentures' A/c (Being cancellation of own debentures of the value of Rs. 1,00,000 purchased last year for Rs. 1,98,500)		2,00,000	1,98,500 1,500
1999 Jan. 1	Profit on Cancellation of Own Debentures' A/c Dr. To Capital Reserve Account (Being profit on cancellation transferred to Capital Reserve)		1,500	1,500

Illustration 19

X Ltd. had 1,000 12% debentures of Rs. 100 each outstanding on 1st January, 1988.

It purchased 300 debentures on 1-4-1988 at Rs. 95 ex-interest and 200 debentures at Rs. 96 cum-interest on 1-7-1988. These were cancelled on 31-12-1988.

Assuming that interest is due on 31st December every year, pass entries relating to redemption of debentures and interest payment.

(K.U.D., Oct., 1989)

Solution :

In the Books of X Co. Ltd.
Journal Entries

Date	Particulars		L.F.	Dr. Rs.	Cr. Rs.
1-4-88	Own Debentures' Account	Dr.		28,500	
	Interest on Debentures' A/c	Dr.		900	
	To Bank Account				29,400
	(Being purchase of debentures of Rs. 30,000 as investment at Rs. 95 ex-interest)				
1-7-88	Own Debentures' Account	Dr.		18,000	
	Interest on Debentures' A/c	Dr.		1,200	
	To Bank Account				19,200
	(Being purchase of debentures of Rs. 20,000 as investment at Rs. 96 cum-interest)				
31-12-88	12% Debentures' Account	Dr.		30,000	
	To Own Debentures' Account				28,500
	To Profit on Redemption/Cancellation of Debentures' A/c				1,500
	(Being debentures of the face value of Rs. 30,000 purchased as investment at Rs. 95 ex-interest cancelled and difference being profit)				
31-12-88	12% Debentures' Account	Dr.		20,000	
	To Own Debentures' Account				18,000
	To Profit on Redemption/Cancellation of Debentures' A/c				2,000
	(Being debentures of the face value of Rs. 20,000 purchased as investment at Rs. 96 cum-interest cancelled and difference being profit)				

Illustration 20

On 1st Jan. X Ltd. has Rs. 12,000 6% debentures. In accordance with the powers under the deed, the directors acquire in the open market for immediate cancellation of debentures as follows :

March 1— Rs. 2,000 at Rs. 98 cum-interest

August 1— Rs. 4,000 at 100¼ cum-interest

December 15— Rs. 1,000 at Rs. 98½ ex-interest.

Debenture interest is payable half yearly, 30th June, and 31st December. Show the ledger accounts. Ignore income tax.

(C.U., B.Com., Hons.)

Solution :

In the books of X Ltd.

Dr. **6% Debentures' Account** Cr.

19...		Rs.	19...		Rs.
Mar. 1	To Bank A/c (1,960 – 20)	1,940	Jan. 1	By Balance b/d	12,000
	To General Reserve A/c (Profit on cancellation)	60			
Aug. 1	To Bank A/c (4,010 – 20)	3,990			
	To General Reserve A/c (Profit on cancellation)	10			
Dec. 15	To Bank A/c (1000 × 98.5)	985			
	To General Reserve A/c (Profit on cancellation)	15			
Dec. 31	To Balance c/d	5,000			
		12,000			12,000

Dr. **Debentures' Interest Account** Cr.

19...		Rs.	19...		Rs.
Mar. 1	To Bank A/c (2,000 × 6/12 × 2/12)	20.00	Dec. 31	By Profit and Loss A/c (Transfer)	517.50
June 1	To Bank A/c (10,000 × 6/100 × 6/12)	300.00			
Aug. 1	To Bank A/c (40,000 × 6/100 × 1/12)	20.00			
Dec. 15	To Bank A/c (1,000 × 6/100 × 5 ½)	27.50			
Dec. 31	To Bank A/c (5,000 × 6/100 × 6/12)	150.00			
		517.50			517.50

Dr. **General Reserve Account** Cr.

	Rs.	19...		Rs.
		Mar. 1	By 6% Debentures A/c	60
			By P&L (App.) A/c	1,940
		Aug. 1	By 6% Debentures A/c	10
			By P&L (App.) A/c	3,990
		Dec. 1	By 6% Debentures A/c	15
			By P&L (App.) A/c	985

Illustration 21

On 1-7-1990 a company issued 2,000 12% debentures of Rs. 100 each. The interest is payable half yearly on 31st December and 30th June. The company is allowed to purchase its own debentures which may be cancelled or kept alive at the option of the company.

The company has made the following purchases in the open market :

(a) On 30-4-1991, 200 debentures at Rs. 95 ex-interest.

(b) On 31-8-1992, 400 debentures at Rs. 98 cum-interest.

The debentures which were purchased on 30-4-1991 were cancelled on 31-12-1992. All the payments were duly made on the respective due dates.

Pass the necessary journal entries assuming that the accounts are closed by the company on 31st December every year.

(*Gulbarga, April, 1994*)

Solution :

Journal Entries

Date	Particulars		L.F.	Dr. Rs.	Cr. Rs.
1-7-90	Bank Account	Dr.		2,00,000	
	To 12% Debentures' Account				2,00,000
	(Being the issue of 2,000 8% debentures at Rs. 100 each)				
31-12-90	Interest on Debentures' A/c	Dr.		12,000	
	To Bank Account				12,000
	(Being interest paid for six months)				
31-12-90	Profit and Loss Account	Dr.		12,000	
	To Interest on Debentures' A/c				12,000
	(Being transfer of interest)				

(*Contd.*)

Journal Entries (*Contd.*)

30-4-91	Own Debentures' Account Dr.		19,000	
	Interest on Debentures' Account Dr.		800	
	To Bank Account			19,800
	(Being paid for purchase of 200 debentures at Rs. 95 ex-interest and also interest on Rs. 20,000 at 12% for 4 months)			
30-6-91	Interest on Debentures' A/c Dr.		11,200	
	To Interest on Own Debentures' A/c			400
	To Bank Account			10,800
	(Being balance of interest paid after deducting interest on own debentures of Rs. 20,000 at 12% for 2 months)			
31-12-91	Interest on Debentures' A/c Dr.		12,000	
	To Interest on own Debentures' A/c			1,200
	To Bank Account			10,800
	(Being interest paid for six months after deducting interest on own debentures of Rs. 20,000 at 12% for six months)			
31-12-91	Profit and Loss Account Dr.		24,000	
	To Interest on Debentures' A/c			24,000
	(Being interest transferred *i.e.*, 800 + 11,200 + 12,000)			
31-12-91	Interest on Own Debentures' A/c Dr.		1,600	
	To Profit and Loss A/c (400 + 1,200)			1,600
	(Being interest on own debentures transferred)			
30-6-92	Interest on Debentures' A/c Dr.		11,400	
	To Interest on own Debentures' A/c			600
	To Bank Account			10,800
	(Being interest paid for 6 months after deducting interest on own debentures for 6 months on Rs. 20,000 at 12%)			
31-8-92	Own Debentures' Account Dr.		39,200	
	Interest on Debentures' Account Dr.		800	
	To Bank Account			40,000
	(Being paid for purchase of 400 debentures at Rs. 98 cum-interest and also interest on own debentures of Rs. 40,000 for 4 months at 12%)			

(*Contd.*)

Journal Entries (*Contd.*)

Date	Particulars	L.F.	Dr. Rs.	Cr. Rs.
31-12-92	Interest on Debentures' A/c Dr.		11,200	
	To Interest on own Debentures' A/c			2,800
	To Bank Account			8,400
	(Being interest paid for 6 months after deducting interest on own debentures *i.e.*, on Rs. 20,000 for 6 months and on Rs. 40,000 for 4 months at 12%)			
31-12-92	12% Debentures' A/c Dr.		20,000	
	To Own Debentures' A/c			19,000
	To Profit on Redemption of Debentures' A/c			1,000
	(Being the cancellation of Rs. 20,000 debentures purchased for Rs. 19,000 on 30-4-91and difference being profit on cancellation)			
31-12-92	Profit and Loss Account Dr.		24,000	
	To Interest on Debentures' A/c			24,000
	(Being interest transferred *i.e.,* 12,000 + 800 + 11,200)			
31-12-92	Interest on Own Debentures' A/c Dr.		4,000	
	To Profit and Loss A/c (1,200 + 2,800)			4,000
	(Being transfer of interest on own debentures)			

Illustration 22

Indebted Ltd., issued 10% debentures at par for Rs. 8 lakhs on 1st January, 1979. Interest was payable half yearly on 30th June and 31st December every year. Under the terms of the trust deed, the debentures are redeemable at par (after three years of issue) by the company purchasing them in open market and cancelling them with a minimum redemption of Rs. 80,000 every year. In case, there was a shortfall in redemption by the company by open operations, the shortfall would be made good by the company by payment on the last day of the accounting year to the trustees who would draw lots and redeem the debentures.

The company purchased its own debentures for cancellation as under :

(a) 30th Sept., 1982 — Rs. 1,00,000 at Rs. 98 cum-interest
(b) 31st March, 1983 — Rs. 60,000 at Rs. 95 ex-interest
(c) 31st July, 1984 — Rs. 90,000 at Rs. 96 cum-interest.

The company carried out its obligations under the deed. Prepare the following ledger accounts for calendar year 1982, 1983 and 1984.

(i) Debentures Account, (ii) Debentures Redemption Account and (iii) Debenture Interest Account. Ignore taxation.

(C.A. Inter New Scheme, Nov., 1981)

Solution :

In the books of Indebted Ltd.
Ledger Accounts

Dr. **10% Debentures' Account** Cr.

		Rs.			Rs.
1982 Sept. 30	To Debenture Redemption A/c	1,00,000	1982 Jan. 1	By Balance b/d	8,00,000
Dec. 31	To Balance c/d	7,00,000			
		8,00,000			8,00,000
1983 May 31	To Debenture Redemption A/c	60,000	1983 Jan. 1	By Balance b/d	7,00,000
Dec. 31	To Debenture Redemption A/c	20,000			
Dec. 31	To Balance c/d	6,20,000			
		7,00,000			7,00,000
1984 July 31	To Debenture Redemption A/c	90,000	1984 Jan. 1	By Balance b/d	6,20,000
Dec. 31	To Balance c/d	5,30,000			
		6,20,000			6,20,000

Dr. **Debenture Redemption Account** Cr.

		Rs.			Rs.
1982 Sept. 30	To Bank A/c	95,500	1982 Sept. 30	By 10% Debentures' A/c	1,00,000
	To Capital Reserve A/c (Profit on cancellation)	4,500			
		1,00,000			1,00,000
1983 May 31	To Bank A/c	57,000	1983 May 31	By 10% Debentures' A/c	60,000
May 31	To Capital Reserve	3,000	Dec. 31	By 10% Debentures' A/c	20,000
Dec. 31	To Bank	20,000			
		80,000			80,000
1984 July 31	To Bank A/c	85,650	1982 Jan. 1	By 10% Debentures' A/c	90,000
July 31	To Capital Reserve	4,350			
		90,000			90,000

Dr. **Debentures Interest Account** Cr.

		Rs.			Rs.
1982			1982		
June 30	To Bank A/c	40,000	Dec. 31	By Profit and Loss A/c	77,500
Sept. 30	To Bank A/c	2,500		(Transfer)	
Dec. 31	To Bank A/c	35,000			
		77,500			77,500
1983			1983		
May 31	To Bank A/c	2,500	Dec. 31	By Profit and Loss A/c	66,500
June 30	To Bank A/c.	32,000		(Transfer)	
Dec. 31	To Bank A/c	32,000			
		66,500			66,500
1984			1984		
June 30	To Bank A/c	31,000	Dec. 31	By Profit and Loss A/c	58,250
July 31	To Bank A/c.	750		(Transfer)	
Dec. 31	To Bank A/c	26,500			
		58,250			58,250

Working Note :

Calculation of interest paid on debentures

Date	Amount of Debentures Rs.	Period	Amount of Interest Rs.
1982 June 30	8,00,000	6 months	40,000
1982 Sept. 30	1,00,000	3 months	2,500
1982 Dec. 31	7,00,000	6 months	35,000
1983 May 31	60,000	5 months	2,500
1983 June 30	6,40,000	6 months	32,000
1983 Dec. 31	6,40,000	6 months	32,000
1984 June 30	6,20,000	6 months	31,000
1984 July 31	90,000	1 month	750
1984 Dec. 31	5,30,000	6 months	26,500

EXAMINATION QUESTIONS

(A) Answer the following questions in not exceeding 4 lines each :

(*Each Carries two Marks*)

(1) What do you mean by redemption of debentures ?

(2) What do you mean by redemption of debentures out of profit ?

(3) What is meant by redemption of debentures out of capital ?

(4) What do you understand by redemption of debentures out of sinking fund ?

(5) What is a sinking fund ? (*Bangalore, April, 1983*)

(6) Give the entry to close the Sinking Fund A/c on redemption of debentures. (*Bangalore, April, 1980*)

(7) What accounting treatment would you give for interest received on Sinking Fund Investment ? (*Bangalore, April, 1980*)

(8) What is sinking fund method of redemption of debentures ? (*Kar., Oct., 1995*)

(9) What do you mean by redemption on debentures out of insurance policy amount?

(10) How do you treat the profit or loss on the sale of "Debenture Redemption Fund Investment"? (*Bangalore, May, 1981*)

(11) Mention any two methods of redemption of debentures. (*Bangalore, April, 1983 & Karnataka, April, 1995*)

(12) What do you understand by redemption of debentures by annual drawings ?

(13) What is meant by redemption of debentures by conversion ?

(14) What do you mean by redemption of debentures by purchase of own debentures in the open market ?

(15) What is meant by "cum-interest" and "ex-interest" rates? (*Karnataka, April, 1996*)

(B) Answer the following questions/problems :

(*Each Carries two Marks*)

(1) What are the sources for the redemption of debentures ?

(2) What are the methods of redemption of debentures ?

(3) Set out the accounting procedure for redemption of debentures by creation of sinking fund. (*Kerala, Sept., 1982*)

(4) Explain the following :

(a) Purchase of own debentures for immediate cancellation.

(b) Purchase of own debentures as investments.

(*Mysore, April, 1982*)

(5) Pass the journal entries in the following cases :

(i) Purchase of debentures at ex-interest.

(ii) Purchase of debentures at cum-interest.

(*M.K.U., Oct., 1993*)

(6) Hercules Ltd., issued 2,000 8% debentures of Rs. 100 each repayable at a premium of 5% at the end of 4 years out of capital.

Pass the journal entries relating to the issue and redemption of debentures.

(7) On 1st January, 1997, Sunbeam Ltd., issued Rs. 4,00,000 debentures at par repayable at par at the end of four years out of profits.

Pass the necessary journal entries relating to the issue and redemption of debentures.

(8) Rising Star Ltd. issued 2,000 5% debentures of Rs. 100 each repayable at par at the end of 4 years. At the end of 4th year the company issued 2,000 6% debentures of Rs. 100 each at a premium of 5% to raise funds for the redemption of debentures.

Pass the necessary journal entries for 4 years.

(9) Akash Deep Ltd. issued 1,500 9% debentures at Rs. 100 each at par repayable at par at the end of 4 years or any time before the maturity. At the end of fourth year, the company sold the machinery of the book value of Rs. 2,00,000 for Rs. 1,80,000 to raise funds for the redemption of debentures.

Pass the necessary journal entries.

(10) Shri Sai Ltd. issued on 1-1-1994, 2,000 12% redeemable bonds of Rs. 100 each. The company pays interest annually on 31st December. On 1-5-1994 the company bought 300 at Rs. 94 ex-interest and on 30-9-1994 200 own bonds at Rs. 97 cum-interest. These bonds were cancelled on 31-12-1994.

Pass the journal entries relating to issue, purchases and redemption of bonds.

(*Karnataka, Oct., 1995*)

Ans. : Interest paid on debentures : Rs. 21,000 (24,000 – 3,000) after deducting interest of Rs. 3,000 (1,200 + 1800) on own debentures. Profit on cancellation of own debentures Rs. 4,200 (50,000 – 28,200 = 21,800 – 17,600).

(11) The ledger of Zee Ltd., showed the balances of the following accounts as under :

	Rs.
6% Debentures	2,00,000
Debentures Redemption Fund	2,00,000
Premium on Redemption of Debentures	20,000
Debentures Redemption Fund Investment Account (Face value Rs. 1,80,000)	1,75,000

The above investments were sold at 102% and all the debentures were paid. Prepare the above accounts to record the redemption of debentures.

(*Karnataka, April, 1996*)

Ans. : Sale proceeds of investments Rs. 1,83,600 (1,80,000 × 102/100); Profit on sale of investment Rs. 8,500; Balance of Fund Account transferred to General Reserve Rs. 2,08,500; Payment of debentures Rs. 2,20,000 including premium.

(12) Indian Co. Ltd., has issued following debentures :

(a) 9%, 6,000 debentures of 100 each issued at 5% discount for a period of 3 years and repayable at par value.

(b) 11%, 4,000 debentures of 100 each issued at 10% discount for 4 years and repayable at 5% premium.

Pass the journal entries in the journal books.

(*Karnataka, April, 1997*)

Hints : (a) (i) For issue : Debit Bank A/c (5,70,000) and Discount on Issue of Debentures' A/c (30,000) and Credit 9% Debentures' A/c.

(ii) For repayable : Debit 9% Debentures' A/c and Credit Bank A/c.

(b) (i) For issue : Debit Bank A/c (3,60,000), Discount on Issue of Debentures A/c (40,000) and Loss on Redemption of Debentures' A/c (20,000) and Credit 11% Debentures' A/c (4,00,000) and Premium on Redemption of Debentures' A/c (20,000).

(ii) For repayable : Debit 11% Debentures' A/c (4,00,000) and Premium on Redemption of Debentures' A/c (20,000) and Credit Bank A/c (4,20,000).

(C) Solve the following problems :

(*Each Carries 16 Marks*)

(1) X Co. Ltd. issued 4,000 6% debentures of Rs. 100 each at par on 1-1-1997 redeemable at the end of 4 years at a premium of 5%. A sinking fund was established for this purpose. It was expected that the investments would earn 4% net. The sinking fund table shows that Re. 0.235490 annually amounts to one rupee at the end of 4 years at 4%.

On 31-12-1980 the investments realised Rs. 3,13,600. On that date the bank balance stood at Rs. 1,18,000. The debentures were duly redeemed.

Prepare : (1) Debentures Account, (2) Sinking Fund Account and (3) Sinking Fund Investment Account.

(Gulbarga, Oct., 1984 and April, 1988)

Ans. : Loss on issue of debentures Rs. 20,000 debited to Fund Account; Profit on sale of investments Rs. 4,856; Balance of Fund A/c transferred to General Reserve Rs. 4,04,856; Annual instalment amount Rs. 98,906 (*i.e.*, 0.235490 × 4,20,000); Amount required to redemption Rs. 4,20,000.

(2) Dasappa Ltd. issued on 1-1-1970 Rs. 1,00,000 5% debentures of Rs. 100 each at par redeemable in 5 years. It was decided to create a sinking fund for redemption and it should have investments to yield 5% compound interest.

The sinking fund table shows that an investment of Re. 0.180975 annually over 5 years fetches Re. 1 at 5%. The investments realised 10% less than the book value.

Write up the necessary accounts and show the redemption of debentures.

(Gulbarga, April, 1984)

Ans. : Loss on sale of investment Rs. 7,800.25; Annual instalment amount Rs. 18,097.50 (*i.e.*, 0.180975 × 1,00,000); Balance of Fund A/c transferred to General Reserve Rs. 92,199.75.

(3) On 1st January, 1977, the Metal Product Ltd. issued debentures for Rs. 1,00,000 redeemable at par at the end of five years and it was resolved that a sinking fund should be formed and invested in tax-free securities.

Give the journal entries and show the ledger accounts for 5 years, assuming that the interest received on the investments was at the rate of 5 per cent on cost, that the interest was received yearly and immediately invested and that the investments were realised at a loss of Rs. 300 at the end of 5 years.

Reference to the table shows that Re. 0.180975 invested at the end of each year, at 5 per cent compound interest, will produce Re. 1 at the end of five years.

(Adapted from I.C.W.A. Inter)

Ans. : Annual Instalment amount Rs. 18,097.50 (*i.e.*, 0.180975 × 1,00,000); Loss on sale of investment Rs. 300; Balance of Fund A/c transferred to General Reserve Rs. 99,700.11.

(4) A company issued 5,000 debentures of Rs. 100 each at par on 1st January, 1976 redeemable at par on 31st December, 1980. A sinking fund was established for the purpose. It was expected that investment would earn 5% net. Sinking fund tables show that Re. 0.180975 amount to Re. 1 at the end of 5 years at 5%. On 31st December, 1980 the investments were sold for Rs. 3,90,000. On that date the company's bank balance stood at Rs. 1,45,600. The debentures were duly redeemed. Give the necessary ledger accounts assuming that the investments are made in multiples of Rs. 100.

(*Adapted from Mysore University, B.Com.*)

Ans. : Annual instalment amount Rs. 90,487.50; Profit on sale of investments Rs. 200; Balance of Fund A/c transferred to General Reserve Rs. 5,00,187.50.

Note : Investments— 1976 Rs. 90,400; 1977 Rs. 95,000; 1978 Rs. 99,700; 1979 Rs. 1,04,700 *i.e.*, Investments are made in multiples of Rs. 100.

(5) In 1st January, 1974, debentures of the face value of Rs, 7,500 were issued at par, repayable at par at the end of 5 years. In terms of the Trust Deed, Sinking Fund was to be created for the purpose of accumulating sufficient funds for the purpose. Investments were made, yielding 5% interest received at the end of each year. All investments, including investments of interest received, were made at the end of the year.

You are required to show for 5 years, the

(a) Sinking Fund Account and

(b) Sinking Fund Investment Account.

Note : Rs. 2.71462 invested at the end of each year at 5 per cent compound interest will amount to Rs. 15 at the end of 5 years.

(*Adapted from C.A. Inter*)

Ans. : Annual instalment amount Rs. 1,357.31 (*i.e.*, 2.71462 × 7,500/15); Investment realised at par Rs. 5,850.16; Balance of Fund A/c transferred to General Reserve Rs. 7,500.

(6) Beta Ltd., had Rs. 3,00,000, 8% debentures outstanding on January 1, 1983. On that date the Debenture Redemption Fund had Rs. 2,50,000 invested in Rs. 2,65,000, 6% (1992) Government Loan Bonds. The annual appropriation from profits to the fund was Rs. 41,150.

On December 31, 1983 the interest on investments had been collected. The bank balance was Rs. 78,200. The debentures were redeemed by realising the bonds at 87%. Show all relevant Ledger Accounts.

(*M.K.U., B.Com., April, 1984*)

Ans. : Loss on sale of investment Rs. 19,450; Interest Rs. 15,900; Balance of Fund A/c transferred to General Reserve Rs. 2,87,600.

(7) R Ltd., had Rs. 3,00,000 5% debentures outstanding on 1-4-1982. On that date the Debentures Redemption Fund stood at Rs. 2,50,000 represented by Rs. 2,95,000, 3% (1988). Loan of the Govt. of India. The annual instalment added to the Debentures Redemption Fund was Rs. 41,150.

On 31-3-1983, the balance at Bank was Rs. 70,000. On that date, the interest on investments was received, the investments were sold at 83% and the debentures were paid off.

Show necessary ledger accounts for the year ended 31-3-1983.

(*I.C.W.A. - Adapted*)

Ans. : Sale proceeds of investments Rs. 2,44,850; Loss on sale of investment Rs. 5,150; Interest Rs. 8,850; Balance of Fund A/c transferred to General Reserve Rs. 2,94,850; Bank balance Rs. 23,700.

(8) Vijay Engineering Works Ltd., had issued 300 6% debentures of Rs. 100 each 1-1-1974. The above debentures are redeemable at 5% premium on 31-12-1980. On that date the concerned ledger accounts showed the following balances :

	Rs.
6% Debentures Account	3,00,000
Debentures Redemption Fund Account	3,15,000
Debenture Redemption Fund Investment Account	2,71,500
(in 5% Govt. of India Loan of the face value Rs. 2,77,500)	
Bank Account	3,32,250
Premium on Redemption of Debentures	15,000

On 31-12-1980 investments were sold at 101% and all the debentures were duly redeemed.

Record the above in the concerned ledger accounts of the company.

(*Karnataka, April, 1981 and Gulbarga, Oct., 1986*)

Ans. : Sale proceeds of investments Rs. 2,80,275; Profit on sale of investments Rs. 8,775; Balance of Fund A/c transferred to General Reserve Rs. 3,23,775; Bank balance Rs. 2,97,525.

(9) The Debenture Redemption Account of X Ltd. stood at Rs. 80,000 represented by Rs. 1,00,000 (Nominal) investments. The debentures stood at Rs. 3,00,000 and the company sold Rs. 60,000 (Nominal) investments at 84 for the purpose of redeeming Rs. 50,000 debentures at 100½.

Show ledger accounts, ignoring interest and brokerage.

(*I.C.W.A., Dec., 1975*)

Ans. : Sale proceeds of investments Rs. 50,400; Profit on sale of investment Rs. 2,400; Debenture Redemption Fund A/c balance Rs. 32,150; Debenture Redemption Fund Investment A/c balance Rs. 3,200; Bank balance Rs. 150.

(10) On January 1, 1986, 'KJ' Ltd., issued 3,000 12% debentures of Rs. 100 each repayable at the end of three years at par. For the redemption of these debentures company took an insurance policy to provide the necessary cash. Premium of Rs. 82,395 was paid every year and an interest of 10% p.a. at compound rate was expected. Policy amount was received at the expiry of three years and the debentures were redeemed. Show ledger accounts in the books of 'KJ' Ltd.

(*I.C.W.A. Inter*)

Ans. : Interest : 1986 Rs. 8,239; 1987 Rs. 17,303 and 1988 Rs. 27,273.

(11) A Limited Company has made an issue of Rs. 2,00,000 9% Debentures on 1st January, 1980, the terms of which include that the company must take a 5 years Sinking Fund Insurance Policy for the redemption. The annual premium is Rs. 37,000. The value of the policy increases each year by 4%. Give the important Ledger Accounts to record the above transactions for 5 years.

(*C.A. Inter*)

Ans. : Interest : 1980 Rs. 1,480; 1981 Rs. 3,019; 1982 Rs. 4,620; 1983 Rs. 6,285 and 1984 Rs. 8,016.

(12) On 1-1-1976, P Ltd., issued 4,000 6% debentures of Rs. 100 each at a discount of 10% repayable in 4 years by annual equal instalments.

(a) Give Journal entries on the date of issue.

(b) Show the Debenture Account, Discount on Debenture Account and Debenture Interest Account till the date of redemption.

(*C.U., B.Com.*)

Ans. : Loss on issue of debentures written off : 1976 Rs. 16,000; 1977 Rs. 12,000 1978 Rs. 8,000 and 1979 Rs. 4,000; Interest : 1976 Rs. 24,000; 1977 Rs. 18,000; 1978 Rs. 12,000 and 1979 Rs. 6,000.

(13) On 1st January, 1978, Sunbeam Ltd., issued Rs. 3,00,000 debentures at a discount of 5% repayable at a premium of 5% by annual drawings of Rs. 1,00,000 out of profits.

Give the necessary journal entries and the ledger accounts relating to the issue and redemption of debentures over the period of debentures.

(*I.C.W.A. Inter*)

Ans. : Loss on issue of debentures Rs. 30,000 (15,000 + 10,000 + 5,000); Premium on Redemption of Debentures Rs. 15,000 (5,000 + 5,000 + 5,000).

(14) On January 1, 1984, a company issued 400, 5 per cent debentures of Rs. 1,000 each at Rs. 980. Holders of these debentures had an option to convert their holdings into 8 per cent preference shares of Rs. 100 each, at a premium of Rs. 20 per share at any time within five years.

On December 31, 1984, one year's interest had accrued on the debentures and remained unpaid. A holder of 24 debentures notified his intention to exercise the above options.

Pass the necessary Journal Entries.

[C.U., B.Com. (Hons.)]

Ans. : Discount on issue of debentures Rs. 8,000; Interest on debentures Rs. 20,000; Share Premium Rs. 4,000 and Proportionate amount of discount written off Rs. 480 *i.e.*, 8,000 × 24,000/4,00,000.

(15) On January 1, 1981, Green Limited issued 250, 5% debentures of Rs. 1,000 each at Rs. 950. The debentureholders have an option to convert at par their holdings into 7% preference shares of Rs. 100 each at a premium of Rs. 25 per share at any time after three years. Interest payable half yearly. Ignore income tax.

On 1st January, 1984, holders of 50 debentures exercised their option. Show journal entries relating to issue and conversion of debentures. Also show company's balance sheet as at 1-1-1984 (relevant items only) assuming no other transaction during the period.

(C.A. Adapted & B.Com., Nagpur)

Ans. : Discount on issue of debentures Rs. 10,000 (*i.e.*, 12,500 – 2,500); Interest on debentures Rs. 6,250; every year on 30th June and 31st December, till 1983; Share Premium Rs. 10,000 i.e. 25% on Rs. 40,000 or 20% on 50,000; Preference Share Capital Rs. 40,000 and 200, 5% debentures Rs. 20,00,000.

(16) On 1-1-1973 Exporters Ltd. issued Rs. 20,00,000 7% Debentures at 5% discount repayable in 5 years at par. The company reserved the right to redeem to the extent of Rs. 2,00,000 in any year by purchasing in the open market. The interest was payable half yearly on 30th June and on 31st December and the same was duly paid.

On 3-9-1973 the company purchased Rs. 2,00,000 worth of debentures for investment at a cost of Rs. 1,91,000.

Pass the necessary journal entries in the books of the company up to the end of 31-12-1973.

(Karnataka, Oct., 1978)

Ans. : Interest on own debentures on 31-12-1973 Rs. 3,500.

Hint : The purchase price is ex-interest unless otherwise stated.

(17) Journalise the following transactions in the books of X Co. Ltd. Purchased 60, 5% debentures of Rs. 100 each of its own at Rs. 95 per debenture for cancellation on 1-4-1979. The company pays interest half yearly on 30th June and 31st December. Show how the entries will appear if the debentures are purchased under : (i) Ex-interest and (ii) Cum-interest.

(Karnataka, 1980)

Ans. : (i) Profit on redemption of debentures Rs. 300.

(ii) Profit on redemption of debentures Rs. 375.

(18) On 1-7-1976 a company issued 2,000 6% debentures of Rs. 100 each. The interest is payable on 30th June and 31st December every year. The company is allowed to purchase its own debentures which may be cancelled or kept or re-issued at the option of the company.

The company made the following purchases in the open market :

(i) On 31-5-1977, 200 debentures at Rs. 98 ex-interest

(ii) On 30-9-1978, 100 debentures at Rs. 97 cum-interest.

The debentures which were purchased on 31-5-77 were cancelled on 31-12-1978. All the payments were made on due dates.

Give the necessary journal entries.

(*Karnataka, April, 1984 & Gulbarga, April, 1994*)

Ans. : Interest on own debentures : 30-6-1977 Rs. 100, 31-12-1977 Rs. 600, 30-6-1978 Rs. 600 and 31-12-78 Rs. 750; Profit on redemption of debentures Rs. 400; Balance of Own Debentures A/c Rs. 9,550.

(19) On January 1, 1976, a company had a balance of Rs. 5,00,000 in its 10% Debenture Accounts, Rs. 3,60,000 in the Debenture Redemption Fund Account and Rs. 3,60,000 in the Debenture Redemption Fund Investment Account represented by Government Securities at cost at Rs. 90.

The company purchased from the open market Rs. 1,00,000 debentures at Rs. 98 (ex-interest) on April 30, 1976 and cancelled them. On the same date, the company sold investments of face value Rs. 1,00,000 at Rs. 95 (ex-interest).

Show the Debenture Account, Debenture Redemption Fund Account and the Debentures Redemption Fund Investment Account for the whole year 1976.

(*I.C.W.A., June, 1978*)

Ans. : Profit on cancellation of debentures transferred to Capital Reserve Rs. 2,000; Balance in Debentures Redemption Fund A/c Rs. 2,65,000; Balance in Debenture Redemption Fund Investment A/c Rs. 2,34,000.

(20) (A) Bharat Ltd. issued 1,000 6% debentures of Rs. 500 each. Give the journal entries if the debentures are :

(i) issued at par

(ii) issued at a discount of 10% and

(iii) issued at a premium of 10%.
(redemption being in all cases at par).

(B) Also show the entries which will be made if the debentures are payable at a premium of 5% but are issued :

(i) at par, and

(ii) at a discount of 10%.

(*Gulbarga, April, 1989*)

Hints : (A) (i) Bank A/c is debited and Debentures' A/c is credited Rs. 5,00,000.

(ii) Bank (4,50,000) and Discount on Issue of Debentures' (50,000) A/c's are debited and Debentures' A/c is credited Rs. 5,00,000.

(iii) Bank A/c is debited Rs. 5,50,000 and Debentures (5,00,000) and Premium on Issue of Debentures' A/cs (Rs. 50,000) are credited.

(B) (i) Bank (5,00,000) and Loss on Issue of Debentures' A/cs (25,000) are debited and Debentures (5,00,000) and Premium on Redemption of Debentures' A/cs (25,000) are credited.

(ii) Bank (4,50,000), Discount on Issue of Debentures (50,000) and Loss on Issue of Debentures' A/cs (25,000) are debited and Debentures (5,00,000) and Premium on Redemption of Debentures' A/cs (25,000) are credited.

(21) Journalise the following transactions in the books of Reliance Co. Ltd.

(i) 5,000 7% debentures of Rs. 100 each issued at par and redeemable after 5 years at par.

(ii) 10,000 6% debentures of Rs. 100 each issued at par and redeemable at 5% premium after 10 years.

(iii) 4,000 10% debentures of Rs. 100 each issued at 5% discount but repayable at par after 20 years.

(iv) 5,000 5% debentures of Rs. 100 each issued at 10% discount but repayable at 5% premium after 10 years.

(*Gulbarga, April, 1990 and Karnataka, April, 1991*)

Hints : (i) Bank A/c is debited and Debentures A/c is credited Rs. 5,00,000.

(ii) Bank (10,00,000) and Loss on Issue of Debentures (50,000) A/cs are debited and Debentures (10,00,000) and Premium on Redemption (50,000) A/cs are credited.

(iii) Bank (3,80,000) and Discount on Issue of Debentures (20,000) A/cs are debited and Debentures A/c (Rs. 4,00,000) is credited.

(iv) Bank (4,50,000), Discount on Issue of Debentures' (50,000) and Loss on Issue of Debentures' (25,000) A/cs are debited and Debentures' (5,00,000) and Premium on Redemption (25,000) A/cs are credited.

15

ROYALTY ACCOUNTS

Royalty

Royalty is the consideration or an amount payable by one person to another person for using the rights vested in him. In other words, it is the payment made by one person called lessee, to another person called lessor, for using the rights vested in the lessor. For instance, the consideration or payment made by the tenant to the landlord for raising minerals, coals, stones etc., or the consideration or payment made by the publisher to the author for using the copyright, or the consideration or payment made by the patentor (manufacturer) to the patentee (owner of the patent) for using the patent right is called royalty. The person who makes the payment to the owner for using his asset is called as lessee or licensee and the owner of the asset to whom the payment is made is called as lessor.

Royalty account is a nominal account. Royalty is an expense to the lessee. Hence, it should be debited in the books of lessee. At the end of the accounting period royalty account is closed by transferring the balance to manufacturing account, trading account or profit and loss account as the case may be. If the royalty is based on the output, it should be transferred to manufacturing or trading account. If the royalty is based on sales, it should be transferred to the profit and loss account.

Royalty is an income to the lessor. Therefore, it should be credited in the books of lessor. At the end of the accounting period royalty account is closed by transferring the balance to the profit and loss account and not to the manufacturing or trading account, whether it is based on output or sales. Because, royalty is considered as an ordinary income to the lessor.

Minimum Rent

It is a guaranteed minimum amount which the lessee is required to pay to the lessor irrespective of the production (output) or sales on which the royalty is based. It is also called 'Dead Rent', 'Fixed Rent' or 'Rock Rent'. It provides a guarantee to the lessor regarding the receipt of minimum amount in case of low production or sales. If the actual royalty is less than the minimum rent, then, the lessor is entitled to get fixed minimum rent. If the actual royalty is more than the minimum rent, then, the lessor will get the actual royalty.

Minimum Rent or Royalty in case of strike, lockout etc.

Sometimes, due to strike, lockout, accident or any other unforeseen contingency, the work will be stopped and the output or sales will be reduced. In such a cash, it is not possible to the lessee to pay the usual minimum rent to the lessor. Then, as per the agreement (a) the minimum rent shall be reduced proportionately to the period of strike or (b) the actual royalty will discharge all the rental obligations for that year or period even if it is less than the minimum rent.

Surplus

It is the excess of actual amount of royalty over the shortworking. For example, if the actual royalty is Rs. 20,000 and the minimum rent is only Rs. 15,000, then, surplus will be Rs. 5,000 (*i.e.*, excess of Rs. 20,000 over Rs. 15,000). As per the royalty agreement lessee or licensee has a right to use such surplus to recover the shortworkings of the earlier years, within the period that is allowed to him. After recovering the shortworkings, if the surplus amount is still remained, that amount will go to the lessor.

Shortworkings

The excess of minimum rent over the actual royalty based on the output or sales is called shortworkings. It is also termed as 'shortage' or 'deficiency'. Shortworkings arise only for those years when the actual royalty is less than the minimum rent payable. For example, if the minimum rent payable is Rs. 15,000 and the actual royalty during the period is only Rs. 12,000, then, shortworking will be Rs. 3000 (*i.e.*, excess of Rs. 15,000 over Rs. 3,000).

Recoupment of Shortworkings

Usually, in every royalty agreement it is provided that shortworkings of the earlier years are to be recovered by the lessee in the subsequent years when the actual royalty is more than the minimum rent. The right of getting back from the lessor, excess payment made by the lessee in the earlier years is called recoupment of shortworkings. Recoupment of shortworkings is also called as 'Redeemable Dead Rent'. The right of recoupment of shortworkings may be given to the lessee by the lessor for a limited period or unlimited period. If the shortworkings are recouped or recovered fully within the allowed period, it is well and good. If such a recovery is not made within the allowed period, it is considered as a loss to the lessee and transferred to his profit and loss account. The balance of shortworkings recoupable or recoverable is to be shown as a liability in the Balance Sheet of lessor and shown as an asset in the Balance Sheet of lessee.

Accounting Entries

The following tables show the accounting entries to be passed in the books of lessee (*i.e.* tenant) and the lessor (*i.e.* landlord).

(1) *When the account of royalty is equal to minimum rent.*

	In the books of lessee	In the books of lessor
(a) For amount of royalty due	Royalty Payable A/c Dr. To Lessor's A/c (Landlord A/c)	Lessee's A/c Dr. To Royalty Receivable A/c
(b) For payment of royalty	Lessor's A/c Dr. To Bank A/c	Bank A/c Dr. To Lessee's A/c
(c) For transfer of royalty to Profit and Loss A/c	Profit and Loss A/c Dr. To Royalty Payable A/c	Royalty Receivable A/c Dr. To P & L A/c

(2) *When the amount of royalty is less than the amount of minimum rent.*

	In the books of lessee	In the books of lessor
(a) For amount of royalty and short-workings due	*Royalty Payable A/c Dr. Shortworkings Recoverable A/c Dr. To Lessor's A/c	Lessee's A/c Dr. To Royalty Receivable A/c To Shortworkings Allowable A/c
(b) For payment of minimum rent	Lessor's or Landlord A/c Dr. To Bank A/c	Bank A/c Dr. To Lessee's A/c
(c) For transfer of royalty to P&L A/c	P & L A/c Dr. To Royalty Payable A/c	Royalty Receivable A/c Dr. To P & L A/c

***Note :** When the minimum rent account is required to prepare, it is to be prepared only if the actual royalty is less than the minimum rent (*i.e.*, short-workings). In such a case, the following two entries are to be prepared in the place of entry 'a' of No. 2 table.

(i) When the royalty is less than the minimum rent :

Minimum Rent or Dead Rent A/c	Dr.	With the amount of minimum rent.
To Landlord A/c		

(ii) For closing the minimum rent account :

Royalty A/c	Dr.	With royalty.
Shortworkings Receivable A/c	Dr.	With deficiency.
To Minimum or Dead Rent A/c		With minimum rent.

(3) *When the amount of royalty is more than the amount of minimum rent.*

	In the books of lessee	In the books of lessor
(a) When amount of royalty due	Royalty Payable A/c Dr. To Lessor's A/c	Lessee's A/c Dr. To Royalty Receivable A/c
(b) For recoupment of shortworkings	Lessor's A/c Dr. To Shortworkings Recoupable A/c	Shortworkings Allowable A/c Dr. To Lessee's A/c
(c) For payment of royalty	Lessor's A/c Dr. To Bank A/c	Bank A/c Dr. To Lessee's A/c
(d) For transfer of royalty and unrecoupable shortworkings to P & L A/c	Profit & Loss A/c Dr. To Royalty Payable A/c To Shortworkings Recoupable A/c	Royalty Receivable A/c Dr. Shortworkings Allowable A/c Dr. To P & L A/c

Note : Shortworkings Receivable Account is also called as shortworkings Recoverable Account or short workings Recoupable Account.

Analytical Table or Royalty and Shortworkings Chart

Year	Output	Royalty	Minimum Rent	Short-workings	Surplus	Shortworkings		Payment to Landlord
						Re-couped	Irrecouped	

Illustration 1

On 1st January, 1994, the Mysore Collieries leased a piece of land for a minimum rent of Rs. 12,000 merging into a royalty of 75p. per ton sold with power to recoup shortworkings over the first three years of the lease. The output of the colliery sold for the first three years was 10,000, 16,000, and 20,000 tons respectively.

You are required to pass the necessary journal entries and prepare ledger accounts in the books of both lessee and lessor.

Solution :

Calculation of Royalty and Shortworkings

Year	Output (tonnes)	Royalty at 75 paise	Minimum Rent	Short-workings	Surplus	Shortworkings Re-couped	Shortworkings Irrecouped	Payment to Landlord
		Rs.	Rs.	Rs.	Rs.	Rs.	Rs.	Rs.
1994	10,000	7,500	12,000	4,500	—	—	—	12,000
1995	16,000	12,000	12,000	—	—	—	—	12,000
1996	20,000	15,000	12,000	—	3,000	3,000	1,500	12,000

Journal Entries in the books of Mysore Collieries (Lessee)

Date	Particulars		L.F.	Debit Rs.	Credit Rs.
1994	Royalty Payable A/c	Dr.		7,500	
Dec. 31	Shortworkings Recoupable A/c	Dr.		4,500	
	To Landlord (Lessor) A/c				12,000
	(Being royalty and shortworkings due)				
1994	Landlord A/c	Dr.		12,000	
Dec. 31	To Bank A/c				12,000
	(Being payment made to landlord)				
1994	Profit and Loss Account	Dr.		7,500	
Dec. 31	To Royalty Payable Account				7,500
	(Being transfer of royalty to P&L A/c)				
1995	Royalty Payable A/c	Dr.		12,000	
Dec. 31	To Landlord A/c				12,000
	(Being royalty due)				
1995	Landlord Account	Dr.		12,000	
Dec. 31	To Bank Account				12,000
	(Being payment made to landlord)				
1995	Profit and Loss Account	Dr.		12,000	
Dec. 31	To Royalty Payable A/c				12,000
	(Being transfer of royalty to P & L A/c)				
1996	Royalty Payable A/c	Dr.		15,000	
Dec. 31	To Landlord A/c				15,000
	(Being royalty due)				

1996 Dec. 31	Landlord Account Dr. To Bank To Shortworkings Recoupable A/c (Being minimum rent paid and shortworkings recouped to the extent of Rs. 3,000)		15,000	 12,000 3,000
1996 Dec. 31	Profit and Loss Account Dr. To Royalty Payable A/c To Shortworkings Recoupable A/c (Being royalty payable and shortworkings unrecoupable transferred to P&L A/c)		16,500	 15,000 1,500

Ledger Account

Royalty (Payable) Account

Dr. Cr.

		Rs.			Rs.
31-12-94	To Landlord	7,500	31-12-94	By P & L A/c	7,500
		7,500			7,500
31-12-95	To Landlord	12,000	31-12-95	By P & L A/c	12,000
		12,000			12,000
31-12-96	To Landlord	15,000	31-12-96	By P & L A/c	15,000
		15,000			15,000

Landlord's Account

Dr. Cr.

		Rs.			Rs.
31-12-94	To Bank/Cash	12,000	31-12-94	By Short workings A/c	4,500
				By Royalty (Payable) A/c	7,500
		12,000			12,000
31-12-95	To Bank/Cash	12,000	31-12-95	By Royalty (Payable) A/c	12,000
		12,000			12,000
31-12-96	To Shortworkings A/c	3,000	31-12-96	By Royalty (Payable) A/c	15,000
	To Bank/Cash	12,000			
		15,000			15,000

Shortworkings (Recoupable) Account

Dr. Cr.

		Rs.			Rs.
31-12-94	To Landlord	4,500	31-12-94	By Balance c/d	4,500
		4,500			4,500
1-1-95	To Balance b/d	4,500	31-12-95	By Balance c/d	4,500
		4,500			4,500
1-1-96	To Balance b/d	4,500	31-12-96	By Landlord	3,000
				By P & L A/c	1,500
		4,500			4,500

Journal Entries in the books of Landlord (Lessor)

Date	Particulars		L.F.	Debit Rs.	Credit Rs.
1994	Mysore Collieries A/c (Lessee's A/c)	Dr.		12,000	
Dec. 31	To Royalty Receivable A/c				7,500
	To Shortworkings Allowable A/c				4,500
	(Being royalty and shortworkings due from Mysore Collieries)				
1994	Bank A/c	Dr.		12,000	
Dec. 31	To Mysore Collieries A/c				12,000
	(Being cash received from Mysore Collieries)				
1994	Royalty Receivable A/c	Dr.		7,500	
Dec. 31	To Profit and Loss Account				7,500
	(Being transfer of royalty to P & L A/c)				
1995	Mysore Collieries A/c	Dr.		12,000	
Dec. 31	To Royalty Receivable A/c				12,000
	(Being royalty due from Mysore Collieries)				
1995	Bank Account	Dr.		12,000	
Dec. 31	To Mysore Collieries A/c				12,000
	(Being cash received from Mysore Collieries)				
1995	Royalty Receivable A/c	Dr.		12,000	
Dec. 31	To Profit and Loss A/c				12,000
	(Being transfer of royalty to P & L A/c)				
1996	Mysore Collieries A/c	Dr.		15,000	
Dec. 31	To Royalty Receivable A/c				15,000
	(Being royalty due from Mysore Collieries)				
1996	Bank Account	Dr.		12,000	
Dec. 31	Shortworkings Allowable A/c	Dr.		3,000	
	To Mysore Collieries A/c				15,000
	(Being minimum rent received and short-workings allowed to the extent of Rs. 3,000)				
1996	Royalty Receivable A/c	Dr.		15,000	
Dec. 31	Shortworkings Allowable A/c	Dr.		1,500	
	To Profit and Loss A/c				16,500
	(Being royalty receivable and shortworkings not allowed transferred to P & L A/c)				

Ledger Accounts :

Dr. **Royalty (Receivable) Account** Cr

		Rs.			Rs.
31-12-94	To P & L A/c	7,500	31-12-94	By Mysore Collieries	7,500
		7,500			7,500
31-12-95	To P & L A/c	12,000	31-12-95	By Mysore Collieries	12,000
		12,000			12,000
31-12-96	To P & L A/c	15,000	31-12-96	By Mysore Collieries	15,000
		15,000			15,000

Dr. **Mysore Collieries Account** Cr.

		Rs.			Rs.
31-12-94	To Royalty (Receivable) A/c	7,500	31-12-94	By Bank/Cash	12,000
	To Shortworkings A/c	4,500			
		12,000			12,000
31-12-95	To Royalty (Receivable) A/c	12,000	31-12-95	By Bank/Cash	12,000
		12,000			12,000
31-12-96	To Royalty (Receivable) A/c	15,000	31-12-96	By Shortworkings A/c	3,000
				By Bank/Cash	12,000
		15,000			15,000

Dr. **Shortworkings (Allowable) A/c or Royalty Suspense A/c** Cr.

		Rs.			Rs.
31-12-94	To Balance c/d	4,500	31-12-94	By Mysore Collieries	4,500
		4,500			4,500
31-12-95	To Balance c/d	4,500	1-1-95	By Balance b/d	4,500
		4,500			4,500
31-12-96	To Mysore Collieries	3,000	1-1-96	By Balance b/d	4,500
	To P & L A/c	1,500			
		4,500			4,500

Illustration 2

Mr. Rakesh wrote a book on Accountancy and got it published with Mangalore Publishers on the terms that royalties will be paid at Rs. 5 per copy sold subject to a minimum rent of Rs. 15,000 per year with a right of recoupment of shortworkings over the first three years of the royalty agreement.

Year	No. of copies printed	No. of copies of closing stock
1985	2,000	100
1986	3,000	200
1987	4,000	400
1988	5,000	500

Prepare Minimum Rent Account, Royalties Account, Shortworkings Account and Mr. Rakesh's Account in the books of Mangalore Publishers.

(*Mangalore, B.Com., April, 1984*)

Solution :

Calculation of Royalty Payable

Year	Copies Sold	Royalty at Rs. 5	Minimum Rent	Short-workings	Surplus	Shortworkings Re-couped	Shortworkings Irrecouped	Payment to Author
		Rs.	Rs.	Rs.	Rs.	Rs.	Rs.	Rs.
1985	1,900	9,500	15,000	5,500	—	—	—	15,000
1986	2,900	14,500	15,000	500	—	—	—	15,000
1987	3,800	19,000	15,000	—	4,000	4,000	2,000	15,000
1988	4,900	24,500	15,000	—	9,500	—	—	24,500

Note : No. of copies sold 1985 – 1,900 (*i.e.*, 2,000 – 100), 1986 – 2,900 (*i.e.*, 3,000 – 100 *i.e.*, 200 – 100), 1987 – 3,800 (4,000 – 200 *i.e.*, 400 – 200) and 1988 – 4,900 (*i.e.*, 5000 – 100 *i.e.*, 500 – 400).

Dr. **Minimum Rent Account** Cr.

		Rs.			Rs.
1985	To Mr. Rakesh (Author)	15,000	1985	By Royalty	9,500
				By Shortworkings	5,500
		15,000			15,000
1986	To Mr. Rakesh (Author)	15,000	1986	By Royalty	14,500
				By Shortworkings	500
		15,000			15,000

Note : Minimum Rent Account is prepared only when the actual royalty is less than minimum rent. Therefore, it appears only in the first two years.

Dr. **Royalty (Payable) Account** Cr.

		Rs.			Rs.
1985	To Minimum Rent	9,500	1985	By Profit & Loss A/c	9,500
		9,500			9,500
1986	To Minimum Rent	14,500	1986	By Profit & Loss A/c	14,500
		14,500			14,500
1987	To Mr. Rakesh (Author)	19,000	1987	By Profit & Loss A/c	19,000
		19,000			19,000
1988	To Mr. Rakesh (Author)	24,500	1988	By Profit & Loss A/c	24,500
		24,500			24,500

Dr. **Mr. Rakesh's Account (Author's A/c)** Cr.

		Rs.			Rs.
1985	To Bank/Cash	15,000	1985	By Minimum Rent	15,000
		15,000			15,000
1986	To Bank/Cash	15,000	1986	By Minimum Rent	15,000
		15,000			15,000
1987	To Bank/Cash	15,000	1987	By Royalty	19,000
	To Shortworkings	4,000			
		19,000			19,000
1988	To Bank/Cash	24,500	1988	By Royalty	24,500
		24,500			24,500

Dr. **Shortworkings (Recoupable) Account** Cr.

		Rs.			Rs.
1985	To Minimum Rent	5,500	1985	By Balance c/d	5,500
		5,500			5,500
1986	To Balance b/d	5,500	1986	By Balance c/d	6,000
	To Minimum Rent	500			
		6,000			6,000
1987	To Balance b/d	6,000	1987	By Mr. Rakesh	4,000
				By P & L A/c	2,000
		6,000			6,000

Illustration 3

Mr. Anand an Engineer owned a patent of Safety Locks. Badoda Lockers Ltd. acquired the rights to manufacture and sell locks for seven years on the following terms :

(a) Badoda Lockers Ltd. to pay Mr. Anand Royalty of Rs. 5 for each lock sold with a minimum annual payment of Rs. 50,000. Accounts are to be settled on 31st December every year.

(b) If in any year the royalty calculated on locks sold does not reach the minimum amount of Rs. 50,000, the Badoda Lockers Ltd., has a right to deduct the deficiency from the Royalty payable in excess of that sum in the two following years. Number of locks sold was as under :

1992 - 8,000 1994 - 11,000
1993 - 9,000 1995 - 18,000

You are required to prepare Royalty Account, Shortworkings Account and Mr. Anand's Account in the books of Badoda Lockers Ltd.

(*Kar., Oct., 1977 & Bangalore, Oct., 1985*)

Solution :

Calculation of Royalty Payable

Year	No. of Locks Sold	Royalty at Rs. 5	Minimum Rent	Short-workings	Surplus	Shortworkings		Payment to Landlord
						Re-couped	Irrecouped	
		Rs.	Rs.	Rs.	Rs.	Rs.	Rs.	Rs.
1992	8,000	40,000	50,000	10,000	—	—	—	50,000
1993	9,000	45,000	50,000	5,000	—	—	—	50,000
1994	11,000	55,000	50,000	—	5,000	5,000	5,000	50,000
1995	18,000	90,000	50,000	—	40,000	5,000	—	85,000

In the books of Badoda Lockers Ltd.

Royalty (Payable) Account

Dr. Cr.

		Rs.			Rs.
1992	To Mr. Anand	40,000	1992	By Profit & Loss A/c	40,000
		40,000			40,000
1993	To Mr. Anand	45,000	1993	By Profit & Loss A/c	45,000
		45,000			45,000
1994	To Mr. Anand	55,000	1994	By Profit & Loss A/c	55,000
		55,000			55,000
1995	To Mr. Anand	90,000	1995	By Profit & Loss A/c	90,000
		90,000			90,000

Dr. **Mr. Anand's Account** Cr.

		Rs.			Rs.
1992	To Bank	50,000	1992	By Royalty	40,000
				By Shortworkings	10,000
		50,000			50,000
1993	To Bank	50,000	1993	By Royalty	45,000
				By Shortworkings	5,000
		50,000			50,000
1994	To Shortworkings	5,000	1994	By Royalty	55,000
	To Bank	50,000			
		55,000			55,000
1995	To Shortworkings	5,000	1995	By Royalty	90,000
	To Bank	85,000			
		90,000			90,000

Dr. **Shortworkings (Recoupable) Account** Cr.

		Rs.			Rs.
1992	To Mr. Anand	10,000	1992	By Balance c/d	10,000
		10,000			10,000
1993	To Balance b/d	10,000	1993	By Balance c/d	15,000
	To Mr. Anand	5,000			
		15,000			15,000
1994	To Balance b/d	15,000	1994	By Mr. Anand	5,000
				By P & L Account	5,000
				By Balance c/d	5,000
		15,000			15,000
1995	To Balance b/d	5,000	1995	By Mr. Anand	5,000
		5,000			5,000

Illustration 4

On 1st January, 1989, Hiren, patentee of a new type of article required in Engineering Concern, issued a licence to Subir for three years for the manufacture and sale of the article on the following terms and conditions :

(a) Royalty of Rs. 5 per article manufactured.

(b) Minimum rent of Rs. 5,000 per annum.

(c) Recoupment of shortworkings out of the royalties in excess of minimum rent during the two years immediately following subject to a maximum of Rs. 2,000 per annum.

(d) Accounts were to be settled annually on 31st December. The number of article manufactured for the three years were as follows :

1989 – 100, 1990 – 1,100 and 1991 – 2,600.

You are required to show Royalty A/c, Short workings A/c & Hiren's A/c in the books of Subir.

(*I.C.W.A. Inter & Bombay, Oct., 1985*)

Solution :

Calculation of Royalty Payable

Year	No. of Articles Manu-factured	Royalty Rs. 5 per Article	Minimum Rent	Short-workings	Surplus	Shortworkings Re-couped	Shortworkings Irrecouped	Payment to Landlord
		Rs.	Rs.	Rs.	Rs.	Rs.	Rs.	Rs.
1989	100	500	5,000	4,500	—	—	—	5,000
1990	1,100	5,500	5,000	—	500	500	—	5,000
1991	2,600	13,000	5,000	—	8,000	2,000	2,000	11,000

Dr. **Royalty (Payable) Account** Cr.

		Rs.			Rs.
1989	To Hiren's A/c	500	1989	By Manufacturing A/c	500
		500			500
1990	To Hiren's A/c	5,500	1990	By Manufacturing A/c	5,500
		5,500			5,500
1991	To Hiren's A/c	13,000	1991	By Manufacturing A/c	13,000
		13,000			13,000

Dr. **Shortworkings (Recoupable) Account** Cr.

		Rs.			Rs.
1989	To Hiren's A/c	4,500	1989	By Balance c/d	4,500
		4,500			4,500
1990	To Balance b/d	4,500	1990	By Hiren's A/c	500
				By Balance c/d	4,000
		4,500			4,500
1991	To Balance b/d	4,000	1991	By Hiren's A/c	2,000
				By P & L A/c	2,000
		4,000			4,000

Dr. **Hiren's Account** Cr.

		Rs.			Rs.
1989	To Bank A/c	5,000	1989	By Royalty A/c	500
				By Shortworkings A/c	4,500
		5,000			5,000
1990	To Bank A/c	5,000	1990	By Royalty A/c	5,500
	To Shortworkings A/c	500			
		5,500			5,500
1991	To Bank A/c	11,000	1991	By Royalty A/c	13,000
	To Shortworkings A/c	2,000			
		13,000			13,000

Illustration 5

'M' wrote a book and got it published with 'P' on the following terms :

(1) Royalty would be 15% of the sale proceeds of each year.

(2) Minimum amount Rs. 10,000 p.a.

(3) The deficiency in sales, if any, of one year could be recouped out of the excess in the immediate next year.

(4) 'M' to revise the book when requested by the publisher and submit the revised edition within 6 months of the request. If 'M' delays beyond 6 months, he has to pay 'P' at Rs. 500 per month for the period of delay, further in the year of delay minimum rent clause was not apply.

The number of copies sold and the sales price of each copy were as follows :

	No. of copies sold	Sales price of each copy
Ist year	2,000	Rs. 20
IInd year	4,000	Rs. 20
IIIrd year	5,000	Rs. 25
IVth year	2,000	Rs. 25
Vth year	6,000	Rs. 30

'M' was requested to revise the book on Ist January of IVth year. The revised manuscript reached the publisher 'P' only on 1st November of IVth year.

Give the important ledger accounts in the books of 'P'.

(Bangalore, Oct., 1982 & Mysore, April, 1972)

Solution :

Calculation Royalty Payable

Year	No. of Copies Sold	Royalty	Minimum Rent	Short-workings	Surplus	Shortworkings Re-couped	Shortworkings Irrecouped	Payment to Author
		Rs.	Rs.	Rs.	Rs.	Rs.	Rs.	Rs.
Ist yr.	2,000	6,000	10,000	4,000	–	–	–	10,000
IInd yr.	4,000	12,000	10,000	–	2,000	2,000	2,000	10,000
IIIrd yr.	5,000	18,750	10,000	–	8,750	–	–	18,750
IVth yr.	2,000	7,500	7,500	–	–	–	–	7,500
Vth yr.	6,000	27,000	10,000	–	17,000	–	–	27,000

Note: (i) Royalty Ist yr. Rs. 6,000 *i.e.*, 15% on 40,000

Royalty IInd yr. Rs. 12,000 *i.e.*, 15% on 80,000

Royalty IIIrd yr. Rs. 18,750 *i.e.*, 15% on 1,25,000

Royalty IVth yr. Rs. 7,500 *i.e.*, 15% on 50,000

Royalty Vth yr. Rs. 27,000 *i.e.*, 15% on 1,80,000.

(ii) In the IVth year, due to delay in sending revised manuscript, the actual royalty earned for that year will be the minimum rent.

Dr. **Royalty Payable Account** Cr.

		Rs.			Rs.
Ist yr.	To M's A/c	6,000	Ist yr.	By Profit & Loss A/c	6,000
		6,000			6,000
IInd yr.	To M's A/c	12,000	IInd yr.	By Profit & Loss A/c	12,000
		12,000			12,000
IIIrd yr.	To M's A/c	18,750	IIIrd yr.	By Profit & Loss A/c	18,750
		18,750			18,750
IVth yr.	To M's A/c	7,500	IVth yr.	By Profit & Loss A/c	7,500
		7,500			7,500
Vth yr.	To M's A/c	27,000	Vth yr.	By Profit & Loss A/c	27,000
		27,000			27,000

Dr. **M's (Author) Account** Cr.

		Rs.			Rs.
Ist yr.	To Bank	10,000	Ist yr.	By Royalty	6,000
				By Shortworkings	4,000
		10,000			10,000
IInd yr.	To Shortworkings	2,000	IInd yr.	By Royalty	12,000
	To Bank	10,000			
		12,000			12,000
IIIrd yr.	To Bank	18,750	IIIrd yr.	By Royalty	18,750
		18,750			18,750
IVth yr.	To Fines A/c	2,000	IVth yr.	By Royalty	7,500
	To Bank	5,500			
		7,500			7,500
Vth yr.	To Bank A/c	27,000	Vth yr.	By Royalty	27,000
		27,000			27,000

Dr. **Shortworkings (Recoupable) Account** Cr.

		Rs.			Rs.
Ist yr.	To M's Account	4,000	Ist yr.	By Balance c/d	4,000
		4,000			4,000
IInd yr.	To Balance b/d	4,000	IInd yr.	By M's A/c	2,000
				By P & L A/c	2,000
		4,000			4,000

Dr. **Fines Account** Cr.

		Rs.			Rs.
IVth yr.	To P & L A/c	2,000	IVth yr.	By M's A/c	2,000
		2,000			2,000

Illustration 6

Minerals Ltd. leased a property from Mr. Shankar at a royalty of Rs. 1.50 per ton raised with a minimum rent of Rs. 10,000 per annum. Each year's excess of minimum rent over the royalty is recoverable out of the royalties of the next three years. In the event of strike in any year, the lease provides for the proportionate reduction of minimum rent for that year. Accounts are to be settled every year on 31st December.

The annual out put of the first five years is as follows :

Year ending 31st December	Output (in tons)
1981	4,000
1982	5,000
1983	6,000
1984	10,000
1985 (strike for 3 months)	4,000

Prepare (a) Royalty Account (b) Shortworkings Account (c) Shankar's Account in the books of Minerals Ltd.

(*Gulbarga, Oct., 1987*)

Solution :

Calculation of Royalty Payable

Year	Output in tons	Royalty at Rs. 1.50	Minimum Rent	Short-workings	Surplus	Shortworkings		Payment to Landlord
						Re-couped	Irrecouped	
		Rs.	Rs.	Rs.	Rs.	Rs.	Rs.	Rs.
1981	4,000	6,000	10,000	4,000	—	—	—	10,000
1982	5,000	7,500	10,000	2,500	—	—	—	10,000
1983	6,000	9,000	10,000	1,000	—	—	—	10,000
1984	10,000	15,000	10,000	—	5,000	5,000	—	10,000
1985 (Strike)	4,000	6,000	7,500	1,500	—	—	1,500	7,500

Note : There was a strike in the year 1985. Therefore, the minimum rent has been reduced proportionately which comes to Rs. 7,500 (*i.e.*, ¾ of 10,000).

Dr. **Royalty (Payable) Account** Cr.

		Rs.			Rs.
1981	To Landlord	6,000	1981	By Manufacturing A/c	6,000
		6,000			6,000
1982	To Landlord	7,500	1982	By Manufacturing A/c	7,500
		7,500			7,500
1983	To Landlord	9,000	1983	By Manufacturing A/c	9,000
		9,000			9,000
1984	To Landlord	15,000	1984	By Manufacturing A/c	15,000
		15,000			15,000
1985	To Landlord	6,000	1985	By Manufacturing A/c	6,000
		6,000			6,000

Dr. **Shortworkings (Recoupable) Account** Cr.

		Rs.			Rs.
1981	To Landlord	4,000	1981	By Balance c/d	4,000
		4,000			4,000
1982	To Balance b/d	4,000	1982	By Balance c/d	6,500
	To Landlord	2,500			
		6,500			6,500
1983	To Balance b/d	6,500	1983	By Balance c/d	7,500
	To Landlord	1,000			
		7,500			7,500
1984	To Balance b/d	7,500	1984	By Landlord	5,000
				By Balance c/d	2,500
		7,500			7,500
1985	To Balance b/d	2,500	1985	By P & L A/c	1,500
	To Landlord	1,500		By Balance c/d	2,500
		4,000			4,000

Dr. **Landlord's Account** Cr

		Rs.			Rs.
1981	To Bank	10,000	1981	By Royalty	6,000
				By Shortworkings	4,000
		10,000			10,000
1982	To Bank	10,000	1982	By Royalty	7,500
				By Shortworkings	2,500
		10,000			10,000
1983	To Bank	10,000	1983	By Royalty	9,000
				By Shortworkings	1,000
		10,000			10,000
1984	To Bank	10,000	1984	By Royalty	15,000
	To Shortworkings	5,000			
		15,000			15,000
1985	To Bank	7,500	1985	By Royalty	6,000
				By Shortworkings	1,500
		7,500			7,500

Illustration 7

A Colliery Co. Ltd. leased a property from B at a royalty of Re. 1 per tonne with a minimum rent of Rs. 3,000 in the first year, Rs. 4,000 in the second year and thereafter Rs. 5,000 per annum. Each years excess of minimum rent over royalties is recoverable out of the royalties in the next two years. In the event of strike and the minimum rent is not reached, the lease provided that the actual royalties earned for the year discharged all the rental obligations for that year.

Year	1992	1993	1994	1995	1996
Output in tonnes	1,500	3,500	5,500	4,000 (Strike)	6,000

Prepare Royalty Account and Shortworkings Account in the books of Colliery Co. Ltd. for the above five years.

Solution :

Calculation of Royalty Payable

Year	Output in tonnes	Royalty at Re. 1	Minimum Rent	Short-workings	Surplus	Shortworkings Re-couped	Shortworkings Irrecouped	Payment to Landlord
		Rs.	Rs.	Rs.	Rs.	Rs.	Rs.	Rs.
1992	1,500	1,500	3,000	1,500	—	—	—	3,000
1993	3,500	3,500	4,000	500	—	—	—	4,000
1994	5,500	5,500	5,000	—	500	500	1,000	5,000
1995 (Strike)	4,000	4,000	4,000	—	—	—	500	4,000
1996	6,000	6,000	5,000	—	1,000	—	—	6,000

Note : The actual royalty of Rs. 4,000 in the year 1995 (strike year) itself is treated as minimum rent payable to landlord (*i.e.*, B).

In the books of Colliery Co. Ltd.

Royalty (Payable) Account

Dr. Cr.

		Rs.			Rs.
1992	To B's A/c	1,500	1992	By Manufacturing A/c	1,500
		1,500			1,500
1993	To B's A/c	3,500	1993	By Manufacturing A/c	3,500
		3,500			3,500
1994	To B's A/c	5,500	1994	By Manufacturing A/c	5,500
		5,500			5,500
1995	To B's A/c	4,000	1995	By Manufacturing A/c	4,000
		4,000			4,000
1996	To B's A/c	6,000	1996	By Manufacturing A/c	6,000
		6,000			6,000

Dr. **Shortworkings (Recoupable) Account** Cr.

		Rs.			Rs.
1992	To B's A/c	1,500	1992	By Balance c/d	1,500
		1,500			1,500
1993	To Balance b/d	1,500	1993	By Balance c/d	2,000
	To B's A/c	500			
		2,000			2,000
1994	To Balance b/d	2,000	1994	By B's A/c	500
				By P & L A/c	1,000
				By Balance c/d	500
		2,000			2,000
1995	To Balance b/d	500	1995	By P & L A/c	500
		500			500

Illustration 8

The Assam Coal Ltd. holds a lease of coal mine for the period of 10 years commencing from 1991. According to the lease, the Co. is to pay 75 paise royalty per tonne with minimum rent of Rs. 15,000 a year. Shortworkings can however, be recovered out of the royalty in excess of the minimum rent of the next two years only. In the year of strike the minimum rent is to be reduced to 60%. The output for the six years has been as under :

Year	Tonnes (production)
1991	10,000
1992	12,000
1993	28,000
1994	25,000
1995 (Strike)	15,000

Show the landlord account and shortworkings account in the books of the company.

(Bangalore, Oct., 1986 & ICWA Inter)

Solution :

Calculation of Royalty Payable

Year	Output in tonnes	Royalty at 75 Paise	Minimum Rent	Short-workings	Surplus	Shortworkings Re-couped	Shortworkings Irrecouped	Payment to Landlord
		Rs.	Rs.	Rs.	Rs.	Rs.	Rs.	Rs.
1991	10,000	7,500	15,000	7,500	—	—	—	15,000
1992	12,000	9,000	15,000	6,000	—	—	—	15,000
1993	28,000	21,000	15,000	—	6,000	6,000	1,500	15,000
1994	25,000	18,750	15,000	—	3,750	3,750	2,250	15000
1995 (Strike)	15,000	11,250	9,000	—	2,250	—	—	11,250

In the Books of Assam Co. Ltd.

Dr. **Landlord Account** Cr.

		Rs.			Rs.
1991	To Bank	15,000	1991	By Royalty (Payable) A/c	7,500
				By Shortworkings	7,500
		15,000			15,000
1992	To Bank	15,000	1992	By Royalty	9,000
				By Shortworkings	6,000
		15,000			15,000
1993	To Bank	15,000	1993	By Royalty	21,000
	To Shortworkings	6,000			
		21,000			21,000
1994	To Bank	3,750	1994	By Royalty	18,750
	To Shortworkings	15,000			
		18,750			18,750
1995	To Bank	11,250	1995	By Royalty	11,250
		11,250			11,250

Dr. **Shortworkings (Allowable) Account** Cr.

		Rs.			Rs.
1991	To Landlord	7,500	1991	By Balance c/d	7,500
		7,500			7,500
1992	To Balance b/d	7,500	1992	By Balance c/d	13,500
	To Landlord	6,000			
		13,500			13,500
1993	To Balance b/d	13,500	1993	By Landlord	6,000
				By P&L A/c	1,500
				By Balance c/d	6,000
		13,500			13,500
1994	To Balance b/d	6,000	1994	By Landlord	3,750
				By P&L A/c	2,250
		6,000			6,000

Illustration 9

Dharwar Coal Company acquired on lease a coal mine on a royalty of 50 paise per tonne of coal brought on the surface with a minimum rent of Rs. 56,000 a year with no right to recover shortworkings except the shortworkings of the strike period which can be recovered in the next year.

10% of the coal taken out from the mine is lost in weight in bringing the coal on surface.

Dharwar Coal Company took out the mine as under :

Ist year 20,000 tonnes, IInd year 80,000 tonnes, IIIrd year 1,20,000 tonnes, IVth year 1,70,000 tonnes and Vth year 80,000 tonnes (Strike).

Show minimum rent account, royalty account and shortworkings account for the years.

(*KUD, 1964 & C.A. Intermediate, 1993*)

Solution :

Calculation of Royalty Payable

Year	Output in tonnes	Output bringing on surface	Royalty at 50 paise	Minimum Rent	Short-workings	Surplus	Shortworkings		Payment to Landlord
							Re-couped	Irrecouped	
			Rs.	Rs.	Rs.	Rs.	Rs.	Rs.	Rs.
Ist yr.	20,000	18,000	9,000	56,000	47,000	—	—	47,000	56,000
IInd yr.	80,000	72,000	36,000	56,000	20,000	—	—	20,000	56,000
IIIrd yr.	1,20,000	1,08,000	54,000	56,000	2,000	—	—	2,000	56,000
IVth yr.	1,70,000	1,53,000	76,500	56,000	—	20,500	—	—	76,500
Vth yr.	80,000 (Strike)	72,000	36,000	56,000	20,000	—	—	—	56,000

Notes : (i) There is no right to recover shortworkings except the shortworkings of the strike period. Therefore, the shortworkings of each year should be considered as irrecoupable shortworking.

(ii) There is a right to recover shortworkings of strike year. So, the shortworkings of strike period can be recovered in the next year.

Dr. **Minimum Rent Account** Cr.

		Rs.			Rs.
Ist yr.	To Landlord	56,000	Ist yr.	By Royalty	9,000
				By Shortworkings	47,000
		56,000			56,000
IInd yr.	To Landlord	56,000	IInd yr.	By Royalty	36,000
				By Shortworkings	20,000
		56,000			56,000
IIIrd yr.	To Landlord	56,000	IIIrd yr.	By Royalty	54,000
				By Shortworkings	2,000
		56,000			56,000
Vth yr.	To Landlord	56,000	Vth yr.	By Royalty	36,000
				By Shortworkings	20,000
		56,000			56,000

Note : Minimum rent account is prepared only when the actual royalty is less than minimum rent. Hence, it does not appear in the IVth year.

Dr. **Royalties (Payable) Account** Cr.

		Rs.			Rs.
Ist yr.	To Minimum Rent	9,000	Ist yr.	By Manufacturing A/c	9,000
		9,000			9,000
IInd yr.	To Minimum Rent	36,000	IInd yr.	By Manufacturing A/c	36,000
		36,000			36,000
IIIrd yr.	To Minimum Rent	54,000	IIIrd yr.	By Manufacturing A/c	54,000
		54,000			54,000
IVth yr.	To Landlord	76,500	IVth yr.	By Manufacturing A/c	76,500
		76,500			76,500
Vth yr.	To Minimum Rent	36,000	Vth yr.	By Manufacturing A/c	36,000
		36,000			36,000

Dr. **Shortworkings (Recoupable) Account** Cr.

		Rs.			Rs.
Ist yr.	To Minimum Rent	47,000	Ist yr.	By P&L A/c	47,000
		47,000			47,000
IInd yr.	To Minimum Rent	20,000	IInd yr.	By P&L A/c	20,000
		20,000			20,000
IIIrd yr.	To Minimum Rent	2,000	IIIrd yr.	By P&L A/c	2,000
		2,000			2,000
Vth yr.	To Minimum Rent	20,000	Vth yr.	By Balance c/d	20,000
		20,000			20,000
VIth yr.	To Balance b/d	20,000			

Sub-Lease

Sometimes a lessee or licensee may transfer a part or whole of his rights acquired by him to another person called sub-lessee or sub-tenant. In such a case, the lessee acts as a landlord and sub-lessee acts as a tenant. In case of sub-lease three parties are involved.

(1) Landlord : He is original owner of the right. He will continue to get the royalty on the total output or sales. The contract between him and lessee will not be affected on account of granting sub-lease.

(2) Lessee : When sub-lease is granted by the lessee, lessee acts in dual capacity *i.e.*, tenant as well as landlord. He acts as a tenant for the original owner and acts as a landlord for the sub-lessee. He will receive the royalty from the sub-lessee as per the agreement in between him and sub-lessee and will pay the royalty to the original owner as per the agreement in between him and the owner.

(3) Sub-lessee : Sub-lessee will pay royalty to lessee as per the agreement in between him and lessee. In this case, the lessee is the landlord for the sub-lessee.

Accounting Entries

The procedure of passing the accounting entries is the same as explained in case of ordinary lease. But in the books of lessee, the number of accounts will be more due to his dual capacity. The following are the accounts to be opened in the books of lessee :

(i) Royalty Receivable Account.

(ii) Royalty Payable Account.

(iii) Shortworkings Recoupable or Recoverable A/c (*i.e.*, Account for recoupment of shortworkings from the landlord as per the agreement).

(iv) Shortworkings Allowable Account or Royalty Suspense Account (*i.e.*, Account for shortworkings allowed to be recouped by the sub-lessee.

Royalty Receivable Account is credited with the amount of royalty receivable from the sub-lessee and Royalty Payable Account is debited with the total amount of royalty payable to the landlord. Usually, the lessee gets more royalty from sub-lessee than the royalty which he pays to the original owner (*i.e.*, original landlord). The difference is treated as a profit of lessee. This profit is transferred from the Royalty Receivable Account to Profit and Loss Account. The balance of Royalty Receivable Account is transferred to the Royalty Payable Account and balance of Royalty Payable Account is ultimately transferred to Manufacturing, Trading or Profit and Loss Account.

Illustration 10

ABC Co. Ltd. holds a lease of minerals from 'R' for a period of 40 years from 1-1-1990. Under this lease there is payable a royalty of a rupee per tonne, merging in a minimum rent of Rs. 20,000 a year payable half-yearly on 30th June and 31st December each year. They granted a sub-lease for 20 years from 1-7-1990 to 'X' Co. Ltd. of one-half of the area for a royalty of Rs. 1.50 per tonne merging in a minimum rent of Rs. 15,000 per half-year, payable half-yearly on 30th June and 31st December each year.

ABC Co. Ltd. is entitled under the lease from 'R' to recoup shortworkings out of the excess workings throughout the term of lease, but sub-lease allows 'X' Co. Ltd. to recoup the shortworkings only out of excess workings in any of the three half-years immediately following that in which the shortworkings accrued.

Minerals are worked as follows :

	By ABC Co., Ltd.	By X Co., Ltd.
Half-year ended 30-6-1990	5,000 tonnes	—
Half-year ended 31-12-1990	5,000 tonnes	5,000 tonnes
Half-year ended 30-6-1991	20,000 tonnes	6,000 tonnes
Half-year ended 31-12-1991	30,000 tonnes	6,000 tonnes
Half-year ended 30-6-1992	25,000 tonnes	12,000 tonnes

Show the necessary ledger accounts in the books of ABC Co. Ltd. and its books are balanced each year on 30th June.

(*KUD, Oct., 1971 & Shivaji, April, 1992*)

Solution :

Calculation of Royalty Payable to 'R'

Year	Output in tonnes	Royalty Re. 1	Minimum Rent	Short-workings	Surplus	Shortworkings Re-couped	Shortworkings Irrecouped	Payment to Landlord
		Rs.	Rs.	Rs.	Rs.	Rs.	Rs.	Rs.
30-6-90	5,000	5,000	10,000	5,000	—	—	—	10,000
31-12-90	10,000	10,000	10,000	—	—	—	—	10,000
30-6-91	26,000	26,000	10,000	—	16,000	5,000	—	21,000
31-12-91	36,000	36,000	10,000	—	26,000	—	—	36,000
30-6-92	37,000	37,000	10,000	—	27,000	—	—	37,000

Calculation of Royalty Receivable from 'X' Co. Ltd.

Year	Output in tonnes	Royalty at Re. 1.5	Minimum Rent	Short-workings	Surplus	Shortworkings Re-couped	Shortworkings Irrecouped	Payment to Landlord
		Rs.	Rs.	Rs.	Rs.	Rs.	Rs.	Rs.
31-12-90	5,000	7,500	15,000	7,500	—	—	—	15,000
30-6-91	6,000	9,000	15,000	6,000	—	—	—	15,000
31-12-91	6,000	9,000	15,000	6,000	—	—	—	15,000
30-6-92	12,000	18,000	15,000	—	3,000	3,000	4,500	15,000

In the books of ABC Co. Ltd.

Dr. **Royalty Payable Account** Cr.

		Rs.			Rs.
30-6-90	To R's Account	5,000	30-6-90	By Manufacturing A/c	5,000
		5,000			5,000
31-12-90	To R's Account	10,000	30-6-91	By Royalty Receivable A/c	11,000
30-6-91	To R's Account	26,000		(5,000 + 6,000 from	
				31-12-90 to 30-6-1991)	
				By Manufacturing A/c	25,000
		36,000			36,000
31-12-91	To R's Account	36,000	30-6-92	By Royalty Receivable A/c	18,000
30-6-92	To R's Account	37,000		(6,000 + 12,000)	
				By Manufacturing A/c	55,000
		73,000			73,000

Royalty Receivable Account

Dr.		Rs.		Cr.	Rs.
30-6-91	To Royalty Payable A/c (5,000 + 6,000)	11,000	31-12-90	By X Co. Ltd.	7,500
			30-6-91	By X Co. Ltd.	9,000
	To Profit & Loss A/c	5,500			
		16,500			16,500
30-6-92	To Royalty Payable A/c (6,000 + 12,000)	18,000	31-12-91	By X Co. Ltd.	9,000
			30-6-92	By X Co. Ltd.	18,000
	To Profit & Loss A/c	9,000			
		27,000			27,000

R's Account (Landlord's A/c)

Dr.		Rs.		Cr.	Rs.
30-6-90	To Bank or Cash	10,000	30-6-90	By Royalty Payable	5,000
				By Shortworkings Recoupable	5,000
		10,000			10,000
31-12-90	To Cash	10,000	31-12-90	By Royalty Payable	10,000
30-6-91	To Shortworkings Recoupable	5,000	30-6-91	By Royalty Payable	26,000
30-6-91	To Cash	21,000			
		36,000			36,000
31-12-91	To Cash	36,000	31-12-91	By Royalty Payable	36,000
30-6-92	To Cash	37,000	30-6-92	By Royalty Payable	37,000
		73,000			73,000

X Co. Ltd. (Sub-lessee) Account

Dr.		Rs.		Cr.	Rs.
31-12-90	To Royalty Receivable	7,500	31-12-90	By Cash	15,000
	To Shortworkings Allowable	7,500	30-6-91	By Cash	15,000
30-6-91	To Royalty Receivable	9,000			
	To Shortworkings Allowable	6,000			
		30,000			30,000
31-12-91	To Royalty Receivable	9,000	31-12-91	By Cash	15,000
	To Shortworkings Allowable	6,000	30-6-92	By Shortworkings Allowable	3,000
30-6-92	To Royalty Receivable	18,000	30-6-92	By Cash	15,000
		33,000			33,000

Dr. **Shortworkings Recoupable Account** Cr.

		Rs.			Rs.
30-6-90	To R's A/c	5,000	30-6-90	By Balance c/d	5,000
		5,000			5,000
1-7-90	To Balance b/d	5,000	30-6-91	By R's Account	5,000
		5,000			5,000

Dr. **Shortworkings Allowable A/c (Royalty Suspense A/c)** Cr.

		Rs.			Rs.
30-6-91	To Balance c/d	13,500	31-12-90	By X Co. Ltd.	7,500
			30-6-91	By X Co. Ltd.	6,000
		13,500			13,500
30-6-92	To X Co. Ltd.	3,000	1-7-91	By Balance b/d	13,500
	To P & L A/c	4,500	31-12-91	By X Co. Ltd.	6,000
	To Balance c/d	12,000			
		19,500			19,500
			1-7-92	By Balance b/d	12,000

Illustration 11

On 1st January, 1985 'A' Co. Ltd. took a coalfield on a lease from Landlord 'B' on a minimum rent of Rs. 2,000 p.a., merging into a royalty at 25 paise per tonne of coal raised. The company could recoup shortworkings during the first four years of the lease. On the same date 'A' Co. Ltd., granted a sub-lease of a part of the coalfield to sub-lessee 'C' on a royalty of 50 paise per tonne merging into a minimum rent of Rs. 1,000 per annum with a right of recoupment of shortworkings during the two years following the year in which shortworking arises.

The mineral worked as follows :

Year	'A' Co. Ltd.	'C' Co. Ltd.
1985	4,000 tonnes	1,000 tonnes
1986	4,500 tonnes	1,200 tonnes
1987	5,200 tonnes	2,700 tonnes
1988	6,800 tonnes	3,500 tonnes
1989	7,000 tonnes	4,800 tonnes

Prepare Royalty Payable A/c, Royalty Receivable A/c and Shortworkings A/c in the books of 'A' Co. Ltd.

(*Mysore, Oct., 1980 & ICWA Inter*)

Solution :

Calculation of Royalty Payable to 'B'

Year	Output in tonnes	Royalty at 25 paise	Minimum Rent	Short-workings	Surplus	Shortworkings Re-couped	Shortworkings Irrecouped	Payment to Landlord
		Rs.	Rs.	Rs.	Rs.	Rs.	Rs.	Rs.
1985	5,000	1,250	2,000	750	—	—	—	2,000
1986	5,700	1,425	2,000	575	—	—	—	2,000
1987	7,900	1,975	2,000	25	—	—	—	2,000
1988	10,300	2,575	2,000	—	575	575	775	2,000
1989	11,800	2,950	2,000	—	950	—	—	2,950

Calculation of Royalty Receivable from 'C'

Year	Output in tonnes	Royalty at 50 paise	Minimum Rent	Short-workings	Surplus	Shortworkings Re-couped	Shortworkings Irrecouped	Payment to Landlord
		Rs.	Rs.	Rs.	Rs.	Rs.	Rs.	Rs.
1985	1,000	500	1,000	500	—	—	—	1,000
1986	1,200	600	1,000	400	—	—	—	1,000
1987	2,700	1,350	1,000	—	350	350	150	1,000
1988	3,500	1,750	1,000	—	750	400	—	1,350
1989	4,800	2,400	1,000	—	1,400	—	—	2,400

In the books of 'A' Co. Ltd.

Royalty Payable Account

Dr. Cr.

		Rs.			Rs.
1985	To B's A/c (*i.e.*, Landlord's A/c)	1,250	1985	By Royalty Receivable A/c	250
				By Manufacturing A/c	1,000
		1,250			1,250
1986	To B's A/c	1,425	1986	By Royalty Receivable A/c	300
				By Manufacturing A/c	1,125
		1,425			1,425
1987	To B's A/c	1,975	1987	By Royalty Receivable A/c	675
				By Manufacturing A/c	1,300
		1,975			1,975
1988	To B's A/c	2,575	1988	By Royalty Receivable A/c	875
				By Manufacturing A/c	1,700
		2,575			2,575
1989	To B's A/c	2,950	1989	By Royalty Receivable A/c	1,200
				By Manufacturing A/c	1,750
		2,950			2,950

Dr. **Royalty Receivable Account** Cr.

		Rs.			Rs.
1985	To Royalty Payable A/c	250	1985	By C's Account	500
	To P & L A/c	250			
		500			500
1986	To Royalty Payable A/c	300	1986	By C's Account	600
	To P & L Account	300			
		600			600
1987	To Royalty Payable A/c	675	1987	By C's Account	1,350
	To P & L Account	675			
		1,350			1,350
1988	To Royalty Payable A/c	875	1988	By C's Account	1,750
	To P & L A/c	875			
		1,750			1,750
1989	To Royalty Payable A/c	1,200	1989	By C's Account	2,400
	To P & L Account	1,200			
		2,400			2,400

Dr. **Shortworkings Recoupable Account** Cr.

		Rs.			Rs.
1985	To B's Account	750	1985	By Balance c/d	750
		750			750
1986	To Balance b/d	750	1986	By Balance c/d	1,325
	To B's Account	575			
		1,325			1,325
1987	To Balance b/d	1,325	1987	By Balance c/d	1,350
	To B's Account	25			
		1,350			1,350
1988	To Balance b/d	1,350	1988	By B's Account	575
				By P & L Account	775
		1,350			1,350

Dr. **Shortworkings Allowable Account** Cr.

		Rs.			Rs.
1985	To Balance c/d	500	1985	By C's Account	500
		500			500
1986	To Balance c/d	900	1986	By Balance b/d	500
				By C's Account	400
		900			900
1987	To C's Account	350	1987	By Balance b/d	900
	To P & L Account	150			
	To Balance c/d	400			
		900			900
1988	To C's Account	400	1988	By Balance b/d	400
		400			400

EXAMINATION QUESTIONS

(A) Answer the following questions in not exceeding 4 lines each :

(*Each Carries 2 Marks*)

(1) What is "Royalty"? (*Bangalore, Nov., 1983*)

(2) What do you mean by Minimum Rent?
(*Bangalore, Oct., 1985 & Karnataka, Oct., 1996*)

(3) What do you mean by Surplus?

(4) What is dead rent? (*Bangalore, April, 1984*)

(5) What do you mean by Shortworking?
(*B'lore, April, 1985 & Karnataka, April, 1995*)

(6) What is recoupment of Shortworking?

(7) What will be the minimum rent in case of strike?

(8) What entry is passed for irrecoverable shortworking by lessee?
(*Karnataka, April, 1996*)

(9) Give meaning of the following :

(a) Royalty

(b) Minimum rent (*Karnataka, Oct., 1995*)

(10) Who is landlord? (*M.K.U., Oct., 1995*)

(11) What is the meaning of Sub-lease? (*B'lore, April, 1986*)

(12) Who is Sub-lessee?

(13) What is minimum rent? (*Bangalore, April, 1998*)

(14) Give the meaning of royalty and mention four kinds of royalty.
(*Karnataka, April, 1998*)

(15) What do you mean by lessor and lessee?
(*Karnataka, April, 1997*)

(16) What is the basis on which royalty is calculated in the following cases :

(a) Author of a book, (b) Owner of mine, (c) A scientist holding a patent, (d) An owner of an oil well.

(*Bangalore, April, 1998*)

Hints : (a) No. of copies, (b) No. of tonnes, (c) No. of products and (d) No. of barrels.

(B) Answer the following questions/problems :

(Each Carries 8 Marks)

(1) What do you mean by royalty? What is the minimum rent in case of lockout etc.?

(M.K.U., Oct., 1994)

(2) Give the journal entries when the amount of royalty is equal to minimum rent.

(3) Pass the accounting entries when the amount of royalty is less than the amount of minimum rent.

(4) Pass the journal entries when the amount of royalty is more than the amount of minimum rent.

(5) Record the following in the journal of mining company (lessees) :

(a) Minimum rent Rs. 10,000 p.a.

(b) Recoupment period is next one year only.

(c) Royalty earned : 1st year Rs. 6,000 and 2nd year Rs. 12,000.

(Karnataka, April, 1995)

Ans. : Shortworkings : 1st year Rs. 4,000;
Recouped : 2nd year Rs. 2,000 and Irrecouped : 2nd year Rs. 2,000.

(6) A mining company acquires the lease of coal mines on the following terms :

(a) Royalty is to be paid Rs. 10 per tonne of coal raised.

(b) Minimum rent is Rs. 10,000 per annum.

(c) Shortworkings, if any, of any year can be recovered in the next two years. Coal raised during the first 4 years were :

Ist year 800 tonnes	IInd year 1,100 tonnes
IIIrd year 900 tonnes	IVth year 1,500 tonnes

Prepare landlords account in the books of the company.

(Gulbarga, April, 1983 & Oct., 1993)

Ans. : Shortworkings : Ist year Rs. 2,000 and IIIrd year Rs. 1,000.
Recouped : IInd year Rs. 1,000 & IVth year Rs. 1,000.
Irrecouped : IIIrd year Rs. 1,000.

(7) The Santosh Mines Ltd. took from Shahabad Co. a lease of mine for a period of 25 years from 1-1-1981 on a royalty of Rs. 5 per tonne of minerals got with a dead rent of Rs. 20,000 and power the recoup shortworkings during the first five years of the lease. The annual output were as follows :

1981	2,000 tonnes
1982	3,000 tonnes

1983	4,000 tonnes
1984	4,500 tonnes
1985	5,000 tonnes

Pass the journal entries in the books of Santosh Mines Ltd.

(*Gulbarga, Oct., 1982 & Karnataka, April, 1987*)

Ans. : Shortworkings : 1981 Rs. 10,000 and 1982 Rs. 5,000.
Recouped : 1984 Rs. 2,500 and 1985 Rs. 5,000.
Irrecouped : 1985 Rs. 7,500.

(8) The Ideal Minerals Ltd. has taken a lease a mine on a royalty of 50 paise per tonne of iron ore raised with an annual minimum rent of Rs. 20,000 and power to recoup the shortworkings during the first 4 years of the lease. The output was as under :

First year	10,000 tonnes
Second year	24,000 tonnes
Third year	40,000 tonnes
Fourth year	90,000 tonnes

Prepare Royalty Payable Chart and Royalty Account in the books of lessees.

(*Karnataka, Oct., 1995*)

Ans. : Shortworkings : Ist year 15,000 and IInd year 8,000.
Recouped : IVth year 23,000.

(9) On 1-1-1991 the Chittapur Collieries Ltd. leased a land for a minimum rent of Rs. 5,000 in the first year, Rs. 10,000 in the second year and thereafter Rs. 15,000 p.a. merging into a royalty of Rs. 2.50 per tonne of coal raised with a power to recoup shortworkings over the first 3 years only. The annual output for the 4 years ending with 31-12-1994 was 500; 3,000; 8,000 and 12,000 tonnes respectively.

Prepare royalty payable chart and royalty account in the books of the lessees.

(*Karnataka, April, 1996*)

Ans. : Shortworkings : 1991 Rs. 3,750 and 1992 Rs. 2,500.
Recouped : 1993 Rs. 5,000 and 1994 Rs. 1,250.

(10) Raj has patented a quick-boiling kettle and granted the right of manufacture and market the same to Home Equipment Ltd., under a licence subject to the following terms :

(a) A royalty of Rs. 2 to be paid for each kettle sold.

(b) A minimum payment of Rs. 10,000 p.a.

(c) The right to deduct in the two following years any excess of the minimum rent over the actual royalties.

The number of kettles sold were :

1993 — 1,000, 1994 — 4,500, 1995 — 5,400 and 1996 — 6,500.

Draft Statement of Royalty and write Royalty Account in the books of Home Equipment Ltd.

(*Karnataka, April, 1998*)

Ans. : Shortworkings : 1993 Rs. 2,000 and 1994 Rs. 1,000.
Recouped : 1995 Rs. 800 and 1996 Rs. 1,000.
Irrecouped : 1995 Rs. 1,200.

(11) On 1st Jan., 1993 'X' Collieries leased out some land for a minimum rent of Rs. 3,000 for the 1st Year, Rs. 5,000 in the IInd Year and thereafter Rs. 10,000 p.a. merged into a royalty of 50 paise per tonne with power to recoup shortworking over two years after occurring the shortworking. The annual output for the 4 years ending are :

1993	3,000 tonnes
1994	8,600 tonnes
1995	22,000 tonnes
1996	18,000 tonnes (strike for 3 months)

There was a provision in the lease that in the event of a strike and the minimum rent not being reached the actual royalties earned for the year discharged all rental obligations for that year. Show Shortworking A/c.

(*Bangalore, April, 1998*)

Ans. : Shortworkings : 1993 Rs. 1,500 and 1994 Rs. 700.
Recouped : 1995 Rs. 1,000.
Irrecouped : 1995 Rs. 500 and 1996 Rs. 700.

(C) Solve the following problems :

(*Each Carries 16 Marks*)

(1) Mrs. Parvati Amar Tandel took lease land from Fish Federation of Karnataka for prawn culturing in Tadadi at Aghanashine river belt.

The royalty is agreed to be Rs. 500 per tonne of prawns, subjected to minimum amount of Rs. 5,00,000 and shortworkings recoupment period extending to two succeeding years only.

The output over 5 years were :

31st March 1987	500 tonnes
1988	800 tonnes
1989	1,100 tonnes

1990	1,300 tonnes
1991	1,500 tonnes

Pass necessary journal entries in the books of Mrs. Parvati Amar Tandel.

(*Karnataka University, April, 1994*)

Ans. : Shortworkings : 1987 Rs. 2,50,000; 1988 Rs. 1,00,000.
Recouped : 1989 Rs. 50,000; 1990 Rs. 1,00,000.
Irrecouped : 1989 Rs. 2,00,000.

(2) Mr. Ishwar of Belgaum a professional author of Managerial Techniques, has entered into an agreement with India Publishing House, Delhi on 1-1-1986 for publication and sale of the book. The terms agreed were as under :

(a) Royalty payable is 20% on the sales amount of the book.

(b) The author is to be paid the minimum amount of Rs. 50,000 per annum.

(c) Each year's excess of minimum amount over royalties earned is recoverable out of the surplus royalties of the next 3 years subject to the maximum amount of Rs. 6,000 in that particular years of recovery.

The following are the particulars of sales :

Year ending	Number of books sold
1986	2,000 copies
1987	2,800 copies
1988	4,500 copies
1989	6,000 copies
1990	4,000 copies

Prepare the Royalty Account, Author's Account and Shortworkings Account in the books of India Publishing House.

(*Karnataka, April, 1992*)

Ans. : Shortworkings : 1986 Rs. 20,000; 1987 Rs. 8,000.
Recouped : 1988 Rs. 6,000; 1989 Rs. 6,000; 1990 Rs. 6,000.

(3) Dhaneshwari Publishers agreed to take up the printing and sales of book from the author, Somnath on 1-1-1986. The following are the terms of agreement :

(a) Royalty payable at 20% on the sale price of the book. The book is priced at Rs. 30 per copy.

(b) The author is to be paid the minimum amount of Rs. 20,000 per annum.

(c) Each year's excess of minimum amount over the actual royalties is recoverable out of the royalties of the next two years. The details are as under :

Year ending	No. of copies printed	No. of copies of closing stock
31-12-1986	3,000	250
31-12-1987	3,200	300
31-12-1988	3,500	100
31-12-1989	3,650	200

Record the journal entries in the books of Dhaneshwari Publishers.

(*Karnataka, Oct., 1990 & April, 1995 Mod.*)

Ans. : Shortworkings : 1986 Rs. 3,500; 1987 Rs. 1,100.
Recouped : 1988 Rs. 2,200 and 1989 Rs. 1,100.
Irrecouped : 1988 Rs. 1,300.

(4) Mr. Kiran owned the patent of a safety lock. The Alighar Lockers Ltd. acquired the right to manufacture and sell the locks for seven years on the following terms :

(1) Alighar Lockers Ltd. to pay a royalty of Rs. 2.50 for each lock with a minimum annual payment of Rs. 1,00,000.

(2) If in any year the royalty calculated on locks manufactured and sold amounts to less than Rs. 1,00,000 the Alighar Lockers Ltd. is to have the right to deduct the deficiency from the royalty payable in excess of that sum in the two following years.

(3) In the event of strike in any year, the lease provides for the proportionate reduction of minimum rent for that year.

(4) The accounts are to be settled annually on 31st December.

The number of locks manufactured and sold was as follows :

Year ending 31st December	Rs.
1977	32,000
1978	35,000
1979	46,000
1980 (Strike for three months)	28,000
1981	60,000

Pass the journal entries in the books of Alighar Lockers Ltd. to record the above.

(*Gulbarga, Oct., 1983*)

Ans. : Shortworkings : 1977 Rs. 20,000; 1978 Rs. 12,500 and 1980 Rs. 5,000.
Recouped : 1979 Rs. 15,000.
Irrecouped : 1979 Rs. 5,000 and 1980 Rs. 12,500.

Note : Minimum Rent in the strike year is Rs. 75,000 *i.e.*, 1,00,000 × 3/4.

(5) On 1st Jan., 1992, the Chittapur Collieries Ltd. leased a piece of land for Minimum Rent of Rs. 500 in the first year, Rs. 1,000 in the second year and thereafter Rs. 1,500 per annum, merging into a royalty of 25 paise per tonne, with power to recoup shortworkings over the first three years ending 31st December, 1995 was 500, 3,000, 8,000 and 12,000 tonnes respectively. Show how the accounts would appear in the books of the Colliery company.

(*B'lore, Oct., 1993 & Panjab, April, 1982*)

Ans. : Shortworkings : 1992 Rs. 375 and 1993 Rs. 250.
Recouped : 1994 Rs. 500; Irrecouped : 1994 Rs. 125.

(6) The Quick Coal Ltd. are the lease of coal mines on a royalty of 50 paise per tonne of coal raised with a minimum rent of Rs. 10,000. Each year excess of minimum rent over royalties is recoverable out of the royalties of next two years. In the event of strike the lease provides for the proportionate reduction in a minimum rent, the output for the first five years is as follows :

Year ending 31st Dec.	Output (tonnes)
1994	10,000
1995	16,000
1996	25,000
1997	30,000
1998 (Strike for 3 months)	12,000

Prepare Minimum Rent A/c, Royalty A/c and Shortworkings A/c in the books of Quick Coal Limited.

(*Shivaji, April, 1992 & KUD, Oct., 1992*)

Ans. : Shortworkings : 1994 Rs. 5,000 and 1995 Rs. 2,000.
Recouped : 1996 Rs. 2,500 and 1997 Rs. 2,000.
Irrecouped : 1996 Rs. 2,500.

(7) A Coal Company took amine on lease from X at a royalty of Re.1 per tonne of coal raised with a minimum rent of Rs. 10,000 per annum. Each year's excess of minimum rent over royalties, is recoverable out of the royalties of the next two years. In the event of a strike and the minimum rent is not reached, the lease provided that the actual royalties earned for the year discharge all the rental obligations for that year.

The results of the working for four years were as under :

Year	Output in tonnes
1980	7,000
1981	9,000
1982	11,000
1983 (Strike)	8,000

Pass the necessary journal entries in the books of the coal company for the above period.

(*KUD, April, 1984 & Oct., 1996*)

Ans. : Shortworkings: 1980 Rs. 3,000 and 1981 Rs. 1,000.
Recouped : 1982 Rs. 1,000.
Irrecouped : 1982 Rs. 2,000 and 1983 Rs. 1,000.

(8) Vasavi Ltd. took a 20-year lease of a gold mine from Mr. Vasant on a royalty of Rs. 2 per ton with a minimum rent of Rs. 20,000 per annum. Each year's excess of minimum rent over royalties is recoverable out of the royalties of the next two years only. The output of the first six years was as follows :

Year	Output in tonnes
Ist	4,000
IInd	7,000
IIIrd	8,000
IVth	12,000
Vth	19,000
VIth	20,000

Prepare the necessary accounts in the book of Vasavi Ltd. for the above period.

(*KUD, April, 1986*)

Ans. : Shortworkings : Ist year Rs. 12,000; IInd year Rs. 6,000 and IIIrd year Rs. 4,000
Recouped : IVth year Rs. 4,000; Vth year Rs. 4,000
Irrecouped : IIIrd year Rs. 12,000 and IVth year Rs. 2,000.

(9) M Co. Ltd. took a mine on lease from N Co. Ltd. at a given rate of royalty with a minimum rent of Rs. 10,000 a year. Each year's excess of minimum rent over royalties is recoverable out of the royalties of the next year only. In the event of a strike and the minimum rent not being reached, it was provided that the actual royalties earned for the year would be the full royalty obligation for the year.

The results of the working of M Co. Ltd. were as follows :

Year	Actual Royalty
	Rs.
First year	Nil
Second year	12,000
Third year (Strike)	8,000
Fourth year	9,000

Pass the journal entries in the books of M Co. Ltd. for the first three years only.

(*B'lore, April, 1991 & Gulbarga, Oct., 1980*)

Ans. : Shortworkings : Ist year Rs. 10,000 and IVth year Rs. 1,000.
Recouped : IInd year Rs. 2,000.
Irrecouped : IInd year Rs. 8,000.

(10) On 1-1-1985 the Mysore Collieries Ltd. leased a piece of land for a minimum rent of Rs. 2,000 in the first year Rs. 4,000, in the second year and thereafter Rs. 6,000 per annum merging into a royalty of 25 paise per tonne of coal raised with power to recoup shortworkings over the first three years only. The annual output for the four years ending with 31st December, 1988 was 2,000, 12,000, 32,000 and 48,000 tonnes respectively.

Write up Minimum Rent Account, Shortworkings Account and Landlord's A/c in the books of Mysore Collieries Ltd.

(*KUD, April, 1989 & Mysore, April, 1964*)

Ans. : Shortworkings : 1985 Rs. 1,500 and 1986 Rs. 1,000.
Recouped : 1987 Rs. 2,000.
Irrecouped : 1987 Rs. 500.

(11) A owned certain patent rights. He granted a licence to B to use such rights on royalty basis. The following are the relevant particulars:

Year	Minimum Rent	Royalty Earned
	Rs.	Rs.
1st year	750	500
2nd year	1,000	800
3rd year	1,250	900
4th year	1,500	1,750
5th year	1,500	1,600

The deficiency of any one year is to be set off against excess payable within the next two years.

Give the entries and the shortworkings account in the books of 'B'.

(*Mysore, September, 1984*)

Ans. : Shortworkings : Ist year Rs. 250, IInd year Rs. 200; and IIIrd year Rs. 350.
Recouped : IVth year Rs. 250 and Vth year Rs. 100
Irrecouped : IIIrd year Rs. 250; Vth year Rs. 200.

(12) Mr. Anand has developed a kitchen appliance items. The Kitchen Appliance Manufacturing Co. Ltd. has entered into agreement on 1-1-1985 with Mr. Anand to acquire the patent right for manufacture and sale of the appliances.

The terms of agreement were as under :

1. The period of lease shall be 7 years from 1-1-1985.
2. The company shall pay minimum amount of Rs. 60,000 per annum merging into a royalty of 20% of sales payable on 31st December every year.
3. The shortworkings of each year shall be recovered from the excess of royalty earned over the minimum amount in the next two years.

The sales of the appliances during 5 years are as follows :

Year	Sales Rs.
1985	2,00,000
1986	2,80,000
1987	3,90,000
1988	4,10,000
1989	4,60,000

Prepare royalty account, shortworkings account and Mr. Anand's account in the books of Kitchen Appliance Manufacturing Company Limited.

(*B.Com. Hon., Calcutta & KUD, Oct., 1991*)

Ans. : Shortworkings : 1985 Rs. 20,000 and 1986 Rs. 4,000.
Recouped : 1987 Rs. 18,000 and 1988 Rs. 4,000.
Irrecouped : 1987 Rs. 2,000.

(13) Srikant had patented a new type of pocket transistor. On 1st January, 1988 he granted Parker a licence for 20 years to manufacture and sell the transistor on the following terms :

(a) Parker to pay a royalty of Rs. 5 for each transistor manufactured and further royalty of Rs. 3 for each transistor sold with a minimum rent of Rs. 8,000 per annum.

(b) If in any year, the royalties calculated on the transistors manufactured and sold be less than the minimum rent, Parker to have the right to recoup shortworkings out of the royalties in excess of the minimum rent during the two years immediately following, subject to a maximum amount of Rs. 2,000 per annum.

The number of transistors manufactured and sold for the first four years were as follows :

Year	Manufactured	Sold
1988	800	500
1989	1,000	700
1990	2,500	1,500
1991	500	2,000

All the payments were made by Parker on the due date.

Prepare : (i) Parker's Account;

(ii) Royalties Receivable Account; and

(iii) Shortworkings Suspense Account for the first four years as they would appear in the books of Srikant.

(*B.Com., Delhi & ICWA Inter*)

Ans. : Shortworkings : 1978 Rs. 2,500 and 1979 Rs. 900.
Recouped : 1990 Rs. 2,000 and 1991 Rs. 500.
Irrecouped : 1990 Rs. 500 and 1991 Rs. 400.

(14) A mining Company acquires the lease of coal mines on the following terms :

(a) Royalty is to be paid Rs. 10 per tonne of coal raised.

(b) Minimum rent is Rs. 10,000 per annum.

(c) Shortworkings, if any, of any year can be recovered in the next two years.

Coal raised during the four years were :

Year	Output in tonnes
1st	800
2nd	1,100
3rd	900
4th	1,500

Prepare Landlords Accounts, Shortworkings Account and Royalties Account in the books of the company.

(*Gulbarga, April, 1983 & Oct., 1993*)

Ans. : Shortworkings : Ist year Rs. 2,000; IIIrd year Rs. 1,000.
Recouped : IInd year Rs. 1,000; IVth year Rs. 1,000.
Irrecouped : IIIrd year Rs. 1,000.

Sub-Lease

(15) Asha Ltd. work minerals under a lease from M.N. the landlord. The lease was for a period of 20 years from 1st Jan., 1993, the terms being a royalty of 40 paise a tonne of mineral raised subject to a minimum rent of Rs. 2,000 a year with a right to recoup shortworkings in the first four years of the lease.

Asha Ltd. granted a sub-lease to Prakash Ltd. of the 1/3 of the area for a period of 8 years from 1st Jan., 1994, for Minimum Rent of Rs. 750 a year merging in a royalty of 60 paise a tonne of minerals raised with a right to recover shortworkings during the first two years from the date of sub-lease.

The output for the first four years was as under :

Year	Asha Ltd.	Prakash Ltd.
1993	2,200 tonnes	–
1994	2,400 tonnes	1,120 tonnes
1995	3,000 tonnes	1,600 tonnes
1996	3,200 tonnes	1,920 tonnes

Show the necessary Ledger Accounts in the books of Asha.

(Karnataka & Bombay)

Ans. : (a) As per royalty payable chart :
Shortworkings : 1993 Rs. 1,120; 1994 Rs. 592 and 1995 Rs. 160.
Recouped : 1996 Rs. 48.
Irrecouped : 1996 Rs. 1,824.

(b) As per royalty receivable chart :
Shortworkings : 1994 Rs. 78.
Recouped : 1995 Rs. 78.

(16) The Bangalore Colliery Co. acquired the lease of a coal mine on a minimum rent of Rs. 5,000 per annum merging into a royalty of Re. 1 per tonne of coal raised with the right of recouping shortworkings during the first two years only. The company granted a sub-lease to the Mysore Colliery Co. on a minimum rent of Rs. 3,000 per annum merging into a royalty of Rs. 2 per tonne of coal raised with the right of recouping each year's shortworkings within the next year only.

The output was :

Year	B'lore Colliery Co.	Mysore Colliery Co.
Ist	2,000 tonnes	750 tonnes
IInd	3,880 tonnes	1,600 tonnes
IIIrd	4,000 tonnes	2,000 tonnes
IVth	5,000 tonnes	3,000 tonnes

Write up the shortworkings recoupable, royalty receivable and the shortworkings allowable accounts in the books of the Bangalore Colliery Company.

(Bangalore, Oct., 1985 old)

Ans. : (a) As per royalty payable chart :
Shortworkings : Ist year Rs. 2,250.
Recouped : IInd year Rs. 400.
Irrecouped : IInd year Rs. 1,850.

(b) As per royalty receivable chart :
Short workings : Ist year 1,800 and IInd year Rs. 100.
Recouped : IIIrd year Rs. 100.
Irrecouped : IInd year Rs. 1,800.

Additional Problems

(17) Kaveri Ltd. obtained on 1-1-1986 the use of patent right of a grinding machine from Krishna Ltd. under the following terms :

(a) A royalty of 2% on sales subject to a minimum amount of Rs. 20,000 per annum payable at the end of each year.

(b) Kaveri Ltd. will have the right of recouping shortworkings in the next two years period only.

The sales in the first five years were :

Years	Sales Rs.
1986	4,00,000
1987	7,00,000
1988	10,00,000
1989	12,00,000
1990	19,00,000

Prepare the royalty account, short workings account and Krishna Ltd. account in the books of Kaveri Ltd.

(*Karnataka, April, 1993*)

Ans. : Shortworkings : 1986 Rs. 12,000 and 1987 Rs. 6,000.
Recouped : 1989 Rs. 4,000.
Irrecouped : 1988 Rs. 12,000 and 1989 Rs. 2,000.

(18) Mysore Soaps Ltd. entered into agreement with Mr. Vinayak who had developed Ayurvedic Soap to acquire the patent right for manufacture and sale of the soaps. The soap was priced at Rs. 10 each. The terms of agreement were :

(a) The period of lease shall be for 10 years from 1-1-1988.

(b) The Company shall pay a minimum amount of Rs. 20,000 per annum merging into a royalty of 10% on sales payable on 31st December every year.

(c) The shortworkings can be recovered from the excess of royalty earned over the minimum rent during the first four years of the lease.

Year	Output (numbers)	Closing (numbers)
1988	10,000	200
1989	16,000	100
1990	19,000	—
1991	22,000	1,000
1992	32,000	4,000

Prepare Royalties A/c, Shortworkings A/c and Vinayak's A/c in the books of the company.

(Karnataka, Oct., 1994)

Ans. : Shortworkings : 1988 Rs. 10,200; 1989 Rs. 3,900; 1990 Rs. 900.
Recouped : 1991 Rs. 1,000 and Irrecouped : 1991 Rs. 14,000.
No. of soaps sold : 1988—9,800; 1989—16,000; 1990—19,100; 1991 — 21,000 and 1992 — 29,000.

(19) A Coal Company took a lease from Mr. Kumar of Coal mine for period of 25 years from 1988 on a royalty of Rs. 2.50 per tonne of Coal raised with a minimum rent of Rs. 25,000 per annum and power to recoup the shortworkings during the first 5 years of the lease. The annual output in tonnes was as follows :

1988 — 6,000 tonnes; 1989 — 9,000 tonnes; 1990 — 11,000 tonnes; 1991 — 12,000 tonnes; 1992 — 15,000 tonnes.

Prepare Royalty A/c, Shortworkings A/c and Kumar's A/c in the books of Coal Company.

(Gulbarga, April, 1996)

Ans. : Shortworkings : 1988 Rs. 10,000 and 1989 Rs. 2,500.
Recouped : 1990 Rs. 2,500; 1991 Rs. 5,000 and 1992 Rs. 5,000.

(20) On 1st January, 1992. Ilkal Co. leased a piece of land for a minimum rent of Rs. 5,000 in the first year, Rs. 10,000 in the second year and thereafter Rs. 15,000 per annum merging into a royalty of Rs. 2.50 per tonne with power to recoup shortworkings over first 3 years only. The annual output for four years ending 31-12-92, was 500; 3,000; 8,000 and 12,000 tons respectively.

Show the Accounts that would appear in the books of Company.

(Karnataka, April, 1997)

Ans. : Shortworkings : 1989 Rs. 3,750 and 1990 Rs. 2,500.
Recouped : 1991 Rs. 5,000.
Irrecouped : 1991 Rs. 1,250.

(21) Options Minerals and Boxite Ltd., has taken lease of a mine on the following terms :

(a) Minimum rent of Rs. 12,000 is to be paid per year and it shall merge into a royalty of Rs. 5 per tonne of mineral ore raised.

(b) Each year's excess of minimum rent over actual royalties is recoverable out of excess royalties of the next three years.

(c) Proportionate reduction in the minimum rent is to be made in the event of strike or lock out.

The results of the working for five years are as below :

For the year ended	Actual royalty
	Rs.
(1) 31-12-1990	1,200
(2) 31-12-1991	8,400
(3) 31-12-1992	13,200
(4) 31-12-1993	22,800
(5) 31-12-1994	9,600

During the year ended 31-12-1994 because of a strike by the workers demanding higher wages, the ore extraction work had been stopped for three months' period.

Prepare in the books of the company:

(a) Royalty account.

(b) Landlord account.

(c) Shortworkings account.

(*Karnataka, April, 1998 old*)

Ans. : Shortworkings : 1990 Rs. 10,800 and 1991 Rs. 3,600.

Recouped : 1992 Rs. 1,200; 1993 Rs. 10,800 and 1994 Rs. 600.

Irrecouped : 1994 Rs. 1,800.

Note : In the year of strike, the amount payable to landlord is Rs. 9,000.

16

FIRE CLAIM OR INSURANCE CLAIM

Meaning

When a fire occurs in a business premises, it destroys a number of assets such as building, machinery, stock etc. Therefore, the businessmen, usually, take a fire insurance policy to indemnify the loss of stock and other assets resulting from fire. A fire insurance contract is a contract of indemnity under which one of the parties who is called the **insurer** agrees or undertakes to indemnify (*i.e.,* to compensate) the loss suffered by the other party called the **insured** on the happening of a contingent (*i.e.*, unforeseen) event in consideration of a payment called the premium. When the assets are destroyed by the fire, then, the actual loss of the assets is to be claimed from the insurance company. The insurance company usually appoints skilled persons called the loss **assessors** to estimate the loss of damage. On the basis of report of the assessor, the insurance company makes the payment of the claim. A formal demand submitted by the insured in respect of the loss by fire to be compensated by the insurer is called as a **'claim' or insurance claim or fire claim.**

Types of Fire Claim

Depending upon the risk covered by an insurance policy, claims against the insurer can be divided as below :

(I) Claim for loss of stock.

(II) Claim for loss of fixed assets.

(III) Claim for loss of profit or claim for consequential loss.

(I) Claim for Loss of Stock

If the stock is insured against the fire and if it is destroyed by fire, the value of stock in trade on the date of fire should be properly estimated and the claim should be lodged or presented by the insured to the insurer (*i.e.*, the insurance company) for the loss of stock.

If stock records are properly maintained and if such stock records are not destroyed by fire, the estimation of stock on hand on the date of fire does not pose any problem. On the other hand, in case the proper records of stocks are not maintained or the records are destroyed by fire, it is really somewhat difficult task to estimate the stock on hand on the date of fire. In such a case, the following steps should be considered in estimating the stock in hand on the date of fire.

(1) Rate of gross profit of the previous year : Sometimes, the ratio or percentage or rate of gross profit on sales of the previous year is taken as the rate applicable for the current year. If the ratio of gross profit on sales of the previous year is given in the problem, the same may be made applicable to the current period for estimating the value of stock as at the date of fire. In case the ratio of gross profit is not given in the problem, Memorandum Trading Account for the previous year should be prepared for computing the rate of gross profit.

(2) Average rate of gross profit of number of previous years : Some times, the average rate of gross profit on sales of number of previous years is taken as the rate applicable for the current year for estimating the value of stock as at the date of fire. If this average rate is not given in the problem, the same is to be computed from the given rates of the previous years or from the gross profits of the previous years. In the absence of both of them, the Memorandum Trading Account for all such previous years are to be prepared to compute the gross profits and ratios thereon. Then, the average of such ratios will be computed for ascertaining the gross profit ratio of the current year.

But, it is not the proper way to consider the average rate of gross profit of the previous years as the rate is applicable for the current year, if there is considerable fluctuation in the rates of the previous years. In such a case, it is better to estimate the rate of gross profit that is likely to prevail in the current year and consider that rate for the current year for estimating the value of stock. Suppose the gross profit ratio in the previous three years have been 10%, 15% and 20%, in this case in stead of taking the average rate of gross profit *viz.* 15% $\frac{10 + 15 + 20}{3}$ it is better to take the rate of gross profit that is likely to prevail in the current year *viz.* 25% and take 25% as the rate applicable for the current year. In case of continuous fall in the rate of gross profit, the same procedure should be followed to determine the rate applicable for the current year.

(3) Memorandum Trading Account of current year up to the date of fire : The next step is to prepare the Memorandum Trading Account for the period from the beginning of the current year up to the date of fire to compute the value of stock as at the date of fire. The opening stock, the purchases, the manufacturing expenses and the estimated gross profit on sales (*i.e.*, from the beginning of the current year up to the date of fire) should be entered on the debit side of the Memorandum Trading Account and the sales (*i.e.*, from the beginning of the current year up to the date of fire) should be entered on the credit side of the Memorandum Trading Account. Then, the Memorandum Trading Account should be balanced. The balancing figure in the Memorandum Trading Account will be the estimated value of stock as on the date of fire. The following is the form of Memorandum Trading Account :

Memorandum Trading Account

(For the period from beginning of the current year to the date of fire)

	Rs.		Rs.
To Opening Stock	xxxx	By Sales	xxxx
To Purchases	xxxx	By Closing Stock	xxxx
To Manufacturing Expenses	xxxx	(Balancing figure being	
To Gross Profit	xxxx	the value of stock)	
(---- % on sales)			
	xxxx		xxxx

(4) Stock salvaged and retained : Salvage refers to the goods or stocks saved from fire. If the salvage is retained by the insured, then, the value of stock salvaged should be deducted from the value of stock as on the date of fire, and the remaining amount should be considered as the value of stock lost by fire. On the other hand, if the salvage is taken over by the insurer, the entire value of stock (*i.e.*, value of stock + value of salvage) as on the date of fire should be considered as the amount of stock lost by fire.

Usually, the salvage is retained by the insured himself. Therefore, the amount of stock lost by fire is calculated as below :

Value of stock as on the date of fire (As shown by the Memorandum Trading A/c)	xxxx
Less : Value of stock salvaged or saved	xxxx
Value of stock lost on account of fire	xxxx

(5) Average clause in the insurance policy : Some times, the businessmen may think to undertake over–insurance or under-insurance. If the insured amount is more than the actual value of stock, it is known as over-insurance. In this case, the insurance company will not pay the claim more than the actual amount of stock lost by fire. If the insured amount is lower than the actual value of stock, it is known as under-insurance. In other words, under-insurance means insuring for a lesser value. This is undertaken to save the some amount of premium. Another reason is also there *i.e.*, usually the loss will not be total and therefore, inspite of under-insurance, the businessman can recover his loss. For example, stock worth Rs. 65,000 may by insured by the businessman for Rs. 30,000, because the businessman knows from the experience that in the event of the fire—all the stocks cannot likely to be lost. As per his assumption, if the fire is occurred and the actual loss is Rs. 20,000, the businessman can recover actual amount of loss in the absence of an "average clause". In order to avoid such misuse of insurance, the insurance policy includes 'average clause'.

To discourage under-insurance, usually the 'averaged clause' inserted in all contracts of fire insurance. The main object of inserting this clause is to make the insured also liable to bear the portion of the loss. Under this clause the loss is suffered by both insurer and insured proportionately. The effect of this clause is that if the value of stock or any other asset insured on the date of fire is much higher than the amount of policy taken, the full value of stock or any other asset destroyed by the fire does not become payable to the insured but insurance company pays only the proportion of actual loss which the amount of the policy taken bears to the actual value of stock or any other asset on hand on the date of fire. This is explained as below :

	Rs.
Value of the insurance policy	5,00,000
Value of stock or any other asset on hand in the godown on the date of fire	8,00,000
Stock or any other asset destroyed by fire	4,00,000

$$\text{Amount of claim} = \frac{\text{Value of insurance policy}}{\text{Value of stock or any other asset on hand on the date of fire}} \times \text{Value of stock or any other asset destroyed}$$

$$= \frac{5{,}00{,}000 \times 4{,}00{,}000}{8{,}00{,}000} = \text{Rs. } 2{,}50{,}000$$

In this case, even though the loss is Rs. 4,00,000 the insured is entitled to get only Rs. 2,50,000, because the policy covers only 62.50%

$\left(\frac{5{,}00{,}000 \times 100}{8{,}00{,}000}\right)$ of the stock or asset in the godown on the date of fire. The remaining loss of Rs. 1,50,000 is not admissible to the insured. This loss should be borne by insured. Therefore, the purpose of inserting of this clause in the insurance policy, is to discharge under insurance. But, if the value of stock or asset, on hand is equal or more than the value of policy, the average clause will not be applicable.

(6) Expenses incurred by the insured for extinguishing fire : Some times, the insured may incur some expenses to extinguish (*i.e.*, to put down) the fire, such expenses are recoverable from the insurance company. Therefore, the amount of such expenses should be added to the value of stock or any other asset lost by fire for the purpose of claims. The following is the statement of fire claim :

Statement of Fire Claim

	Rs.
Value of stock or any other asset on the date of fire	xxxx
Less : Value of stock or any other asset salvaged	xxxx
	xxxx
Add : Expenses incurred for extinguishing fire	xxx
Amount of fire claim	xxxx

Accounting entries in the books of insured in respect of fire claim for the loss of stock :

The following are the accounting entries to be passed in the books of the insured for the amount of stock lost by fire and the amount of claim for loss of stock.

(1) For the amount of stock lost by fire :

Loss of Stock by Fire Account Dr. } With the amount of
To Trading Account } loss by fire

(2) For the value of stock salvaged and retained :

Salvaged Stock Account Dr. } With the amount of
To Loss of Stock by Fire Account } salvaged

(3) For the amount of claim admitted by insurance company :

Insurance Company Account Dr. } With the amount of
To Loss of Stock by Fire Account } claim admitted

(4) For the amount claim not admitted by insurance company :

Profit and Loss Account Dr. } With the amount of
To Loss of Stock by Fire Account } claim not admitted (due to under-insurance)

(5) For the receipt of claim from the insurance company :

Cash or Bank Account Dr. } With the amount of
To Insurance Company A/c } claim received

Adjustments in the Memorandum Trading Account

While preparing the Memorandum Trading Account, certain adjustments are required to be made. They are :

(1) Stock over-valued or under-valued : If the opening stock or closing stock of any previous year has been over-valued or under-valued, it should be properly adjusted and shown in the concerned Memorandum Trading Account at cost, before finding out the rate of gross profit or the value of stock on hand on the date of fire.

(2) Increase or decrease in the selling price or purchases price : If the selling price or purchase price of goods has been increased or decreased during the current year, it should be properly taken and shown in the Memorandum Trading A/c before finding out the gross profit.

(3) Unrecorded purchases and sales : If any purchases and sales are unrecorded during the current year, they should be properly adjusted and shown in the Memorandum Trading Account.

(4) Abnormal line of goods : If there are any abnormal line of goods, say, a slow moving item or poor selling line of goods included in the opening stock, purchases, sales or closing stock of any previous year or current year, they should be eliminated from the concerned item in the Memorandum Account of concerned year.

Illustration 1

Fire occurred in the business premises of Nishan Trading Company on 1-7-1999 and the entire stock was destroyed. But business books and records were saved. The following information was obtained :

	Rs.
Stock on 31-12-1997	70,000
Stock on 31-12-1998	80,000
Purchases from 1-1-1999 to 30-6-1999	86,000
Sales from 1-1-1999 to 30-6-1999	1,20,000
Purchases for the year ending 31-12-1998	1,70,000
Sales for the year ending 31-12-1998	2,00,000

Calculate the amount of claim to be presented to the insurance company in respect of the loss by fire.

Solution :

Memorandum Trading Account
(For the previous year ending 31-12-1998)

	Rs.		Rs.
To Opening Stock (1-1-1998)	70,000	By Sales (For 1998)	2,00,000
To Purchases (For 1998)	1,70,000	By Closing stock	80,000
To Gross Profit (B. F.)	40,000	(31-12-1998)	
	2,80,000		2,80,000

Note : The above account is prepared to find out the rate of gross profit of the previous year. The rate of gross profit on sales of the previous year is at 20% $\left(\frac{40,000 \times 100}{2,00,000}\right)$. This rate is applied to find out the closing stock of current year.

Memorandum Trading Account
(From 1-1-1999 to 30-6-1999)

	Rs.		Rs.
To Opening Stock (1-1-1999)	80,000	By Sales	1,20,000
To Purchases	86,000	(From 1-1-99 to 30-6-99)	
(1-1-1999 to 30-6-1999)		By Closing Stock (30-6-99)	70,000
To Gross Profit	24,000	(Balancing figure)	
	1,90,000		1,90,000

Note : The closing stock of the previous year is the opening stock for the current year.

Statement of Fire Claim

Value of stock on the date of fire (*i.e.*, on 30-6-1999)	70,000
Less : Value of stock salvaged	—
Amount of claim	70,000

Illustration 2

A fire occurred in the premises of a trader on 25-12-1998 and destroyed most of the stock. The following particulars were however, available :

	Rs.
Stock on 1-1-1998	65,000
Purchases from 1-1-1998 to 25-12-1998	1,50,000
Sales from 1-1-1998 to 25-12-1998	2,20,000

It is further stated that the trader in fixing the selling price has added 25% on the cost of the goods.

The value of the salvaged stock was agreed at Rs. 9,000. Prepare a statement showing the amount of claim in respect of loss of stock by fire.

Solution :

Memorandum Trading Account
(From 1-1-1998 to 25-12-1998)

	Rs.		Rs.
To Opening Stock (1-1-98)	65,000	By Sales	2,20,000
To Purchases	1,50,000	By Closing Stock	39,000
To Gross Profit	44,000	(25-12-1998)	
(20% of Rs. 2,20,000)		(Balancing Figure)	
	2,59,000		2,59,000

Notes : (1) The above account is prepared to ascertain the value of stock on the date of fire.

(2) An addition of 25% in fixing the selling price is the same as 20% on sales. Hence, the rate of gross profit on sales is 20%.

Statement of Fire Claim

	Rs.
Value of stock on the date of fire (25-12-1998)	39,000
Less : Value of stock salvaged	9,000
Amount of fire claim	30,000

Illustration 3

On 30-6-1998 of fire breakout in the premises of a trader and a considerable stock was destroyed. The stock records were not maintained. However, the following information is available :

	Rs.
Value of stock on 1-1-1998	48,000
Purchases from 1-1-1998 to 30-6-1998	1,55,000
Sales in the above period	2,10,000
Value of stock salvaged	3,000

Particulars :	1995	1996	1997
Purchases	5,50,000	5,20,000	3,80,000
Sales	6,00,000	5,00,000	4,00,000
Gross Profit	72,000	50,000	44,000

Prepare the statement of fire claim.

Solution :

Calculation of rate of gross profit of the past years and the average rate of gross profit

(A) Rate of gross profit $= \dfrac{\text{Gross profit}}{\text{Net sales}} \times 100$

1995

$\dfrac{72{,}000}{6{,}00{,}000} \times 100 = 12\%$

1996

$\dfrac{50{,}000}{5{,}00{,}000} \times 100 = 10\%$

1997

$\dfrac{44{,}000}{4{,}00{,}000} \times 100 = 11\%$

(B) Average rate of gross profit $= \dfrac{12 + 10 + 11}{3} = \dfrac{33}{3} = 11\%$

Memorandum Trading Account
For the period between 1-1-1998 to 30-6-1998
(To Find out the value of closing stock as on the date of fire)

	Rs.		Rs.
To Opening Stock	48,000	By Sales (1-1-98 to 30-6-98)	2,10,000
To Purchases (1-1-98 to 30-6-98)	1,55,000	By Closing Stock (30-6-1998) (Balancing figure)	16,100
To Gross Profit (11% on Rs. 2,10,000)	23,100		
	2,26,100		2,26,100

Note : The average rate of gross profit is applied for the above period.

Statement of Fire Claim

Value of stock as on the date of fire	16,000
Less : Value of stock salvaged	3,000
Amount of fire claim	13,100

Illustration 4

A fire occurred in the business premises of Sri Das on 15th April, 1998 and all the stock were destroyed. The salvaged was taken at the agreed valuation of Rs. 10,000. From the last balance sheet, the following details were found :

Stock on 1-1-1998	1,50,000
Purchases less returns up to 15-4-98	4,80,000
Sales less returns up to 15-4-98	5,20,000

Gross Profit on sales during the last five years were : 28%, 26%, 27%, 28% and 26% respectively.

The salvage stock was renovated and made fit for sale at a cost of Rs. 7,000. A part of this stock was sold for Rs. 12,000 and the balance was valued at Rs. 8,000.

Calculate the amount of fire claim and show the salvaged stock account.

Solution :

Memorandum Trading Account
For the period from 1-1-98 to 15-4-98

(To find out the value closing stock as on the date of fire)

	Rs.		Rs.
To Opening Stock	1,50,000	By Sales (Net)	5,20,000
To Purchases	4,80,000	By Closing Stock	2,50,400
To Gross Profit	1,40,400	(Balancing figure)	
(27% of Rs. 5,20,000)			
	7,70,400		7,70,400

Note : The average rate gross profit

$$\left(i.e., 27\%\ i.e., \frac{28+26+27+28+26}{5} \right)$$ is applied for the above period.

Statement of Fire Claim

Value of closing stock as on the date of fire	2,50,400
Less : Agreed value of stock salvaged	10,000
Amount of fire claim	2,40,400

Note : While calculating the amount fire claim, the expenses incurred in renovating sale proceeds and balance of salvaged stock should not be taken into account. They should be taken to salvaged stock account.

Dr. **Salvaged Stock Account** Cr.

	Rs.		Rs.
To Stock Destroyed (Agreed value of salvaged stock)	10,000	By Bank (Sale proceeds of part of salvaged stock)	12,000
To Bank (Cost of renovating)	7,000	By Balance c/d (Stock on hand)	8,000
To Profit and Loss A/c (Profit transferred)	3,000		
	20,000		20,000

Illustration 5

A fire occurred in the premises of Sri Ramanand on April, 1998 and considerable part of the stock was destroyed. The stock salvaged was Rs. 56,000. Sri Ramanand has taken a fire insurance policy for Rs. 3,42,000 to cover up the loss of stock by fire.

You are required to ascertain the insurance company claim which Sri Ramanand should claim from the insurance company for the loss of stock by fire. The following particulars are available :

	Rs.
Purchases for the year 1997	18,76,000
Sales for the year 1997	23,20,000
Purchases from 1-1-98 to 1-4-98	3,64,000
Sales from 1-1-98 to 1-4-98	4,80,000
Stock on 1-1-1997	2,88,000
Stock on 31-12-1997	4,84,000
Wages paid during the year 1997	2,00,000
Wages paid during 1-1-98 to 1-4-98	36,000

Sri Ramanand, in June, 1997, consigned goods worth Rs. 1,00,000 which unfortunately, were lost in transit. Since there was no insurance cover taken, the loss had to be borne by him in full.

Stock at the end of each year for and till the end of calendar year 1996 had been valued at cost less 10%. From 1997, however, there was change in the valuation of closing stock, which was ascertained by adding 10% to its cost.

(*Adapted from Madras Uni. and C.A. Inter*)

Solution :

Memorandum Trading Account
For the year ended 31st December, 1997

	Rs.		Rs.
To Opening Stock (at cost)	3,20,000	By Sales	23,20,000
To Purchases	18,76,000	By Goods Sent on	
To Wages	2,00,000	Consignment	
To Gross Profit	4,64,000	(Goods lost in transit)	1,00,000
(Balancing figure)		By Closing Stock	4,40,000
	28,60,000		28,60,000

Notes : (i) The above account is prepared to find out the gross profit of the previous year and the rate of gross profit on sales.

The rate of gross profit is 20% $\left(i.e., \frac{4,64,000}{23,20,000} \times 100\right)$

(ii) Opening stock has been valued at cost less 10%. Therefore, it should be properly adjusted to bring it to its value of cost. So, the cost of opening stock as on 1-1-97 will be Rs. 3,20,000 $\left(\frac{2,88,000}{90} \times 100\right)$. Similarly, the closing stock has been valued at cost + 10%. So, the cost of closing stock as on 31-12-1997 will be Rs. 4,40,000 $\left(i.e., \frac{4,84,000}{110} \times 100\right)$.

Memorandum Trading Account
For the period from 1-1-1998 to 1-4-1998
(To find out the value of closing stock on the date of fire)

	Rs.		Rs.
To Opening Stock (at cost)	4,40,000	By Sales	4,80,000
(*i.e.*, Closing stock of 1997)		By Closing Stock	4,56,000
To Purchases	3,64,000	(On the date of fire)	
To Wages	36,000	(Balancing figure)	
To Gross Profit	96,000		
(20% on Rs. 4,80,000)			
	9,36,000		9,36,000

Note : The rate of gross profit (*i.e.*, 20%) of previous year is applied for the current year on sales.

Statement of Fire Claim under Average Clause

Value of closing stock affected by fire	4,56,000
Less : Value of stock salvaged	56,000
Actual value of stock lost	4,00,000
Claim amount under average clause :	
Loss of stock by fire × $\frac{\text{Amount of the policy}}{\text{Value of stock on hand}}$	
$4{,}00{,}000 \times \frac{3{,}42{,}000}{4{,}56{,}000}$ = Amount to be claimed	3,00,000

Illustration 6

A fire occurred in the premises of A & Co. Ltd. on 1-9-89 and the stock of the value of Rs. 1,01,000 was salvaged and the business books and records were saved. The following information was obtained :

	Rs.
Purchases for the year ended 31-3-1989	6,80,000
Sales for the year ended 31-3-1989	11,00,000
Purchases from 31-3-89 to 1-9-89	2,50,000
Sales from 31-3-89 to 1-9-89	3,60,000
Stock on 31-3-1988	3,00,000
Stock on 31-3-1989	3,40,000

Further information given is that the stock on 31-3-1989 was over-valued by Rs. 20,000. Calculate the amount of claim. In April, 1989 selling price was lowered by 10%.

(*Adapted from C.A. Inter & Gulbarga, Oct., 1993*)

Solution :

Memorandum Trading Account
For the previous year ending 31-3-1989
(To find out gross profit of the year 1989)

	Rs.		Rs.
To Opening Stock	3,00,000	By Sales	11,00,000
To Purchases	6,80,000	By Closing stock	3,20,000
To Gross Profit (Balancing figure)	4,40,000		
	14,20,000		14,20,000

Notes : (1) Rate of gross profit is 40% on sales $\left(i.e., \frac{4,40,000}{11,00,000} \times 100\right)$

(2) The actual cost of closing stock is Rs. 3,20,000 (*i.e.*, 3,40,000 – 20,000 over-valued).

Memorandum Trading Account
For the period from 1-4-89 to 1-9-89
(To find out closing stock as on the date of fire)

	Rs.			Rs.
To Opening stock (*i.e.*, Closing stock of previous year)	3,20,000	By Sales	3,60,000	
		Add : Decrease in selling price (3,60,000 × 1/9)	40,000	4,00,000
To Purchases	2,50,000			
To Gross Profit (40% on Rs. 4,00,000)	1,60,000	By Closing stock (Balancing figure)		3,30,000
	7,30,000			7,30,000

Notes : The selling price has been reduced by 10% during the above period. Hence, it should be properly adjusted before finding out the gross profit. So, the adjusted sales amount will be Rs. 40,000 (*i.e.*, 3,60,000 × 100/90) for the calculation of gross profit at 40%.

Statement of Fire Claim

Value of closing stock affected by fire	3,30,000
Less : Value of stock salvaged	1,01,000
Amount of fire claim	2,29,000

Illustration 7

Coastal Traders have taken out a fire policy of Rs. 80,000 covering its stock in trade. A fire occurred on 31st March, 1996 and stock was destroyed with the exception of Rs. 20,680. The following particulars are available from the books of account of the firm :

	Rs.
Stock on 1st January, 1996	30,000
Purchases to the date of fire	1,30,000
Sales to the date of fire	90,000
Commission paid to the purchase Manager on purchases	2%
Carriage paid on purchases	800
Average gross profit on cost	50%

The policy was subject to average clause. You are required to calculate :

(1) Total loss of stock.

(2) Amount of claim to be made against the insurance company.

(*Adapted from Mangalore University*)

Solution :

Memorandum Trading Account
For the period from 1-1-1996 to 31-3-1996
(To find out the closing stock as on the date of fire)

	Rs.		Rs.
To Opening Stock	30,000	By Sales	90,000
To Purchases	1,30,000	By Closing Stock	1,03,400
To Commission (2% on Rs. 1,30,000)	2,600	(Balancing figure)	
To Carriage	800		
To Gross Profit (90,000 × 50/150)	30,000		
	1,93,400		1,93,400

Note : Average gross profit is 50% on cost. It means, if the cost is 100, the selling price will be 110, then for 90,000, the gross profit will be Rs. 30,000 $\left(i.e., 90,000 \times \frac{50}{150}\right)$.

Statement of Fire Claim under Average Clause

Value of closing stock on the date of fire	1,03,400
Less : Value of stock salvaged or saved	20,680
Total (actual) value of stock lost	82,720
Claimed amount under average clause :	
Loss of stock by fire × $\frac{\text{Amount of the Policy}}{\text{Value of stock on hand}}$	
$82,720 \times \frac{80,000}{1,03,400}$ = Amount to be claimed	64,000

Illustration 8

A fire occurred on 21st April, 1996, in the premises of Jwalamukhi and the stock in trade was destroyed. The following information is, however, available to you :

	Rs.
Opening stock on 1-1-1996	22,000
Purchases up to 21-4-1996	45,000
Sales up to 21-4-1996	68,000
Goods drawn for personal use	5,000

The stock on hand was always valued at cost price or market price whichever is lower. However, the closing stock as on 31st December, 1995 was valued at market price which was 10% above cost.

The percentage of profit usually obtained in the business was 15%. The salvaged realised only Rs. 400.

Prepare a statement of fire claim in respect of stock destroyed assuming that Jwalamukhi incurred an expenses of Rs. 500 to extinguish fire recoverable from the insurance company.

(*Adapted from Mysore & Bangalore University*)

Solution :

Memorandum Trading Account
For the period from 1-1-1996 to 21-4-1996
(To find out the value of closing stock as on the date of fire)

		Rs.		Rs.
To Opening Stock $\left(22{,}000 \times \frac{100}{110}\right)$		20,000	By Sales	68,000
To Purchases	45,000		By Closing Stock	2,200
Less : Goods used	5,000	40,000	(Balancing figure)	
To Gross Profit		10,200		
(15% on Rs. 68,000)				
		70,200		70,200

Note : The Opening stock has been valued at 10% above cost. So, it should be reduced to cost price. It is reduced to cost price as below :

If the value given is 110, its cost is 100.

If the value is Rs. 22,000, the cost price will be Rs. 20,000 $\left(i.e., 22{,}000 \times \frac{100}{110}\right)$

Statement of Fire Claim

Closing stock as on the date of fire	2,200
Less : Value of stock salvaged	400
Actual amount of stock	1,800
Add : Fire extinguishing expenses	500
Amount of fire claim	2,300

Illustration 9

The premises of a merchant caught fire on November 1996 and his stock was damaged. The stock was fully insured. The merchant had made up his accounts to 31st December, each year. The following information was available:

	Rs.
Stock on 31st December, 1995	1,32,720
Stock on 31st December, 1994	96,140
Purchases from 1st January, 1996 to the date of fire	3,48,270
Purchase up to 31st December, 1995	4,52,580
Sales up to 31st December, 1995	5,20,000
Sales from 1st January, 1996 to the date of fire	4,91,700

You are given further information :

(1) In May 1996, goods costing Rs. 10,000 were given as free samples for advertising purpose. No entry was made in the books.

(2) During 1996, a clerk had misappropriated unrecorded cash sales of Rs. 4,000.

(3) The rate of gross profit is constant.

(4) The stock salvaged was agreed to be worth Rs. 3,000 and the expenses incurred to extinguish the fire amounted to Rs. 200.

From the above information, make an estimate of stock in hand on the date of fire and prepare a statement showing the claim for the loss of stock.

(*Adapted from Mangalore University Bangalore, Nov., 1993*)

Solution :

Memorandum Trading Account
For the previous year ending 31-12-95
(To find out the amount of gross profit)

	Rs.		Rs.
To Opening Stock	96,140	By Sales	5,20,000
To Purchases	4,52,580	By Closing Stock	1,32,720
To Gross Profit (Balancing figure)	1,04,000		
	6,52,720		6,52,720

Calculation of rate of gross profit of the year 1995 :

$$\frac{\text{Gross profit of the year 1995}}{\text{Sales of the year 1995}} \times 100$$

$$= \frac{1,04,000}{5,20,000} \times 100 = 20\%$$

Memorandum Trading Account
For the period from 1-1-96 to 1-11-96
(To find out the value of closing stock as on the date of fire)

		Rs.			Rs.
To Opening Stock (*i.e.*, Closing stock of previous year)		1,32,720	By Sales	4,91,700	
			Add : Unrecorded Sales	4,000	4,95,700
To Purchases	3,48,270		By Closing Stock (Balancing figure)		74,430
Less : Unrecorded free samples	10,000	3,38,270			
To Gross Profit (20% on Rs. 4,95,700)		99,140			
		5,70,130			5,70,130

Statement of Fire Claim

Value of closing stock on the date of fire	74,430
Less : Value of stock salvaged	3,000
Actual value of stock lost by fire	71,430
Add : Expenses incurred to extinguish fire	200
Amount of fire claim	71,630

Illustration 10

Mohan owns a retail stationery shop which was partly destroyed by fire on 27th June, 1996. The stock was insured for Rs. 13,000.

The balance sheet drawn on 31st December, 1995 included, *inter alia*, the following items :

	Rs.
Stock	12,000
Creditors	3,500

On examination of the books of account for the subsequent period up to the date of fire, the following particulars were obtained :

Sales	88,800
Payments to creditors for goods	75,000
Creditors as on 27-6-1996	1,800
A physical check of stock after the fire showed that items undamaged were	7,000

The normal rate of gross profit is 25% on purchases, but on 31st December, 1995, the included items of discontinued line totalling Rs. 3,800 which were all sold during the next two months at cost.

You are required to compute the amount of claim to be made to the insured.

(Adapted from C.A. Inter & B.Com., Osmania)

Solution :

Total Creditors' Account

Dr. (To find out credit purchases during the current year) Cr.

	Rs.		Rs.
To Cash (Payments made to creditors)	75,000	By Balance b/d (Opening creditors)	3,500
To Balance c/d (Closing creditors)	1,800	By Credit purchases (Balancing figure)	73,300
	76,800		76,800

Memorandum Trading Account
For the period from 1-1-1996 to 27-6-1996

(To find out the value of closing stocks as on the date of fire)

		Rs.			Rs.
To Opening Stock	12,500		By Sales	88,800	
Less : Abnormal items (*i.e.*, discontinued line)	3,800	8,700	*Less* : Abnormal items (*i.e.*, discontinued line)	3,800	85,000
To Purchases : Cash	—		By Closing Stock (Balancing figure)		14,000
Credit	73,000	73,000			
To Gross Profit (20% on sales of Rs. 85,000)		17,000			
		99,000			99,000

Notes : (i) The cost of stock of discontinued line is Rs. 3,800. Hence, it is deducted from the opening stock. The discontinued line of stock has been sold at cost during the current year. Hence, there is no loss by sale. Therefore, the same amount (Rs. 3,800) should be deducted from sales.

(ii) The normal rate of gross profit is 25% on purchases. It means, it is 25% on cost. If the rate of gross profit is 25% on cost, it will be 20% on sales. It is calculated as below :

Cost	Profit	Sales	Ratio
Rs. 100	Rs. 25	Rs. 125 (100 + 25)	$\frac{\text{Profit}}{\text{Sales}} \times 100 = \frac{25}{125} \times 100 = 20\%$

Statement of Fire Claim under Average Clause

	Rs.
Value of closing stock as on the date of fire	14,000
Add : Value of stock of abnormal items, *i.e.*, discontinued line (if any)	Nil
	14,000
Less : Value of stock undamaged (saved)	7,000
Actual value of stock lost by fire	7,000
Claim amount under average clause :	
Loss of stock by fire $\times \dfrac{\text{Amount of the policy}}{\text{Value of stock on hand}}$	
$7{,}000 \times \dfrac{13{,}000}{14{,}000}$ = Amount to be claimed	6,500

Illustration 11

On 1st April, 1996, Godown of Marble Ltd., was destroyed by fire. The records of the company revealed the following particulars :

	Rs.
Stock on 1st January, 1995	75,000
Stock on 1st December, 1995	80,000
Purchases during 1995	3,10,000
Sales during 1995	4,00,000
Purchases from 1-1-1996 to the date of fire	75,000
Sales from 1-1-1996 to the date of fire	1,00,000

In valuing the closing stock of 1995 Rs. 5,000 were written off whose cost was Rs. 4,800. Part of this stock originally costing Rs. 2,400 was sold in 1996 at a loss of Rs. 400. Stock salvaged was Rs. 5,000. The stock in the godown was fully insured.

Indicate from the above, the amount of the claim to be made against the insurance company.

(*Adapted from Mangalore University*)

Solution :

Memorandum Trading Account
For the previous year ended 31st December, 1995
(To find out the amount of gross profit on goods or normal selling line items)

		Rs.			Rs.
To Opening Stock		75,000	By Sales		4,00,000
To Purchases	3,10,000		By Closing Stock	80,000	
Less : Cost of abnormal Goods	4,800	3,05,200	*Add :* Excess amount written off as		
To Gross Profit (Balancing figure)		1,00,000	abnormal goods (5,000 – 4,800)	200	80,200
		4,80,200			4,80,200

Calculation of rate of gross profit of the year 1995

$$\frac{\text{Gross Profit}}{\text{Sales}} \times 100 = \frac{1,00,000}{4,00,000} \times 100 = 25\%$$

Notes : (i) It is assumed that the abnormal goods were purchased during the year 1995 and were not in stock at the beginning of the year 1995. Hence, the cost of abnormal goods (Rs. 480) is deducted from the purchases.

(ii) The abnormal items *i.e.*, goods purchased during the year 1995 were not sold in that year. It means they were in the stock at the end of the year 1995. Therefore, closing stock of abnormal goods is adjusted in the total closing stock to ascertain the value of closing stock of goods of normal selling items.

Memorandum Trading Account
For the period from 1-1-1996 to 1-4-1996
(To find out the value of closing stock of goods or normal items)

	Rs.			Rs.
To Opening Stock (*i.e.*, Closing stock of previous year)	80,200	By Sales	1,00,000	
		Less : Sale of abnormal goods		
To Purchases	75,000	(2,400 – 400)	2,000	98,000
To Gross Profit (25% on Rs. 98,000)	24,500	By Closing Stock (Balancing figure)		81,700
	1,79,700			1,79,700

Notes : (i) Of the total sale of Rs. 1,00,000, the sale of abnormal goods is Rs. 2,000. The remaining sales of Rs. 98,000 will be the sale of good selling items.

(ii) The abnormal goods are sold at Rs. 2,000 (*i.e.*, original cost Rs. 2,400 *minus* selling loss Rs. 400).

Alternative Method (*i.e.*, in the columnar form)

Memorandum Trading Account

For the previous year ended 31st Dec., 1995

(To find out the amount of gross profit)

Particulars	Normal Goods	Abnormal Goods	Total	Particulars	Normal Goods	Abnormal Goods	Total
To Opening Stock	75,000	—	75,000	By Sales	4,00,000	—	4,00,000
To Purchases	3,05,200	4,800	3,10,000	By Closing Stock	80,200	– 200	80,000
To Gross Profit	1,00,000	—	1,00,000	By Gross Loss	—	5,000	5,000
	4,80,200	4,800	4,85,000		4,80,200	4,800	4,85,000

Calculation of rate of normal gross profit of previous year

$$\frac{\text{Gross Profit of Normal Goods}}{\text{Sales of Normal Goods}} \times 100 = \frac{1,00,000}{4,00,000} \times 100 = 25\%$$

Memorandum Trading Account

For the period from 1-1-96 to 1-4-96

(To find out the value of closing stock as on the date of fire)

Particulars	Normal Goods	Abnormal Goods	Total	Particulars	Normal Goods	Abnormal Goods	Total
To Opening Stock	80,200	– 200	80,000	By Sales	98,000	2,000	1,00,000
To Purchases	75,000	—	75,000	By Closing Stock	81,700	2,400	84,100
To Gross Profit	24,500	4,600	29,100	(Balancing figure)			
	1,79,700	4,400	1,84,100		1,79,700	4,400	1,84,100

Note : Calculation of closing stock of abnormal goods :

	Rs.
Total cost of abnormal goods	4,800
Less : Cost of abnormal goods sold during 1996	2,400
Value of closing stock of abnormal goods	2,400

Statement of Fire Claim

	Rs.
Value of closing stock of normal goods on the date of fire	81,700
Add : Value of closing stock of abnormal goods on the date of fire	2,400
Actual value of closing stock affected by fire	84,100
Less : Value of stock salvaged	5,000
Amount of fire claim	79,100

Illustration 12

Bharati Ltd. suffered a loss of stock due to fire on May 15, 1996. From the following information, prepare a statement showing the claim to be lodged :

	Rs.
Stock on 1-1-1995	38,400
Purchases less returns during 1995	1,60,000
Sales less returns during 1995	2,02,600
Closing stock on 31-12-1995	31,800
Purchases less returns from 1-1-1996 to 15-5-1996	54,000
Sales less returns from 1-1-1996 to 15-5-1996	61,400

An item of stock purchased in 1994 at a cost of Rs. 10,000 was valued at Rs. 6,000 on 31-12-1994. Half of this stock was sold in 1995 for Rs. 2,600, the remaining was valued at Rs. 2,400 on 31-12-95. One fourth of the original stock was sold in March, 1996 for Rs. 1,400 and the remaining stock was considered to be worth 60% of the original cost. Salvage was Rs. 12,000. The amount of the policy was Rs. 30,000 and there was an average clause in the policy.

(*Adapted from B.Com., Bharathiar*)

Solution :

Memorandum Trading Account
For the previous year ended 31st Dec., 1995
(To find out the amount of gross profit of normal items)

		Rs.			Rs.
To Opening Stock	38,400		By Sales	2,02,600	
Less : Abnormal items included in the above stock	6,000	32,400	*Less :* Sales of abnormal items	2,600	2,00,000
To Purchases		1,60,000	By Closing stock	31,800	
To Gross Profit (Balancing figure)		37,000	*Less :* Abnormal items included in above stock	2,400	29,400
		2,29,400			2,29,400

Calculation of rate of gross profit on sales of normal items

$$\frac{\text{Gross Profit}}{\text{Sales}} \times 100 = \frac{37{,}000}{2{,}00{,}000} \times 100 = 18.5\%$$

Memorandum Trading Account
For the period from 1-1-1996 to 15-5-1996
(To find out the value of closing stock of normal items as on the date of fire)

	Rs.			Rs.
To Opening Stock (*i.e.*, Closing stock of previous year)	29,400	By Sales	61,400	
		Less : Sales of abnormal items	1,400	60,000
To Purchases	54,000	By Closing Stock (Balancing figure)		34,500
To Gross Profit (18.5% on Rs. 60,000)	11,100			
	94,500			94,500

Alternative Method (*i.e.*, in the columnar form)

Memorandum Trading Account
For the previous year ended 31-12-1996
(To find out the amount of gross profit)

Particulars	Normal Items	Abnormal Items	Total	Particulars	Normal Items	Abnormal Items	Total
To Opening Stock	32,400	10,000	42,400	By Sales	2,00,000	2,600	2,02,600
To Purchases	1,60,000	—	1,60,000	By Closing Stock	29,400	5,000	34,400
To Gross Profit (Balancing figure)	37,000	—	37,000	By Gross Loss (Balancing figure)	—	2,400	2,400
	2,29,400	10,000	2,39,400		2,29,400	10,000	2,39,400

Calculation of rate of gross profit on sales of normal items

$$\frac{\text{Gross profit of normal items}}{\text{Sales of normal goods}} \times 100 = \frac{37,000}{2,00,000} \times 100 = 18.5\%$$

Notes : (i) The value of opening stock is included the abnormal items (6,000) as given in the problem. Therefore, the abnormal items should be deducted to ascertain the value of opening stock of normal items (*i.e.*, 38,400 – 6,000 = 32,400).

(ii) Value of closing stock of abnormal items is Rs. 5,000 (*i.e.*, half of the total stock of Rs. 10,000).

Memorandum Trading A/c
For the period from 1-1-96 to 15-5-96
(To find out the value of closing stock as on the date of fire)

Particulars	Normal Items	Abnormal Items	Total	Particulars	Normal Items	Abnormal Items	Total
To Opening Stock (*i.e.*, Closing Stock of previous year)	29,400	5,000	34,400	By Sales	60,000	1,400	61,400
To Purchases	54,000	—	54,000	By Closing Stock (Balancing figure in case of normal items and 60% of 2,500 (*i.e.*, 1/4 × 10,000) in case of abnormal items)	34,500	1,500	36,000
To Gross Profit (18.5% on Rs. 60,000)	11,100	—	11,100	By Gross Loss (B.F.)	—	2,100	2,100
	94,500	5,000	99,500		94,500	5,000	99,500

Statement of Fire Claim under Average Clause

Value of closing stock of normal goods on the date of fire	34,500
Add: Value closing stock of abnormal goods on the date of fire $\left(10{,}000 \times \frac{1}{4} \times \frac{60}{100}\right)$	1,500
	36,000
Less : Value of stock salvaged	12,000
Actual value of stock lost by fire	24,000
Claim amount under average clause	
Claim amount under average clause $\left(24{,}000 \times \frac{30{,}000}{36{,}000}\right)$	20,000
$\left(\textit{i.e.,}\text{ Loss of stock by fire} \times \frac{\text{Amount of the policy}}{\text{Value of stock on hand}}\right)$	

(II) Claim for Loss of Fixed Assets

When the fixed assets such as building, machinery, furniture etc., are insured against the fire and are destroyed by a fire, then, the claim can be lodged with the insurance company for the loss suffered. The statement of claim can be prepared with the help of accounts maintained and records saved. The fixed assets are valued at their book values appearing in the books of the insured on the date of fire. While preparing fire claim, value of salvage and the average clause inserted in the policy should be considered as in case of stock.

The accounting entries to be passed in the books of the insured in respect of fire claim for the loss of fixed assets will be as follows :

(1) For the claim amount admitted by insurance company :

Insurance Company Account	Dr.	With the amount of
To Concerned Asset Account		claim admitted

(2) For the claim amount received from insurance company :

Bank *or* Cash Account	Dr.	With the amount of
To Insurance Company A/c		claim received

(3) For the transfer of profit on any fixed assets :

Concerned Asset Account	Dr.	With the amount of
To Profit and Loss Account		profit, if any

(4) For the transfer of loss on any fixed assets :

P & L A/c *or* Capital Reserve A/c	Dr.	With the amount of
To Concerned Asset Account		loss, if any.

Illustration 13

The Karnataka Ltd. fully insured their factory, which was damaged by fire on 31st March, 1998. The Management asks you to file insurance claim for the damages from the following particulars available from the Balance sheet as on 30th November, 1997 :

Stock	...... Rs. 3,64,956;	Machinery	...... Rs. 1,85,820
Building	...... Rs. 1,38,420	and Furniture	...... Rs. 8,400

Transactions from 1st December, 1997 to 31st March, 1998 were :

Purchases Rs. 5,88,276; Sales Rs. 3,38,829 and Wages Rs. 1,49,538.

Salvage recovered were :

Building Rs. 6,000; Machinery Rs. 9,000 and Furniture Rs. 1,500.

The average profit percentage is 23 of sales.

Draw up a statement of claim.

(*Adapted from Karnataka University*)

Solution :

Memorandum Trading Account
For the period 1-12-1997 to 1998
(To find out the value of closing stock as on the date of fire)

	Rs.		Rs.
To Opening Stock (30-11-97)	3,64,956	By Sales	3,38,829
To Purchases	5,88,276	By Closing Stock	8,41,872
To Wages	1,49,538	(Balancing Figure)	
To Gross Profit	77,931		
(23% on Rs. 3,38,829)			
	11,80,701		11,80,701

Statement of Fire Claim

	Rs.	Rs.
In respect of Stock :		
Value of Closing Stock on the date of fire	8,41,872	
Less : Value of Stock salvaged	Nil	8,41,872
In respect of Building :		
Value of Building on the date of fire	1,38,420	
Less : Value of Building salvaged	6,000	1,32,420
In respect of Machineıy		
Value of Machinery on the date of fire	1,85,820	
Less : Value of Machinery salvaged	9,000	1,76,820
In respect of Furniture :		
Value of Furniture on the date of fire	8,400	
Less : Value of Furniture salvaged	1,500	6,900
Total amount of fire claim		11,58,012

Illustration 14

Insolvent Ltd. caught fire on the morning of 1-7-1998. The records at the factory were all destroyed, though the office records supplied the following information for the months from 1st January to 30th June, 1998.

	Rs.
Sale	2,40,000
Sales returns and allowances	10,000
Purchases	1,90,000
Purchases returns and allowances	4,000
Carriage inwards	6,000
Stock in Hand on 31-12-1997	30,000
Building (Valued on 31-12-1997)	80,000

Equipment (valued on 31-12-1997)	16,000
Depreciation Reserve on :	
Building	25,000
Equipment	4,500

No depreciation has been provided since 31st December, 1997. The usual rate for charging depreciation is 3% per annum on the building and 8% per annum on equipment.

Normally, the business makes a gross profit of 30% on net sales. Cost of salvage amounted to Rs. 3,360.

On a claim being made on the insurance company with which the factory was insured, the claim was settled by a cash payment of Rs. 1,00,000.

Give journal entries to close the accounts concerned and write up the fire loss account to show the net loss on account of fire.

(*Adapted from Karnataka University*)

Solution :

Memorandum Trading Account
For the period from 1-1-1998 to 30-6-1998
(To find out the value of closing stock as on the date of fire)

		Rs.			Rs.
To Opening stock (1-1-98)		30,000	By Sales	2,40,000	
To Purchases	1,90,000		*Less* : Returns and Allowances	10,000	2,30,000
Less : Returns and Allowances	4,000	1,86,000	By Closing Stock (Balancing figure)		61,000
To Carriage Inwards		6,000			
To Gross Profit (30% on Rs. 2,30,000)		69,000			
		2,91,000			2,91,000

Statement of Fire Claim

In respect of Stock :			
Value of Closing Stock on the date of fire		61,000	
Less : Value of Stock salvaged		4,000	57,000
In respect of Building :			
Value of Building as on 31-12-97 or 1-1-98		80,000	
Less : Existing depreciation reserve	25,000		
Depreciation charged for current six months at 3% on Rs. 80,000	1,200		
Value of Building salvaged	800	27,000	53,000

(*Contd.*)

In respect of Equipment :			
Value of Equipment as on 31-12-97 or 1-1-98		16,000	
Less : Existing depreciation reserve	4,500		
Depreciation charged for current six months at 8% on Rs. 16,000	640		
Value of equipment salvaged	500	5,640	10,360
			1,20,360
Add : Cost of extinguishing fire			3,360
			1,23,720

Journal Entries

Sl. No.	Particulars	L.F.	Dr. Rs.	Cr. Rs.
1.	Insurance Company Account Dr. (Total claim made)		1,23,720	
	To Stock Destroyed A/c (Claim in respect of stock)			57,000
	To Building A/c (Claim in respect of building)			53,000
	To Equipment A/c (Claim in respect of equipment)			10,360
	To Cost of Salvage A/c (Claim in respect of cost of salvage)			3,360
	(Being the various claims made)			
2.	Bank A/c (Amount of claim received) Dr.		1,00,000	
	Loss on Fire A/c Dr. (Balance of claim not admitted) (*i.e.*, Balancing figure *i.e.*, 1,23,720 – 1,00,000)		23,720	
	To Insurance Company Account			1,23,720
	(Being claim received and claim not admitted transferred to loss on fire account)			
3.	Profit and Loss Account Dr.		23,720	
	To Loss on Fire Account			23,720
	(Being loss transferred to P & L A/c)			

Illustration 15

A severe fire occurred on 1st March, 1998 at the factory of Bharat Co. Ltd. by which practically the whole of the buildings and contents were destroyed, with exception of the offices.

The Insurance company paid a lump sum of Rs. 1,00,000 in respect of the building, Rs. 15,000 for the machinery and plant and Rs. 1,20,000 for the stock, the salvage being sold to Bharat Co. Ltd. for Rs. 10,000 and deducted from the insurance money on settlement. Bharat Co. Ltd. realised Rs. 20,000 from the salvage.

In Bharat Co. Ltd.'s books, land and buildings stood at Rs. 1,75,000 and the value of buildings not destroyed was Rs. 10,000, the land being valued at Rs. 50,000. Machinery and plant stood at Rs. 16,000 and was all destroyed. The stock at the date of the last balance sheet, 30th June, 1997 stood at Rs. 1,35,000.

The sales for the eight months amounted to Rs. 3,00,000 and the purchases and expenses for that period amounted to Rs. 2,60,000. Expenses in connection with the fire claim were Rs. 2,000.

Show the Stock Destroyed Account, Land and Buildings Account, Machinery Account and Insurance Company's Account and the Trading and Profit and Loss Account in the books of Bharat Co. Ltd. Make the necessary assumption.

(*Adapted from Madras University*)

Memorandum Trading Account
For the period from 1-7-1997 to 1-3-1998
(To find out the value of closing stock as on the date of fire)

	Rs.		Rs.
To Opening Stock (30-6-97)	1,35,000	By Sales	3,00,000
To Purchases and expenses	2,60,000	By Closing stock (Balancing figure)	1,55,000
To Gross Profit (20% on Rs. 3,00,000)	60,000		
	4,55,000		4,55,000

Note : In this problem, the percentage of gross profit is not given. Hence, the rate of gross profit on sales is assumed to be 20%.

In the Books of Bharat Co. Ltd.
Stock Destroyed Account

Dr. Cr.

	Rs.		Rs.
To Trading A/c (As per above account)	1,55,000	By Insurance Company (Claim amount)	1,20,000
To Insurance Co. A/c (Salvaged stock taken over)	10,000	By Bank (Salvage realised)	20,000
		By Profit and Loss A/c (Balancing figure) (Loss transferred)	25,000
	1,65,000		1,65,000

Dr. **Land and Buildings Account** Cr.

	Rs.		Rs.
To Balance b/d (Book value on 30-6-97)	1,75,000	By Insurance Company (Claim amount)	1,00,000
		By Profit & Loss A/c (B.F.) (Loss transferred)	15,000
		By Balance c/d (50,000 + 10,000)	60,000
	1,75,000		1,75,000

Dr. **Plant and Machinery** Cr.

	Rs.		Rs.
To Balance b/d (Book value on 30-6-97)	16,000	By Insurance Company (Claim amount)	15,000
		By Profit & Loss A/c (B.F.) (Loss transferred)	1,000
	16,000		16,000

Dr. **Fire Claim Expenses Account** Cr.

	Rs.		Rs.
To Bank (Expenses incurred)	2,000	By Profit and Loss A/c (B.F.) (Loss transferred)	2,000
	2,000		2,000

Dr. **Insurance Company Account** Cr.

	Rs.		Rs.
To Stock Destroyed	1,20,000	By Stock Destroyed/ Salvaged A/c (Salvaged stock taken over)	10,000
To Land & Building	1,00,000		
To Plant & Machinery (Admitted claim amount)	15,000		
		By Bank (B.F.) (Total claim received)	2,25,000
	2,35,000		2,35,000

Note : It is assumed that the expenses incurred in connection with fire are not admitted by the insurance company. Hence, they are not debited to insurance company account. They should be debited to P & L A/c.

Trading and Profit and Loss Account

Dr. **For the period from 1-7-1997 to 1-3-1998** Cr.

	Rs.		Rs.
To Opening Stock	1,35,000	By Sales	3,00,000
To Purchases & Expenses	2,60,000	By Closing Stock	1,55,000
To Gross Profit c/d	60,000		
	4,55,000		4,55,000
To Stock Destroyed	25,000	By Gross Profit b/d	60,000
To Land & Building	15,000		
To Plant & Machinery	1,000		
To Fire Claim Expenses	2,000		
To Net Profit c/d (Balancing figure)	17,000		
	60,000		60,000

(III) Claim for Loss of Profits *Or* Claim for Consequential Loss

When a fire occurs in a business premises, it destroys not only stock and the fixed assets of the business, but also it affects the profits or earning capacity of the business for sometime due to dislocation of the business. Due to dislocation of the business temporarily, the sales of the business will fall, the standing or fixed charges of the business will continue to be the same and the cost of working of a business will increase. Consequently, there will be loss of profits. To cover such losses, a separate policy called the Loss of Profits Policy or Consequential Loss Policy will be taken to indemnify the loss on account of dislocation temporarily for conducting business operations. An ordinary fire insurance policy covers only the loss on account of stock or properties destroyed by fire, but it does not cover the consequential losses. Therefore, a separate 'Loss of Profits Policy' is taken to cover the following losses due to fire :

(i) Loss of profits due to stoppage of business.

(ii) Loss of standing (or fixed) charges.

(iii) Increased cost of working.

Loss of profit policy gives future protection to the insured. It covers revenue losses. But, ordinary fire policy covers only capital losses. Hence, the insured should take both the policies to get complete protection.

Explanation of Certain Terms

The explanation or the meaning of certain terms which are commonly used in a consequential policy is given as below :

(1) Period of indemnity: This is a period of dislocation of business as result of fire. This period varies from business to business depending upon the time to be taken to restore the normalcy of business operations. It starts with the occurrence of the fire and ends with restoration of normalcy. Normal period of indemnity is one year. If the period of indemnity is longer, the amount of premium charged by the insurance company is higher. The period of indemnity is mentioned in the policy. But the insurance company makes good loss of profit during the period mentioned in the policy or the actual period of dislocation, whichever is shorter. For instance, if the indemnity period mentioned in the policy is 8 months and the period of dislocation is 7 months, then, the period of claim is 7 months. Similarly, if the indemnity period specified in the policy is 5 months and the period of dislocation is 6 months, then, the period of claim is 5 months.

(2) Standard turnover or sales : It refers to the sales made during the period in the preceding financial year corresponding to the period of indemnity. This is to be adjusted for valuation in the light of the trend in the current year, by including a clause to that effect in the policy. For instance, if the standard turnover for the corresponding period in the previous year was Rs. 1,00,000 and there is an increase of 10% every year, the figure is to be adjusted by adding Rs. 10,000, then, the adjusted turnover would be Rs. 1,10,000.

(3) Short sales or loss of turnover : It refers to shortfall in the sales volume during the period of business dislocation. The loss of turnover during the period of indemnity is arrived by comparing the actual turnover for the period with the standard turnover. In other words, the difference between the standard sales and the actual sales is treated as short sales or loss of turnover.

(4) Standing charges or fixed charges : They refer to those fixed expenses, which are incurred irrespective of the reduction in the business during the period of dislocation. These are incurred inspite of stoppage of business. For example, salaries, rent, rates and taxes, lighting and heating, repairs and maintenance, depreciation, directors fees, interest on debentures issued, interest on loan borrowed, etc. The insured has to specify the standing charges in the policy which he would like to insure. The standing charges which are specified in the policy are called **'Insured Standing Charges'** and the standing charges which are not specified in the policy are called **'Uninsured Standing Charges'**. If there is no information about the standing charges in the policy, all the standing charges should be assumed as insured standing charges.

(5) Rate of gross profit : The term gross profit has got a different meanings than the gross profit used in the other contexts. In this context, gross profit means the net profit of the business during the last financial year plus insured standing charges. In case there is net loss, it is necessary to deduct the same from the insured standing charges. The rate of gross profit is calculated as below :

$$\frac{\text{Net profit} + \text{Insured standing charges}}{\text{Turnover or sales of the preceding financial year}} \times 100$$

In case of net loss, the rate is calculated as below :

$$\frac{\text{Insured standing charges} - \text{Net loss}}{\text{Sales of the preceding financial year}} \times 100$$

Note : If the above gross profit ratio is adjusted in the light of the trend in the current year, if any, the resulting ratio is called the adjusted gross profit ratio.

(6) Loss of profit during the period of dislocation : The loss of profit during the period of dislocation or interruption is calculated by applying the rate of gross profit or the rate of adjusted gross profit to the short sales. For instance, if the short sales are Rs. 25,000 and the rate of gross profit is 25% then, the loss of profit during the period of dislocation would be Rs. 6,250 (25,000 × 25/100).

(7) Increased cost of working : The insured may have to incur certain additional expenses during the period of dislocation to reduce the loss of turnover. Such expenses are called increased working expenses. For example, rent paid for premises hired from other party temporarily for running the business during the period of dislocation. The claim for increased cost of working is restricted to the lowest of the following amount :

(i) Actual increased working expenses.

(ii) $$\frac{\text{Net profit} + \text{Insured standing charges}}{\text{Net profit} + \text{All standing charges}} \times \text{Increased cost of working}$$

(iii) Short sales avoided through increased cost of working × Rate of gross profit.

(8) Saving in expenses : Expenses which are avoided or not incurred during the period of dislocation are called saving in expenses. The amount of expenses saved as a result of fire should be deducted from the total claim for loss of profit.

(9) Average clause : As it has been explained already, when there is under-insurance, the insured is entitled to get only a proportion of his claim. For the verification of the fact whether there is under-insurance or not, we should find out the amount of the policy ought to have been taken. The amount of the policy ought to have been taken is to be calculated as below in this context :

Adjusted turnover for the 12 months before fire or

Annual sales preceding the date of fire × Rate of Gross Profit.

Then, we should compare it with the insured amount.

If there is under-insurance, the actual amount of claim for consequential loss should be calculated as below :

$$\text{Total amount of claim} \times \frac{\text{Amount of the policy taken or sum insured}}{\text{Amount of the policy ought to have been taken}}$$

Steps Involved in Computation of Claim

The following are the various steps involved in the computation of the amount of claim for consequential loss :

(1) Fixation of period of claim (*i.e.*, period of indemnity or period of dislocation whichever is lower).

(2) Calculation of short sales.

(3) Calculation of gross profit ratio.

(4) Computation of loss of profit.

(5) Addition of increased cost of working subject to the limit.

(6) Deduction of saving in expenses.

(7) Application of average clause and ascertainment of net claim for consequential loss.

Illustration 16

From the following, calculate the amount of short sales :

Fire occurred on 1st January, 1998.

Period of indemnity from 1-1-1998 to 1-6-1998.

Sales from 1-1-1998 to 1-6-1998	Rs. 1,20,000
Sales from 1-1-1997 to 1-6-1997	Rs. 3,00,000

Turnover before 1st January showed an increase of 15% as compared with the preceding year.

Solution :

Calculation of short sales for the period of dislocation :

Short sales = Standard sales in the preceding period minus Actual sales during the period of dislocation.

	Rs.
Sales in the preceding period (*i.e.*, from 1-1-1997 to 1-6-1997)	3,00,000
Add : 15% increase in sales	45,000
Standard sales	3,45,000
Less : Actual sales during the period of dislocation	1,20,000
Amount of short sales	2,25,000

Illustration 17

From the following information, calculate the amount of permissible increased working expenses :

	Rs.
Net profit	8,000
Rate of gross profit	25%
Short sales	15,000
Insured standing charges	12,000
Uninsured standing charges	3,000
Short sales avoided through increased cost of working	7,500
Increased working expenses	2,000

Solution :

Calculation of permissible increased working expenses :

(1) $$\frac{\text{Net profit + Insured standing charges}}{\text{Net profit + All standing charges}} \times \text{Increased working expenses}$$

$$\frac{8{,}000+12{,}000}{8{,}000+15{,}000} \times 2{,}000 = \text{Rs. } 1{,}600$$

(2) Short sales avoided through increased cost of working × Rate of gross profit

$$7{,}500 \times 25\% = 7{,}500 \times \frac{25}{100} = \text{Rs. } 1{,}875$$

The amount of increased working expenses will be the lower of two limits calculated as above. Therefore, the amount of increased working expenses will be allowed only to the extent of Rs. 1,600.

Illustration 18

From the following particulars, prepare a claim for loss of profit covering consequential loss :

(a) Accounts are prepared on 31st December, the profit for 1978 amounted to Rs. 65,000 after debiting constant expenses totalling Rs. 75,000. Sales for 1978 were Rs. 11,20,000.

(b) Fire occurred on June 1, 1979 and affected sales for four months.

(c) Sales for four months ending Sept. 30, in 1978 and 1979 were respectively Rs. 3,00,000 and Rs. 40,000.

(d) The policy was Rs. 2,00,000; the sales for the year ending on May 31, 1979, were Rs. 12,50,000.

(*B.Com., M.K.U.(s), April, 1982*)

Solution :

(a) Calculation of short sales :

	Rs.
Standard sales during 1-6-1978 to 30-9-1978	3,00,000
Less : Actual sales during interruption	40,000
Short sales	2,60,000

(b) Calculation of rate of gross profit for claim purpose :

$$\text{Rate of G.P.} = \frac{\text{Net profit + Insured standing charges}}{\text{Sales of the preceding financial year}} \times 100$$

$$\frac{65{,}000 + 75{,}000}{11{,}20{,}000} \times 100 \quad = 12.5\%$$

(c) Calculation of loss of profit :

Short sales × Rate of gross profit

$$\frac{2{,}60{,}000 \times 125}{100 \times 10} = \text{Rs. } 32{,}500.$$

(d) Claim to be admitted :

	Rs.
Sales during the preceding 12 months	12,50,000
Policy required for Rs. 12,50,000	1,56,250
(Annual sales preceding the date of fire ×	
Rate of G.P. = Rs. 12,50,000 ×12.5%)	
Policy taken for	2,00,000
As the policy taken is sufficient, the claim is admitted in full	32,500.

Illustration 19

A company was insured for consequential loss. A fire occurred on 31st March, 1996, and as a result there was diminished turnover, as compared with the corresponding months of the preceding year of Rs. 20,000. The company was insured for a period which adequately covered the dislocation and no special factors existed.

The account for last accounting period of a year to 31st January, 1996 showed a net profit of Rs. 4,000 after debiting standing charges (all insured) Rs. 6,000 and turnover being Rs. 1,00,000. The company had taken a loss of profit policy of Rs. 4,800 and the turnover for the year immediately preceding the fire was Rs. 64,000. Calculate the claim on average basis.

(*Adapted from B.Com., Madurai University*)

Solution :

(a) Calculation of gross profit :

G.P.= Net profit of preceding financial year + Insured standing charges.

= 4,000 + 6,000

= Rs. 10,000

(b) Rate of gross profit :

$$\frac{\text{Gross profit}}{\text{Annual sales of preceding financial year}} \times 100 = \frac{10,000}{1,00,000} \times 100 = 10\%.$$

(c) Loss of profit for the period of dislocation :

$$\text{Short sales} \times \text{Gross profit ratio} = 20,000 \times \frac{10}{100} = \text{Rs. } 2,000$$

(d) Claim to be admitted :

Sales during the preceding 12 months	64,000
Policy required or ought to have been taken	6,400
(Adjusted turnover for the 12 months before fire × Rate of gross profit = 64,000 × 10/110)	
Policy taken for	4,800

Since the actual policy amount is less than the policy ought to have been taken, it involved under-insurance. Therefore, the actual claim for loss of profit can be calculated as below :

$$\text{Total claim} \times \frac{\text{Policy taken}}{\text{Policy ought to have been taken}}$$

$$= 2,000 \times \frac{4,800}{6,400} = \text{Rs. } 1,500$$

Illustration 20

Items related to the previous year :

Rate of gross profit	25%
Insured standing charges	10,000
Total standing charges	15,000
Net Profit	25,000

Items related to the current year :

Short sales	20,000
Increased working expenses	2,000
Saving in expenses	750
Short sale avoided through increased cost of working	5,000
Amount of policy	20,000

Sales during 12 months immediately preceding the fire being Rs. 1,00,000, the sales of the current year up to the date of fire has increased by 10% over the sales of the same period in the previous year.

Calculate the amount of claim to be admitted by the Insurance company.

(*A.C.S., Inter, June, 1994*)

Solution :

(a) Calculation of allowable limit of the increased working expenses :

(i) $$\frac{\text{Net profit+Insured standing charges}}{\text{Net profit + All standing charges}} \times \text{Increased working expenses}$$

$$\frac{25{,}000+10{,}000}{25{,}000+15{,}000} \times 2{,}000 = \text{Rs. } 1{,}750$$

(ii) Short sales avoided through increased cost of working × Rate of gross profit

$$\frac{5{,}000 \times 25}{100} = \text{Rs. } 1{,}250$$

Rs. 1,250 being the lower of the above two calculations is allowable by the insurance company.

(b) Calculation of total claim *i.e.*, claim for loss of profit and claim for increased cost of working :

	Rs.
Loss of profit during the period of dislocation (Short sales × Rate of G.P. = 20,000 × 25/100)	5,000
Add : Increased working expenses	1,250
	6,250
Less : Saving in expenses	750
Claim for loss of profit and increased working expenses	5,500

(c) Claim to be admitted :

Sales during 12 months immediately preceding the fire	1,00,000
Add : 10% increase in the current year trend	10,000
	1,10,000

Amount of the policy should have been taken for

$$\text{Rs. } 1{,}10{,}000 \left(\frac{1{,}10{,}000 \times 25}{100} = \text{Rs. } 27{,}500\right) \qquad 27{,}500$$

Amount of the policy taken 20,000

Here, there is an under-insurance. Hence, the actual loss of profit should be calculated as below :

$$\text{Amount of claim} \times \frac{\text{Amount of the policy taken}}{\text{Amount of the policy ought to have been taken}}$$

$$5{,}500 \times \frac{20{,}000}{27{,}500} = \text{Rs. } 4{,}000$$

So, the claim for consequential loss will be Rs. 4,000.

Illustration 21

The following are the details relating to a company for the year ended 31st December, 1995 :

	Rs.
Total variable expenses	3,50,000
Total fixed expenses	1,20.000
Non-operating income	60,000
Net profit	90,000

The company took a decision to arrange for a loss of profits insurance for the year 1996. It is expected that the turnover might increase by 15% and all the fixed standing charges will remain constant. Ascertain the extent to which the company should finalise the amount to be insured under loss of profit policy.

(*Adapted from B.Com., Madurai University*)

Solution :

(a) Calculation of gross profit of preceding financial year :

Total net profit of the preceding financial year	90,000
Less : Non-operating income of the preceding financial year	60,000
Operating net profit of the preceding financial year	30,000
Add : Total fixed expenses	1,20,000
Gross profit of the preceding financial year	1,50,000

(b) Calculation of gross profit of the current financial year :

Gross profit of the preceding financial year (As calculated above)	1,50,000
Add : 15% increase in the gross profit of the current financial year because of 15% increase in sales $\left(\frac{1{,}50{,}000 \times 15}{100}\right)$	22,500
	1,72,000

(c) Calculation of the sum to be insured for loss of profit :

The gross profit of current financial year is Rs. 1,72,000

So, the policy for the loss of profit must cover the entire loss of gross profit. Hence, the sum to be insured on the policy amount should be Rs. 1,72,000.

Illustration 22

From the following information, find the claims under a 'loss of profit' policy.

	Rs.
Sales in 1991	1,00,000
Sales in 1992	1,20,000
Sales in 1993	1,44,000
Sales in 1994	1,72,800
Net Profit in 1994	10,000
(All insured) Standing charges in 1994	7,280
Date of dislocation by fire : 1-1-1995	
Period of dislocation : 3 months	
Sales from 1-1-1994 to 31-3-1994	43,200
Sales from 1-1-1995 to 31-3-1995	11,840
Indemnity period : 9 months	
Policy value	50,000

There was no reduction in standing charges during the dislocation period, nor were there any additional costs.

(*Adapted from C.A. Inter*)

Solution :

(a) Calculation of gross profit of preceding financial year :

Net Profit + Insured standing charges

10,000 + 7,280 = Rs. 17,280.

(b) Calculation of rate of gross profit :

$$\frac{\text{Gross profit}}{\text{Annual sales of preceding financial year}} \times 100 = \frac{17{,}280}{1{,}72{,}800} \times 100 = 10\%$$

(c) Calculation of adjusted standard sales :

Standard sales (1-1-94 to 31-3-94)	43,200
Add : 20% Increase in sales	8,640
Adjusted standard sales	51,840

Note : From the information given in the problem, it is clear that there is an annual increase of 20% in the sales during the period 1991-94

$$\left(1992 = \frac{20{,}000 \times 100}{1{,}00{,}000} = 20\%;\ 1993 = \frac{24{,}000 \times 100}{1{,}20{,}000} = 20\% \text{ and } 1994 = \frac{28{,}800 \times 100}{1{,}44{,}000} = 20\%\right).$$

So, while calculating the standard sales for the period of dislocation, 20% adjustment must be made to reflect the trend of the business.

(d) Calculation of short sales, for the period of dislocation :

Adjusted standard sales	51,840
Less : Actual sales for the period of dislocation	11,840
Short sales for the period of dislocation	40,000

(e) Loss of profit during the period of dislocation :

$$\text{Short sales} \times \text{Rate of G.P.} = 40{,}000 \times \frac{10}{100} = \text{Rs. } 4{,}000$$

(f) Claim to be admitted :

Sales during the preceding 12 months (1,72,800 + 20% increase in sales *i.e.*, 34,560)	2,07,300
Policy required (2,07,300 × 10/100)	20,736
Policy taken	50,000

Here, there is no under-insurance. Therefore, there is no need of application of average clause. So, the full claim of Rs. 4,000 will be admitted by the insurance company.

Illustration 23

The premises of a company were destroyed by fire which took place on 1st March, 1992, and as a result of which the business was disorganized from 1st March to 31st July, 1992. Accounts are closed on 31st December every year. The company is insured under a loss of profit policy for Rs. 7,50,000. The period of indemnity specified in the policy is 6 months. From the following information, you are required to compute the amount of claim under the loss of profit policy.

Turnover for the year 1991	40,00,000
Net profit for the year 1991	2,40,000
Insured standing charges	4,80,000
Uninsured standing charges	80,000
Turnover during the period of dislocation *i.e.*, from 1-3-92 to 31-7-92	8,00,000
Standard turnover for the corresponding period in the preceding year *i.e.*, from 1-3-91 to 31-7-91	20,00,000
Annual turnover for the year immediately preceding the fire *i.e.*, from 1-3-91 to 28-2-92	44,00,000
Increased cost of working	1,50,000
Saving in insured standing charges	30,000
Reduction in turnover avoided through increased working cost	4,00,000

Owing to reason acceptable to the insurer, the "Special Circumstances Clause" stipulates for :

(a) Increase of turnover (standard and annual) by 10% and

(b) Increase of rate of gross profit by 2%.

(*Adapted from C.A. Inter N.S.*)

Solution :

(a) Calculation of rate gross profit :

$$\text{Rate of G.P.} = \frac{\text{Net profit + Insured standing charges}}{\text{Sales of the preceding financial year}} \times 100$$

$$= \frac{2{,}40{,}000 + 4{,}80{,}000}{40{,}00{,}000} \times 100 = 18\%$$

Add : Increase in the rate of gross profit	= 2%
Adjusted gross profit ratio	= 20%.

(b) Calculation of short sales during the period of dislocation :

Standard turnover from 1-3-91 to 31-7-91	20,00,000
Add : 10% Increase in turnover	2,00,000
Adjusted standard turnover	22,00,000
Less : Actual sales from 1-3-92 to 31-7-92	8,00,000
Short sales	14,00,000

(c) Calculation of allowable limit of the working expenses :

(i) $\frac{\text{Net profit+Insured standing charges}}{\text{Net profit + All standing charges}} \times \text{Increased working expenses}$

$$= \frac{2{,}40{,}000 + 4{,}80{,}000}{2{,}40{,}000 + 5{,}60{,}000} \times 1{,}50{,}000 = \frac{7{,}20{,}000}{8{,}00{,}000} \times 1{,}50{,}000 = \text{Rs. } 1{,}35{,}000$$

(ii) Short sales avoided through increased cost of working × Rate of gross profit

$$\frac{4{,}00{,}000 \times 20}{100} = \text{Rs. } 80{,}000$$

Rs. 80,000 being the lowest of the above two calculations is allowed by the insurance company.

(d) Calculation of total claim *i.e.*, loss for profit and increased cost of working :

Loss for profit (Short sales × Rate of gross profit) (14,00,000 × 20%)	2,80,000
Add : Increased cost of working	80,000
	3,60,000
Less : Saving in expenses	30,000
	3,30,000

Rs. 3,60,000 is within the overall limit of 20% of Rs. 22,00,000 (Adjusted standard turnover).

(e) Claim to be admitted :

Sales during the preceding 12 months from the date of fire	44,00,000
Add : 10% Increase in turnover	4,40,000
	48,40,000
Policy should have been taken (for Rs. 48,40,000) $\left(\frac{48,40,000 \times 20}{100} = 9,68,000\right)$	9,68,000
Policy taken for	7,50,000

Here, there is an under-insurance. Hence, the actual claim to be admitted should be calculated as below :

$$\text{Amount of claim} \times \frac{\text{Amount of the policy taken}}{\text{Amount of the policy should have been taken}}$$

$$3,30,000 \times \frac{7,50,000}{9,68,000} = 2,55,681.8 \text{ or } 2,55,682$$

So, the claim for consequential loss will be Rs. 2,55,682.

EXAMINATION QUESTIONS

(A) Answer the following questions in two sentences each :

(*Each Carrying 2 Marks*)

(1) What do you mean by contract of fire insurance?

(2) What is fire claim ?

(3) What do you mean by salvage?

(*Bangalore, April, 1991*)

(4) What is average clause ?

(*Kuvempu, April, 1994*)

(5) What is 'average' in fire insurance claim ?

(*M.K.U., April, 1994*)

(6) Give the meaning of average clause with an example.

(*Bangalore, April, 1997*)

(7) What is meant by under-insurance?

(8) How do you calculate the amount of claim under average clause?

(9) What are abnormal items?

(10) How do you ascertain the claim for loss of stock?

(11) What is consequential loss?

(12) What do you mean by period of indemnity?

(13) What is standard turnover?

(14) What is meant by short sales?

(15) What are standing charges?

(16) What are savings in expenses?

(17) How do you ascertain the claim for loss of profit?

(18) What are increased working expenses?

(19) Find out the actual claim in the following case :

Value of stock on the date of fire	Rs. 25,000
Value of stock saved from fire	Rs. 5,000
Value of insurance policy	Rs. 20,000

There is an average clause in the policy.

(*Bangalore, November, 1993*)

Ans. : Claim amount under average clause Rs. 16,000.

(20) Loss of stock by fire Rs. 4,00,000

Amount of policy Rs. 3,42,000

Total value stock destroyed by fire Rs. 4,56,000

Calculate the amount of fire claim by applying average clause.

(*Bangalore, April, 1998*)

Ans. : Claim amount under average clause Rs. 3,00,000.

(B) Answer the following questions :

(*Each Carrying 8 Marks*)

(1) What is Average Clause? How is the claim ascertained if average clause is included in a fire policy?

(*Kuvempu, April, 1994*)

(2) Describe the procedure to be followed for calculating the fire loss claim for the loss of goods.

(*Andra, Oct., 1994*)

Simple Problems

(3) A fire occurred on September 30, 1996, in the godown of Mr. Anand. From the following figures ascertain the claim to be lodged :

Stock on January 1, 1996	17,000
Purchases from January 1, 1996 to date of fire	1,70,000
Wages and other manufacturing expenses	17,000
Sales from January 1, 1996, to date of fire	2,00,000

The rate of gross profit is 25% on cost. The stock salvaged was valued at Rs. 4,000.

(*Adapted from M.K.U., April, 1996*)

Ans. : Value of closing stock on the date of fire Rs. 44,000 and Amount of claim Rs. 40,000.

(4) On 15th June, 1986, the premises and stock of a firm was destroyed by fire but the accounting records were saved from which the following particulars were available :

Stock on 1-1-1985	73,500
Stock on 31-12-1985	81,900
Purchases for the year 1985	3,98,000
Sales for the year 1985	4,87,000
Purchases from 1-1-1986 to 15-6-1986	1,62,000
Sales from 1-1-1986 to 15-6-1986	2,31,200

The stock salvaged was Rs. 5,300. Show the amount of claim.

(*Bangalore, Oct., 1991*)

Ans. : Rate of gross profit 20%; Value of closing stock on the date of fire Rs. 58,940 and Amount of claim Rs. 53,640.

(5) A fire occurred in Hubli Provision Stores on 21-7-1995. The stock was fully covered by insurance company :

Stock on 1-4-1995	95,000
Purchases from 1-4-1995 to 21-7-1995	3,75,000
Sales from 1-4- 1995 to 21-7-1995	4,00,000

The stock has been always valued at less by 5%.

The gross profit for the past three years ending 31-3-1993, 31-3-1994 and 31-3-1995 was 30%, 25% and 20% respectively after adjustment for the opening and closing stock of the respective years to the proper valuation. Stock salvaged was agreed to Rs. 8,000.

From the above particulars, prepare a statement of fire claim to be submitted to the insurance company.

(*Adapted from K.U.D.*)

Ans. : Rate of gross profit 15%; Value of closing stock on the date of fire Rs. 1,35,000 and Amount of claim Rs. 1,27,000.

(6) On 15-2-1990, a fire occurred in the premises of a company. From the following particulars, ascertain the amount of claim to be lodged in case of stock which was insured :

Stock on 1-1-1990	1,00,000
Purchases from 1-1-1990 to the date of fire	1,50,000
Wages	50,000
Manufacturing expenses	30,000
Sales from 1-1-1990 to the date of fire	2,40,000

The gross profit ratio is 25%. The stock salvaged was valued at Rs.19,500.

(*Kerala, April, 1990*)

Ans. : Value of closing stock on the date of fire Rs. 1,50,000 and Amount of claim Rs. 1,30,500.

(7) A fire occurred in the premises of a merchant on 30-6-1998; destroying a greater part of his stock. The following information was found from the records available :

Value of stock on 1-1-1998	12,500
Purchases from 1-1-1998 to 30-6-1998	45,500
Sales from 1-1-1998 to 30-6-1998	56,500

The percentage of gross profit on sales for the year 1995, 1996 and 1997 were 30% , 20% and 10% respectively.

Prepare a statement of fire claim on the insurance company for the stock destroyed by fire assuming that the value of stock salvaged was Rs. 1,500.

(*Adapted from K.U.D.*)

Ans. : Value of closing stock on the date of fire Rs. 1,500 and Amount of claim is Nil (Stock Rs. 1,500 – salvage Rs. 1,500).

Hint : Since the rate of gross profit of previous years are consistently falling, the average rate of gross profit should not be taken. Hence, the rate of gross profit is Nil.

(8) A fire occurred on 30-6-1991 in the premises of a Company and stock-in-trade was destroyed. The following information is however available :

Opening stock on 1-1-1991	11,000
Purchases up to 30-4-1991	45,000
Sales up to 30-6-1991	60,000

The closing stock on 31-12-1990 was valued at market price which was 10% above cost.

The usual percentage of gross profit in the business was 15% on sales. Salvaged stock was valued at Rs. 400.

Compute the fire claim.

(*Adapted from My. U. & Gulbarga, Oct., 1995*)

Ans. : Value of opening stock Rs. 10,000 (11,000 × 100/110); Value of closing stock on the date of fire Rs. 4,000 and Amount of claim Rs. 3,600.

(9) A fire occurred in a textile mill on 15-9-1990 and a considerable part of the stock was destroyed. The stock was fully insured.

The books revealed the following information :

(i) The stock on 1-1-1990 was 28,567 (as per business convention the stock was valued at 10% more than cost).

(ii) The purchases and sales to the date of fire amounted to Rs. 57,628 and Rs. 93,900 respectively.

(iii) The stock salvaged was agreed to be worth Rs. 3,200.

(iv) The average rate of gross profit for the past three years on sales was 36%.

Prepare the statement showing the amount of claim with the insurance company.

(*Gulbarga, Oct., 1994*)

Ans. : Value of opening stock Rs. 25,970 (28,567 × 100/110); Value of closing stock Rs. 23,502 and Amount of claim Rs. 20,302.

(10) On 15-12-97 fire occurred in godown of Shri Kumar and stock was destroyed. The books of account were however saved. From the information available it was ascertained that the average gross profit of Kumar was $33^1/_3$% on cost of sales.

The stock on 31-3-1997 valued as per the business convention at 10% above cost was Rs. 67,100. The purchases, wages and sales from 1-4-1997 to the date of fire were ascertained at Rs. 1,28,000, Rs. 27,500 and Rs. 1,84,000 respectively. Prepare statement of fire claim on the insurance company.

(*Adapted from K.U.D.*)

Ans. : Value of opening stock Rs. 61,000 (67,100 × 100/110); Gross profit Rs. 46,000; Value of closing stock on the date of fire Rs. 78,500 and Amount of fire claim Rs. 78,500.

Hint : $33^1/_3$% on cost is same as 25% on sales.

(11) Fire occurred in the premises of Anna & Co., on 1st September, 1996 and the stock of the value of Rs. 1,01,000 was salvaged and the business books and records were saved.

The following information was obtained :

Purchases of the year ended 31-3-1996	6,80,000
Sales for the year ended 31-3-1996	11,00,000
Purchases from 31-3-1996 to 1-9-1996	2,50,000
Sales from 31-3-1996 to 1-9-1996	3,60,000
Stock on 31-3-1995	3,00,000
Stock on 31-3-1996	3,40,000

Further information is that the stock on 31-3-1996 was over-valued by Rs. 20,000. Calculate the amount of claims to be presented to the insurance company in respect of the loss. In April, 1996, selling price was lowered by 10%.

(*Adapted from Mangalore University*)

Ans. : Rates of gross profit 40% and $33^1/_3$%; Value of opening stock Rs. 3,20,000 (3,40,000 – 20,000); Value of closing stock on the date of fire Rs. 3,30,000 and Amount of claim Rs. 29,000.

Hint : Previous year's gross profit ratio is 40% (4,40,000 × 100/11,00,000). In the current year, the selling price is lowered by 10%. This affects the rate of gross profit. It has to be revised in the light of the change in the selling price. The revised rate of gross profit (*i.e.*, $33^1/_3$%) is to be used for the current period. It is calculated as below :

Year	Cost	Profit	Selling Price
Previous year	Rs. 60 (100 – 40)	Rs. 40	Rs. 100.
Current year	Rs. 60	Rs. 30 (90 – 60)	Rs. 90 (100–10)

Revised Rate of G.P. $= \frac{\text{Gross profit}}{\text{Sales}} \times 100$ *i.e.,* $\frac{30}{90} \times 100 = 33\frac{1}{3}\%$

(12) A fire broke-out in the warehouse of Mercantile Traders Ltd. on 30-9-1983. The company desires to file a claim with the insurance company for loss of goods and gives you the following information to enable you to prepare a statement showing the amount to be claimed :

(a) The last account of the company was prepare on 31-12-1982.

(b) Sundry debtors on 31-12-1982 were Rs. 40,000.

(c) Sundry debtors on 30-9-83 were Rs. 30,000.

(d) Cash received from debtors was Rs. 1,44,000.

(e) Stock on 31-12-1982 was Rs. 15,000.

(f) Purchases from 1-1-1983 to 30-9-1983 Rs. 1,25,000.

(g) Rate of gross profit to cost of sales 25%.

(*Gulbarga, Oct., 1991*)

Ans. : Credit sales in Total Debtors A/c Rs. 1,34,000; Gross profit Rs. 26,800; Value of closing stock on the date of fire Rs. 32,800 and Amount of fire claim Rs. 32,800.

Note : 25% on cost is same as 20% on sales.

(13) A fire accident occurred in the shop of M. Devappa on 15-10-1991. Calculate the loss from the fire and the claim to be made to the insurance company.

Stock on hand on 1-1-1990	30,600
Purchases from 1-1-1990 to 31-12-1990	1,22,000
Sales from 1-1-1990 to 31-12-1990	1,80,000
Stock on hand on 31-12-1990	27,000
Purchases from 1-1-1991 to 14-10-1991	1,47,000
Sales from 1-1-1991 to 14-10-1991	1,50,000

M. Devappa always valued stock on hand at 90% at cost price. Goods worth Rs. 18,000 had been salvaged from fire. He had taken out an insurance policy of Rs. 63,000 on the goods and this policy contained the average clause.

(*Bangalore, April, 1993*)

Ans. : Value of opening stock (1-1-90) Rs. 34,000 (30,600 × 100/90); Value of closing stock (on 31-12-90) Rs. 30,000 (27,000 × 100/90); Rate of gross profit 30%; Closing Stock on the date of fire Rs. 72,000 and Amount of claim Rs. 47,250 (63,000 × 54,000/72,000).

(14) A fire occurred in the godown of M/s Nagesh Bros. on 31-3-90 and a considerable part of the stock was destroyed. The value of the salvaged stock was agreed at Rs. 4,600. The following information is available from their books :

Stock on 1-1-1990	Rs. 62,100
Sales from 1-1-1990 to 31-3- 1990	Rs. 3,84,000
Purchases from 1-1-1990 to 31-3-1990	Rs. 2,52,000

Average gross profit to sales is 20%. Stocks were always valued at 90% of cost. The policy was for Rs. 9,600. There was an average clause in the policy.

Prepare a statement of claim.

(*Mysore, April, 1992*)

Ans. : Value of opening stock Rs. 69,000 (62,100 × 100/90); Rate of gross profit 20% ; Value of closing stock on the date of fire Rs. 13,800 and Amount of claim Rs. 6,400 (9,600 × 9,200/13,800).

(15) Fire occurred in the premises of Unluky Company Ltd. on 1-9-94 and the stock of the value of Rs. 40,000 was salvaged and the business books and records were saved. The following information was obtained :

Purchases for the year ended 31-3-94	Rs. 3,50,000
Sales for the year ended 31-3-94	Rs. 5,50,000
Purchases from 1-4-94 to 1-9-94	Rs. 1,00,000
Sales from 1-4-94 to 1-9-94	Rs. 1,50,000
Stock on 1-4-93	Rs. 1,50,000
Stock on 31-3-94	Rs. 1,70,000

The stock on 31-3-94 was over-valued by Rs. 10,000. Calculate the amount of claim to be presented to the Insurance Company in respect of losses. Rate of gross profit is to be based on the year ended 31-3-94.

(*Bangalore, April, 1997*)

Ans. : Rate of gross profit 38.18%; Value of closing stock on the date of fire Rs. 1,67,270 and Amount of claim Rs. 1,27,270.

Hint : Value of opening stock Rs. 1,60,000 (1,70,000 – 10,000).

(16) From the following information, calculate the amount of claim to be admitted by the insurance company :

	Rs.
Short sales	20,000
Increased working expenses	1,000
Rate of gross profit	20%
Saving in expenses	200
Sales during 12 months immediately preceding the fire	1,00,000
Amount of policy	15,000

The sales are showing an increasing trend since the commencement of the accounting year.

(Kerala, April, 1998)

Ans. : Claim for loss of the profit and increased working expenses Rs. 4,800 [4,000 (*i.e.*, 20% of 20,000) + 1,000 – 200]; Amount of the policy should have been taken Rs. 22,000 (20% of 1,10,000 *i.e.*, 1,00,0000 + 10%) and Amount of claim Rs. 3,273 (4,800 × 15,000/22,000).

(C) Solve the following problems :

(Each Carrying 15/16 Marks)

Loss of Stock

(1) A fire broke out in the premises of Rock and Stone on 30th June, resulting in the destruction of a greater part of the stock. Stock records have not been maintained. The following information is however, available. Value of stock on 1-1-1996 Rs. 25,000 and purchases and sales from 1-1-1996 to 30-6-1996 were Rs. 91,000 and Rs. 1,13,200 respectively. Value of stock salvaged Rs. 2,000.

Other Particulars	1993	1994	1995
Purchases	4,20,000	3,50,000	3,00,000
Sales	5,00,000	3,20,000	3,80,000
Gross profit	65,000	32,000	38,000

Prepare a statement showing the amount to be claimed from the insurance company.

(Adapted from K.U.D.)

Ans. : Average rate of gross profit 11% (13 + 10 + 10/3); Value of closing stock Rs. 15,252; Memorandum Trading Account total Rs. 1,28,452 and Amount of fire claim Rs. 13,252.

(2) A fire broke out in the godown of Sohan Lal & Co. on 30-4-1993 and destroyed the entire stock therein. The books of the firm are balanced on 31st December every year and you are required to estimate the value of stock lost from the following particulars :

1990	Sales	Rs. 3,00,000;	Gross Profit	Rs. 75,000
1991	Sales	Rs. 2,80,000;	Gross Profit	Rs. 56,000
1992	Sales	Rs. 2,60,000;	Gross Profit	Rs. 54,000

Up to the end of 30-4-1993 :

Purchases	Rs. 48,000;	Wages	Rs. 12,000
Sales	Rs. 76,000;	Carriage inwards	Rs. 2,000

The stock on 31-12-1992 was Rs. 62,000.

(Bangalore, April, 1992 Mod. & Adapted from K.U.D.)

Ans. : Average rate of gross profit on sales 22% $\left(\frac{25 + 20 + 21}{3}\right)$; Value of closing stock on the date of fire Rs. 64,720; Memorandum Trading Account total Rs. 1,40,720 and Amount of fire claim Rs. 64,720.

Hint : The percentage is calculated directly on sales, since the gross profit of previous years are given.

(3) Fire occurred in the premises of A & Company on 1st September, 1995 and stock of the value of Rs. 5,05,000 was salvaged and the business books and records were saved. The following information was obtained :

	Rs.
Purchases for the year ended 31-3-1995	35,00,000
Sales for the year ended 31-3-1995	55,00,000
Purchases from 1-3-1995 to 1-9-1995	12,00,000
Sales from 1-3-1995 to 1-9-1995	18,00,000
Stock on 31-3-1994	15,00,000
Stock on 31-3-1995	17,00,000

Further information is also given that the stock on 31-3-1995 was over-valued by Rs. 1,00,000.

Calculate the amount of the claim to be presented to the insurance company in respect of losses. Rate of Gross Profit is to be based on the year ended 31-3-1995.

(Adapted B.Com. (Hons.), Calcutta)

Ans. : Rate of gross profit 38.18%; Value of opening stock Rs. 16,00,000 (17,00,000 – 1,00,000); Value of closing stock on the date of fire Rs. 16,72,700 and Amount of fire claim Rs. 11,67,700.

Note : Purchases and sales for 6 months (*i.e.*, from 1-3-95 to 1-9-95) include purchases and sales of March 1995. But, they should be reduced to 5 months sales and purchases from April 1, 1995 to September 1, 1995. Then, the sales and purchases would be Rs. 15,00,000 (18,00,000 × 5/6) and 10,00,000 (12,00,000 × 5/6) respectively.

(4) The premises of Bombay Sports House caught fire on 1st April, 1995 and its stock was damaged. The firm had made up accounts to 31st May each year. The following information is available :

	1st June, 1993 to 31st May, 1994	1st June, 1994 to 1st April, 1995
	Rs.	Rs.
Stock at commencement conventionally valued at 10% above cost	1,05,754	1,45,992
Purchases	4,52,580	3,48,270

Sales	5,20,000	4,91,700

In December, 1994 goods which cost Rs. 10,000 were given away to Gymkhana Secretaries of various colleges for advertising purpose. No entry was made in the books. During the same month salesman had misappropriated unrecorded cash sales of Rs. 4,000. The rate of gross profit is constant. From the above make an estimate of stock on hand on the date of fire.

(Adapted from B.Com., Bombay)

Ans. : Value of opening stock (on 1-6-93) Rs. 96,140 (100/110 × 1,05,754); Rate of gross profit 20%; Value of closing stock on the date of fire Rs. 74,430; Amount of fire claim Rs. 74,430 and Value of closing stock on 31-5-94 Rs. 1,32,720 (1,45,992 × 100/110).

Note : Goods given away for advertisement purpose are deducted from purchases and cash sales misappropriated are added to sales on the date of fire.

(5) A fire occurred in the premises of Vinod Co. Ltd. on 4th March, 1994. All the stock with the exception of Rs. 13,000 was destroyed by fire. From the following figures ascertain the loss suffered by the company :

	Rs.
Stock on 31-3-1993	36,000
Stock on 31-1-1994	66,000
Purchases during 1993	4,70,000
Sales during 1993	6,00,000
Purchases during 1994 up to the date of fire	2,30,000
Sales during 1994 up to the date of fire	3,00,000

There was a practice in the company to value stock at cost less 10%. But they changed this practice and valued stock on 31st December, 1993 at cost plus 10%. The amount of the policy was Rs. 40,000 and claim was subject to an average clause.

(B.Com., Mysore, April, 1994)

Ans. : Rate of gross profit 25%; Value of stock destroyed Rs. 65,000 and Amount of fire claim Rs. 32,000.

(6) A fire occurred on October 1, 1993 and destroyed the stock of a firm. The business records were saved and from them the following particulars were ascertained :

	Rs.
Stock at cost on April 30, 1992	44,300
Stock at cost on April 30, 1993	37,550
Purchases for the year to April 30, 1993	1,03,850
Sales for the year to April 30, 1993	1,52,500
Purchases from May 1st, 1993 to September 30, 1993	59,000

In valuing the stock on April 30, 1993 to Rs. 800 had been written off a particular line of goods which had originally cost Rs. 1,800 and which were sold in June 1993 for Rs. 1,750. Except as regards this transaction, the ratio of gross profit had remained unchanged throughout. The value of stock salvaged from fire was Rs. 5,105.

Calculate the amount of the claim to be submitted to the insurance company in respect of the loss of stock.

(*B.Com., Bangalore, Nov., 1994*)

Ans. : Rate of gross profit 28%; Value of closing stock on the date of fire Rs. 32,680 and Amount of fire claim Rs. 27,575.

(7) The following information is made available from the records of the "Adventure Limited" whose premises were destroyed by fire on 31st May, 1987. The salvage was Rs. 15,000.

	Rs.
Stock on 31-12-1986	1,32,000
Sales during 1-1-1986 to 31-12-1986	5,42,000
Stock on 1-1-1986	90,000
Purchases during 1-1-1986 to 31-12-1986	4,48,000
Returns outward in May 1986	4,000
Returns inward in June 1986	42,000

The inventories on 1-1-1986 were valued at 10% below cost. However, this practice was suddenly changed and the inventories at 31st December, 1986 was valued at 10% above the cost.

After the finalisation of accounts for the year ended 31st December, 1986 it was discovered that purchase of furniture of Rs. 24,000 was erroneously included in the figure of purchases are given above.

The information for the period 1-1-1987 to 31-5-1987 is as follows :

Purchases	3,20,000
Return outwards	20,000
Sales (excluding goods sent on approval)	4,00,000

On 31st May, 1987 goods of the cost price of Rs. 40,000 were lying with prospective customers on approval basis (Sale or Return basis) on the date of fire. Customers had approved half the value of goods sent to them on approval. The gross profit margin charged on the above is the normal margin.

Calculate the amount of claim to be submitted to the Insurance Company.

(*B.Com., Bombay, April, 1988 and Bangalore, 1994*)

Ans. : Value of opening stock on 1-1-86 Rs. 1,00,000 (90,000 × 100/90); Value of closing stock on 31-12-86 Rs. 1,20,000 (1,32,000 × 100/110); Rate of gross profit 20%; Value of closing stock on the date of fire Rs. 60,000 and Amount of fire claim Rs. 45,000.

Notes : (i) Purchases of furniture of Rs. 24,000 should be deducted from the purchases in the Memorandum Trading A/c of 1986.

(ii) Goods sold on sale or approval basis are as below :
50% of Rs. 40,000 at a profit of 20% on sales or 25% on lost Rs. 25,000; 50% of Rs. 40,000 lying with customers Rs. 20,000.

Goods approved by the customers of Rs. 25,000 should be added to sales and Stock lying with customers at cost 20,000 should be shown on the credit side of Memorandum Trading A/c for the period 1-1-87 to 31-5-87.

(8) The premises and stock of Karam Chand Stores were totally destroyed by fire on 31st January, 1995. From the account books and other records that were saved, the following information is available. The stock on hand has always been valued at 10% less than cost.

	1992	1993	1994	1995
Opening Stock as valued	27,090	32,400	36,000	36,900
Purchases less Returns	74,900	80,000	81,000	6,000
Sales less Returns	1,20,000	1,32,000	1,40,000	12,000
Wages	17,400	16,400	23,600	2,000
Closing Stock as valued	32,400	36,000	36,900	—

Prepare a statement of submission to the Insurance Company in support of the claim for loss of stock.

(Poona, Oct., 1996)

Ans. : Rates of gross profit : 1992—28%; 1993—30% and 1994—28%.
Amount of gross profit : 1992—Rs. 33,600; 1993—Rs. 39,600; 1994—Rs. 36,400 and 1995—Rs. 3,360.
Value of opening stock : 1992—Rs. 30,100 (27,090 × 100/90); 1993—Rs. 36,000 (32,400 × 100/90); 1994—Rs. 40,000 (36,000 × 100/90) and 1995—Rs. 41,000 (36,900 × 100/90).
Value of closing stock : 1992—36,000 (32,400 × 100/90); 1993—Rs. 40,000 (36,000 × 100/90) & 1994—Rs. 41,000 (36,900 × 100/90).
Value of closing stock on the date of fire Rs. 40,360 & Amount of fire claims Rs. 40,360.

(9) On 15th June, 1996, the premises of Beech & Pine were destroyed by fire, but sufficient records were saved from which the following particulars were ascertained :

	Rs.
Stock at cost—1st January, 1995	7,350
Stock at cost—31st December, 1995	7,960
Purchases less returns for the year ended 31st December, 1995	39,800
Sales less returns for the year ended 31st December, 1995	48,700
Purchases less returns from 1st January, 1996 to 15th June, 1996	16,200
Sales less returns from 1st January, 1996 to 15th June, 1996	23,120

In valuing the stock for the Balance sheet at 31st December, 1995 Rs. 230 had been written off certain stock which was a poor selling line having cost Rs. 690 portion of these goods were sold in March, 1996 at a loss of Rs. 25 on original cost of Rs. 345. The remainder of this stock was now estimated to be worth the original cost, subject to the above exception, gross profit had reminded at a uniform rate throughout.

The stock salvaged was Rs. 580. Show the amount of the claim.

(Adapted from Madras University B.Com.)

Ans. : Rate of gross profit 20%; Total value of closing stock Rs. 5,805 (Normal items 5,460 + 345 abnormal items) and Amount of fire claims Rs. 5,225.

(10) From the following figures, calculate the amount of claim to be lodged with the insurance company for loss of stock :

Stock at cost on 1st January, 1993	90,000
Stock at cost on 1st January, 1994	70,000
Purchases during 1993	4,00,000
Purchases from 1st January, 1994 to 30th September	6,00,000
Sales during 1993	6,00,000
Sales from 1st January, 1994 to 30th September	8,80,000

You are informed that :

(a) In 1994 the cost of purchases have risen by 20% above the level prevailing in 1993;

(b) In 1994 the selling prices have gone up by 10% over the levels prevailing in 1993;

(c) Salvage value is Rs. 5,000.

(Adapted from B.Com., Bombay)

Ans. : Rate of gross profit 30%

Gross profit on the date of fire :	
On sales of opening stock (1,10,000 – 70,000)	40,000
On sales out of current purchases (7,70,000 × 26/110)	1,82,000
Total	2,22,000
Sales on the date of fire :	
Out of opening stock (70,000 × 110/70)	1,10,000
Out of current purchases (8,80,000 – 1,10,000)	7,70,000
Total	8,80,000
Closing stock on the date of fire	Rs. 12,000
Amount of claim to be lodged	Rs. 7,000

Notes : (i) Sales of out of opening stock : Cost of sales in 1993—70 (100 sales – 30 G.P.) and Selling price in 1994—110 (100 sales + 10% increase) then G.P. will be 40 (110 – 70).

(ii) Sales of current purchases and profit there on : Sales in 1993—100 and Sales in 1994—110 (100 sales + 10% increase) less cost of sales —84 (*i.e.*, cost of sales in 1993—70 + 20% increase), then, G.P. will be 26.

Loss of Fixed Assets

(11) A heavy fire took place in the factory of Karma Ltd. on 1-7-1993 and almost the entire factory was destroyed in fire. Their stock on 31-12-1992 was worth Rs. 12,243, machinery appeared in the books at Rs. 6,301 and furniture at Rs. 440.

Their purchases for the six months ending 30-6-1993 were Rs. 24,803, sales Rs. 25,648 and wages Rs. 11,081.

No addition was made to any fixed asset except to furniture of Rs. 100 during the above period.

From the examination of their books for the previous three years it was found that the gross profit on sales is at 20% on an average.

The factory building was not the property of the company.

The salvage was valued at Rs. 1,400.

Prepare a statement of fire claim.

(*Adapted from Karnataka University*)

Ans. : Amount of fire claim : Stock Rs. 26,209; Machinery Rs. 6,301 and Furniture Rs. 540. Total claim Rs. 33,050.

(12) A severe fire occurred on 1-3-1998 at the factory of Bombay Co. Ltd. by which the whole of the building and the contents were destroyed with the exception of the offices.

The insurance company paid a lump sum of Rs. 2,00,000 in respect of the buildings, Rs. 30,000 for machinery & plant and Rs. 2,40,000 for stock, the salvage being purchased by the Bombay Co. Ltd. for Rs. 20,000 and deducted the same from insurance money on settlement. The Bombay Co. Ltd. realised Rs. 40,000 from the salvage.

In the books of Bombay Co. Ltd., land & buildings stood at Rs. 3,50,000 and the value of buildings not destroyed was Rs. 20,000, the land being valued at Rs. 1,00,000. Machinery & plant stood at Rs. 32,000 and was all destroyed. The stock on the date of the last balance sheet as at 30-6-1997 stood at Rs. 2,70,000.

The sales for the eight months ending 29-2-1998 amounted to Rs. 6,00,000 and the purchases Rs. 5,20,000. Expenses in connection with fire claim were Rs. 4,000. The normal rate of gross profit is 20% on sales.

Show the necessary ledger accounts for the above in the books of Bombay Co. Ltd.

(*Adapted from Karnataka University*)

Ans. : Value of Stock on the date of fire Rs. 3,10,000; Loss on stock destroyed transferred to P & L A/c Rs. 50,000; Loss on land & building destroyed transferred to P & L A/c Rs. 30,000; Loss on plant and machinery destroyed transferred to P & L A/c Rs. 2,000.

Expenses of fire claim not admitted transferred to P&L A/c Rs. 4,000, Gross profit Rs. 1,20,000 and Net profit Rs. 34,000.

(13) The fire proof was fully insured against the premises and the insurance company settles the claims for Rs. 20,000 as follows :

Plant & Machinery		5,000
Buildings		7,000
Stock Damaged (50% of the value)		1,800
Stock Destroyed		3,000
Consequential Losses :		
Wages paid to retain men	700	
Incidental outlay	400	
Loss of profit	2,100	3,200
	Total Rs.	20,000

The plant & machinery lost was old and had been entirely written off. The building was repaired at a cost of Rs. 4,500. By expending Rs. 500 on damaged stock, the firm was able to sell it at the full price.

Set out the accounts to record the above, showing how you would finally deal with the various differences.

(*Adapted from Karnataka University*)

Ans. : Profit on plant & machinery transferred to P & L A/c Rs. 5,000
Profit on building transferred to P & L A/c Rs. 2,500
Value of stock destroyed transferred to Trading A/c Rs. 3,000
Profit on damaged stock transferred to P & L A/c. Rs. 1,300.
Loss on profit claim admitted transferred to P & L A/c Rs. 2,100.

Note : Wages of Rs. 700 and incidental outlay of Rs. 400 are paid in cash *i.e.*, they are transferred to Cash A/c.

Consequential Loss or Loss on Profits

(14) From the following details, find out the claim under a loss of profit policy :

Indemnity period—6 months
Policy value—Rs. 75,000
Date of fire—1st April, 1985
Dislocation period is up to 1st August, 1985
Sales for the accounting year 1984—Rs. 3,60,000.

Net profit for the accounting year 1984—Rs. 39,000.
Standing charges for the accounting year 1984 (all insured) Rs. 51,000.
Sales from 1st April, 1984 to 31st March, 1985—Rs. 4,80,000.
Sales from 1st April, 1985 to 1st August, 1985—Rs. 60,000.
Sales from 1st April, 1984 to 1st August, 1984—Rs. 1,50,000.
There is a clear 10% upward trend in business.

(B.Com., Poona, April, 1987)

Ans. : Short sales Rs. 1,05,000; Rate of gross profit 25%; Loss of profit Rs. 26,250; Claim for increased working Nil and Amount of claim on average clauses basis Rs. 16,406.

(15) A businessman holds a loss of profit policy. From the following information, prepare a claim for consequential loss :

(a) The accounts are prepared annually on 31st December. The net profit plus insured standing charges for the year ended 31st Dec., 1996 amounted to Rs. 2,00,000.

(b) A fire occurred on 30th April, 1997. The period of indemnity is six months.

(c) The sales for the year ended 30th April, 1997 were Rs. 5,24,000 and for the year ended 31st Dec., 1996 were Rs. 5,00,000.

(d) The sales during the period of dislocation were Rs. 80,000 and for the corresponding period in the preceding year were Rs. 1,80,000.

(e) The expenses incurred to mitigate loss were Rs. 8,000.

(f) The saving on insured standing charges due to fire amounted to Rs. 2,000.

(g) The amount insured was Rs. 1,57,200.

(B.Com., Poona, Oct., 1997)

Ans. : Short sales of Rs. 1,00,000; Gross profit Rs. 2,00,000; Rate of gross profit 40%; Loss of profit Rs. 40,000; Total claim *i.e.*, claim for loss of profit and claim for increased cost of working Rs. 46,000 and Amount of claim on average clause Rs. 34,500.

(16) From the following particulars, find the claims lodged under loss of profit policy :

Loss of profit policy : Rs. 1,65,000
Indemnity period : 6 months
Fire occurred on : 1-7-1989

Sales particulars :	Rs.
Sales from 1-7-1989 to 30-10-1989	60,000
Sales from 1-7-1988 to 30-10-1988	2,00,000
Net profit for the last financial year	90,000

Insured standing charges for last financial year	60,000
Turnover for the last financial year	5,00,000
Turnover for the year ending 30-6-1989	5,50,000
Total standing charges for the year	72,000
Additional expenses to reduce the loss of turnover	9,000
Saving during indemnity period	2,486

Adjustment of 20% be made in respect of upward trend in turnover.

(*B.Com., Bharathidasan, April, 1994*)

Ans. : Short sales of Rs. 1,80,000; Rate of gross profit 32.4%; Loss of profit Rs. 58,320; Total claims for loss of profit and increased cost of working Rs. 64,834; and Amount of fire claims Rs. 50,000.

(17) On 31st December, 1995 a fire occurred in the premises of a firm and the business of the firm was disorganized until 31st March, 1996. The firm was insured under a loss of profit policy for Rs. 26,000 with a six months period of indemnity.

The firm's accounts for the year ended 31st October, 1995 showed a turnover of Rs. 70,000 with a net profit of Rs. 8,000. The amount of standing charges covered by the insurance and debited in that year was Rs. 20,000. The turnover for the twelve months ended 31st December, 1995 was Rs. 78,000. The turnover (during the period the business was dislocated) amounted to Rs. 8,000, while during the corresponding period in the preceding year, it was Rs. 17,000. A sum of Rs. 2,000 was spent as additional expenses to mitigate the effects of the loss, there being, however, no saving in standing charges as a result of the fire.

Prepare a claim to be submitted in respect of the consequential loss policy.

(*Adapted from C.A. Inter*)

Ans. : Short sales of Rs. 9,000; Rate of gross profit 40%; Insured cost of working Rs. 2,000; Total claim for loss of profit and increased cost of working Rs. 5,600 and amount of fire claim on average clauses Rs. 4,667.

(18) Comet Ltd. has "Loss of Profit Insurance Policy" of Rs. 21,00,000. The period of indemnity is three months. A fire occurred on 31st March, 1996. The following information is available :

Sales :	Rs.
For the year ended 31st December, 1995	70,00,000
For the period from 1st April, 1995 to 31st March, 1996	80,00,000
For the period from 1st April, 1995 to 30th June, 1995	18,00,000
For the period from 1st April, 1996 to 30th June, 1996	1,20,000
Standing charges for 1995	16,00,000

Profit for 1995	5,00,000
Saving in standing charges because of fire	50,000
Additional expenses to reduce loss of turnover	1,00,000

Assuming that no adjustment has to be made for the upward trend in the turnover, compute the claim to be made on the Insurance Company.

(*Bharathidasan, April, 1993*)

Ans.: Gross profit Rs. 21,00,000; Rate of gross profit 30%; Short sales Rs. 16,80,000; Loss of profit Rs. 5,04,000; Insurance cost of working Rs. 36,000; Total claim for loss of profit and increased cost of working Rs. 4,90,000 and Amount of claim on average clauses Rs. 4,28,750.

(19) From the following information, you are required to work out claim under the loss of profits insurance policy.

(1) Cover – Gross profit – Rs. 1,00,000.

(2) Indemnity period – Six months.

(3) Damage – due to a fire accident on 28th December accounting year ends on 31st December.

(4) Net profit plus all standing charges in the prior accounting year Rs. 1,50,000.

(5) Standing charges uninsured Rs. 25,000.

(6) Turnover of the last accounting year was Rs. 5,00,000, the rate of gross profit being 25%.

(7) The annual turnover namely, the turnover for 12 months immediately preceding the fire— Rs. 5,20,000.

(8) As a consequence of fire, there was a reduction in certain insured standing charges at the rate of Rs. 25,000 per annum.

(9) The standard turnover Rs. 2,60,000.

(10) Increased cost of working during the period of indemnity was Rs. 20,000.

(11) Turnover during the period of indemnity was Rs. 1,00,000 and out of this turnover of Rs. 80,000 was maintained due to increased and cost of working.

(*Madras, April, 1993*)

Ans. : Short sales of Rs. 1,60,000; Rate of gross profit 25%; Increased cost of working Rs. 16,774; Total claim for loss of profit and increased cost of working Rs. 44,274 and amount of claim on average clause Rs. 34,057.

(20) On 1st November, 1995 a severe fire broke out in the premises of Ill Luck Co. Ltd. The indemnity period lasted for 4 months during which the sales of the company were reduced to Rs. 2,00,000 only. The company closes its account on 30th June every year. The profit & loss account for the year ended 30th June, 1995 is given below :

Profit and Loss Account for the year ended 30th June, 1995

Particulars	Rs.	Particulars	Rs.
To Opening stock	5,00,000	By Sales	47,50,000
To Purchases	30,00,000	By Closing Stock	2,50,000
To Variable expenses	7,87,500		
To Standing charges	3,62,500		
To Net profit	3,50,000		
	50,00,000		50,00,000

The company took a loss of profit policy for a sum of Rs. 6,00,000. The sales of the company for the 12 months ending the date of fire were Rs. 50,00,000 and for the 4 months from 1st November, 1994 to 28th February, 1995 were Rs. 15,00,000.

It was noted that the sales for the first four months of the year under indemnity were 20% higher than previous year. Compute the claim for loss of profit.

(*Bombay, Oct., 1994*)

Ans. : Short sales of Rs. 16,00,000 (15,00,000 + 3,00,000 – 2,00,000); Rate of gross profit 15%; Loss of profit Rs. 2,40,000; Gross profit on sales for 12 months ending the date of fire Rs. 9,00,000 and Amount of claim on average clause Rs. 1,60,000.

(21) There was a serious fire in the premises of M/s Fortunate on 1st September, 1994. Their business activities were interrupted until 31st December, 1994, when normal trading conditions were re-established. M/s Fortunate have insured under the loss of profit policy for Rs. 42,000, the period of indemnity being six months.

You are able to ascertain the following information :

(1) The net profit for the year ended 31st December, 1993 was Rs. 20,000.

(2) The annual insurable standing charges amounted to Rs. 30,000 of which Rs. 2,000 were not included in the definition of insured standing charges under the policy.

(3) The additional cost of working in order to mitigate the damage caused by the fire amounted to Rs. 600 and but for this expenditure the business would have had to shut down.

(4) The saving in insured charges in consequence of the fire amounted to Rs. 1,500.

(5) The turnover for the period of four months ended on April 30,

August 31 & December 31, for each of the year 1993 & 1994 was as under :

1993	65,000	80,000	95,000
1994	70,000	80,000	15,000

You are required to compute the relevant claim under the terms of the loss of profit policy.

(*Kerala, Oct., 1996*)

Ans. : Short sales Rs. 80,000;

Rate of gross profit 20% $\left(\frac{20,000 \times 28,000}{65,000 + 80,000 + 95,000} \times 100\right)$;

Increased cost of working Rs. 576; Total claim for loss of profit and increased cost of working Rs. 15,076 and Amount of fire claim on average clause Rs. 12,922.

Note : Gross sales on 12 months sales preceding the date of fire Rs. 2,45,000 (sales for 1st September, 1993 to 31st August, 1994, *i.e.*, 95,000 + 70,000 + 80,000).

Additional Problems

(22) The premises of Fire Stone Company caught fire on 22nd October, 1991 and the stock was damaged. The firm had made up accounts to 31st December each year, and on 31st December, 1990, Stock at cost was Rs. 1,32,720 as against Rs. 96,140 on 31st December, 1989.

Purchases from 1st January, 1991 to the date of fire were Rs. 3,48,270 as against Rs. 4,52,580 for the year 1990 and the corresponding sales figures were Rs. 4,91,700 and 5,20,000 respectively. You are given the following further information :

(1) In April 1991 goods which cost Rs. 10,000 were given away for advertising, no entries having been made in the books.

(2) During 1991 a clerk had misappropriated unrecorded cash sales. It is estimated that the defalcation averaged Rs. 200 per week from 1st January, 1991 until the clerk was dismissed on 21st May, 1991.

(3) The rate of gross profit is constant.

(4) The goods salvaged was Rs. 23,680.

Calculate the value of goods destroyed by fire.

(*Bangalore, Nov., 1989*)

Ans. : Rate of gross profit 20%; Closing stock on 22-10-91 (Balancing Figure) Rs. 74,590; Unrecorded cash sales Rs. 3,800 (Rs. 200 × 19 weeks) and amount of fire claim Rs. 50,910.

Notes : (i) Unrecorded advertisement should be deducted from the purchases.

(ii) Unrecorded cash sales should be added to the sales.

(23) On 1st April, 1997, a fire destroyed the stock of a business firm. From the records which were saved, the following information was obtained :

	Rs.
Stock :	
1-1-1996	45,000
1-1-1997	55,000
Purchases :	
Calendar year 1996	1,29,250
3 months to 31-3-1997	60,000
Sales :	
Year ended 31-12-1996	1,70,000
Upto the date of fire	1,00,000
Manufacturing Expenses :	
Calendar year 1996	21,000
3 months to 31-3-1997	?

In February, 1997, goods valued at a Sale Price of Rs. 5,000 were distributed as samples. Manufacturing expenses were normally found to be constant. The Salvages Stock was estimated at Rs. 7,000.

Prepare a Statement showing the amount of claim.

(*Bangalore, April, 1991*)

Ans. : Rate of gross profit 17.5%; Closing stock as on 31-3-97 (Balancing Figure) Rs. 37,750 and Amount of fire claim Rs. 30,750.

Notes : (i) As the manufacturing expenses are normally found to be constant in 1997 for 3 months, it will be (Rs. 21,000 × 3/12) Rs. 5,250.

(ii) It is assumed that goods distributed as samples have been included in sales because they are issued at sales price.

(24) The Head Office of a Concern usually sends goods to its Branch at cost plus 25%. Once there was a small fire accident in the Branch and portion of the goods was destroyed. The relevant details have been given from the books of the Head Office.

	Rs.
Goods despatched to the Branch	2,00,000
Sales made by the Branch	1,80,000

Sales Returns	4,000
Opening Stock	25,000
Closing Stock	10,000
Goods returned by the Branch to the H.O.	20,000
Loss of goods due to theft	1,000
Receipts from sale of salvage	2,000

Prepare the Branch Stock Account in the Books of the Head Office and find out the net loss of stock due to the fire accident. Assume that the Branch has earned a profit of 20% on sales made.

(*Bangalore, Nov., 1992*)

Ans. : Stock on the date of fire (Balancing figure) Rs. 14,400; Total of Branch Stock Account Rs. 2,15,200 and Net Loss of stock due to fire Rs. 12,400 (14,400 – 2,000).

Hints : In this problem the students should prepare Branch Stock Account and not to prepare the Memorandum Trading A/c since the fire is occurred at the branch and goods with the branch should be a part of goods received from head office, they will be at invoice price. As the stock has to be valued at cost price or at market price whichever is lower, the cost price of goods has been ascertained (since it is lower) as shown below :

(i) Opening Stock Rs. 20,000 (25,000 × 100/125)

(ii) Goods sent to Branch Rs. 1,60,000 (2,00,000 × 100/125)

(iii) Goods returned to Head Office Rs. 16,000 (20,000 × 100/125)

(iv) Closing Stock Rs. 8,000 (10,000 × 100/125)

(v) Loss by theft Rs. 800 (1,000 × 100/125).

In the Books of Head Office

Branch Stock Account

Dr. Cr.

	Rs.			Rs.
To Opening Stock	20,000	By Sales	1,80,000	
To Goods Sent to Branch A/c	1,60,000	*Less* : Returns	4,000	1,76,000
To Gross Profit (1,76,000 × 20/100)	35,200	By Goods Returned		16,000
		By Loss by Theft		800
		By Closing Stock		8,000
		By Stock on the date of Fire (B.F.)		14,400
	2,15,200			2,15,200

(25) The following information is available from the records of Reckless Limited whose premises were destroyed by Fire on 31st May, 1993. The salvage was Rs. 15,000.

	Rs.
Stock on 31st December, 1992	1,32,000
Sales during 1-1-1992 to 31-12-1992	5,42,000
Stock on 1-1-1992	90,000
Purchase during 1-1-1992 to 31-12-1992	4,48,000
Returns outwards in May 1992	4,000
Returns inwards in June 1992	42,000

The stock on 1st January, 1992 was valued at 10% below cost. This practice was changed and the Stock on 31-12-1992 was valued at 10% above cost.

After finalisation of accounts for the year ended 31-12-92 it was discovered that purchase of furniture of Rs. 24,000 was wrongly included in the purchases given above.

The information for the period 1-1-1993 to 31-5-1993 is follows :

Purchases	3,20,000
Returns outwards	20,000
Sales (excluding sent on approval)	4,00,000

On 31-5-1993, goods of the cost price of Rs. 40,000 were lying with customers on approval basis. On the date of the fire the customers approved half the value of goods sent to them on approval.

The gross profit margin charged on the above is normal margin.

Calculate the amount of claim to be submitted to the Insurance Company.

(*Bangalore, April, 1994*)

Ans. : Rate of gross profit 20%; Closing Stock on 31-5-93 (Balancing figure) Rs. 60,000; Total of Trading A/c Rs. 6,20,000; Total of Memorandum Trading A/c Rs. 5,05,000 and Amount of fire claim Rs. 45,000.

Notes : (i) Stock of January, 1992 has been increased (90,000 × 100/90 = 1,00,000) and reduced on December, 1992 (1,32,000 × 100/110 = 1,20,000).

(ii) Purchase of Furniture should be deducted from purchases.

(iii) The goods which are approved by the customers are treated as sales. The sales price of the goods approved should (20,000 + 5,000 profit = Rs. 25,000) be added to sales. The goods which are not approved by the customers should be deducted (at their cost price *i.e.*, 20,000) from the purchases.

(iv) Gross profit percentage on sale is 20% or 25% on cost.

INDEX-I

List of Accounting Standards

(As on July 1, 2002)

S. No.	Accounting Standard (AS) No.	Title of the Accounting Standard	Date from which mandatory (Accounting periods commencing on or after)	Mandatory*
1.	AS 1	Disclosure of Accounting Policies	1-4-1991 for companies governed by the Companies Act, 1956, as well as for enterprises other than those specified in Note 1. 1-4-93— for all enterprises, including those specified in Note 1.	for all enterprises
2.	AS 2 (Revised)	Valuation of Inventories	1-4-1999	for all enterprises
3.	AS 3 (Revised)	Cash Flow Statements	1-4-2001	See Note 2
4.	AS 4 (Revised)	Contingencies and Events Occurring After the Balance Sheet Date	1-4-1995	for all enterprises
5.	AS 5 (Revised)	Net Profit or Loss for the Period, Prior Period Items and Changes in Accounting Policies	1-4-1996	for all enterprises
6.	AS 6 (Revised)	Depreciation Accounting	1-4-1995	for all enterprises
7.	AS 7	Accounting for Construction Contracts	As in case of AS 1 above (See also Note 3)	for all enterprises
8.	AS 8**	Accounting for Research and Development	As in case of AS 1 above	for all enterprises
9.	AS 9	Revenue Recognition	As in case of AS 1 above	for all enterprises
10.	AS 10	Accounting for Fixed Assets	As in case of AS 1 above	for all enterprises

(*Contd.*)

S. No.	Accounting Standard (AS) No.	Title of the Accounting Standard	Date from which mandatory (Accounting periods commencing on or after)	Mandatory*
11.	AS 11 (Revised)	Accounting for the Effects of Changes in Foreign Exchange Rates	1-4-1995	for all enterprises (See also Announcement IX)
12.	AS 12	Accounting for Government Grants	1-4-1994	for all enterprises
13.	AS 13	Accounting for Investments	1-4-1995	for all enterprises
14.	AS 14	Accounting for Amalgamations	1-4-1995	for all enterprises
15.	AS 15	Accounting for Retirement Benefits in the Financial Statements of Employers	1-4-1995	for all enterprises
16.	AS 16	Borrowing Costs	1-4-2000	for all enterprises
17.	AS 17	Segment Reporting	1-4-2001	See Note 2
18.	AS 18	Related Party Disclosers	1-4-2001	See Note 2
19.	AS. 19	Leases	in respect of all assets leased during accounting periods commencing on or after 1-4-2001	for all enterprises
20.	AS 20	Earnings Per Share	1-4-2001 (See also Note 4)	See Note 4
21.	AS 21	Consolidated Financial Statements	1-4-2001 (See also Note 5)	See Note 5
22.	AS 22	Accounting for Taxes on Income	See Note 6	See Note 6
23.	AS 23	Accounting for Investments in Associates in Consolidated Financial Statements	1-4-2002 (See also Note 7)	See Note 7

(*Contd.*)

S. No.	Accounting Standard (AS) No.	Title of the Accounting Standard	Date from which mandatory (Accounting periods commencing on or after)	Mandatory*
24.	AS 24	Discounting Operations	See Note 8	See Note 8
25.	AS 25	Interim Financial Reporting	1-4-2002 (See also Note 9)	See Note 9
26.	AS 26	Intangible Assets	See Note 10	See Note 10
27.	AS 27	Financial Reporting of Interests in Joint Ventures	1-4-2002 (See also Note 11)	See Note 11
28.	AS 28	Impairment of Assets	See Note 12	See Note 12

* Reference may be made to the foregoing Announcements for a detailed discussion on the implications of the mandatory status of an accounting standard.

** AS 8 would stand withdrawn with effect from the date AS 26, 'Intangible Assets', becomes mandatory (See Note 10 to this Table).

Note 1 : (a) Sole proprietary concerns/individuals.

(b) Partnership Firms

(c) Societies registered under the Societies Registration Act

(d) Trusts

(e) Hindu undivided families

(f) Associations of persons

Note 2 : AS 3, AS 17 and AS 18 have been made mandatory in respect of following enterprises :

(i) Enterprises whose equity or debt securities are listed on a recognised stock exchange in India, and enterprises that are in the process of issuing equity or debt securities that will be listed on a recognised stock exchange in India as evidenced by the board of directors' resolution in this regard.

(ii) All other commercial, industrial and business reporting enterprises, whose turnover for the accounting period exeeds Rs. 50 crore.

Note 3 : This standard has been revised as Accounting Standard (AS) 7, 'Construction Contracts'. The revised standard would come into effect in respect of all contracts entered into during accounting periods commencing on or after 1-4-2003 and will be mandatory in nature from that date.

Accordingly, Accounting Standard (AS) 7, 'Accounting for Construction Contracts', issued by the Institute in December 1983, will not be applicable in respect of such contracts.

Note 4 : AS 20 is mandatory in nature in respect of enterprises whose equity shares or potential equity shares are listed on a recognised stock exchange in India. An enterprise which has neither equity shares nor potential equity shares which are so listed but which discloses earnings per share, should calculate and disclose earnings per share in accordance with AS 20. It has been clarified that every company, which is required to give information under Part IV of the Schedule VI to the Companies Act, 1956, should calculate and disclose earnings per share in accordance with AS 20, whether its equity shares or potential equity shares are listed on a recognised stock exchange in India or not.

Note 5 : AS 21 is mandatory if an enterprise presents consolidated financial statements. In other words, the accounting standard does not mandate an enterprise to present consolidated financial statements but, if the enterprise presents consolidated financial statements for complying with the requirements of any statute or otherwise, it should prepare and present consolidated financial statements in accordance with AS 21.

Note 6 : AS 22 comes into effect in respect of accounting periods commencing on or after 1-4-2001. It is mandatory in nature for :

(a) All the accounting periods commencing on or after 1-4-2001, in respect of the following :

  (i) Enterprises whose equity or debt securities are listed on a recognised stock exchange in India and enterprises that are in the process of issuing equity or debt securities that will be listed on a recognised stock exchange in India as evidenced by the board of directors' resolution in this regard.

  (ii) All the enterprises of a group, if the parent presents consolidated financial statements and the Accounting Standard is mandatory in nature in respect of any of the enterprises of that group in terms of (i) above.

(b) All the accounting periods commencing on or after 1-4-2002, in respect of companies not covered by (a) above.

(c) All the accounting periods commencing on or after 1-4-2003, in respect of all other enterprises.

Note 7 : AS 23 comes into effect in respect of accounting periods commencing on or after 1-4-2002. AS 23 is mandatory if an enterprise presents consolidated financial statements. In other words, if an enterprise presents consolidated financial statements, it should account for investments in associates in the consolidated financial statements in accordance with AS 23 from the date of its coming into effect, *i.e.*, 1-4-2002.

Note 8 : AS 24 will be mandatory in nature in respect of accounting periods commencing on or after 1-4-2004 for the following :

(i) Enterprises whose equity or debt securities are listed on a recognised stock exchange in India, and enterprises that are in the process of issuing equity or debt securities that will be listed on a recognised stock exchange in India as evidenced by the board of directors' resolution in this regard.

(ii) All other commercial, industrial and business reporting enterprises, whose turnover for the accounting period exceeds Rs. 50 crore.

In respect of all other enterprises, the Accounting Standard will be mandatory in nature in respect of accounting periods commencing on or after 1-4-2005.

Note 9 : AS 25 comes into effect in respect of accounting periods commencing on or after 1-4-2002. This Accounting Standard does not mandate which enterprises should present interim financial reports, how frequently, or how soon after the end of an interim period. If an enterprise is required or elects to prepare and present an interim financial report, it should comply with this Accounting Standard.

Note 10 : AS 26 will come into effect in respect of expenditure incurred on intangible items during accounting periods commencing on or after 1-4-2003 and will be mandatory in nature from that date for the following :

(i) Enterprises whose equity or debt securities are listed on a recognised stock exchange in India, and enterprises that are in the process of issuing equity or debt securities that will be listed on a recognised stock exchange in India as evidenced by the board of directors' resolution in this regard.

(ii) All other commercial, industrial and business reporting enterprises, whose turnover for the accounting period exceeds Rs. 50 crore.

In respect of all other enterprises, the Accounting Standard will come into effect in respect of expenditure incurred on intangible items during accounting periods commencing on or after 1-4-2004 and will be mandatory in nature from that date.

In respect of intangible items appearing in the balance sheet as on the aforesaid date, *i.e.*, 1-4-2003 or 1-4-2004, as the case may be, AS 26 has limited application as stated in paragraph 99 of this Standard.

Note 11 : AS 27 comes into effect in respect of accounting periods commencing on or after 1-4-2002. In respect of separate financial statements of an enterprise, this Accounting Standard is mandatory in nature from that date. In respect of consolidated financial statements of an enterprise, this Standard is mandatory in nature where the enterprise prepares and presents the consolidated financial statements in respect of accounting periods commencing on or after 1-4-2002.

Note 12 : AS 28 will come into effect in respect of accounting periods commencing on or after 1-4-2004 and will be mandatory in nature from that date for the following :

(i) Enterprises whose equity or debt securities are listed on a recognised stock exchange in India and enterprises that are in the process of issuing equity or debt securities that will be listed on a recognised stock exchange in India as evidenced by the board of directors' resolution in this regard.

(ii) All other commercial, industrial and business reporting enterprises, whose turnover for the accounting period exceeds Rs. 50 crore.

In respect of all other enterprises, the Accounting Standard will come into effect in respect of accounting periods commencing on or after 1-4-2005 and will be mandatory in nature from that date.

Source : Announcement of the Council, Institute of Chartered Accountants of India.

Comparative Statement of International Accounting Standards and Indian Accounting Standards (As on July 1, 2002)

I. Accounting Standards already issued by the Institute corresponding to the International Accounting Standards

	International Accounting Standards*		Indian Accounting Standards	
Sl. No.	IAS No.	Title of the Standard	AS No.	Title of the Standard
1.	1	Presentation of Financial Statements	1	Disclosure of Accounting Policies
2.	2	Inventories	2	Valuation of Inventories
3.	4	Corresponding IAS has been withdrawn since the matter is now covered by IAS 16, 22 and 38	6	Depreciation Accounting
4.	7	Cash Flow Statements	3	Cash Flow Statements
5.	8	Net Profit or Loss for the Period, Fundamental Errors and Changes in Accounting Policies.	5	Net Profit or Loss for the Period, Prior Period Items and changes in Accounting Policies
6.	10	Events after the Balance Sheet Date	4	Contingencies and Events Occurring after the Balance Sheet Date
7.	11	Construction Contracts	7	Accounting for Construction Contracts
8.	12	Income Taxes	22	Accounting for Taxes on Income
9.	14	Segment Reporting	17	Segment Reporting
10.	16	Property, Plant and Equipment	10	Accounting for Fixed Assets
11.	17	Leases	19	Leases
12.	18	Revenue	9	Revenue Recognition
13.	19	Employee Benefits	15	Accounting for Retirement Benefits in the Financial Statements of Employers

* It may he noted that International Accounting Standards no. 3, 4, 5, 6, 9, 13 and 25 have already been withdrawn by the International Accounting Standards Committee (now International Accounting Standards Board).

	International Accounting Standards		Indian Accounting Standards	
Sl. No.	**IAS No.**	**Title of the Standard**	**AS No.**	**Title of the Standard**
14.	20	Accounting for Government Grants and Disclosure of Government Assistance	12	Accounting for Government Grants
15.	21	The Effects of Changes in Foreign Exchange Rates	11	Accounting for the Effects of Changes in Foreign Exchange Rates
16.	22	Business Combinations	14	Accounting for Amalgamations
17.	23	Borrowing Costs	16	Borrowing Costs
18.	24	Related Party Disclosures	18	Related Party Disclosures
19.	27	Consolidated Financial Statements and Accounting for Investments in Subsidiaries	21	Consolidated Financial Statements
20.	28	Accounting for Investments in Associates	23	Accounting for Investments in Associates in Consolidated Financial Statements
21.	31	Financial Reporting of Interests in Joint Ventures	27	Financial Reporting of Interests in Joint Ventures
22.	33	Earnings Per Share	20	Earnings Per Share
23.	34	Interim Financial Reporting	25	Interim Financial Reporting
24.	35	Discontinuing Operations	24	Discontinuing Operations
25.	36	Impairment of Assets	28	Impairment of Assets
26.	38	Intangible Assets	26	Intangible Assets
27.		Corresponding IAS has been withdrawn since the matter is now covered by IAS 38	8	Accounting for Research and Development (It will also be withdrawn from the date of AS 26, Intangible Assets, becoming mandatory)
28.		Corresponding IAS has been withdrawn since the matter is now covered by IAS 32, 39 and 40	13	Accounting for Investments
29.	40	Investment Property	–	Dealt with by Accounting Standard 13

II. Guidance Note issued by the Institute on the subject corresponding to the International Accounting Standard

International Accounting Standard (IAS) 15, Information Reflecting the Effects of Changing Prices.

III. International Accounting Standards not considered relevant for issuance of either Accounting Standards or the Guidance Notes by the Institute for the reasons indicated

	International Accounting Standards		
Sl. No.	**IAS No.**	**Title of the Standard**	**Reasons**
1.	29	Financial Reporting in Hyper-inflationary Economies	The International Accounting Standard is applicable only in those countries where the inflationary rate is extremely high, *i.e.*, where hyper-inflationary situation exists. The Institute notes that the hyper-inflationary conditions do not prevail in India. Accordingly, there is no justification to issue an Accounting Standard on the subject.
2.	30	Disclosures in Financial Statements of Banks and Similar Financial Institutions	Covered by the Banking Regulations Act, 1949; also certain disclosure norms have been prescribed by the Reserve Bank of India. Therefore, Accounting Standard on the subject is not considered necessary at present.

IV. Accounting Standards presently under preparation corresponding to the International Accounting Standards

	International Accounting Standards		
Sl. No.	**IAS No.**	**Title of the Standard**	**Status**
1.	32	Financial Instruments : Disclosure and Presentation	Under Preparation
2.	37	Provisions, Contingent Liabilities and Contingent Assets	Under Preparation (at present covered by AS 4)
3.	41	Agriculture (effective from 1-1-2003)	Under preparation

V. **In respect of International Accounting Standard (IAS) 39, Financial Instruments: Recognition and Measurement, Accounting Standards Board of the Institute has decided not to issue a corresponding Indian Accounting Standard since the IAS 39 is based on fair value approach for which time is not ripe enough in India at present. Accordingly, it was decided that the aspects of the IAS would be covered by the Guidance Notes already issued* and to be issued by the Research Committee.**

VI. **In respect of International Accounting Standard (IAS 26) on 'Accounting and Reporting by Retirement Benefit Plans', the Institute has decided to prepare a Guidance Note on the subject in view of the fact that at the moment there are not many retirement benefit plans apart from LIC and Government run plans. However, as soon as significant number of private players enter the sector, the guidance note may be converted into an accounting standard.**

---

* Guidance Notes on accounting for the following financial instruments have been issued :

(1) Equity Index Futures

(2) Investments by Mutual Funds

(3) Equity Index Options and Equity Stock Options

Reconciliation of the International Accounting Standards with the Indian Accounting Standards

(As on July 1, 2002)

(A)	Number of International Accounting Standards (IASs) issued by the International Accounting Standards Committee (IASC)	41
	Less : Number of IASs since withdrawn by the IASC	– 7
	Add : IAS 4 which has been withdrawn, however, included here for reconciliation purposes because corresponding Accounting Standard of the ICAI (*i.e.* AS 6) is in force	1
		35
(B)	Accounting Standards (ASs) and other documents issued by the Institute of Chartered Accountants of India	
1.	Number of Indian Accounting Standards issued (except AS 8 which will be withdrawn after AS 26 becoming mandatory)	27
2.	Number of Guidance Notes issued	1
3.	IAS irrelevant to the Indian Economic conditions	1
4.	IAS in respect of which the disclosure requirements are prescribed under the relevant Indian Statutes	1
5.	Number of Accounting Standards under preparation	3
6.	IAS 39 to be covered by the Guidance Notes already issued and to be issued	1
7.	Number of Guidance Notes under preparation	1
		35

Source : Compendium of Accounting Standards.

INDEX–II

ANNEXURE – 5

Disclosure on Accounting Standards

AS - 1

Disclosure of Accounting Policies

18. To ensure proper understanding of financial statements, it is necessary that all significant accounting policies adopted in the preparation and presentation of financial statements should be disclosed.
19. Such disclosure should form part of the financial statements.
20. It would be helpful to the reader of financial statements if they are all disclosed as such in one place instead of being scattered over several statements, schedules and notes.
21. Examples of matters in respect of which disclosure of accounting policies adopted will be required are contained in paragraph 14. This list of examples is not, however, intended to be exhaustive.
22. Any change in an accounting policy which has a material effect should be disclosed. The amount by which any item in the financial statements is affected by such change should also be disclosed to the extent ascertainable. Where such amount is not ascertainable, wholly or in part, the fact should be indicated. If a change is made in the accounting policies which has no material effect on the financial statements for the current period but which is reasonably expected to have a material effect in later periods, the fact of such change should be appropriately disclosed in the period in which the change is adopted.
23. Disclosure of accounting policies or of changes therein cannot remedy a wrong or inappropriate treatment of the item in the accounts.

AS - 2 (Revised)

Valuation of Inventories

Disclosure

26. The financial statements should disclose :
    (a) the accounting policies adopted in measuring inventories, including the cost formula used; and

(b) the total carrying amount of inventories and its classification appropriate to the enterprise.

27. Information about the carrying amounts held in different classifications of inventories and the extent of the changes in these assets is useful to financial statement users. Common classifications of inventories are raw materials and components, work in progress, finished goods, stores and spares, and loose tools.

AS - 3 (Revised)

Cash Flow Statements

Other Disclosures

45. An enterprise should disclose, together with a commentary by management, the amount of significant cash and cash equivalent balances held by the enterprise that are not available for use by it.

46. There are various circumstances in which cash and cash equivalent balances held by an enterprise are not available for use by it. Examples include cash and cash equivalent balances held by a branch of the enterprise that operates in a country where exchange controls or other legal restrictions apply as a result of which the balances are not available for use by the enterprise.

47. Additional information may be relevant to users in understanding the financial position and liquidity of an enterprise. Disclosure of this information, together with a commentary by management, is encouraged and may include :

(a) the amount of undrawn borrowing facilities that may be available for future operating activities and to settle capital commitments, indicating any restrictions on the use of these facilities; and

(b) the aggregate amount of cash flows that represent increases in operating capacity separately from those cash flows that are required to maintain operating capacity.

48. The separate disclosure of cash flows that represent increases in operating capacity and cash flows that are required to maintain operating capacity is useful in enabling the user to determine whether the enterprise is investing adequately in the maintenance of its operating capacity. An enterprise that does not invest adequately in the maintenance of its operating capacity may be prejudicing future profitability for the sake of current liquidity and distributions to owners.

AS - 4

Contingencies and Events occurring after the Balance Sheet Date

9.1. The Disclosure requirements herein referred to apply only in respect of those contingencies or events which affect the financial position to a material extent.

9.2. If a contingent loss is not provided for, its nature and an estimate of its financial effect are generally disclosed by way of note unless the possibility of a loss is remote (other than the circumstances mentioned in paragraph 5.5) if a reliable estimate of the financial effect cannot be made, this fact is disclosed.

9.3. When the events occurring after the balance sheet date are disclosed in the report of the approving authority, the information given comprises the nature of the events and an estimate of their financial effects of a statement that such an estimate cannot be made.

16. If disclosure of contingencies is required by paragraph 11 of this statement, the following information should be provided :

(a) the nature of the contingency;

(b) the uncertainties which may affect the future outcome;

(c) an estimate of the financial effect, or a statement that such an estimate cannot be made

17. If disclosure of events occurring after the balance sheet date in the report of the approving authority is required by paragraph 15 of this statement, the following information should be provided :

(a) the nature of the event;

(b) an estimate of the financial effect, or a statement that such.

AS - 5

Net Profit or Loss for the period, prior period items and changes in Accounting Policies

27. The nature and amount of a change in an accounting estimate which has a material effect in the current period, or which is expected to have a material effect in subsequent periods, should be disclosed. If it is impracticable to quantify the amount, this fact should be disclosed.

32. Any change in an accounting policy which has a material effect should be disclosed. The impact of and the adjustments resulting from, such change, if material, should be shown in the financial statements of the period in which such change is made, to reflect the effect of such change. Where the effect of such change is not ascertainable wholly or in part, the fact should be indicated. If a change is made in the

accounting policies which has no material effect on the financial statements for the current period but which is reasonably expected to have a material effect in later periods, the fact of such change should be appropriately disclosed in the period in which the change is adopted.

AS - 6 Depreciation Accounting

17. The depreciation methods used, the total depreciation for the period for each class of assets, the gross amount of each class of depreciable assets and the related accumulated depreciation are disclosed in the financial statements alongwith the disclosure of other accounting policies. The depreciation rates or the useful lives of the assets are disclosed-only if they are different from the principal specified in the statute governing the enterprise.

18. In case the depreciable assets are revalued, the provision for depreciation is based on the revalued amount on the estimate of the remaining useful life of such assets. In case the revaluation has a material effect on the amount of depreciation, the same is disclosed separately in the year in which revaluation is carried out.

19. A change in the method of depreciation is treated a change in an accounting policy and is disclosed accordingly.

AS - 7

Accounting for Construction Contracts

20. There should be disclosure in the financial statements of

    (i) the amount of construction work-in-progress;

    (ii) progress payments received and advances and retentions on account of contracts included in construction work-in-progress; and

    (iii) the amount receivable in respect of income accrued under cost plus contracts not included in construction work-in-progress.

    If both the percentage of completion method and the completed contract method are simultaneously used by the contractor, the amount of contract work described in (I) above should be analysed to disclose separately the amounts attributable to contracts accounted for under each method.

Note : For details of various paragraphs, please refer 'Chartered Accountant Office Manual' 2nd March, 2002.

21. Disclosure of changes in an accounting policy used for construction contracts should be made in the financial statements giving the effect of the change and its amount. However if a contractor changes from the percentage of completion method to the completed contract method for contracts in progress at the beginning of the year it may not be possible to quantify the effect of the change. In such cases disclosure should be made of the amount of attributable profits reported in prior years in respect of contracts in progress at the beginning of the accounting period.

AS - 8

Accounting for Research and Development

6.1. The accounting policy adopted for the costs of research and development is included in the statement of accounting policies (see AS 1 on 'Disclosure of Accounting Policies'). Information about amortisation practices is also disclosed when research and development costs are deferred.

The disclosure of

(i) research and development costs, inclu
ding the amortisation of deferred costs, charged as an expense of each period, and

(ii) the unamortised balance, if any, of deferred research and development costs, enables the users of financial statements to consider the significance of such activities in relation to those of other enterprises as well as to the other activities of the enterprise itself.

AS - 9

Revenue Recognition

14. In addition to the disclosures required by Accounting Standard 1 on 'Disclosure of Accounting Policies' (AS 1), an enterprise should also disclose the circumstances in which revenue recognition has been postponed pending the resolution of significant uncertainties.

AS - 10

Accounting for Fixed Assets

17.1. Certain specific disclosures on accounting for fixed assets are already required by Accounting Standard 1 on 'Disclosure of Accounting Policies' and 'Accounting Policies' and Accounting Standard 6 on 'Depreciation Accounting'.

17.2. Further disclosures that are sometimes made in financial statements include :

(i) gross and net book values of fixed assets at the beginning and end of an accounting period showing additions, disposals, acquisitions and other movements;

(ii) expenditure incurred on account of fixed assets in the course of construction or acquisition; and

(iii) revalued amounts substituted for historical costs of fixed assets, the method adopted to compute the revalued amounts, the nature of any indices used, the year of any appraisal made, and whether an external valuer was involved, in case where fixed assets are stated at revalued amounts.

AS - 11

Accounting for the Effects of Changes in Foreign Exchange Rates

26. An enterprise should disclose—

(i) the amount of exchange difference included in the net profit or loss for the period;

(ii) the amount of exchange differences adjusted in the carrying amount of fixed assets during tne accounting period; and

(iii) the amount of exchange differences in respect of forward exchange contracts to be recognised in the profit or loss for one or more subsequent accounting periods, as required by paragraph 13.

27. Disclosure is also encouraged of an enterprise's foreign currency risk management policy.

AS - 12

Accounting for Government Grants

23. The following should be disclosed :

(i) the accounting policy adopted for government grants, including the methods of presentation in the financial statements.

(ii) the nature and extent of government grants recognised in the financial statements, including grants of non-monetary assets given at a concessional rate or free of cost.

AS - 13

Accounting for Investments

25. The following disclosures in financial statements in relation to investments are appropriate—

(a) the accountirc policies for the determination of carrying amount of investments;

(b) the amounts included in profit and loss statement for :

(i) interest, dividends (showing separately dividends from subsidiary companies), and rentals on investments showing separately such income from long term and current investments. Gross income should be stated, the amount of income tax deducted at source being included under Advance Taxes Paid;

(ii) Profits and losses on disposal of current investments and changes in carrying amount of such investments;

(iii) Profits and losses on disposal of long term investments and changes in the carrying amount of such investments;

(c) significant restrictions on the right of ownership, realisability of investments or the remittance of income and proceeds of disposal;

(d) the aggregate amount of quoted and unquoted investments, giving the aggregate market value of quoted investments;

(e) Other disclosures as specifically required by the relevant statute governing the enterprise.

35. The following information should be disclosed in the financial statements :

(a) the accounting policies for determination of carrying amount of investments;

(b) classification of investments as specified in paragraphs 26 and 27 above;

(c) the amounts included in profit and loss statement for :

(i) interest, dividends (showing separately dividends from subsidiary companies), and rentals on investments showing separately such income from long term and current investments. Gross income should be stated, the amount of income-tax deducted at source being included under Advance Taxes Paid;

(ii) profits and losses on disposal of current investments and changes in carrying amount of such investments;

(iii) profits and losses on disposal of long term investments and changes in the carrying amount of such, investments;

(d) signification restrictions on the right of ownership, realisability of investments or the remittance or the remittance of income and proceeds of disposal;

(e) the aggregate amount of quoted and unquoted investments, giving the aggregate market value of quoted investments;

(f) other disclosures as specifically required by the relevant statute governing the enterprise.

AS - 14 Recounting for Amalgamations

43. For all amalgamations, the following disclosures should be made in the first financial statements following the amalgamation :

    (a) names and general nature of business of the amalgamating companies;

    (b) effective date of amalgamation for accounting purposes;

    (c) the method of accounting used to reflect the amalgamation; and

    (d) particulars of the scheme sanctioned under a statute.

44. For amalgamations accounted for under the purchase method, the following additional disclosures should be made in the first financial statements following the amalgamation :

    (a) consideration for the amalgamation and a description of the consideration paid or contingently payable; and

    (b) the amount of any difference between the consideration and the value of net identifiable assets acquired, and the treatment thereof including the period of amortisation of any goodwill arising on amalgamation.

AS - 15

Accounting for Retirement Benefits in the financial statements of Employers

31. The financial statements should disclose the method by which retirement benefit costs for the period have been determined. In case the costs related to gratuity and other defined benefit schemes are based on an actuarial valuation, the financial statements should also disclose whether the actuarial valuation was made at the end of the period or at an earlier date. In the latter case, that date of the actuarial valuation should be specified and the method by which the accrual for the period has been determined should also be briefly described, if the same is not based on the report of the actuary.

45. In view of the diversity of practices used for accounting of retirement benefits costs, adequate disclosure of method followed in accounting for them is essential for an understanding of the significance of such costs to an employer.

46. Retirement benefit costs are sometimes disclosed separately for statutory compliance. In other cases, they are considered to be an element of employee remuneration and their separate disclosure is not usually made.

AS - 16

Borrowing Costs

22. The financial statements should disclose :

(a) the accounting policy adopted for borrowing costs; and

(b) the amount of borrowing costs capitalised during the period.

AS - 17

Segment Reporting

This Standard requires disclosure of certain financial information about the enterprise based on its major business/geographical operations.

Under primary reporting format, the enterprise should disclose :

- segment revenue from sales to external customers
- segment revenue from transactions with other segments
- segment results
- total carrying amount of segment assets
- total amount of segment liabilities
- additions to assets during the period (tangible and intangible)
- depreciation and amortization for the period, and
- significant other non-cash expenses, included in segment results.

AS - 18

Related Party Disclosures

In case there have been transaction with related parties, the following disclosures are required :

- Name of the party
- Description of the relationship between the parties
- Description of the nature of transactions
- Volume of the transaction either as an amount or a proportion
- Any other elements of the transactions necessary for an understanding of the financial statements
- The amount or proportion of dues/payables from/to such parties and provisions there against; and
- Amount written off/back in respect of related parties.

AS - 19

Leases

Treatment in case of finance lease

In the books of the lessee - The following should be disclosed :

- Assets acquired under finance lease
- The net carrying amount of such assets
- The total amount and present value of minimum lease payments for specified periods
- Reconciliation between total minimum lease payments and their present value
- Contingent rents recognised as income
- The total future minimum payments expected to be received under subleases, and
- General description of significant leasing arrangements.

In the books of the lessor - The following should be disclosed :

- The total gross investment in the lease and the present value of minimum lease payments receivable for specified future periods
- Reconciliation between the total gross investment in the lease and the present value of minimum lease payments receivable
- Unearned finance income
- Unguaranteed residual values accruing to the lessor
- Accumulated provision for uncollectible minimum lease payments receivable
- Contingent rents recognized as income
- General description of significant leasing arrangements, and
- Accounting policy for initial direct costs.

Treatment in case of operating lease

In the books of the lessee - The following should be disclosed :

- The total amount of minimum lease payments for specified future periods
- The total future minimum payments expected to be received under subleases
- The lease payment (showing the minimum lease and contingent rent separately) recognized in the profit and loss statement

- Sub-lease payments recognized in the statement of profit and loss for the period, and
- General description of significant leasing arrangements.

In the books of the lessor - The following should be disclosed :

- The gross carrying amount, accumulated depreciation and impairment losses
- Depreciation charged during the period
- Impairment losses recognised or reversed
- The future minimum lease payments in the aggregate and for specified periods
- Contingent rents recognised as income
- General description of significant lease arrangements, and
- Accounting policy for initial direct costs

AS - 20

Earning Per Share

This standard requires an enterprise to disclose 'basic' and 'diluted' earnings per share, the profit and loss statement for all periods, such disclosure is required even if the amount is negative (*i.e.*, loss per share) :

- Amounts of earnings used as numerator in calculating basic and diluted EPS and its reconciliation with the net profit or loss for the period;
- Weighted average number of equity shares used as the denominator in calculating basic and diluted EPS, and a reconciliation of these denominators to each other;
- The nominal value of shares along with the earning per share figures.

AS - 21

Consolidated Financial Statements

- The name, country of incorporation, residence, proportion of ownership and voting right, if different, of all the subsidiaries;
- The nature of the relationship if the parent does not hold majority voting power;
- The effect of acquisition and disposal of subsidiaries on the financial position;
- The subsidiary(ies) with differing reporting date and the difference.

AS - 22

Accounting for Taxes on Income

- Related assets and liabilities representing current tax should usually be set-off with each other.
- An enterprise should offset deferred tax assets and liabilities if it has a right to set off the assets against current tax liabilities; and the relevant asset and liability are covered by the same governing taxation laws.
- Deferred tax assets and liabilities should be disclosed separately from current assets and current liabilities in the balance sheet. The break-up of deferred tax assets and liabilities into major components should be disclosed.
- If an enterprise has unabsorbed depreciation or carry forward of tax losses, the nature of evidence to justify the recognition of deferred tax assets should be disclosed.

AS - 23

Accounting for investments in Associates in Consolidated Financial Statements

- A list of associates along with ownership interest and, if different, the voting right, the share of profits or losses, or any extraordinary or prior period items, should be separately disclosed.
- The associate(s) with different reporting dates and the difference.
- The difference in accounting policies between the investor and the associate(s).
- On the first implementation of this standard, the value of investments should be brought to the amount, as if the equity method of accounting was followed since the acquisition, and necessary adjustment made in the retained earnings.

Source : Chartered Accountants Manual by S. Krishnaswamy, 2nd March, 2002.